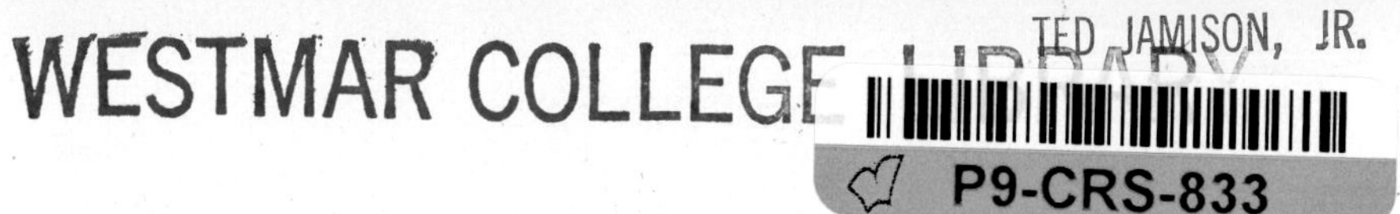

WORLD POLITICS

WORLD POLITICS

THE WRITINGS OF THEORISTS AND PRACTITIONERS, CLASSICAL AND MODERN

EDITED BY *AREND LIJPHART*

UNIVERSITY OF CALIFORNIA, BERKELEY

ALLYN AND BACON, INC.

BOSTON / 1966

Library of Congress Catalog Card Number: 66–20991

Printed in the United States of America

TO ANTONY SUNE

PREFACE

THIS BOOK OF READINGS IS DESIGNED SPECIFICALLY FOR USE IN THE introductory course in International Relations as a companion volume to the textbook. It presents provocative and authoritative materials on the basic concepts and persistent issues of world politics. Among the authors are the classical political theorists—Plato, Thucydides, Machiavelli, Dante, Bodin, Grotius, Hobbes, Hume, Rousseau, Kant, Von Clausewitz, and De Tocqueville; the acknowledged leaders among contemporary theorists—political scientists Deutsch, Haas, Hoffmann, Kaplan, Mitrany, Thompson, and Wright; theologian Niebuhr; historian Langer; geographer Jones; psychiatrist Frank; and political practitioners who can speak authoritatively on world affairs, from Theodore Roosevelt and Woodrow Wilson to Kennedy, De Gaulle, Hallstein, U Thant, and Khrushchev.

The readings are supplementary in nature, and do not attempt to substitute for the International Relations text or the tasks of the instructor. The introductory sections in each of the chapters are deliberately kept very brief; they are introductory only, rather than full expositions or outlines of the topic under consideration or interpretations and summaries of the readings which follow.

Any book of readings on world politics can only include an infinitesimal portion of the vast and ever-growing literature in the field; the selection of specific readings was, therefore, no simple task. In compiling this reader, I was guided by several criteria, not all of which were easily reconcilable. The most important criterion was over-all quality of analysis and exposition. The selections had to treat the fundamental concepts and issues in an intellectually challenging and stimulating fashion. Furthermore, I thought it desirable to present the authors' ideas in their entirety rather than in truncated form. This goal conflicted with the aims of comprehensiveness and balance of topics, viewpoints, and approaches, and with the practical necessity of keeping the length of this volume within reasonable bounds. The inevitable result was a compromise. Wherever possible, entire articles, speeches, or chapters from books are reprinted. And when any pieces had to be abridged, the excerpts represent consecutive material as much as possible.

I acknowledge with gratitude the helpful comments and suggestions I have received from my colleagues Professors Saul N. Silverman and M. George Zaninovich. And my wife deserves special thanks, in particular for her help with translations.

A.L.

CONTENTS

THE STUDY OF INTERNATIONAL RELATIONS

part I

INTERNATIONAL RELATIONS AS AN ACADEMIC DISCIPLINE

I

WHAT IS THE ACADEMIC DISCIPLINE VARIously labeled "International Relations," "International Politics," "International Studies," "Foreign Affairs," "World Affairs," or "World Politics"? What are its distinguishing characteristics? What is its scope? Is it truly an academic discipline? These and other fundamental questions are discussed in the first selection by Morton A. Kaplan of the University of Chicago. Kaplan is the author of *System and Process in International Politics* and many other books and articles.

In the second selection, which is an excerpt from a longer article, William T. R. Fox and Annette Baker Fox analyze the teaching of International Relations at both the undergraduate and the graduate level in

American colleges and universities. William T. R. Fox is Professor of International Relations at Columbia University. Annette Baker Fox is a member of the Department of Political Science at Hunter College. She is the author of *The Power of Small States* and other scholarly publications.

1. *IS INTERNATIONAL RELATIONS A DISCIPLINE?* * / *MORTON A. KAPLAN*

Is international relations a distinctive discipline—different from sociology, for instance, in the same way in which sociology is distinctive from political science or economics? Can it be studied independently, or must it be studied as a sub-discipline of some other discipline such as political science? Is the subject matter of international relations susceptible to disciplinary study in some coherent fashion or is it a mere grab bag from which we pick and choose according to momentary interests and to which we can apply no coherent theory, sets of generalizations, or standardized methods?

That we are asked to discuss the topic "Is International Relations a Discipline?" is indicative of a state of unease in the profession. One would find it difficult to imagine similar questions asked of economics, sociology, or political science in general. The practitioners in these fields assume that they practice a discipline and turn their attention immediately to the important substantive and methodological questions raised by their subject matter. They may be concerned with the proper methods of conducting research but not with their title to conduct research. The difficulties that cause students of international relations to raise such a fundamental question must be sought, I believe, in the nature of the subject matter and the history of the discipline.

Before raising the problem in a more general way, I should like briefly and in an over-simplified fashion to mention one aspect of

* Morton A. Kaplan, "Is International Relations a Discipline?" *The Journal of Politics*, Vol. 23, No. 3 (August 1961), pp. 462–76. Reprinted by permission.

the history of international relations studies that is perhaps in part responsible for this state of affairs. When political science separated itself from historical or legal studies, it turned to factual studies of existing political institutions. Then it began to raise questions about comparative institutional differences and to study the inter-relationships between different kinds and levels of political organizations. When interdisciplinary political scientists came on the scene, they were able to apply their theories and insights to an established body of factual data and an established body of theory. Although in their time, they were controversial, they enriched both our factual knowledge and our theoretical understanding. They permitted us to develop broader and more complex theories and to investigate new and interesting factual problems. The relationships between politics and boundary conditions, for example, political personality, elite structures, and voting behavior, could be explored systematically and scientifically for the first time. But however revolutionary these inter-disciplinary methods appeared at the time, they were related to the traditional problems of political science. They were concerned ultimately with institutional and organizational regularities of a political nature even where these problems were raised and studied in novel ways. And findings based on these new methods have been absorbed so successfully by the discipline that they are now even regarded by some as "old hat."

International relations broke away from its historical base at the time when interdisciplinary research in political science first began to develop. It inherited the new approach without having a traditional body of theory or factual data to apply it to (aside perhaps from some earlier and rather vague generalities about the "balance of power"). It could not use interdisciplinary data and theories to enrich and deepen our knowledge of international politics because that was still largely an unexplored subject. In addition, international relations broke loose as an independent discipline during a period in the 1920's when idealism was high and the urge to solve practical problems great. As a consequence, there were sometimes fantastic schemes for world government. The object was to produce international peace rather than disciplinary knowledge. Some scholars did recognize the need for theory and data if such objectives were to be achieved; although this led to an occasional monumental work, such as Quincy Wright's *The Study of War*, the international system as a complex social and political system still remained largely unexplored. This is not to deny that very useful knowledge was sometimes attained. Staley's *War and the Private Investor* added to our knowledge of imperialism and Lasswell's *World Politics and Personal Insecurity* was a major contribution to our knowledge of the psychodynamics of aggressive international behavior. There were of course other important pieces of research that could have been named in place of these examples. But, at least in my opinion, all these works, however valuable they may have been individually, did not add up to a discipline of international relations because there was no common disciplinary core to be enriched as there had been in the companion subject matter of political science.

In short, international relations, although a subject matter, had not become a discipline. Now, although this distinction is perhaps elementary, it might be useful to say a few words about it. Different abstract phases of the same concrete subject matter can be studied by different disciplines. For instance, the economic institutions of society can be studied by the economist, sociologist, psychologist, political scientist, and so forth. The economist studies the flow of resources and the allocative mechanisms; the psychologist may study the effects of different economic systems on personality; the sociologist may study the interrelationships of the economic sub-system with other sub-systems of the society; the political scientist may study the relationships between political and economic organization or the political aspects of economic organization. But only the study by the economist concerns economics.

A discipline implies a set of skills and techniques; a body of theory and of propositions; and a subject matter. This assertion is perhaps necessarily a bit vague and subject to judgmental discriminations, for the astrophysicist, the biophysicist, and the microphysicist share some skills and techniques, some matters of theory and of propositional import, and the common subject matter of physics only at an appropriate level of generalization. This vagueness at the boundary, however, need not distress us, for when we turn to international relations, as the subject matter involving transactions across national boundaries, it is immediately evident that these transactions come within the purview of many different recognized disciplines. For example, international trade comes within the purview of economics; international religious movements and cultural diffusion patterns may be studied by the sociologist; international tensions may come within the province of the psychologist; and wars, international political movements, and patterns of alliance fall within the realm of political science.

The Problem of a Discipline of International Relations

The preceding discussion, discursive as it may have been, raises at least two general questions worth some discussion and exploration. Are any international transactions properly to be studied by a discipline that is specifically international or do we merely apply an already existing discipline to some aspects of international transactions? If there is any such discipline, then it deserves to become the focus of international relations research. If there is no such discipline, then there is no discipline of international relations although there may be disciplines of political science, economics, sociology, and so forth, that can be applied to the study of international relations. In this case, as political scientists, we would expect the student of political science to be concerned primarily with political aspects of international relations. And although as modern political scientists we would also expect him to have some knowledge of economics, sociology, and psychology, we would expect him to use this knowledge in structuring primarily political research problems. We might, however, recognize international politics as a sub-discipline of political science in the same sense in which astrophysics is a sub-discipline of physics.

I know of no convincing discussion that a specifically international relations discipline exists. But, before we can therefore assume that international politics can be studied as a sub-discipline of political science, we must ask whether the conditions appropriate for the existence of such a sub-discipline exist. There are at least three sets of circumstances which would suffice to contra-indicate this. If international events were epiphenomena of national events, that is, mere consequences of national events not requiring for their understanding study of the international matrix, we would deny the validity of a sub-discipline. If international events were to be studied primarily by non-political techniques, we would deny the existence of such a sub-discipline. And, if the subject matter of international politics were recalcitrant to systematic political exploration, we might be led to deny the feasibility of a sub-discipline of international politics. In this latter case, we might have to restrict ourselves to historical investigations.

I am under no illusions concerning my ability to settle definitively the question raised above, particularly within the limitations of the present paper. None the less some partial answers may be attempted. There is no doubt that some wars were caused in some important sense by intra-national considerations, by the need for markets, because of internal political crises, or even perhaps by the influence of a king's mistress. The last illustration is not intended in any sense as humorous, for in those cases where such an influence operated, the failure to take it into account would impoverish our understanding of the actual event. If and to the extent to which some intra-national factor played a systematic role in international events, the study of international relations would have to rely upon the discipline or body of factual information that elucidated this matter and, if possible, would have to incorporate such findings into its own analysis. But it is difficult to believe that the differences between the Italian city state system, the national state politics of nineteenth century Europe, and the present bipolar system can be accounted for in all important senses without an analysis of the number of participating actors, their relationship to non-members of the system and to their environment, their capabilities and geographic relations, and their modes of political intercourse. And, to the extent that this is true, non-political or non-international analyses, although perhaps important and even essential supplements to the analysis of international political events, are not substitutes for such analysis.

Nor, do I think, can international relations be reduced to a discipline other than political science. Even if Lenin's theory of imperialism were correct—and the evidence is conclusively against it—the fact that the declining rate of profit inspired the drive for colonies and trade wars would only serve to provide a motivating factor for international politics and would no more eliminate the need for studying the specifically international political factors than would any of the intra-national factors mentioned in the paragraph above. Lenin's was perhaps the most sophisticated attempt that has been made to reduce international relations to a discipline other than politics, in this case economics. Other attempts have been made in the case of psychological factors. Harold Lasswell pioneered in showing the relationship between personality and behavior within institutional settings. With particular reference to our subject, he explored the shadowland area in which personality has its effects upon aggressive and warlike behavior. Unfortunately, in the hands of psychologists and sociologists who lacked Lasswell's political knowledge and sophistication, Lasswell's theories were misused and attempts were made to reduce wars and arms races to personality maladjustments, as if rational or non-psychological factors never could account for such behavior. Such attempts suffered from grave theoretical and factual faults. No account of international events which leaves out the political can provide satisfactory systematic knowledge.

There is finally a third possibility, namely that the subject matter of international politics, although important, is recalcitrant to the kinds of studies that would have to be made if systematic knowledge were to become available. It might be argued that there is only one international system (except perhaps in time) and that therefore comparative analysis could not be used. The changes that occur through time may occur in so many aspects of the action pattern that ascription of the change in international politics to a particular factor may not be capable of even imprecise empirical confirmation. These factors may include weapons technology, transportation and communication improvements, changes in national economic strength, changes in the number of significant nations, changes in the form of international organization and formal governmental organization, and changes in national values and belief patterns, and so forth. In addition, in the international system, there are a smaller number of events than within the domestic arena; we cannot gamble on the general run, but usually must bank our fate on particular decisions. Thus one cannot necessarily expect the kind of generalized system of roles and role expectations one finds within national systems. This means more unpredictability for individual decisions and less in common between successive decisions. The "deviant" decision is less likely to wash out in the general average and a "deviant" actor has a greater potential for revolutionizing the system than within national systems.

One could multiply the reasons just given. They explain the preference of some for historical investigation or case study. But such investigation or studies are not and cannot be substitutes for political analysis of a systematic nature. A historical study represents an attempt to account for a particular historical sequence of events. In making his study, the historian may employ knowledge from economics, politics, psychology, sociology, technology, and so forth, in evaluating his data. The problem of how he engineers his data when considering the combined effects of events analyzed from the standpoint of many different disciplines is still largely unexplored in the methodological literature and is an art. This means the historian's results are limited by his intuitive ability and judgment in handling combinations of factors. To the extent that factors other than the international political influence the historic sequence of events, the historian is not embarrassed by the absence of a discipline of international politics. To the extent that events are influenced by international political factors—and in the discussion of the first two objections an attempt was made to show briefly that they will be in most important cases—he cannot make his generalizations without employing the same methods which a discipline of international politics would employ. And if such a discipline is not possible, the generalization of the historian is not possible either.

Although this is obvious theoretically, it is not obvious practically for reasons that are easy to understand. The historian or the case study analyst, because he analyzes a concrete sequence of events and tries to take into account all factors influencing that event rather than the class of factors influencing the type of event as in scientific disciplinary studies, engages in a pseudo-recreation of the event and, if he is able, employs the skill of a novelist to create an atmosphere of reality that is psychologically compelling. The nature of his generalizations is hidden by his inexplicit and unsystematic—at least from the standpoint of a generalized science—mode of analysis; and indeed his style of story telling is not conducive to making such analysis explicit or systematic. As a consequence he is usually unaware that his generalization does not follow from the concrete story but can only follow from an abstract argument which, if it is consistent, will be isomorphic with the model that a political scientist would employ.

There can be no quarrel with good historical studies. They do a job that has to be done and for which no other discipline is a substitute. If the historian is not always as sophisticated as he should be with respect to the ways in which he uses scientific theories, the social scientist is often neglectful of the complexity of historical life. And if the historian often fails to provide the social scientist with the data he requires, this is sometimes at least the fault of the social scientist for failing to state his theories in ways that encourage and facilitate related historical investigation. But, when all this is said, the historical investigation is not a substitute for the job a discipline of international politics would be required to perform.

Of course the fact that no substitute exists and that the task such a discipline would perform is quite important does not imply that such a discipline is possible. But the arguments against it are by no means definitive. Nor is it really clear that we are really so much worse off than the other social science disciplines that an effort in this direction would not be worthwhile.

The Requirements of a Discipline of International Politics

It seems to me that regardless of how advanced some of us may consider the techniques we employ, the primary focus of a discipline of international politics must be related to the traditional focus of political science in general. If we cannot escape the methodological advances that have been made in the last thirty years—and there is no reason why we should want to—it may still be important for us to direct these methods and techniques to the study of traditional political problems, at least as they are relevant to international politics. These core problems, so to speak, involve the institutional means by which political problems are solved and political values distributed within the international system.

We are interested in patterns of actions, not with particular cases. Just as we might be interested in a particular cabinet dispute for the light it sheds on the means by which cabinet disputes might be settled in Great Britain or on the range of solution formulas and the constraining factors that predispose toward a particular type of solution, so a study of international conflict or problem settlement would be concerned primarily not with elucidating the particular case but with elucidating the general mode of settlement or the range of settlement and the relevant constraining factors. Even though these institutional patterns may be informal rather than formal, we are concerned with human behavior as it manifests itself in institutions with respect to political matters. That these problems look somewhat different substantively from the problems we are normally used to in political science stems from the fact that the institutional setting of international politics is somewhat different from that of national politics. And, to the extent that this is the case, the sub-discipline of international politics may differ from that of political science in general as much as that of astrophysics differs from microphysics.

The differences between international politics and national politics are fairly obvious. They can be exaggerated and many of these differences may fail to apply to unstable national systems. But the statement of the major differences still should help to clarify the situation. The state as we know it is in some sense the ultimate seat of political authority within which political decisions are made and political values allocated. It attempts to maintain its jurisdiction at the expense of any external or putatively superior authority. The quest for control of the state gives rise to the traditional problems of the form of government, the authority and scope of jurisdiction of officials, the rights of citizens, problems of responsibility and accountability, and so forth. International politics, on the other hand, is the arena in which these ultimately authoritative states, almost like Leibnizian monads, have to come into contact with each other and settle their conflicts without the supravention of any external political authority or master monad. Standardized rules of behavior, if they develop at all, must occur as a consequence of coordination rather than of imposition.

Within national political systems, political organization is formal and durable. Its maintenance does not require explanation although its working processes require study. The organizational forms of international politics, at least those of central importance, like the alliance or bloc, are more often than not of an informal nature, if not with respect to their own organization then at least with respect to relations among them. The memberships of such alignments may be shifting and, although alliances may be a recurrent feature of a particular kind of international system, particular alliances may come into and pass out of existence with relative rapidity. The maintenance of a particular kind of alliance system through changes in actual alliances may indeed require explanation and hence different techniques of investigation from those applied to formal governmental organizations operating within nation states.

Within most national systems, decisions normally are made by voting, whether for candidates for office or on legislative matters. The character of the voting may depend on the kind of electoral or on legislative system; surely votes in the American Congress, the British House of Commons, and the Supreme Soviet are of a different order. But, even where decisions do not occur as a consequence of voting, there are formally determined methods for making the decisions. And in all cases political scientists have developed techniques for studying these processes. In international politics, decisions are made as a consequence of formal or informal bargaining, inexplicit coordination of policy, or the application of force. Techniques for studying these procedures have not been well developed in political science, although the economist has paid considerable attention to bargaining problems that may be considered similar.

Political scientists have paid careful attention to the pressure group in their study of decision processes in national politics. Certainly the pressure group has played an important role in the making of international decisions. The Southern cotton lobby played a role in the revocation of the Aswan Dam offer by John Foster Dulles, the oil lobby plays a role in the current coddling of the Arab states, and the sugar lobby influences American relations with Cuba and the Philippines. Yet, when this is admitted, it remains true that foreign policy is oriented more toward problems produced by the international environment than toward demands of self-interested domestic pressure groups. This is not to say that foreign policy is not responsive to domestic pressures. Unfortunately the ill-advised interwar neutrality legislation was in large part a response to such pressures. But these pressures were based more upon a conception of what American interests were than upon a consideration of what a particular group gained from the legislation. Although their differences are not absolute, it is possible that at least somewhat different methods may be required in investigating the two fields of legislation.

Within the nation state there are millions of voters and still additional millions of citizens. There are parties, labor unions, industrial organizations, religious groups, and so on. They participate in a web of social relations by means of cross-cutting social roles. In the international system, the primary actor is the nation state. In the nineteenth century the number of the most important actors could have been counted on the fingers of one's hands. In the present bipolar system, the United States and the Soviet Union are the most important actors, there is a small number in the second rank, and a total of over one hundred nations. With such small numbers, the statistical averaging out that can occur in domestic social and political processes is not to be expected. This point, however, was made earlier, and need not be expanded here.

Although perhaps overemphasized in earlier writings, nations are characterized by a certain amount of consensus and many of the cross-cutting social roles within them are solidary, that is, based on diffuse affective support or loyalty, rather than of an instrumental character. The relations of individuals and groups toward the nation are themselves solidary; loyal support is expected and those from whom it is expected themselves expect to give it. In general the relations of nations toward each other or toward the international system tend to be instrumental, that is, to be based on considerations of immediate advantage rather than of loyalty, duty, and so forth.

In domestic politics, strategic analysis is not central to investigation. Although the techniques for pushing bills through the legislature may involve a number of strategic elements, the character of the political system is not at stake and the general content of most domestic legislation is oriented toward the broad middle spectrum of opinion in democratic countries or toward the objectives of a dominant party or dictatorship. Ultimate strategic considerations govern domestic politics primarily in transitional periods, for example, the Chinese Civil War, and the periods in Soviet party politics after the deaths of Lenin and Stalin. In the first case, the form of the governmental system was at stake; in the latter, the specification of the winning dictator. It is normally the case in international politics that the major decisions involve the existence of the parties to the decision and the nature of the international political system. And for this reason the decisions are of a highly strategic character. In a general sense the participants in the international political process are engaged in a game or struggle involving honor, fortune, and life. The fact that there are only a small number of them and hence that the system is subsystem dominant, that is, that the patterns of behavior are not parametric givens for the actors but may be influenced by the actions of the actors, reinforces the strategic nature of the decision process, and requires a strategic focus to the analysis of these matters.

If the preceding factors are taken not as absolutes but merely as indications of important differences between national and international politics, they may help to indicate some respects in which the problems of international politics may differ from those of national politics—even though in both cases, we are concerned with institutional patterns of political behavior—and the ways in which somewhat different techniques of analysis profitably may be employed. In general in the international system the most important organizational forms and patterns are the informal rather than the formal. As far as governmental features of the international system are concerned, formally organized systems like the League of Nations and the United Nations, at least so far as past history is concerned, have been peripheral rather than central. The absence of a formal political system in the international arena does not imply the absence of the political management of problems. This political management, with its informal organizational forms, should be regarded as the central focus of the discipline of international politics.

The primary techniques of international government are bargaining and conflict. Bargaining may involve not merely the withholding of the item offered in exchange but the implicit or explicit threat of the use of force. An important instrument in the imposition of goals and goal patterns is the coalition, alignment, bloc, or concert. These are the means by which particular objectives are attained or which may be used to maintain norms of conduct. The criteria for admission to membership, the duration of membership, the types of goals pursued by given kinds of organized international groupings, the limits placed upon these goals, and the factors that constrain all the preceding subjects are among the most important items of the subject matter of the discipline of international politics.

But it is not enough merely to name these features; they must be studied as part of a coherent system of international political relations. The political scientist studying the American legislative system can understand it only as part of a presidential system of government and a federal system of political relationships, for these other aspects of the American political system constrain and qualify the legislative system. In the same way alliance patterns, with respect to durability of specific memberships and goal patterning, depend upon the kinds of national actors who participate, the number of national actors in the entire international system, their relative capabilities, the state of military technology and economic growth, scales of capabilities, the existence or non-existence of supranational types of political organization, and the political organization and goal systems of the participating national actors. The shifting membership and limited goal pattern of most eighteenth and nineteenth century international politics and the rigid membership patterns and relatively unlimited objectives of late nineteenth and early twentieth century international politics must have some relationship to specifiable differences in the international system if there is to be a discipline of international politics. This holds also for present-day bipolar developments.

The study of the discipline of international politics probably will make use of many of the same kinds of institutional analysis as does the discipline of political science in general. But the strategic nature of the activity in the international system indicates that considerable insights may possibly be gained from strategic theory. The absence of durable formal organization, the small number of important or essential actors, and the strategic character of decision making indicate that normative models may be useful to explore the subject matter. The fact that the international system is subsystem dominant and the consequent influence of the decisions of the particular actor upon the state of equilibrium of the system—a situation quite different from that of national politics—tend to reinforce this conclusion. A normative model employs motivational assumptions (in this sense there is a similarity to economic theory) and permits us to study abstractly the relations between a few selected variables of the system. This may be an aid to analysis for, although a change in formal organizational patternings requires explanation in the study of national political systems, it is the maintenance of the informal organizational patterns of international politics that requires explanation. The coordination of independent nation states on particular patterns of alignment and on certain kinds of goal limitations for reasonably long periods of time is not at all easy to understand. A normative model possibly may help to explain how independently chosen strategies converge toward a particular equilibrium—an equilibrium with respect to types of alignment patterns, types and limits of goal objectives, and norms and normative patterns.

There is an important difference, however, between the situation facing the economist and that encountered by the student of international politics. Most economic analysis deals with systems in which irrational behavior by an entrepreneur has the effect only of driving him out of business. If the market is perfect—in our terms, system dominant—this affects only the individual entrepreneur and not the nature of the market. If the market is oligopolistic—subsystem dominant—then individual irrationality may drive the economic system toward a more monopolistic situation. But the irrational entrepreneur does not weaken the position of any of his competitors by collapsing unless his collapse, for specific reasons, favors a particular one of his competitors. Moreover, the economist tends not to analyze these situations because he is more interested in types of markets than in changes from one form of market to another; and present day economies provide him with an abundance of types.

In the international arena, there is only one market, so to speak, rather than many markets co-existing within an economic system. That market is the market of nation states. A change in the configuration of the market is usually a change once and for all. And therefore dynamic aspects of the international system are of the greatest importance. In addition, an irrational strategy in a situation like that of international politics may have a direct effect on the viability of the other actors. Although cartels are known in economics, they do not play the same vital role as alliances, for instance, in the "balance of power" system. Irrationality here of one nation may make ineffective the protective devices normally employed by other nations to maintain the system.

For these reasons the student of international politics cannot assume parametric or environmental conditions in the same way that the economist assumes, for instance, economic rationality. He must be cognizant of all the boundary factors that may produce a dynamic change in the nature of the international system. Although his discipline focuses on the inter-relationships of nations, he does not deify the nation and recognizes that under the skin of the nation, individuals, groups, elites, various kinds of processes, factors, and so forth, may produce novel kinds of international behavior that have the profoundest effect upon the pattern of international politics. And although the discipline of international politics generally assumes the primacy of international factors in its analysis, it is necessary to recognize that occasionally other factors may play a dominant role. The nationalism and anti-Westernism of many of the new nations presents a case in point.

As a consequence the student of international politics will be sensitive to related disciplines that enable him to understand these boundary conditions. Such collateral disciplines include, among others, military science, comparative politics, administrative science and organization theory, economics and studies of economic capabilities, geography, decision-making theory and strategic theory, sociology and related cultural science, and law. No attempt will be made here to specify the role they play in enriching the discipline of international politics other than to assert that they do have a role to play.

I realize that I have merely indicated what the subject matter and methods of the discipline of international politics might look like. I have not established that research in this area can be as successful as in political science generally. But although our methods may have to differ from general political science, we will probably have to turn toward our own version of the traditional problems of politics if we are to succeed in strengthening the discipline. It is not necessary to argue over how fast we should proceed theoretically or formally. Some of the reasons advanced earlier with respect to the need for normative models would seem to indicate at least some effort in a theoretical and at least semi-formal direction. But different political scientists may bring different insights and skills into play in conducting their research. Some research problems may seem to demand more or less theory. And it would seem more fruitful to see what speed turns out best for particular kinds of tasks by applying our insights to these problems than to engage in a methodological debate, which in practice may produce only verbal acrobatics. The discipline should have enough "give" to accommodate different insights, methods, theories, and skills. We have too often seen rejected methods gain new vigor at a new stage of development of a discipline. None of us has achieved such success with his methods that he should be prepared to read others out of court.

2. *THE TEACHING OF INTERNATIONAL RELATIONS IN THE UNITED STATES* / WILLIAM T. R. FOX AND ANNETTE BAKER FOX*

. . . Of the 750 or more accredited American universities and colleges, about 300 have separate departments of political science or of international relations. Only these institutions are likely to offer international relations courses. John Gange estimates that nearly all the significant international relations research comes from forty or fifty of them.[48] This is only a little larger than the number offering the Ph.D. degree in either political science or international relations. For most of the rest, the scope of the international relations courses is largely dictated by the content of the available general textbooks.

* William T. R. Fox and Annette Baker Fox, "The Teaching of International Relations in the United States," *World Politics*, Vol. 13, No. 3 (April 1961), pp. 348–55. Reprinted by permission.

[48] John Gange, *University Research on International Affairs*, Washington, D.C., American Council on Education, 1958, p. 12.

The content of the subject, especially in undergraduate courses, is sharply affected by the goals of the teacher. Although training for citizenship is probably as much of a goal in undergraduate international relations teaching as in the teaching of American government, few professors today see their function as the preaching of salvation via the adoption of some particular grand design for world organization or for American foreign policy. Converting the unwashed isolationist masses to the secular religion of internationalism is not the dominant teaching goal of the international relations scholar. His public service motivation and his voluntaristic predispositions do, however, affect his selection of topics for teaching and research.

Whether because the subject is new or because the world is changing so rapidly, there are few acknowledged classics which every serious American student of international relations will be expected to have read; there are as yet no Paretos or Durkheims, no Marshalls or Keyneses, no Bagehots or Diceys. With no core of acknowledged classics and no system of central examinations, each teacher is free to choose his own approach to a general course in international relations. The large number of introductory textbooks is perhaps one indication of the dissatisfaction which most of their writers have felt with the books written prior to their own. Even the size of the American market cannot by itself account for the continuing production of such books and of collections of annotated readings to supplement or to substitute for them.

Several attempts have been made to classify approaches to international relations teaching and research. In Vernon Van Dyke's 1956 summer seminar on the teaching of international politics, four approaches to the study were identified: the institutional, the historical, the philosophical, and the behavioral.[49] It is noteworthy that the social scientists cited to illustrate these four approaches were as often outside the field of international relations as inside. Heterogeneity of approach is apparently characteristic not just of international relations but of the whole of American social science.

Arnold Wolfers has distinguished the "states as actors," "minds of men," and "corporate actors" approaches.[50] The first takes the nation-states as given and concentrates on the multiple-sovereignty

[49] Vernon Van Dyke, ed., *Some Approaches and Concepts Used in the Teaching of International Politics*, Iowa City, State University of Iowa, 1957.

[50] Arnold Wolfers, "The Actors in International Politics," in William T. R. Fox, ed., *Theoretical Aspects of International Relations*, Notre Dame, Ind., University of Notre Dame Press, 1959, pp. 83–106.

system as an interaction system;[51] it finds the richest materials for study in diplomatic history. The second stresses the unity of intranational and world politics, and makes more use of sociology and social psychology.[52] The third puts "government" rather than "politics" at the center of the study and gives more emphasis to international organization.[53] There are no pure examples of any one of these three approaches at the general textbook level, but the books do differ significantly in their relative emphases.

Still another way of characterizing approaches to the study of international relations is to distinguish the "principles," the "country-by-country," and the "transformations" approaches. Most of the general textbooks exemplify the "principles" approach, although those with a strong historical or geographical emphasis[54] illustrate the second. The experiment at San Francisco State College has emphasized the third, as does the recent text by A. F. K. Organski.[55] These three approaches are complementary rather than incompatible, but the study of such "transformations" as are being wrought by bipolarity, atomic age technology, and the rise of the Afro-Asian nations will receive increasing attention.[56]

Practical limits in approach are set by the gaps in the students'

[51] E.g., Morgenthau, *Politics Among Nations.*

[52] E.g., Harold D. Laswell, *World Politics and Personal Insecurity,* New York, McGraw-Hill, 1935; and Frederick S. Dunn, *War and the Minds of Men,* New York, Council on Foreign Relations, 1951.

[53] E.g., Clyde Eagleton, *International Government,* 3rd ed., New York, Ronald Press, 1957.

[54] A recent example is Lennox A. Mills and Charles H. N. McLaughlin, *World Politics in Transition* (New York, Henry Holt, 1956), in which about half the text is devoted to the foreign policies of particular states; an influential earlier work is Harold and Margaret Sprout, eds., *Foundations of National Power* (2nd ed., New York, Van Nostrand, 1951).

[55] See "San Francisco International Studies Project" and "International Studies," San Francisco State College, 1959 and 1960 (mimeographed); and A. F. K. Organski, *World Politics,* New York, Alfred A. Knopf, 1958.

[56] Among the major transformations, that brought about by scientific and technological change has perhaps been least systematically analyzed. The short-run impact on military policy and strategic theory has been widely discussed, but non-military and long-run aspects have been generally neglected in both teaching and research. A few exceptions are John Herz, *International Politics in the Atomic Age,* New York, Columbia University Press, 1959; Philip C. Jessup and Howard Taubenfeld, *Controls for Outer Space and the Antarctic Analogy,* New York, Columbia University Press, 1959; "Science and World Politics" (a symposium), *Journal of International Affairs,* xiii, No. 1 (1959); and John G. Stoessinger, "Atoms for Peace: The International Atomic Energy Agency," in Commission to Study the Organization of Peace, *Organizing Peace in the Nuclear Age,* New York University Press, 1959, pp. 117–233.

previous historical or social science training.[57] Sometimes this leads the teacher to "do-it-yourself" efforts to be his own historian,[58] his own student of comparative politics, his own sociologist,[59] his own geographer,[60] his own demographer,[61] his own political philosopher,[62] etc. Extensive digressions to make up for the students' presumed deficiencies make it difficult in many cases to discover the integrating approach and sometimes create doubt that the unexplicated approach is even implicit.[63] Texts with a sustained point of view and closely reasoned argument are likely to be addressed to and most suitable for students who begin their study of international relations at a more advanced stage in their educational careers and who have the factual and intellectual resources to evaluate the argument.

There are many subjects which appear in almost all the treatises and course syllabi we have examined, whatever the basic approach of the particular scholar. Grayson Kirk in 1947 identified "five ingredients" which appeared in almost all the treatises and syllabi: (1) the nature and operation of the state system; (2) basic power factors; (3) the special position and policies of the first-ranking powers; (4) the history of international relations since World War I; and (5) the building of a better world order.[64] Richard N. Swift has summarized the changes since 1947 in the following terms: "Courses today stress power and the complexity of world affairs rather than the state system: they probe deeper into the elements of national power, and in so doing take account of the theoretical and

[57] Cf. Grayson Kirk, *The Study of International Relations in American Colleges and Universities*, New York, Council on Foreign Relations, 1947, p. 34: "All social studies are so interrelated that each can best be studied if the beginning student has already studied all the others."

[58] Frederick L. Schuman, *International Politics* (New York, McGraw-Hill, 1st ed., 1933; 6th ed., 1960), is distinctive for its long historical introduction.

[59] Ernst B. Haas and Allen S. Whiting, *Dynamics of International Relations* (New York, McGraw-Hill, 1956), draws on both comparative politics and sociology.

[60] H. and M. Sprout, eds., *op. cit.*

[61] Robert Strausz-Hupé and Stefan T. Possony, *International Relations*, 2nd ed., New York, McGraw-Hill, 1954; and Organski, *World Politics, op.cit.*

[62] Hans J. Morgenthau, *Politics Among Nations*, 3rd ed., New York, Alfred A. Knopf, 1960.

[63] Fred A. Sondermann, in "The Study of International Relations: 1956 Version" (*World Politics*, x, No. 1, October 1957, pp. 102–11), distinguishes the texts with a unified conceptual framework from those "strung together . . . in a more or less random fashion." The latter group often contains more factual data than the former.

[64] Kirk, *op. cit.*, pp. 27–29.

practical results of research in economics, psychology, and sociology. In debating the position of the realists and idealists and presenting the cold war, instructors now pay more attention to theoretical presuppositions; and in presenting accurately the picture of world politics today, they have had to give a larger place than ever before to Africa and Asia."[65] Evidently, fashions in teaching have followed the fashions in research . . ., but usually only after an interval.

In a student's field of undergraduate concentration, courses in international politics, law, and organization are commonly offered. In the more advanced work in the major, students may pursue a variety of courses in non-domestic aspects of economics, law, geography, and possibly other social sciences, and study European and American diplomatic history.

Beyond that, the student often takes special courses in the problems of non-European areas. So little even yet, however, is taught about the non-European world that it is difficult to fill the gaps in knowledge of the history, culture, economy, and politics of various parts of Asia and Africa to the point at which serious analysis becomes possible.[66] Acquiring expertness in any one area is so great a task that it is ususual for a student to be required to do special work in more than one of the areas of non-European culture.

A variety of teaching devices are used to bind together and apply some of the kinds of knowledge that the student has acquired from these varying combinations of courses in international relations, cognate subjects, and area studies. In one sense the course in American foreign policy, which ordinarily deals both with the conduct of American foreign relations and with the analysis of alternative American foreign policies, represents an effort to apply the knowledge previously acquired in courses presented from a "world" point of view. The student looks at the world as seen from Washington, at the situation in which the makers of American foreign policy find themselves, and at the choices which they have to make. Other teaching techniques also have this objective. For

[65] Richard N. Swift, *World Affairs and the College Curriculum*, Washington, D.C., American Council on Education, 1959, pp. 118–19.

[66] Enthusiasm for area studies sometimes goes so far that the task of filling in the gaps of knowledge about unfamiliar parts of the world may be mistaken for the whole study of international relations. This results from a genuine confusion between "foreign" and "international." If "international" were synonymous with "everything foreign," then one would only have to add up his knowledge of individual areas and call the sum total "international relations."

example, there are the recent experiments with political gaming as a teaching device in which the students play roles as representatives of various countries negotiating with each other under specified circumstances and do the research to enable them to play these roles.[67]

Another and more widely used method to promote a vicarious sense of participation is the staging of mock political meetings of various kinds. For example, a mock United Nations General Assembly or a mock disarmament commission or a mock Congressional committee hearing is held in which each student or group of students purports to represent a different country or a different point of view.

Only a relatively small proportion of American students are able to travel abroad and, of these, few in any way that is very helpful to their academic study of international relations. Only a small proportion have the opportunity even to visit Washington. Five institutions, with a grant from the Carnegie Corporation—Colgate, Columbia, Princeton, Rutgers, and Swarthmore—have developed a program to send undergraduate honors students to Europe for independent summer research. The results will be carefully watched for the light they throw on a difficult teaching problem.[68]

At the postgraduate level there are two kinds of programs of study in international relations.[69] One is the program which leads toward the Ph.D. degree and university teaching and research. The other is a quasi-professional program which leads toward a master's degree and employment in government or such private fields of

[67] See Lincoln P. Bloomfield and Norman J. Padelford, "Three Experiments in Political Gaming," *American Political Science Review*, LIII, No. 4 (December 1959), pp. 1105–15; and Herbert Goldhamer and Hans Speier, "Some Observations on Political Gaming," *World Politics*, XII, No. 1 (October 1959), pp. 71–83.

[68] The difficulty of teaching undergraduate students with no foreign travel experience, no direct observation of politics in the national capital, and no simulated international relations experiences in mock meetings and political gaming may be lessened by the rise in standards of television news reporting on world affairs. Documentary presentations on such topics as "The Population Explosion" or "The Munich Crisis" and the showing in full of Nikita Khrushchev's two-hour press conference on the occasion of the abortive summit conference of May 1960 are examples. Harlan Cleveland, "The Real International World and the Academic Lag," in Roy A. Price, ed., *New Viewpoints in the Social Sciences* (28th Yearbook, Washington, D.C., National Council for the Social Studies, 1958, pp. 172–88), emphasizes the importance of immersion in some foreign culture as a "necessary modern supplement" to the education of every American, not just the student with a specialized concern in the field of international relations.

[69] Cf. C. Dale Fuller, *Training of Specialists in International Relations*, Washington, D. C., American Council on Education, 1957.

international affairs as journalism, finance, or trade. The former program culminates in the writing of a dissertation to test the student's independent research abilities. The latter is likely to have a curriculum which is interdisciplinary and largely prescribed and calls for no comparable experience in independent research.[70]

The two types of postgraduate training are not so separate that there are no "cross-over" points. A substantial fraction of the terminal master's degree candidates develop a deeper scholarly interest and become candidates for the Ph.D. degree. On the other hand, many of the Ph.D.'s find careers in government; this appears to be especially true of those with scarce skills in foreign area studies and those with intensive training in economic aspects of international relations.

The traditional three-year period for earning the Ph.D. degree has not ordinarily proved long enough. For the international relations student, all kinds of social science disciplines seem to have tantalizing relevance. More often than not, at least a fourth postgraduate year is required. For the student who is simultaneously pursuing a second program of specialized studies in the problems of some Asian or African or Russian area, it seems to be physically impossible to prepare for the general subjects examinations and to complete a dissertation within the allotted three-year period.

There is no apparent correlation between the organization of international studies within a given university and the availability of courses in special aspects of international relations. Probably, the independent department of international relations or the interdepartmental supervising committee offering a Ph.D. in international relations requires fewer supporting graduate courses in comparative government and political theory and more supporting graduate courses in diplomatic history and the other social sciences. In either case, the choice of options in specialized sub-fields is wide. Each of the leading graduate schools is accordingly turning out men and women of widely varying interests.

[70] It is possible to earn a Ph.D. specializing in international relations and an M.A. as a way-station on the road to the Ph.D. in most of the leading universities, whether in political science or under a separately organized international relations program. The University of Chicago and Yale University were among the first to develop a separately organized Ph.D. program in international relations. The quasi-professional terminal master's degree is offered in a smaller number of institutions. There are separately organized programs for training specialists, for example, at American University, Columbia University, Johns Hopkins University, Princeton University, and Tufts University (Fletcher School of Law and Diplomacy).

One practical consideration may have tended to keep the graduate student in international relations anchored in an established department—usually political science. That consideration is the practical necessity of being employable as an instructor in a department of political science. With the American pattern of requiring the beginning instructor to teach some sections of the introductory course and with that course normally "American Government" if his is a political science department, the prudent graduate student has often combined his international relations studies with enough other political science to compete with political scientists for the available academic vacancies. If there is an increase in the number of independent departments of international relations, prudence may not operate in exactly the same way. . . .

REALISM AND IDEALISM

II

SHOULD STATESMEN BE "IDEALISTS" OR "REALists"? Should students of International Relations be "idealistic" or "realistic" in their analysis of world affairs? Are the two approaches mutually exclusive? Or can one achieve a judicious combination of the two and be a "realist" and an "idealist" at the same time? The selections in this chapter deal with this fundamental and persistent controversy.

Niccolo Machiavelli (1469–1527) gained the reputation of being the realist *par excellence* mainly as a result of his most famous work, *The Prince*. The first selection juxtaposes two chapters breathing vastly different spirits from this one book.

The second selection is a speech by Dean Acheson, a leading critic of the alleged idealism of United States foreign policy, delivered at Amherst College on December 9, 1964. Acheson was Secretary of State from 1949 to 1953, and is the author of *A Citizen Looks at Congress and Power and Diplomacy*.

In the third selection, Stanley H. Hoffmann subjects the realist theory of International Relations, particularly as expounded by Professor Hans J. Morgenthau, to a searching analysis. The selection is an excerpt from his article in *World Politics*. Hoffmann is Professor of Government at Harvard University. He has also written *Contemporary Theory in International Relations* and other works.

3. *THE PRINCE* / NICCOLO MACHIAVELLI*

Whether Princes Ought to Be Faithful to Their Engagements

It is unquestionably very praiseworthy in princes to be faithful to their engagements; but among those of the present day that have been distinguished for great exploits, few indeed have been remarkable for this virtue, or have scrupled to deceive others who may have relied on their good faith.

It should, therefore, be known that there are two ways of deciding any contest: the one by laws, the other by force. The first is peculiar to men, the second to beasts; but when laws are not sufficiently powerful, it is necessary to recur to force. A prince ought, therefore, to understand how to use both these means. This doctrine is admirably illustrated to us by the ancient poets in the allegorical history of the education of Achilles and many other princes of antiquity, by the centaur Chiron, who, under the double form of man and beast, taught those that were destined to govern, that it was their duty to use by turns the arms adapted to both these natures, seeing that one without the other cannot be of any durable advantage. As a prince must learn how to act the part of a beast sometimes, he should make the fox and the lion his patterns. The first can but feebly defend himself against the wolf, and the latter readily falls into such snares as are laid for him. From the fox, therefore, a prince will learn dexterity in avoiding snares; and from

* Niccolo Machiavelli, *The Prince* (New York: The National Alumni, 1907), Chap. 18 (pp. 72–75) and 26 (pp. 106–10).

the lion, how to employ his strength to keep the wolves in awe. But they that entirely rely upon the lion's strength, will not always meet with success: in other words, a prudent prince cannot and ought not to keep his word, except when he can do it without injury to himself, or when the circumstances under which he contracted the engagement still exist.

I should be cautious in inculcating such a precept if all men were good; but as the generality of mankind are wicked, and ever ready to break their word, a prince should not pique himself on keeping his more scrupulously, especially as it is always easy to justify a breach of faith on his part. I could give numerous proofs of this, and show numberless engagements and treaties that have been violated by the treachery of princes, and that those who enacted the part of the fox have always succeeded best in their affairs. But it is necessary to disguise the appearance of craft, and thoroughly to understand the art of feigning and dissembling; for men generally are so simple and so weak that he who wishes to deceive easily finds dupes.

One example, taken from the history of our own times, will be sufficient. Pope Alexander VI played during his whole life a game of deception; and though his faithless conduct was extremely well known, his artifices always proved successful. Oaths and protestations cost him nothing; never did a prince so often break his word or pay less regard to his engagements. This was because he so well understood this chapter in the art of government.

It is not necessary, however, for a prince to possess all the good qualities I have enumerated, but it is indispensable that he should appear to have them. I will even venture to affirm, that it is sometimes dangerous to use them, though it is always useful to appear to possess them. A prince should earnestly endeavor to gain the reputation of kindness, clemency, piety, justice, and fidelity to his engagements. He should possess all these good qualities, but still retain such power over himself as to display their opposites whenever it may be expedient. I maintain that a prince, and especially a new prince, cannot with impunity exercise all the virtues, because his own self-preservation will often compel him to violate the laws of charity, religion and humanity. He should habituate himself to bend easily to the various circumstances that may from time to time surround him. In a word, it will be as useful to him to persevere in the path of rectitude, while he feels no inconvenience in doing so, as to know how to deviate from it when circumstances dictate such a course. He should make it a rule, above all things, never to utter anything that does not breathe of kindness, justice, good faith and piety. This last quality it is most important for him to appear to possess, as men in general judge more from appearances than from reality. All men have eyes, but few have the gift of penetration. Everyone sees your exterior, but few can discern what you have in your heart; and those few dare not oppose the voice of the multitude, who have the majesty of their prince on their side. In forming a judgment of the minds of men, and more especially of princes, as we cannot recur to any tribunal, we must attend only to results. Let it then be the prince's chief care to maintain his authority; the means he employs, be they what they may, will, for this purpose, always appear honorable and meet applause; for the vulgar are ever caught by appearances, and judge only by the event. And as the world is chiefly composed of such as are called the vulgar, the voice of the few is seldom if ever heard or regarded.

There is a prince now living (whose name it may not be proper to mention) who ever preaches the doctrines of peace and good faith; but if he had observed either the one or the other, he would long ago have lost both his reputation and his dominions.*

Exhortation to Deliver Italy from Foreign Powers

When I take a review of the subject-matter treated of in this book, and examine whether the circumstances in which we are now placed would be favorable to the establishment of a new government, alike honorable to its founder and advantageous to Italy, it appears to me that there never was, nor ever will be, a period more appropriate for the execution of so glorious an undertaking.

If it was necessary that the people of Israel should be slaves to Egypt, in order to elicit the rare talents of Moses; that the Persians should groan under the oppression of the Medes, in order to prove the courage and magnanimity of Cyrus; and that the Athenians should be scattered and dispersed, in order to make manifest the rare virtues of Theseus, it will be likewise necessary, for the glory of some Italian hero, that his country should be reduced to its present miserable condition, that the Italians should be greater slaves than the Israelites, more oppressed than the Persians, and still more

* Ferdinand V, King of Aragon and Castile, who thus acquired the kingdoms of Naples and Navarre.

dispersed than the Athenians; in a word, that they should be without laws and without chiefs, pillaged, torn to pieces, and enslaved by foreign powers.

And though it has sometimes unquestionably happened that men have arisen who appeared to be sent by Heaven to achieve our deliverance; yet jealous fortune has ever abandoned them in the midst of their career; so that our unfortunate country still groans and pines away in the expectation of a deliverer that may put an end to the devastations in Lombardy, Tuscany, and the kingdom of Naples. She supplicates Heaven to raise up a prince that may free her from the odious and humiliating yoke of foreigners, may close the numberless wounds with which she has been so long afflicted, and under whose standard she may march against her cruel oppressors.

But on whom can Italy cast her eyes except upon your illustrious house, which, visibly favored by Heaven and the Church, the government of which is confided to its care, possesses also the wisdom and the power necessary to undertake so glorious an enterprise? And I cannot think that the execution of this project will seem difficult if you reflect on the actions and conduct of the heroes whose examples I have adduced. Though their exploits were indeed wonderful, they were still but men; and although their merit raised them above the others, yet none of them certainly were placed in a situation so favorable as that in which you now stand. You have justice on your side; their cause was not more lawful than yours, and the blessing of God will attend you no less than them. Every war that is necessary is just; and it is humanity to take up arms for the defense of a people to whom no other resource is left.

All circumstances concur to facilitate the execution of so noble a project, for the accomplishment of which it will be necessary only to tread in the steps of those great men whom I have mentioned in the course of this work. For though some of them, it is true, were conducted by the hand of God in a wonderful manner—though the sea divided to let them pass, a cloud directed their course, a rock streamed with water to assuage their thirst, and manna fell from heaven to appease their hunger—yet there is no occasion for such miracles at present, as you possess in yourself sufficient power to execute a plan you ought by no means to neglect. God will not do everything for us; much is left to ourselves, and the free exercise of will, that so our own actions may not be wholly destitute of merit.

If none of our princes have hitherto been able to effect what is now expected from your illustrious house, and if Italy has continually been unfortunate in her wars, the evil has arisen from the defects in military discipline, which no person has been able to reform.

Nothing reflects so much honor on a new prince as the new laws and institutions established under his direction, especially when they are good and bear the character of grandeur. It must be acknowledged that Italy soon accommodates herself to new forms. Her inhabitants are by no means deficient in courage, but they are destitute of proper chiefs; the proof of this is in the duels and other individual combats in which the Italians have always evinced consummate ability, while their valor in battle has appeared wellnigh extinguished. This can be attributed only to the weakness of the officers, who are unable to ensure obedience from those who know, or think they know, the art of war. Thus we have seen the greatest generals of the present day whose orders never were executed with exactness and celerity. These are the reasons why, in the wars in which we have been engaged for the last twenty years, the armies raised in Italy have been almost always defeated. Witness Tarus, Alexandria, Capua, Genoa, Vaila, Bologna, and Mestri.

If, therefore, your illustrious house is willing to regulate its conduct by the example of our ancestors, who have delivered their country from the rule of foreigners, it is necessary, above all things, as the only true foundation of every enterprise, to raise a national army. You cannot have better or more faithful soldiers, and though every one of them may be a good man, yet they will become still better when they are all united, and see themselves rewarded by a prince of their own.

It is therefore absolutely necessary to have troops raised in our own country, if we wish to protect it from the invasion of foreign powers. The Swiss as well as the Spanish infantry are highly esteemed, but both have defects that may be avoided in the formation of our troops, which would render them superior to both of those powers. The Spaniards cannot withstand the shock of cavalry, and the Swiss cannot maintain their ground against infantry that is equally resolute.

Experience has fully shown that the Spanish battalions cannot resist the French cavalry, and that the Swiss have been defeated by the infantry of Spain. And though there has not been any thorough trial with regard to the Swiss on this point, yet there was a sort of specimen at the battle of Ravenna, where the Spanish infantry came in contact with the German troops, who fought in the same order as the Swiss. Upon that occasion, the Spanish having, with their accustomed impetuosity, and under the protection of their bucklers, thrown themselves across the pikes of the Germans, the latter were obliged to give way, and would have been decisively defeated, but for their cavalry.

It is necessary, therefore, to institute a military force possessing the defects of neither the Swiss nor the Spanish infantry, and that may be able to maintain its ground against the French cavalry, and this is to be effected, not by changing their arms, but by altering their discipline. Nothing is more likely to make a new prince esteemed and to render his reign illustrious.

Such an opportunity should be embraced eagerly that Italy, after her long sufferings, may at least behold her deliverer appear. With what demonstrations of joy and gratitude, with what affection, with what impatience for revenge, would he not be received by those unfortunate provinces that have so long groaned under such odious oppression? What city would shut her gates against him, and what people would be so blind as to refuse him obedience? What rivals would he have to dread? Is there one Italian that would not hasten to pay him homage? All are weary of the tyranny of these barbarians. May your illustrious house, strong in all the hopes that justice gives our cause, deign to undertake this noble enterprise, that so, under your banners, our nation may resume its ancient splendor, and behold the prophecy of Petrarch at last fulfilled.

When virtue takes the field,
Short will the conflict be,
Barbarian rage shall yield
The palm to Italy:
For patriot blood still warms Italian veins;
Though low the fire, a spark at least remains.

4. *ETHICS IN INTERNATIONAL RELATIONS TODAY: OUR STANDARD OF CONDUCT** / *DEAN ACHESON*

The discussion of ethics or morality in our relations with other states is a prolific cause of confusion. The righteous who seek to deduce foreign policy from ethical or moral principles are as

* Dean Acheson, "Ethics in International Relations Today: Our Standard of Conduct," *Vital Speeches of the Day*, Vol. 31, No. 8 (February 1, 1965), pp. 226–28. Reprinted by permission.

misleading and misled as the modern Machiavellis who would conduct our foreign relations without regard to them.

Most of what we, and a good part of the noncommunist world, regard as ethical principles relates to conduct, the behavior of individuals toward one another. There is pretty general agreement that it is better to act straightforwardly, candidly, honorably, and courageously than duplicitously, conspiratorially, or treacherously. This is true of conduct toward friends and toward those who are ill-disposed to us. It is well that our government should give to foreigners as well as to our own people as clear an idea as possible of its intentions. To do so should inspire confidence and increase stability. One need not counsel perfection—for instance, to tell the whole truth; but it ought not to be too much to advise telling nothing but the truth—advise which might usefully have been given to President Eisenhower before he began issuing statements about the U-2 aircraft shot down some years ago over the Soviet Union.

The French school of diplomacy, founded by Cardinal Richelieu, the dominant school for nearly three centuries, and probably still the best ever devised, was based, as François de Callières stated, upon the principle that "open dealing is the basis of confidence" (a very different idea from President Wilson's ill-considered maxim, "open covenants openly arrived at"). He adds, "The negotiator therefore must be a man of probity and one who loves truth; otherwise he will fail to inspire confidence." And again, "Deceit is the measure of the smallness of mind of him who uses it . . . a lie always leaves behind it a drop of poison. . . . Menaces always do harm to negotiation. . . ."

It does not detract from the purity of his morals that he supports them with worldly wisdom:

> The diplomatist must be . . . a good listener, courteous, and agreeable. He should not seek to gain a reputation as a wit, nor should he be so disputatious as to divulge secret information in order to clinch an argument. Above all the good negotiator must possess enough self control to resist the longing to speak before he has thought out what he wants to say. . . . He should pay attention to women but never lose his heart . . . , possess the patience of a watch-maker . . . should not be given to drink . . . and be able to tell where, in any foreign country, the real sovereignty lies. . . . Finally . . . a good cook is often an excellent conciliator.

For any of you who are contemplating a career in the Foreign Service, François de Callières is as sound an adviser today as he was in 1716.

Without laboring the point further, I take it as clear that, where an important purpose of diplomacy is to further enduring good relations between states, the methods—the modes of conduct—by which relations between states are carried on must be designed to inspire trust and confidence. To achieve this result the conduct of diplomacy should conform to the same moral and ethical principles which inspire trust and confidence when followed by and between individuals.

The purpose of our own diplomacy, as of the French school, requires the inspiring of trust and confidence, for our governmental goal for many years has been to preserve and foster an environment in which free societies may exist and flourish. When we have said this, we had better stop and think before concluding that the policies which will advance us toward this goal can usefully be discussed or evaluated in terms of moral or ethical principles.

In the first place, a little reflection will convince us that the same conduct is not moral under all circumstances. Its moral propriety seems to depend, certainly in many cases, upon the relationship of those concerned with the conduct. For instance, parents have the moral right, indeed duty, to instill moral and religious ideas in their children and correct moral error. Ministers, priests, rabbis, and mullahs have much the same duties to their flocks, including that of correcting heresy, when they can make up their minds what it is.

But these same acts on the part of public officials—certainly in the United States—would be both wrong and a denial of the fundamental rights of the citizen. Indeed, even prayer prescribed and led by teachers in our public schools is condemned by our courts with the approval of some of our churches. The attempt of both governmental and religious bodies to censor literature, painting, sculpture, the theater, and the movies, under the aegis of those alliterative adjectives, lewd and lascivious, seems to me intolerable. Parents, if they are any good, can shield their children from whatever they choose. The rest of us had better take our chances with mortal sin, rather than to have policemen, trained to handle traffic and arrest criminals, become judges of what art we may see or read. And it is just as bad when the local watch and ward society or church body tries to do the same thing.

So, acts, moral in one human relationship, may become quite the reverse in another. Generally speaking, morality often imposes upon those who exercise the powers of government standards of conduct quite different from what might seem right to them as private citizens. For instance, the moral, and indeed the legal, duty of a judge in bringing to bear upon a party before him the coercive power of the state is not to do "what he thinks is right," or by his decision to mould the kind of society which seems to him to accord with divine will or high human aspiration. He has not been given this great power so that he might administer personal justice, even though his conscience be as clear as that of Harun al-Rashid or Henry the Second when they decided disputes by virtuous inspiration. Our courts are supposed to be courts of law; and whatever justice may be (I know of no satisfactory definition of it), it is to be achieved, as the phrase goes, "under law." It is our hope that the consciences of our judges will be guided, not by what they think is right, but what they believe the law requires them to decide, whether they like it or not.

So, too, what may be quite proper and moral for a private citizen—for instance, the pursuit of personal advantage, or the advantage of a group—often, and rightly, is condemned if done when he assumes legislative or executive office. This distinction is not always perceived and has gotten many people into trouble. Even a candidate for office cannot expect the same latitude given private individuals in exposing his ignorance and stupidity. November 3rd last [1964] made that rather clear.

Moreover, the vocabulary of morals and ethics is inadequate to discuss or test foreign policies of states. We are told that what is ethical is characterized by what is excellent in conduct and that excellence may be judged by what is right and proper, as against what is wrong, by existing standards. But when we look for standards we find that none exist. What passes for ethical standards for governmental policies in foreign affairs is a collection of moralisms, maxims, and slogans, which neither help nor guide, but only confuse, decision on such complicated matters as the multilateral nuclear force, a common grain price in Europe, policy in Southeast Asia, or exceptions and disparities under the Kennedy Round of tariff negotiations.

One of the most often invoked and delusive of these maxims is the so-called principle of self-determination. In the continuing dispute over Cyprus it has been invoked by nearly all parties to the struggle to support whatever they were temporarily seeking to achieve—by all Cypriots to justify revolt against British rule, by Archbishop Makarios to support an independent government for the whole island, by Greek Cypriots as foundation for enosis (union) with Greece, and by Turkish Cypriots for partition of the island and double enosis, union of one part with Greece and the other with Turkey.

Despite its approval by Woodrow Wilson, this maxim has a doubtful moral history. He used it against our enemies in the First World War to dismember the Austro-Hungarian and Ottoman Empires with results which hardly inspire enthusiasm today. After the Second World War the doctrine was invoked against our friends in the dissolution of their colonial connections. In all probability these connections would inevitably have been dissolved. But the results were immeasurably improved when considerations other than moralistic maxims were brought to bear on the process.

On the one occasion when the right of self-determination—then called secession—was invoked against our own government by the Confederate States of America, it was rejected with a good deal of bloodshed and moral fervor. Probably you agree that it was rightly rejected. You would doubtless also agree that the dialogue now in progress between the British and French speaking sections of Canada upon the problems of a common national life together would not be helped by conducting it in terms of the principle of self-determination.

Furthermore, this moralistic doctrine is not merely no help to wise policy decisions, it can be a positive menace to them. "Hitler's appeal to national self-determination in the Sudeten crisis in 1938," writes Henry Kissinger, "was an invocation of 'justice,' and thereby contributed to the indecisiveness of the resistance; it induced the Western powers to attempt to construct a 'truly' legitimate order by satisfying Germany's 'just' claims. Only after Hitler annexed Bohemia and Moravia was it clear that he was aiming for dominion, not legitimacy; only then did the contest become one of pure power."

Another set of moralisms and maxims crops up to bedevil discussion and decisions about what is broadly called "foreign aid." A good deal of trouble comes from the anthropomorphic urge to regard nations as individuals and apply to our own national conduct vague maxims for individual conduct—for instance, the Golden Rule—even though in practice individuals rarely adopt it. The fact is that nations are not individuals; the cause and effect of their actions are wholly different; and what a government can and should do with the resources which it takes from its citizens must be governed by wholly different considerations from those which properly determine an individual's use of his own.

This does not mean that considerations of compassion have no place in governmental decisions. It does mean that the criteria are generally quite different and far more complicated. Some of these criteria will determine what funds can be made available; others will determine their allocation among uses always exceeding amounts available.

The overriding guide must be achievement of a major goal of policy—in this case, creating an environment in which free societies may flourish and undeveloped nations who want to work on their own development may find the means to do so. This is an exceedingly difficult matter for both aiding and aided governments. The criteria should be hard-headed in the extreme. Decisions are not helped by considering them in terms of sharing, brotherly love, the Golden Rule, or inducting our citizens into the Kingdom of Heaven.

But, you will say to me, at least one moral standard of right and wrong has been pretty well agreed to be applicable to foreign policy. Surely, the opinion of the world has condemned the use and threat of force by one state against another, as the United Nations Charter bears witness. Does this not give us firm ground on which to stand? Well, does it? Ever since the Charter was signed, those whose interests are opposed to ours have used force, or the threat of it, whenever it seemed to them advisable and safe—in Greece, Czechoslovakia, Palestine, Berlin, Korea, Indochina, and Hungary. Each side used it in regard to Suez.

Is it moral to deny ourselves the use of force in all circumstances, when our adversaries employ it, under handy excuses, whenever it seems useful to tip the scales of power against every value we think of as moral and as making life worth living? It seems to me not only a bad bargain, but a stupid one. I would almost say an immoral one. For the very conception of morality seems to me to involve a duty to preserve values outside the contour of our own skins, and at the expense of foregoing much that is desired and pleasant, including—it may be—our own fortunes and lives.

But, however that may be, those involved in the Cuban crisis of October, 1962, will remember the irrelevance of the supposed moral considerations brought out in the discussions. Judgment centered about the appraisal of dangers and risks, the weighing of the need for decisive and effective action against considerations of prudence; the need to do enough, against the consequences of doing too much. Moral talk did not bear on the problem. Nor did it bear upon the decision of those called upon to advise the President in 1949 whether and with what degree of urgency to press the attempt to produce a thermonuclear weapon. A respected colleague advised me that it would be better that our whole nation and people should perish rather than be party to a course so evil as producing that weapon. I told him that on the Day of Judgment his view might be confirmed and that he was free to go forth and preach the necessity for salvation. It was not, however, a view which I could entertain as a public servant.

What, then, is the sound approach to questions of foreign policy? I suggest that it is what we might call the strategic approach—to consider various courses of action from the point of view of their bearing upon major objectives. On August 22, 1862, President Lincoln wrote to Horace Greeley in response to the latter's question as to how the President viewed the question of slavery in relation to the war then in progress, "my paramount object in this struggle is to save the Union, and is not either to save or destroy slavery. If I could save the Union without freeing any slave, I would do it; and if I could save it by freeing all the slaves, I would do it; and if I could do it by freeing some and leaving others alone, I would also do that. What I do about slavery and the colored race, I do because I believe it helps to save this Union; and what I forbear, I forbear because I do not believe it would help to save the Union. I shall do less whenever I shall believe what I am doing hurts the cause, and I shall do more whenever I shall believe doing more will help the cause."

This is what I mean by the strategic approach. If you object that is no different from saying that the end justifies the means, I must answer that in foreign affairs only the end can justify the means; that this is not to say that the end justifies any means, or that some ends can justify anything. The shifting "combinazioni," sought by the weak Italian city states of the Renaissance to plunder one another, not only failed to justify the means they used, but gave their diplomacy and its expounder, Niccolo Machiavelli, the bad name they have today.

The end sought by our foreign policy, the purpose for which we carry on relations with foreign states, is, as I have said, to preserve and foster an environment in which free societies may exist and flourish. Our policies and actions must be tested by whether they contribute to or detract from achievement of this end. They need no other justification or moral or ethical embellishment. To oppose powerful and brutal states which threaten the independence of others is not less admirable because it helps secure our own as well; nor is it less good to help others improve their lot because it is necessary to keep the free world free and to strengthen it.

In conducting our foreign affairs we can use any amount of intelligence, perseverance, nerve, and luck. But if we have an excess of moral or ethical enthusiasm or idealism, let us not try to find an outlet for it in the formulation of foreign policies. Rather in how we carry them out. In this country we have an unfortunate tendency to do fine and noble things in a thoroughly churlish way. Let us remember that often what we do may be less important than how we do it. "What one lives for may be uncertain," writes Lord Robert Cecil; "How one lives is not." We can be faulted far less in what we do, than in how we do it.

5. *INTERNATIONAL RELATIONS: THE LONG ROAD TO THEORY*/ STANLEY H. HOFFMANN*

. . . The theory which has occupied the center of the scene in this country during the last ten years is Professor Morgenthau's "realist" theory of power politics. It tries to give us a reliable map of the landscape of world affairs,[9] to catch the essence of world politics. The master key is the concept of interest defined in terms of power. The theory succeeds in focusing attention on the principal actors in world affairs: the states, and on the factors that account for the autonomy of international relations: the differences between domestic and world politics which thwart the operation in the latter of ideas and institutions that flourish in the former, the drastic imperatives of survival, self-preservation, and self-help which are both the causes and the products of such differences.

However, as a general theory, the realist analysis fails because it

* Stanley H. Hoffmann, "International Relations: The Long Road to Theory," *World Politics*, Vol. 11, No. 3 (April 1959), pp. 349–54. Reprinted by permission.

[9] Hans J. Morgenthau, "Reflections on the State of Political Science," *Review of Politics*, XVII, No. 4 (October 1955), pp. 455ff.

sees the world as a static field in which power relations reproduce themselves in timeless monotony. The map is inadequate for two main reasons. First, the realist analysis of power is a very debatable one. The decision to equate politics and the effects of man's "lust for power," and the tendency to equate power and evil or violence, mutilate reality.[10] A "power monism" does not account for all politics, when power is so somberly defined. Furthermore, the extent to which power as a carrier of evil and violence expresses a basic human instinct is questionable, for much of the international (or domestic) evil of power is rooted not in the sinfulness of man but in a context, a constellation, a situation, in which even good men are forced to act selfishly or immorally. The discrimination between the inherent or instinctive aspects of the "power drive," and the situational or accidental ones, is an important task, neglected by the theory.

Also, it is dangerous to put in a key position a concept which is merely instrumental. Power is a means toward any of a large number of ends (including power itself): the quality and quantity of power used by men are determined by men's purposes. Now, the realist theory neglects all the factors that influence or define purposes. Why statesmen choose at times to act in a certain way rather than in another is not made clear. The domestic considerations that define national power are either left out or brushed aside. So is the role of internationally shared values and purposes. We get a somewhat mechanistic view of international affairs in which the statesmen's role consists of adjusting national power to an almost immutable set of external "givens." The realist world is a frozen universe of separate essences.[11]

Even if the role of power were as determining as the theory postulates, the question arises whether any scheme can put so much methodological weight upon one concept, even a crucial one; for it seems to me that the concept of power collapses under the burden. Power is a most complex product of other variables which should be allowed to see the light of the theory instead of remaining hidden in

[10] Hans J. Morgenthau, *Scientific Man versus Power Politics*, Chicago, 1946, pp. 50–51 and 188–202.

[11] On these points, see John H. Herz, *Political Realism and Political Idealism*, Chicago, 1951, pp. 3–15 and 63ff.; Robert W. Tucker, "Professor Morgenthau's Theory of Political 'Realism,'" *American Political Science Review*, XLVI, No. 1 (March 1952), pp. 214–24; Herbert Butterfield, "The Scientific versus the Moralistic Approach," *International Affairs*, XXVII, No. 4 (October 1951), pp. 411–22; Harold Sprout, "In Defense of Diplomacy," *World Politics*, I, No. 3, (April 1949), pp. 404–13.

the shadow of power.[12] Otherwise, the theory is bound either to mean different things at different steps of the analysis (or when dealing with different periods), or to end by selecting for emphasis only one aspect of power: either military force or economic strength.[13] Thus, instead of a map which simplifies the landscape so that we can understand it, we are left with a distortion.

There is a second reason for the inadequacy of the map. The clumsiness that comes from the timeless concept of power is compounded by the confusing use of other concepts that are dated in more ways than one, and which the theory applies to situations in which they do not fit. The model of the realists is a highly embellished ideal-type of eighteenth- and nineteenth-century international relations. This vision of the golden age is taken as a norm, both for empirical analysis, and for evaluation. A number of oddities of the theory are explained thereby. First, the lack of an adequuate discussion of ends. For when all the actors have almost the same credo, it becomes easy to forget the effects of the common credo on the actors' behavior, and to omit from among the main variables of the theory a factor whose role seems constant.[14] It is nevertheless an optical illusion to mistake a particular pattern for the norm of a scientific system. Secondly, the conception of an objective and easily recognizable national interest is one which makes sense only in a stable period in which the participants play for limited ends, with limited means, and without domestic kibitzers to disrupt the players' moves. In such a period, the survival of the main players is rarely at stake in the game, and a hierarchy can rather easily be established among the other and far less vital interests that are at stake. Today, survival is almost always in question, and the most divergent courses of action can be recommended as choices for survival.[15] An attempt at using the theory as a key to the under-

[12] It is impossible to subsume under one word variables as different as power as a condition of policy and power as a criterion of policy; power as a sum of resources and power as a set of processes; power as a potential and power in use.

[13] On this last point, see, e.g., A. F. K. Organski's "economic power monism" in his *World Politics*, New York, 1958.

[14] Morgenthau's views on the role of motives and of ideological preferences are to be found in *Politics Among Nations*, New York, 1955, pp. 6–7 and 80ff. Similar views are expressed by Kenneth W. Thompson in Roy Macridis, ed., *Foreign Policy in World Politics*, New York, 1958, pp. 351–55.

[15] See Thomas I. Cook and Malcolm Moos, "Foreign Policy: The Realism of Idealism," *American Political Science Review*, XLVI, No. 2 (June 1952), pp. 342–56; Raymond Aron, "En quête d'une philosophie de la politique étrangère," *Revue Française de Science Politique*, III, No. 1 (January–March 1953), pp. 69–91.

standing of contemporary realities puts one in the position of a Tiresias who recognizes interests which the parties refuse to see, who diagnoses permanence where the parties find confusing change, and whose ex post facto omniscience is both irritating and irrelevant.

Thirdly, the idea that the national interest carries its own morality is also one which makes sense only in a stable period (although it is strangely phrased). For it is in such a period that an international consensus assures at least the possibility of accommodation of national objectives: the conflicts of interests which are involved are not struggles between competing international moralities. The philosophical pluralism implicit in the realist theory (which purports to be both normative and empirical) is hardly tolerable in periods of "nationalistic universalism," and it is unnecessary in periods of stability and moderation, which bloom only because of a basic agreement on values. Fourth, the emphasis on the rationality of foreign policy and the desire to brush aside the irrational elements as intrusions or pathological deviations are understandable only in terms of cabinet diplomacy, where such deviations appear (especially with the benefit of hindsight) to have been rare. There, rationality seemed like the simple adjustment of means to stable and generally recognized ends. These concepts are far less applicable to a period in which the political struggles involve primarily the determination of ends.[16] Thus, behind the claim to realism, we find a reactionary utopia.

The consequence of this inadequacy of the map is that the theory's usefulness as a general theory for the discipline is limited. In the first place, from the point of view of systematic empirical analysis, the theory stresses the autonomy of international relations to the point of leaving beyond its pale the forces which work for change and which, cutting across the states, affect the states' behavior.[17] We are presented both with a single key to the closed room of politics among nations, and with a warning that the room is in a house whose key we cannot have, or whose opening must be

[16] These arguments are developed by Henry A. Kissinger in *A World Restored*, Boston, 1957. The application of a rationality of means to the selection of ends is, it seems to me, one of the fallacies that mar the argument for limited nuclear war.

[17] See Hans J. Morgenthau, "Another 'Great Debate': The National Interest of the United States," *American Political Science Review*, XLVI, No. 4 (December 1952), pp. 973–76; and a critique of this attitude in Reinhold Niebuhr, *The Children of Light and the Children of Darkness*, New York, 1944, pp. 173ff.

left to the "workman-like manipulation of perennial forces."[18] We are not told what they are, or how they operate. We reach at this point one of the most fundamental ambiguities of the theory. The postulate of the permanence of power politics among nations as the core of international relations tends to become a goal. The static qualities of the theory lead to confusion between the phenomenon of power conflicts and the transitory forms and institutions in which such conflicts have been taking place in recent centuries. Why should the sound reminder that power is here to stay mean that the present system of nation-states will continue, or change only through forces that are of no concern to us? Such an attitude is a double evasion: from the empirical duty of accounting for change, and from the normative task of assessing whether the present system should indeed continue. One cannot help but feel that, in spite of Mr. Morgenthau's qualifying statements, there is behind his theory the old position that whatever has been, must continue.

This brings us to a second limitation, which concerns the usefulness of the scheme as a normative theory. It is something of a success philosophy. The criterion of a good foreign policy is its rationality, but the touchstone of rationality is success. Unfortunately the standards of success and failure are not made clear. First, how will we distinguish between the follies of straight utopianism and the fallacies of wrong realism—realism that did not work?[19] Secondly, from what viewpoint shall we decide whether a statesman has succeeded or failed? Shall we turn to history alone? But at what stage? Metternich had succeeded by 1825, failed by 1848, and writers disagree as to whether he had succeeded or failed by 1914.[20] If we set our standards outside and above history, we must avoid trying to prove that history will inevitably recompense policies that meet our standards. Otherwise, we become salesmen for a philosophical stand who travel the roads of history in search of a clientele of confirmations, rather than scholars testing a hypothesis or philosophers interested in an ideal which history cannot promise to bless at all times.

The former position we wish to avoid. It is particularly uncomfortable when one's basic postulate about human nature is such that history cannot be anything but a tale full of sound and fury,

[18] Morgenthau, *Politics Among Nations*, p. 9.

[19] Aron, *op. cit.;* David Thomson in *Contemporary Political Science*, Paris, UNESCO, 1950, pp. 588–89.

[20] See E. H. Carr, *The Twenty Years' Crisis*, London, 1951, pp. 89–91.

signifying nothing.[21] This view makes it impossible to understand how there could be a rational theory of rational human behavior. This is not the last contradiction: the realist theory combines a Hobbesian image of naked power politics with an attempt to show that states are nevertheless not condemned to a life that is "nasty, brutish, and short." Realism thus puts its faith in voluntary restraints, moderation, and the underlying assumption of possible harmony among national interests—points scarcely admitted by the original postulate. Finally, there is a sharp contrast between this postulate, whose logic is a permanent clash of forces of evil, and the norm of eighteenth- and nineteenth-century international relations—the period in which the world's state of nature was most Lockian, and Morgenthau's view of human nature most unjustified.

With such flaws and contradictions, the policy guidance which the realist theory is able to afford is limited. Realism allows us to eliminate those policies that would foolishly forget the prerequisite of power; but it does not go much further. Too many factors are left out for realist advice to avoid the dilemma of homilies and admonishments, or suggestions inappropriate for revolutionary periods.[22] The light that illuminated the landscape in the quiet obscurity of nineteenth-century politics is blown out by today's tempest. . . .

[21] Reason, "far from following its own inherent impulses, is driven toward its goal by the irrational forces the ends of which it serves" (Morgenthau, *Scientific Man versus Power Politics*, p. 154). See Alfred Grosser, "L'étude des relations internationales, spécialité américaine?" *Revue Française de Science Politique*, VI, No. 3 (July–September 1956), pp. 634–51.

[22] This is frequently the case with George Kennan. See William G. Carleton, "Braintrusters of American Foreign Policy," *World Politics*, VII, No. 4 (July 1955), pp. 627–39. On the possibility of justifying in realist terms a policy that can also be advocated on utopian grounds, see Warner R. Schilling, "The Clarification of Ends, or, Which Interest Is the National?" *ibid.*, VIII, No. 4 (July 1956), pp. 566–78.

THE MODERN STATE SYSTEM

part II

SOVEREIGNTY

III

THE PRIME CHARACTERISTIC OF THE MODERN state system is sovereignty. Jean Bodin (1530–96) thoroughly defined and analyzed this concept in his *Six Books of the Commonwealth*, first published in 1576. He wrote this work at a time of political disorders in France, which explains his horror of anarchy and his concern for the establishment of strong governmental authority. The excerpts included in this chapter show, however, that he did not think of sovereignty in terms of completely unlimited power.

Bodin's principal concern was sovereignty within the state. What effect does the existence of many states, each sovereign and under no higher authority, have on the international system? Thomas Hobbes (1588–1679) in his famous work *Leviathan*, from which the second selection is drawn, compared international relations with those of individuals in a "state of nature." In other words, sovereignty equals international anarchy. According to Clement Attlee, British Prime Minister from 1945 to 1951 and Labor Party leader until 1955, this is indeed the root of the world's troubles. The third selection in this chapter is the Annual Memorial Lecture of the David Davies Memorial Institute of International Studies delivered by Lord Atlee in the House of Commons in 1958.

If state sovereignty means anarchy and war, should one conclude that the solution lies in the creation of a single world-state under a single world-government? Yes, according to Dante Alighieri (1265–1321) in his *De Monarchia* or *On World-Government*, both on deductive and empirical grounds. No, says theologian Reinhold Niebuhr in an article in *Foreign Affairs*, which is the fifth selection. Niebuhr is Professor Emeritus at Union Theological Seminary.

6. *ON SOVEREIGNTY* / JEAN BODIN*

Sovereignty is the absolute and perpetual power of a state which in Latin is termed *maiestas* . . . It is perpetual because one may give absolute power to one or more persons for a certain length of time, but once that time has expired they become merely subjects again themselves; even while they are in power, they cannot call themselves sovereign rulers, but only the agents of that power until it pleases the people or the prince to revoke it. The true sovereign always retains his power. Just as he who lends his goods to another remains the lord and owner of them, so he who grants to others the power and authority to judge and command either for a limited time or for as long as it pleases him, actually retains the power and the jurisdiction merely borrowed by those exercising it. That is why the law stipulates that local governors or the prince's lieutenants, as agents of the prince's power, surrender their authority at the end of their terms of office. And in this respect there is no difference between the highest and the lowest officials. For if it were otherwise, and the absolute power granted by a prince to his

* Jean Bodin, *Les Six Livres de la République* (Paris, 1583), Chap. 8. Translated by Eva Tamm Lijphart and Arend Lijphart.

lieutenant should be called sovereignty, he could use it against his prince who would then be a prince in name only: the subject would command his lord and the servant his master. Nothing could be more absurd, because the person of the sovereign is always excepted, as a matter of right, in all grants of power and authority to others. However much he gives, he always keeps more himself. He is never deprived of his power to command or intervene in all matters delegated to his magistrates or officers by way of prevention, confirmation, evocation, or any other way it pleases him. He may also revoke any delegated power or allow it to be exercised only as long as he thinks fit. . . .

Let us now consider the other part of our definition and explain what is meant by the term "absolute power." The people or the lords of a state may simply give to someone the sovereign and perpetual power to dispose of their goods and persons and of the whole state at his pleasure and then leave it to a successor of his choice, in the same way that a property owner may generously make a pure and unconditional gift of his goods to someone. Such a gift is the only true gift—unconditional, unqualified, and irrevocable. Other gifts, burdened by obligations and conditions, are not true gifts. Similarly, sovereignty given to a prince with obligations and conditions attached is neither true sovereignty nor absolute power, unless the conditions of his appointment are only those of the laws of God and of nature . . . If we state that he who has absolute power is not subject to any laws, there is no sovereign prince at all in the world because all the princes of the earth are subject to the laws of God and of nature and to certain human laws common to all nations. . . .

The sovereign cannot in any way be subject to the commands of others, for it is he who makes law for his subjects, abrogates laws that are no longer needed, and replaces them with new laws. No one who is subject to the law or under some other person's authority can do this. That is why according to law the prince is exempt from all laws. The word "law" in Latin also implies the command of the holder of sovereignty. Furthermore, we find in all decrees and statutes the following clause: "Notwithstanding all decrees and statutes from which we have derogated or do hereby derogate." This clause was always added to the ancient laws whether the former law had been promulgated by the prince himself or by his predecessors. For it is quite certain that all laws, ordinances, letters patent, privileges, and grants issued by the prince are in force only during his lifetime, unless they are expressly or at least tacitly confirmed by his successors . . .

If, therefore, the sovereign prince is exempt from the laws of his predecessors, still less can he be bound by his own laws and ordinances. One may impose a law on someone else, but it is impossible to impose a law on oneself or to bind oneself in any matter which depends on one's own free will. As the law states, *Nulla obligatio consistere potest, quae a voluntate promittentis statum capit.* It follows, therefore, that the king cannot be subject to his own laws. Just as, according to the canonists, the Pope can never tie his own hands, the sovereign prince cannot tie his own hands even if he should want to do so. Therefore, we find the following phrase at the end of decrees and statutes: "For such is our good pleasure," indicating that the laws of a sovereign prince, even though founded on good reasons, depend solely on his own free will.

The divine and natural laws present a different case. All princes of the earth are subject to them, and cannot infringe them without being guilty of treason and war against God, under whose majesty all monarchs of the earth must be subjugated and must bow their heads in fear and reverence. Hence the absolute power of princes and sovereign lords does not extend to the laws of God and of nature. He who best understood the meaning of absolute power and made kings and emperors submit to his power [Innocent IV], defined it as being above the ordinary law, but not above the divine and natural laws.

But is not the prince subject to the laws of his country if he has sworn to uphold them? Here we have to distinguish. If the prince swears to himself that he will uphold the law, he is not bound by his oath any more than by a promise to himself. Even subjects are not bound in any way by private oaths to keep agreements. The law permits a breach of such agreements even though they may be fair and reasonable. However, if one sovereign prince promises another prince, whether under oath or not, to uphold the laws which he or his predecessors have made, he is bound to do so if the other prince's interests are involved. If they are not involved, neither the promise nor the oath can bind him.

The same rule applies to promises made by the sovereign prince to his subjects, even if they were made before his election, for this makes no difference. It is not that the prince is bound by his own laws or those of his predecessors. But he is bound by the just covenants and promises he has made, whether under oath or not, just as a private person is bound in such a case. For the same reasons that a private person can be released from a promise which was unjust, unreasonable, or too burdensome, or which was extracted by fraud, error, or force, a sovereign prince can act to reverse any encroachments on his sovereign rights. Hence our maxim stands, that the prince is neither subject to his own laws nor to those of his predecessors, but is bound by the just and reasonable covenants which affect the interests of all or some of his subjects. . . .

We must not confuse laws with covenants. Laws proceed from the sovereign who can bind the subject but cannot bind himself. Covenants are mutually and reciprocally binding on both the prince and his subjects, and cannot be contravened by either party to the prejudice of the other without his consent. In this case, the prince has no more rights than his subjects. . . .

The constitutional laws and the laws concerning the King's estate are, like the salic laws, annexed and united to the Crown, and cannot be infringed by the prince. If he should do so, his successor can always nullify any act prejudicial to the constitutional laws and those of the royal estate on which his sovereign majesty is based. . . .

Is the prince bound to uphold the law of nations? . . . The prince is not bound by the law of nations to a greater extent than by his own laws. If the law of nations is iniquitous, the prince can disregard it when making laws for his own kingdom and can forbid his subjects to observe it, even when it is truly common to all peoples, as was done in this kingdom [France] with regard to slavery. He can also disregard any similar provisions of the law of nations, provided that he does nothing against the law of God. For if justice is the end of the law, the law the work of the prince, and the prince the image of God, the law of the prince should be patterned after the law of God.

7. THE STATE OF NATURE / THOMAS HOBBES*

. . . in the nature of man we find three principal causes of quarrel. First, competition; secondly, diffidence; thirdly, glory.

* Thomas Hobbes, *Leviathan* (London: Andrew Crooke, 1651), Part I, Chap. 13. (Spelling and punctuation modernized.)

The first maketh man invade for gain; the second, for safety; and the third, for reputation. The first use violence, to make themselves masters of other men's persons, wives, children, and cattle; the second, to defend them; the third, for trifles, as a word, a smile, a different opinion, and any other sign of undervalue, either direct in their persons, or by reflection in their kindred, their friends, their nation, their profession, or their name.

Hereby it is manifest that, during the time men live without a common power to keep them all in awe, they are in that condition which is called war, and such a war as is of every man against every man. For "war" consisteth not in battle only or the act of fighting, but in a tract of time wherein the will to contend by battle is sufficiently known, and therefore the notion of "time" is to be considered in the nature of war, as it is in the nature of weather. For as the nature of foul weather lieth not in a shower or two of rain, but in an inclination thereto of many days together, so the nature of war consisteth not in actual fighting, but in the known disposition thereto during all the time there is no assurance to the contrary. All other time is "peace."

Whatsoever therefore is consequent to a time of war, where every man is enemy to every man, the same is consequent to the time wherein men live without other security than what their own strength and their own invention shall furnish them withal. In such condition there is no place for industry, because the fruit thereof is uncertain, and consequently no culture of the earth, no navigation nor use of the commodities that may be imported by sea, no commodious building, no instruments of moving and removing such things as require much force, no knowledge of the face of the earth; no account of time, no arts, no letters, no society, and, which is worst of all, continual fear and danger of violent death, and the life of man solitary, poor, nasty, brutish, and short.

It may seem strange to some man that has not well weighed these things, that Nature should thus dissociate and render men apt to invade and destroy one another; and he may therefore, not trusting to this inference made from the passions, desire perhaps to have the same confirmed by experience. Let him therefore consider with himself, when taking a journey, he arms himself and seeks to go well accompanied; when going to sleep, he locks his doors; when even in his house, he locks his chests; and this when he knows there be laws and public officers armed to revenge all injuries shall be done him; what opinion he has of his fellow-subjects, when he rides armed; of his fellow-citizens, when he locks his doors; and of his children and servants, when he locks his chests. Does he not there as much accuse mankind by his actions as I do by my words? But neither of us accuse man's nature in it. The desires and other passions of man are in themselves no sin. No more are the actions that proceed from those passions, till they know a law that forbids them; which, till laws be made, they cannot know, nor can any law be made till they have agreed upon the person that shall make it.

It may peradventure be thought there was never such a time nor condition of war as this; and I believe it was never generally so over all the world, but there are many places where they live so now. For the savage people in many places of America, except the government of small families the concord whereof dependeth on natural lust, have no government at all, and live at this day in that brutish manner as I said before. Howsoever, it may be perceived what manner of life there would be where there were no common power to fear, by the manner of life which men that have formerly lived under a peaceful government, use to degenerate into in a civil war.

But, though there had never been any time wherein particular men were in a condition of war one against another, yet in all times kings and persons of sovereign authority, because of their independence, are in continual jealousies and in the state and posture of gladiators, having their weapons pointing, and their eyes fixed on one another, that is, their forts, garrisons, and guns, upon the frontiers of their kingdoms, and continual spies upon their neighbours; which is a posture of war. But because they uphold thereby the industry of their subjects, there does not follow from it that misery which accompanies the liberty of particular men. . . .

8. *THE PERILS OF ABSOLUTE SOVEREIGNTY**/ *CLEMENT ATTLEE*

The root of the trouble in today's world is that we believe in anarchy. We believe in the complete, or almost complete, right of

* Clement Attlee, "The Perils of Absolute Sovereignty," *The Saturday Review* (August 23, 1958), pp. 22–23. Reprinted by permission of the David Davies Memorial Institute of International Studies and *The Saturday Review*.

every nation to do what it chooses. One still has the feeling that anything like a surrender of sovereignty is contrary to our human nature. Although every day individuals surrender their sovereignty inside a country for the sake of a larger freedom, we still talk as if we were detached individuals when it comes to international affairs.

What is needed in the world today is the rule of enforceable law enforced. You will find some people who say that all this is high-flying idealistic nonsense. So long as human nature remains human nature this idea of world government will remain nothing but a comfortable dream. I wonder how many people have said that in their time with regard to every possible innovation. But you cannot afford to take that view today. Unless mankind meets the challenge of the present day it will not survive.

The United Nations doesn't yet fill the bill. The U.N. has not yet meant the surrender of sovereignty; it is not an authoritative force—it has no instrument. I am not denying that it is a very powerful forum of public opinion, nor am I denying that it does all kinds of good things, but it doesn't do the *essential* things. But there are some hopeful signs. Leaders in our own country and others no longer shrink from world government. It has been proclaimed by our Government that we must work towards world government—that is a great step forward from the old days when collective security was called midsummer madness. They also declare for absolute disarmament. Thirty or forty years ago anyone who preached that would have been answered, "Human nature never changes—people always fight." Today we have plans for disarmament.

But why do all these admirable plans break down? The late Arthur Henderson worked with great devotion between the wars on disarmament proposals. Other experts are working constantly. Yet why don't we get disarmament? I think the answer is that we always found that between the wars you cannot get disarmament without some security—it always broke down on that. How can you get security? You cannot get security internationally today. You may get a partial security in arrangements of one kind and another—such as NATO and SEATO. But I don't believe we will get real disarmament without an approach to an international force. I say it for this reason: at the present time we are held in uneasy equilibrium by the possession of two groups in the world of nuclear weapons. We hope this means that nuclear warfare will never come to the world. We hope that, but it may be that the mere fact that either side would hesitate to use these nuclear weapons may make them take a chance with what are called "conventional weapons." A good definition of an unconventional weapon was given by Sir Winston Churchill the other day: "Those the other side have got and you have not got." I don't much believe in this distinction. I don't believe that when you arm your forces with nuclear weapons you can then talk of them as conventional weapons. I think the distinction has to do with their mass destructiveness, as contrasted to comparatively light weapons for police purposes.

I think the time has come when, if we are realists, we should say that no major war would be won with nuclear weapons, and therefore if any minor trouble develops we don't want forces which would lead inevitably to the use of nuclear weapons. We want something much smaller and lighter—a form of armed police force. If we had that you could, I believe, have enough to stop incidents where there was danger developing, but we would also be saved all the immense business of these huge land armies that I believe will never fight at all.

How are you going to get such a force? People say that there is not today the necessary unity in the world; power politics are played all the way. I don't see any reason why, apart from power politics, some of these problems that oppress us in various parts of the world should not be settled peaceably, but there are people who have an interest in stirring it up.

Can we get away from this? Let's be realists. If it is really true that the Soviet Union is inspired by a complete desire to enslave the whole world, as a combination of the old-fashioned Russian imperialism and the new Communist ideological imperialism, then the outlook is pretty bad; but I always think we are rather inclined to overestimate the solidarity and strength of the people with whom we can necessarily have only a limited contact. Looking back at the war and reading the memoirs, it is most illuminating to see what they were thinking on the "other side." At the time we were all impressed by the fact of this great military force of Germany, absolutely on top, and yet you find that the inside was quite doubtful. And the idea of an absolutely strong, monolithic power in Russia may be wrong.

I believe that despite the possession of nuclear weapons, the dominating feeling in Russia today is fear. I believe the trouble in America is fear. If we could lift off that fear we might get much further. I don't believe that the holding of the satellite states is essentially due to an imperialist desire to spread Communism. I think it is a desire to have an expendable bursting layer between East and West. I don't think that any of us, any country, even in the most extremist circles in America, imagines that one could conquer Communism by an attack on Russia. I hope Russia also realizes that they will not conquer the world by force, because the forces will be too strong for them—the spiritual forces. They are already finding difficulties in the satellite countries. That is why, I think, that if you could lift off this fear of Russia today an approach might be made which would reconcile things. And even if the nuclear weapons are held by the two rival groups instead of by a world authority it might be possible that the Russians, like everybody else, do not want to have localized little wars because they may not remain localized.

One of our difficulties in all these matters is that it is not as if the world was a very peaceful place. There are an awful lot of sore places. Any suggestion you have to stabilize the world as it is would cause a great outcry from the people under a rule they don't like. Again I don't believe, with all our sympathy for the Hungarians, Poles, Rumanians, and the rest, that one would contemplate embarking on a nuclear war to rescue them, nor do I think they would contemplate it either, because after the rescue there might be very little left of the rescued or the rescuer.

We need to make a start on the idea of an international force. That force would not be European solely, or American or Australian, but should cover Africa and Asia as well. One of the dangers I see today in the world is that out-of-date ideas still hang on. There are still out-of-date ideas about the primacy of Europe. I don't think we have shown an awful lot of commonsense in nearly committing suicide in two world wars, so we might be a bit humble on that.

I think that a world force might make the best approach to world government. I know all the difficulties of world government. You can say, "Where are you going to draw the line between what nations can do and what they cannot do?" But our aim would be to begin with the minimum, just as we did in our own domestic affairs. Our early force was really just to keep law and order, the King's peace, the Police Force gradually coming about, and it has taken very many years before we met society's other needs.

I would like to continue on the widest possible scale the work that is being done to try and raise the standards in the undeveloped countries of the world. I am all for that, but I think one cannot continue without any surrender of sovereignty. Surrender of sovereignty is what you want if you look only at this one aspect of war and peace. Could we make a start on that? I would like to see it pressed further, rather more vigorously than at present. So many of the smaller issues are pressed, but the big major one is not. I don't want it to be done by acrimonious disputes in the U.N.—there are far too many acrimonious debates. I would like it seriously discussed everywhere what the reality is—the reality that faces us, simply, is our civilization going to continue? This question was always at the back of my mind when I was in office. There was always this looming danger. Yet nationalism persists. I refer to the hope that nations may grow upon the question of sovereignty. Sixty years ago, who would have thought of the surrender of sovereignty in the British Commonwealth? Now today in India, Pakistan, Ceylon, Ghana, Malaya and elsewhere we have seen a surrender of sovereignty.

But to whom should sovereignty be surrendered? I believe we must have a wide authority and that that wide authority must cease to be based just on power. All the arguments (we had them all at San Francisco) as to why the power must be placed in the hands of a few big states—are true only if we are going to depend on action of individual states to support the law. If you get away from that there is no reason why we need have this predominance of the bigger states. The interests of the smaller ones are just as great as our own. I am not going to argue on the subject of world government in its detail. I have never felt that technical details were so important. If people want to get these things, they will. I would like a movement in this country and every country in favor of world government, not on the grounds of commonsense. It is commonsense that we who live in a city like London should have all kinds of things controlled—motorists must not pass a red light; drains must be looked after and all that. It is time we realized that the world is also a close-locked community today. We just cannot afford to have the exercise of individual sovereignty.

To whom are you going to hand it over? I am democratic; I am prepared to submit to the will of a properly constituted body representing the world. I am not prepared to submit to a kind of junta of three or four of the strongest powers. I have been accustomed for many years to accept the will of the majority, and I am prepared to do it again. I would like Britain and America and Russia also to be prepared to do it, because I believe that unless we can get this we shall not get peace.

9. *ON WORLD-GOVERNMENT* / DANTE ALIGHIERI*

. . . the proper function of the human race, taken in the aggregate, is to actualize continually the entire capacity of the possible intellect, primarily in speculation, then, through its extension and for its sake, secondarily in action. And since it is true that whatever modifies a part modifies the whole, and that the individual man seated in quiet grows perfect in knowledge and wisdom, it is plain that amid the calm and tranquillity of peace the human race accomplishes most freely and easily its given work. How nearly divine this function is revealed in the words, "Thou hast made him a little lower than the angels." Whence it is manifest that universal peace is the best of those things which are ordained for our beatitude. And hence to the shepherds sounded from on high the message not of riches, nor pleasures, nor honors, nor length of life, nor health, nor beauty; but the message of peace. For the heavenly host said, "Glory to God in the highest, and on earth peace among men in whom he is well pleased." Likewise, "Peace be unto you" was the salutation of the Saviour of men. It befitted the supreme Saviour to utter the supreme salutation. It is evident to all that the disciples desired to preserve this custom; and Paul likewise in his words of greeting.

From these things which have been expounded we perceive through what better, nay, through what best means the human race may fulfill its proper office. Consequently we perceive the nearest way through which may be reached that universal peace toward which all our efforts are directed as their ultimate end, and which is to be assumed as the basic principle of subsequent reasoning.

. . . let the first question be whether temporal Monarchy

* Dante Alighieri, *De Monarchia*, trans. Aurelia Henry (Boston: Houghton, Mifflin and Company, 1904), Book I, Chap. 4, 5, 10, 16.

[world-government] is necessary for the well-being of the world. The necessity of temporal Monarchy can be gainsaid with no force of reason or authority, and can be proved by the most powerful and patent arguments, of which the first is taken on the testimony of the Philosopher in the *Politics*. There this venerable authority asserts that when several things are ordained for one end, one of them must regulate or rule, and the others submit to regulation or rule. This, indeed, not only because of the author's glorious name, but because of inductive reasoning, demands credence.

If we consider the individual man, we shall see that this applies to him, for, when all his faculties are ordered for his happiness, the intellectual faculty itself is regulator and ruler of all others; in no way else can man attain to happiness. If we consider the household, whose end is to teach its members to live rightly, there is need for one called the *pater-familias*, or for some one holding his place, to direct and govern, according to the Philosopher when he says, "Every household is ruled by its eldest." It is for him, as Homer says, to guide and make laws for those dwelling with him. From this arises the proverbial curse, "May you have an equal in your house." If we consider the village, whose aim is adequate protection of persons and property, there is again needed for governing the rest either one chosen for them by another, or one risen to preëminence from among themselves by their consent; otherwise, they not only obtain no mutual support, but sometimes the whole community is destroyed by many striving for first place. Again, if we consider the city, whose end is to insure comfort and sufficiency in life, there is need for undivided rule in rightly directed governments, and in those wrongly directed as well; else the end of civil life is missed, and the city ceases to be what it was. Finally, if we consider the individual kingdom, whose end is that of the city with greater promise of tranquillity, there must be one king to direct and govern. If not, not only the inhabitants of the kingdom fail of their end, but the kingdom lapses into ruin, in agreement with that word of infallible truth, "Every kingdom divided against itself is brought to desolation." If, then, this is true of these instances, and of all things ordained for a single end, it is true of the statement assumed above.

We are now agreed that the whole human race is ordered for one end, as already shown. It is meet, therefore, that the leader and lord be one, and that he be called Monarch, or Emperor. Thus it becomes obvious that for the well-being of the world there is needed a Monarchy, or Empire. . . .

Wherever strife is a possibility, in that place must be judgment; otherwise imperfection would exist without its perfecting agent. This could not be, for God and Nature are not wanting in necessary things. It is self-evident that between any two princes, neither of whom owes allegiance to the other, controversy may arise either by their own fault or by the fault of their subjects. For such, judgment is necessary. And inasmuch as one owing no allegiance to the other can recognize no authority in him (for an equal cannot control an equal), there must be a third prince with more ample jurisdiction, who may govern both within the circle of his right. This prince will be or will not be a Monarch. If he is, our purpose is fulfilled; if not, he will again have a coequal beyond the circle of his jurisdiction, and again a third prince will be required. And thus either the process will be carried to infinity, which is impossible, or that primal and highest judge will be reached, by whose judgments all disputes are settled mediately or immediately. And this judge will be Monarch, or Emperor. Monarchy is therefore indispensable to the world, and this truth the Philosopher saw when he said, "Things have no desire to be wrongly ordered; inasmuch as a multitude of Princedoms is wrong, let there be one Prince." . . .

A phenomenon not to be forgotten attests the truth of all the arguments placed in order above, namely, that condition of mortals which the Son of God, when about to become man for the salvation of man, either awaited, or ordained at such time as He willed. For if from the fall of our first parents, at which point of departure began all our error, we survey the ordering of men and times, we shall find no perfect Monarchy, nor the world everywhere at peace, save under the divine Monarch Augustus. That men were then blessed with the tranquillity of universal peace all historians testify, and all illustrious poets; this the writer of the gentleness of Christ felt it meet to confirm, and last of all Paul, who called that most happy condition "the fulness of the time." Verily, time and all temporal things were full, for no ministry to our happiness lacked its minister. But what has been the condition of the world since that day the seamless robe first suffered mutilation by the claws of avarice, we can read—would that we could not also see! O human race! what tempests must need toss thee, what treasure be thrown into the sea, what shipwrecks must be endured, so long as thou, like a beast of many heads, strivest after diverse ends! Thou art sick in either intellect, and sick likewise in thy affection. Thou healest not thy high understanding by argument irrefutable, nor thy lower by the countenance of experience. Nor dost thou heal thy affection by the sweetness of divine persuasion, when the voice of the Holy Spirit breathes upon thee, "Behold, how good and how pleasant it is for brethren to dwell together in unity!"

10. *THE ILLUSION OF WORLD-GOVERNMENT*/ REINHOLD NIEBUHR*

The trustful acceptance of false solutions for our perplexing problems adds a touch of pathos to the tragedy of our age.

The tragic character of our age is revealed in the world-wide insecurity which is the fate of modern man. Technical achievements, which a previous generation had believed capable of solving every ill to which the human flesh is heir, have created, or at least accentuated, our insecurity. For the growth of technics has given the perennial problems of our common life a more complex form and a scope that has grown to be worldwide.

Our problem is that technics have established a rudimentary world community but have not integrated it organically, morally or politically. They have created a community of mutual dependence, but not one of mutual trust and respect. Without this higher integration, advancing technics tend to sharpen economic rivalries within a general framework of economic interdependence; they change the ocean barriers of yesterday into the battlegrounds of today; and they increase the deadly efficacy of the instruments of war so that vicious circles of mutual fear may end in atomic conflicts and mutual destruction. To these perplexities an ideological conflict has been added, which divides the world into hostile camps.

It is both necessary and laudable that men of good will should, in this situation, seek to strengthen every moral and political force which might give a rudimentary world community a higher degree of integration. It was probably inevitable that the desperate plight of our age should persuade some well meaning men that the gap

* "The Illusion of World Government" (Copyright 1949 Reinhold Niebuhr) is reprinted with the permission of Charles Scribner's Sons from *Christian Realism and Political Problems* by Reinhold Niebuhr.

between a technically integrated and politically divided community could be closed by the simple expedient of establishing a world government through the fiat of the human will and creating world community by the fiat of world government. It is this hope which adds a touch of pathos to already tragic experiences. The hope not only beguiles some men from urgent moral and political responsibilities. It tempts others into irresponsible criticisms of the necessarily minimal constitutional structure which we have embodied in the United Nations and which is as bad as its critics aver only if a better one is within the realm of possibilities.

Virtually all arguments for world government rest upon the simple presupposition that the desirability of world order proves the attainability of world government. Our precarious situation is unfortunately no proof, either of the moral ability of mankind to create a world government by an act of the will, nor of the political ability of such a government to integrate a world community in advance of a more gradual growth of the "social tissue" which every community requires more than government.

Most advocates of world government also assume that nations need merely follow the alleged example of the individuals of another age who are supposed to have achieved community by codifying their agreements into law and by providing an agency of some kind for law enforcement. This assumption ignores the historic fact that the mutual respect for each other's rights in particular communities is older than any code of law; and that machinery for the enforcement of law can be efficacious only when a community as a whole obeys its laws implicitly, so that coercive enforcement may be limited to a recalcitrant minority.

The fallacy of world government can be stated in two simple propositions. The first is that governments are not created by fiat (though sometimes they can be imposed by tyranny). The second is that governments have only limited efficacy in integrating a community.

II

The advocates of world government talk of calling a world constitutional convention which would set up the machinery of a global constitutional order and would then call upon the nations to abrogate or abridge their sovereignty in order that this newly created universal sovereignty could have unchallenged sway. No such explicit abnegation has ever taken place in the history of the world. Explicit governmental authority has developed historically from the implicit authority of patriarchal or matriarchal tribal forms. Governments, so established, have extended their dominion over weaker neighbors. But the abridgment of sovereignty has always been indirect rather than direct; or it has been attained by the superimposition of power.

The notion that world government is a fairly simple possibility is the final and most absurd form of the "social contract" conception of government which has confused modern political thought since Hobbes. It must certainly be obvious by this time that the conception of a state of nature in which all men were at war with all, and of a subsequent social contract through which men established a power over themselves to avoid mutual annihilation, is a pure fiction. A small human community is as primordial as the individual. No group of individuals has ever created either government or community out of whole cloth. One reason why the social contract conception of government has a particular plausibility with us is because the United States came closer to a birth by "contract" than any other nation. But the preamble of our constitution declares that its purpose is to establish a "more perfect union." That is a very telling phrase which presupposes a previous union. This previous union was in fact established on the battlefield in a common struggle against a common foe; it needed only to be made "more perfect." It may be observed in passing that, though the 13 colonies had never enjoyed sovereignty, they did not find it too easy to submit what had only been potential, and not actual, sovereignty to the authority of the federal union. We fought a civil war before it was proved that they had in fact done this without reservations.

When the question is raised whether the nations of the world would voluntarily first create, and then submit to, a super-national authority, the possible reluctance of nations, other than Russia, to take this step is fortunately or unfortunately obscured by the Russian intransigeance. The Russians have declared again and again that they would leave the United Nations if the veto power were abolished. This means that Russia, as a prospective minority in a world community, is not ready to submit her fate to the will of a majority, even in such a loose organization as the United Nations. It is therefore obvious that she would be even more unwilling to submit her sovereignty to a more highly integrated constitutional order.

The proponents of world government have two answers to the problem posed by Russian intransigeance. One is to assert that the Russians never have had the chance to accept or reject a genuinely constitutional world order; and that there are real possibilities of her acceptance of a constitution which is not weighted against her. This answer contains in a nutshell the rationalist illusion implicit in world government theories. It assumes that constitutions can insure the mutual trust upon which community rests. Actually, even the best constitution must, if it is democratic, set up some kind of majority rule. It is not workable if there is not enough common ground between majority and minority to assure that a majority will not take advantage of a minority, or that the minority will not suspect the majority of injustice, even though without cause. There are republics in South America with quite nice constitutions in which a defeated minority starts conspiracies against the government, usually through military channels, on the day after election.

The other answer to the problem of Russian intransigeance is a proposed creation of a "world" government without Russia. Thus in the name of "one world" the world would be divided in two. Proponents of world government are always ready with criticisms of the ambiguities in the Charter of the United Nations, without recognizing that those ambiguities correspond to the actual historical situation. The Security Council is, for instance, a bridge of a sort between the segments of a divided world. They would destroy that bridge for the sake of creating a more logical constitutional system. This done, they look forward to one of two possibilities.

One is that Russia, faced with a united opposition, and concluding that she would not have to sacrifice her Communist Government but only her ambition to spread Communism, would ultimately capitulate and join the world federation. This abstract approach to political problems is completely oblivious of the dynamism of Communism.

The other course chosen by some advocates of world government is to create such a government without Russia and to divide the world more consistently in the name of the principle of "one" world. If this should lead to a world conflict they believe that the agonies of war will be assuaged for us by our knowledge that we are at least fighting for a principle of ultimate validity.

There is, of course, a possibility that a closer political integration of the non-Communist nations may save the world from war by the creation of an adequate preponderance of power in the west. But such an objective is not to be reached by loftily disavowing "power politics" in favor of "law." The world federalists who accept the inevitability of war walk bravely up the hill of pure idealism and down again into the realm of pure power politics. In this journey they rid themselves of the logical and moral ambiguities of the much despised quasi-constitutional system of the United Nations. Their brethren who are in a less exalted frame of mind will continue to put up with the Charter for the sake of preserving a bridge, however slight, between Russia and the west, making the best arrangements they can to restrain Russia, while trying at the same time to strengthen the existing world security agencies.

The ambiguities in the Charter of the United Nations which so outrage the advocates of world government are in fact the consequence of seeking to guarantee two, rather than one, objectives. The one objective is to preserve the unity of one world, even though it be seriously divided, and to provide a meeting ground between east and west where some of the tensions and frictions may be resolved. The other is to preserve the integrity of our "way of life" against a tyrannical system which we abhor. The Russians, in so far as they are honest devotees of a Marxist dream of world order, are presumably in the same position. Each of us hopes ultimately to create a world order upon the basis of our conception of justice. Neither of us is ready, at the moment, to submit our fate to a world authority without reservation, so long as the possibility remains that such an authority could annul a system of law and justice to which we are deeply committed.

III

So far we have considered only the difficulties of creating a world government by constitutional fiat. But a much more serious defect in world government theories is to be found in their conception of the relation of government to community. Governments cannot create communities for the simple reason that the authority of government is not primarily the authority of law nor the authority of force, but the authority of the community itself. Laws are obeyed because the community accepts them as corresponding, on the whole, to its conception of justice. This is particularly true of democratically-organized communities. But it is well to observe that even in traditional, non-democratic communities of the past there was a discernible difference between tyranny and legitimate government. It consisted precisely in the fact that a legitimate government relied primarily upon the implicit consent of the community.

Even in a national constitutional system, such as our own, we have seen how limited is the power of law whenever a portion of the community adheres to moral standards which differ from those of the total community. We have had this experience both with the prohibition movement and with the question of civil rights for Negroes in southern states. And where is the police force, loyal to a world state, to come from? The police power of a government cannot be a pure political artifact. It is an arm of the community's body. If the body is in pieces, the arm cannot integrate it.

The priority of the community to its laws and its use of force does not mean that both law and force may not have limited efficacy in perfecting the organization and preserving the integrity of the community. Good constitutions provide for the rational arbitrament of many conflicting and competing forces which might otherwise tear the community apart. Preponderant force in one part of the community may also so shape the social forces of the total community that its use need not be perpetual. Thus the preponderant force of the northern states decided the issue whether our nation was a nation or merely a federation of states. But force is no longer necessary to guarantee the loyalty of the southern states to our union. The ancient empires of Egypt, Babylon and Persia were created through the preponderant force of a particular city-state; but they finally achieved a unity which did not require the constant application of force. It must be noted that this pattern of coalescence of communities gives us no analogy for the creation of a world community in democratic terms, that is, without the imposition of preponderant power. The best analogy for our present world situation is to be found in Greece rather than in Egypt or Babylon. The Greek city-states never achieved the imperial unity of the oriental empires. The threat of Persia did finally prompt the organization of the Delian League; but the rivalry of Sparta and Athens for the hegemony in the League resulted in its disintegration. The unity of Greece was finally achieved under Philip and Alexander of Macedon. But this imperial unity was also a tyrannical nemesis for Greek culture. The analogy in present global terms would be the final unification of the world through the preponderant power of either America or Russia, whichever proved herself victorious in a final global struggle. The analogy teaches us nothing about the possibilities of a constitutional world state. It may teach us that though the perils of international anarchy are very great, they may still be preferable to international tyranny.

The coalescence of communities from city-states to empires in the ancient world, and from feudal entities to nations in the modern period, was frequently accomplished only by the imposition of preponderant power. The fact is particularly significant, since all of these communities could rely upon all sorts of "organic" factors for their force of cohesion which the rudimentary world community lacks. By organic factors, I mean such forces as the power of ethnic kinship, the force of a common history—particularly the memory of joint struggles against a common foe—a common language, a common culture and a common religion. We do have examples of ethnically and religiously pluralistic nations and empires, but they possess a basic homegeneity of some kind, underlying the differences. In modern India, where religious differences are thoroughgoing and highly localized, it proved impossible to construct a constitutional system which could allay the mutual fears of Hindus and Moslems. The birth in blood of these two nations, once the unifying force of an imperial power was removed, ought to teach our world planners more about the limited efficacy of constitutions than they have evidently learned. There were certainly more common elements in the situation in India than the world community will possess for a long time to come. Despite these common elements, the unity of India proved to be unattainable.

Sometimes the world planners recognize the absence of organic forces of cohesion in the world community. Thus Erich Kahler[1] sees that a world constitution lacks the "substratum" of organic and historical forces, which characterize the constitutions of national governments. But he draws the conclusion that a world constitution "must create the substratum to which it is to be applied." The proposed method of creating the substratum, according to Mr. Kahler, is to use "regions" rather than "extant states" as electoral units in the world constitution, for "if we base the world government on the states, we will fail in the essential task of creating the

[1] Erich Kahler, "The Question of a 'Minimum Constitution.'" *Common Cause,* June 1948.

substratum." The illusions of omnipotence which infect the thought of this kind of political idealism could not be more vividly portrayed. There is no explanation of how states, who have a sovereign voice, would be persuaded to grant this electoral power to "regions" which would have no such voice in a world constitutional convention. The idea probably is that there would be a nonrepresentative constitutional convention of "experts" and the hope is that sovereign states will meekly accept the dictum of the experts that regions offer a better "substratum" for the world community than extant states. Nor is any attempt made to deal with the difficulty that many of the regions which would hopefully be created are so little integrated that an electoral canvass would be completely meaningless in them.

The fact is that even the wisest statecraft cannot create social tissue. It can cut, sew and redesign social fabric to a limited degree. But the social fabric upon which it works must be "given."

IV

The international community is not totally lacking in social tissue; but it is very scant, compared with that of particular states. Let us briefly assess the various factors in it. Most important as a force of social cohesion in the world community is the increasing economic interdependence of peoples of the world. But it is important to contrast this economic interdependence immediately with the wide disparity in the economic strength of various nations. At the climactic dinner of the World Republic convention, held in Chicago in October 1948, Professor Urey, the atomic scientist, expressed the conviction that the "inclusion of the illiterate, poverty-stricken, overnumerous masses of the Far East" constituted the major problem of the world state. He believed that the white race would not tolerate being outvoted by Asiatics. He therefore proposed a system of weighted votes in favor of nations with high literacy and abundance of raw materials and industrial production. He felt certain that the more "enlightened" Orientals would not object to this procedure. But an objection, from Thomas Tchou, sitting two places to the left of Professor Urey, was immediately forthcoming. Weighted representation, he declared, was immoral.[2]

[2] *Common Cause*, December 1948, p. 199.

Thus the real problems have an inconvenient habit of peeking through, even at a dinner of a World Republic convention.

A second factor in the social tissue of the world community is the fear of mutual annihilation, heightened in recent years by the new dimension which atomic discoveries have given to mankind's instruments of death. We must not underestimate this fear as a social force, even as we must recognize that some culturally pluralistic communities of past history have achieved some cohesion through the minimal conviction that order is to be preferred to anarchy. But the fear of destruction in itself is less potent than the fear of specific peril from a particular foe. There is no record in history of peoples establishing a common community because they feared each other, though there are many instances when the fear of a common foe acted as the cement of cohesion.

The final and most important factor in the social tissue of the world community is a moral one. Enlightened men in all nations have some sense of obligation to their fellow-men, beyond the limits of their nation-state. There is at least an inchoate sense of obligation to the inchoate community of mankind. The desperate necessity for a more integrated world community has undoubtedly increased this sense of obligation, inculcated in the conscience of mankind since the rise of universal, rather than parochial, philosophies and religions. This common moral sense is of tremendous importance for the moral and religious life of mankind; but it does not have as much immediate political relevance as is sometimes supposed. Political cohesion requires common convictions on particular issues of justice; and these are lacking. If there is a "natural law" which is "self-evident" to all men, it certainly does not contain very much specific content beyond such minimal rules as the prohibition of murder and theft and such general principles of justice as the dictum that each man is to have his due. There is little agreement on the criteria by which the due of each man is to be measured.

There is a special irony in the fact that the primary differences in the conceptions of justice in the world do not, however, spring from religious and cultural differences between east and west. They can, therefore, not be resolved by elaborate efforts at cultural syncretism between east and west. The primary differences arise from a civil war in the heart of western civilization, in which a fanatical equalitarian creed has been pitted against a libertarian one. This civil war has become nationally localized. Russia has become the national center of the equalitarian creed, while America is the outstanding proponent of the libertarian one. The common use of the word "democracy," together with the contradictory interpretations of the meaning of that word, is the semantic symbol of the conflict. The idea that this conflict could be resolved by greater semantic accuracy is, however, one of the illusions of a too rationalistic culture which fails to understand the power of the social forces expressed in contradictory symbols.

In short, the forces which are operating to integrate the world community are limited. To call attention to this fact does not mean that all striving for a higher and wider integration of the world community is vain. That task must and will engage the conscience of mankind for ages to come. But the edifice of government which we build will be sound and useful if its height is proportionate to the strength of the materials from which it is constructed. The immediate political situation requires that we seek not only peace, but also the preservation of a civilization which we hold to be preferable to the universal tyranny with which Soviet aggression threatens us. Success in this double task is the goal; let us not be diverted from it by the pretense that there is a simple alternative.

We would, I think, have a better chance of success in our struggle against a fanatical foe if we were less sure of our purity and virtue. The pride and self-righteousness of powerful nations are a greater hazard to their success in statecraft than the machinations of their foes. If we could combine a greater degree of humility with our stubborn resolution, we might not only be more successful in holding the dyke against tyranny, but we might also gradually establish a genuine sense of community with our foe, however small. No matter how stubbornly we resist Russian pressure, we should still have a marginal sense of community with the Soviet Union, derived from our sense of being involved in a common fate of tragic proportions and from a recognition of a common guilt of mutual fear. If community in basic terms is established by various organic forces of history, it must finally be preserved by mutual forbearance and forgiveness.

There is obviously no political program which can offer us, in our situation, perfect security against either war or tyranny. Nevertheless we are not prisoners of historical destiny. We shall have constant opportunity to perfect instruments of peace and justice if we succeed in creating some communal foundation upon which constitutional structures can rest. We shall exploit our opportunities the more successfully, however, if we have knowledge of the limits of the will in creating government, and of the limits of government in creating community. We may have pity upon, but can have no sympathy with, those who flee to the illusory security of the impossible from the insecurities and ambiguities of the possible.

NATIONALISM

IV

What is nationalism and what is its role in world affairs? The first selection presents Ernest Renan's classic definition of nationalism. Historian Renan (1823–92) delivered the lecture entitled "What Is a Nation?" at the Sorbonne on March 11, 1882.

The second selection is by the Italian nationalist Giuseppe Mazzini (1805–72). Mazzini is a typical spokesman of nineteenth-century liberal nationalism. It is particularly interesting to note that he regards nationalism not as a factor producing international tension and hostility, but rather as a prerequisite for the establishment of an international brotherhood of free nations. The essay "Duties Toward Your Country" appeared in *Pensiero ed Azione* in 1858.

The final selection in this chapter is taken from an article by Karl W. Deutsch. The excerpts presented here emphasize the aggressive and imperialistic tendencies of successful nationalism. The author, Professor of Political Science at Yale University, is the outstanding contemporary theorist on the question of nationalism. Among his many books and articles are *Nationalism and Social Communication* and *The Nerves of Government.*

11. *WHAT IS A NATION?* / ERNEST RENAN*

I propose to ask you to join with me in analysing an idea which, though it appears simple, yet lends itself to the most dangerous misunderstandings. Human society assumes the most varied forms, great masses of human beings, such as we see in China, in Egypt and in the older Babylonia; the tribe as exemplified by the Hebrews and Arabs; the city, as in Athens and Sparta; the unions of various countries, as in the Achaemenian, Roman and Carlovingian empires; communities having no mother country but held together by the bond of religion, as the Israelites and the Parsees; nations such as France, England and most modern European autonomous States; confederations, as in Switzerland and America; relationships, such as those set up by race, or rather by language, between the different branches of Germans or Slavs: all these various groupings exist, or have existed, and to ignore the differences between them is to create a serious confusion. At the time of the French Revolution it was believed that the institutions of small independent towns, such as Sparta and Rome, could be applied to our great nations comprising thirty or forty million inhabitants. Nowadays, we observe a graver error. The terms "race" and "nation" are confused, and we see attributed to ethnographic, or rather linguistic, groups a sovereignty analogous to that of actually existing peoples. Let us try to arrive at some degree of exactness with regard to these difficult questions in which the least confusion at the outset of the argument as to the meaning of words may lead in the end to the most fatal errors. Our task is a delicate one; it amounts almost to vivisection; and we are going to treat the living as usually we treat the dead. We shall proceed coldly and with the most complete impartiality. . . .

We are told by certain political theorists that a nation is, above

* Alfred Zimmern, ed., *Modern Political Doctrines* (London: Oxford University Press, 1939), pp. 186, 192–96, 198–203. Reprinted by permission.

all, a dynasty representing a former conquest that has been at first accepted, and then forgotten, by the mass of the people. According to these politicians, the grouping of provinces effected by a dynasty, its wars, marriages and treaties, ends with the dynasty that has formed it. It is quite true that most modern nations have been made by a family of feudal origin, which has married into the country and provided some sort of centralizing nucleus. The boundaries of France in 1789 were in no way natural or necessary. The large area that the House of Capet had added to the narrow strip accorded by the Treaty of Verdun was indeed the personal acquisition of that family. At the time when the annexations were made no one thought about natural limits, the right of nations or the wishes of provinces. Similarly, the union of England, Ireland and Scotland was a dynastic performance. The only reason why Italy took so long to become a nation was that, until the present century, none of her numerous reigning families became a centre of union. It is an odd fact that she derives the royal[1] title from the obscure island of Sardinia, a land which is scarcely Italian. Holland, self-created by an act of heroic resolution, has none the less entered into a close bond of marriage with the House of Orange, and would run serious risks, should this union ever be endangered.

Is, however, such a law absolute? Doubtless, it is not. Switzerland and the United States which have been formed, like conglomerates, by successive additions, are based on no dynasty. I will not discuss the question in so far as it concerns France. One would have to be able to read the future in order to do so. Let us merely observe that this great French line of kings had become so thoroughly identified with the national life that, on the morrow of its downfall, the nation was able to subsist without it. Furthermore, the eighteenth century had entirely changed the situation. After centuries of humiliation, man had recovered his ancient spirit, his self-respect and the idea of his rights. The words "mother country" and "citizen" had regained their meaning. Thus it was possible to carry out the boldest operation ever performed in history—an operation that may be compared to what, in physiology, would be an attempt to bring back to its former life a body from which brain and heart had been removed.

It must, therefore, be admitted that a nation can exist without any dynastic principle, and even that nations formed by dynasties

[1] The House of Savoy owes its royal title solely to the possession of Sardinia (1720).

can be separated from them without thereby ceasing to exist. The old principle, which takes into account only the right of princes, can no longer be maintained: and, besides dynastic right, there exists also national right. On what criterion is this national right to be based? By what sign is it to be known? And from what tangible fact is it properly to be derived?

1. Many will boldly reply, from race. The artificial divisions, they say, the results of feudalism, royal marriages and diplomatic congresses, have broken down. Race is what remains stable and fixed; and this it is that constitutes a right and a lawful title. The Germanic race, for example, according to this theory, has the right to retake the scattered members of the Germanic family, even when these members do not ask for reunion. The right of the Germanic family over such-and-such a province is better than the right of its inhabitants over themselves. A sort of primordial right is thus created analogous to the divine right of kings; and the principle of ethnography is substituted for that of nations. This is a very grave error, and if it should prevail, it would spell the ruin of European civilization. The principle of the primordial right of race is as narrow and as fraught with danger for true progress as the principle of nations is just and legitimate.

We admit that, among the tribes and cities of the ancient world, the fact of race was of capital importance. The ancient tribe and city were but an extension of the family. In Sparta and Athens all citizens were related more or less closely to each other. It was the same among the Beni-Israel; and it is still so among the Arab tribes. But let us leave Athens, Sparta and the Jewish tribe and turn to the Roman Empire. Here we have quite a different state of affairs. This great agglomeration of completely diverse towns and provinces, formed in the first place by violence and then held together by common interests, cuts at the very root of the racial idea. Christianity, characteristically universal and absolute, works even more effectively in the same direction. It contracts a close alliance with the Roman Empire, and, under the influence of these two incomparable unifying agents, the ethnographic argument is for centuries dismissed from the government of human affairs.

In spite of appearances, the barbarian invasions were a step further on this road. The barbarian kingdoms which were then cut out have nothing ethnographic about them; they were decided by the forces or whims of the conquerors, who were completely indifferent with regard to the race of the peoples whom they subjugated. Charlemagne reconstructed in his own way what Rome had already built, viz., a single empire composed of the most diverse races. The authors of the Treaty of Verdun, calmly drawing their two long lines from north to south, did not pay the slightest attention to the race of the peoples to right or left of them. The frontier changes which took place in the later Middle Ages were also devoid of all ethnographic tendencies. Let it be granted that the consistent policy of the Capets managed more or less to gather together, under the name of France, the territories of ancient Gaul; yet this was by no means the consequence of any tendency on the part of their inhabitants to unite themselves with their kindred. Dauphiné, Bresse, Provence and Franche-Comté no longer remembered any common origin. The consciousness of Gallic race had been lost since the second century A.D., and it is only in modern times, and retrospectively, that the erudite have unearthed the peculiarities of the Gallic character.

Ethnographic considerations have, therefore, played no part in the formation of modern nations. France is Celtic, Iberic and Germanic. Germany is Germanic, Celtic and Slav. Italy is the country in which ethnography finds its greatest difficulties. Here Gauls, Etruscans, Pelasgians and Greeks are crossed in an unintelligible medley. The British Isles, taken as a whole, exhibit a mixture of Celtic and Germanic blood, the proportions of which are particularly difficult to define.

The truth is that no race is pure, and that to base politics on ethnographic analysis is tantamount to basing it on a chimera. The noblest countries, England, France and Italy, are those where breeds are most mixed. Is Germany an exception in this respect? Is she a purely Germanic country? What a delusion to suppose it! All the South was Gallic; and all the East, starting from the Elbe, is Slav.

2. What we have said about race, applies also to language. Language invites union, without, however, compelling it. The United States and England, as also Spanish America and Spain, speak the same language without forming a single nation. Switzerland, on the contrary, whose foundations are solid because they are based on the assent of the various parties, contains three of four languages. There exists in man a something which is above language: and that is his will. The will of Switzerland to be united, in spite of the variety of these forms of speech, is a much more important fact than a similarity of language, often attained by vexatious measures.

It is to the honour of France that she has never tried to attain unity of language by the use of coercion. Is it impossible to cherish the same feelings and thoughts and to love the same things in different languages? We were talking just now of the objections to making international politics dependent on ethnography. It would be no less objectionable to make them depend on comparative philology. Let us allow full liberty of discussion to these interesting branches of learning, and not mix them up with what would disturb their serenity. The political importance ascribed to languages comes from regarding them as tokens of race. Nothing could be more unsound. In Prussia, where nothing but German is now spoken, Russian was spoken a few centuries ago; in Wales, English is spoken; in Gaul and Spain, the original speech of Alba Longa; in Egypt, Arabic; and we could cite any number of other examples. Even in the beginning of things, similarity of language did not imply that of race. Take the proto-Aryan or proto-Semitic tribe. It contained slaves speaking the same language as their masters, whereas the slave very often differed from his master in race. We must repeat that these divisions into Indo-European, Semitic and other languages, which have been laid down by comparative philologists with such admirable acumen, do not coincide with those laid down by anthropology. Languages are historical formations which afford little clue to the descent of those who speak them and which, in any case, cannot be permitted to fetter human liberty, when it is a question of deciding with what family one is to be linked for life and death.

This exclusive importance attributed to language has, like the exaggerated attention paid to race, its dangers and its objections. If you overdo it, you shut yourself up within a prescribed culture which you regard as the national culture. You are confined and immured, having left the open air of the great world outside to shut yourself up in a conventicle together with your compatriots. Nothing could be worse for the mind; and nothing could be more untoward for civilization. Let us not lose sight of this fundamental principle that man, apart from being penned up within the bounds of one language or another, apart from being a member of one race or another, or the follower of one culture or another, is above all a reasonable moral being. Above French, German or Italian culture, there stands human culture. Consider the great men of the Renaissance. They were neither French, nor Italian, nor German. By their intercourse with the ancient world, they had rediscovered the secret of the true education of the human mind, and to that they devoted themselves body and soul. How well they did!

3. Nor can religion provide a satisfactory basis for a modern nationality. In its origin, religion was connected with the very existence of the social group, which itself was an extension of the family. The rites of religion were family rites. The religion of Athens was the cult of Athens itself, of its mythical founders, its laws and customs. This religion, which did not involve any dogmatic theology, was, in the full sense of the words, a state religion. Those who refused to practice it were not Athenians. At bottom it was the cult of the personified Acropolis; and to swear on the altar of Aglauros[1] amounted to an oath to die for one's country. This religion was the equivalent of our drawing lots for military service or of our cult of the national flag. To refuse to participate in such cult would have been tantamount to a refusal nowadays to serve in the army, and to a declaration that one was not an Athenian. On the other hand, it is clear that such a cult as this meant nothing for those who were not Athenians; so there was no proselytising to compel foreigners to accept it, and the slaves of Athens did not practice it. The same was the case in certain small republics of the Middle Ages. No man was a good Venetian if he did not swear by St. Mark; nor a good citizen of Amalfi if he did not set St. Andrew above all the other saints in Paradise. In these small societies, acts, which in later times became the grounds for persecution and tyranny, were justifiable and were as trivial as it is with us to wish the father of the family many happy returns of his birthday or a happy new year.

What was true of Sparta and Athens was no longer so in the kingdoms that emerged from the conquests of Alexander, and still less so in the Roman Empire. The persecutions carried out by Antiochus Epiphanes to induce the Eastern world to worship the Olympian Jove, like those of the Roman Empire to maintain the farce of a state religion, were mistaken, criminal and really absurd. Nowadays the situation is perfectly clear, since the masses no longer have any uniform belief. Every one believes and practices religion in his own way according to his capacities and wishes. State religion has ceased to exist; and a man can be a Frenchman, an Englishman or a German, and at the same time a Catholic, a Protestant or a Jew, or practice no form of worship at all. Religion has become a matter

[1] Aglauros, who gave her life to save her country, represents the Acropolis itself.

to be decided by the individual according to his conscience, and nations are no longer divided into Catholic and Protestant. Religion which, fifty-two years ago, was so important a factor in the formation of Belgium, is still equally so in the heart of every man; but it is now barely to be reckoned among the reasons that determine national frontiers.

4. Community of interest is certainly a powerful bond between men. But do interests suffice to make a nation? I do not believe it. Community of interest brings about commercial treaties. Nationality, which is body and soul both together, has its sentimental side: and a Customs Union is not a country.

5. Geography, and what we call natural frontiers, certainly plays a considerable part in the division of nations. Geography is one of the essential factors of history. Rivers have guided races: mountains have impeded them. The former have favoured, while the latter have restricted, historic movements. But can one say, as some people believe, that a nation's boundaries are to be found written on the map, and that it has the right to award itself as much as is necessary to round off certain outlines, or to reach such-and-such a mountain or river, which are regarded as in some way dispensing the frontier *à priori?* I know no doctrine more arbitrary or fatal than this, which can be used to justify all kinds of violence. In the first place, is it the mountains, or is it the rivers that constitute these alleged natural frontiers? It is indisputable that mountains separate; but rivers tend rather to bring together. Then again all mountains cannot divide states. Which are those that separate and those that do not? From Biarritz to Tornea there is not one estuary which is more like a boundary than another. If History had so decreed, then the Loire, the Seine, the Meuse, the Elbe and the Oder would have, as much as the Rhine has, this character of national frontier, which has been the cause of so many infringements of that fundamental right, which is the will of men. People talk of strategic grounds. Nothing is absolute; and it is evident that much must be conceded to necessity. But these concessions must not go too far. Otherwise, every one will demand what suits him from a military point of view and we shall have endless warfare. No; it is not the soil any more than the race which makes a nation. The soil provides the substratum, the field for struggle and labour: man provides the soul. Man is everything in the formation of this sacred thing that we call a people. Nothing that is material suffices here. A

nation is a spiritual principle, the result of the intricate workings of history; a spiritual family and not a group determined by the configuration of the earth.

We have now seen those things which do not suffice to create such a spiritual principle. They are race, language, interests, religious affinity, geography and military necessity. What more then is required? In view of what I have already said, I shall not have to detain you very much longer.

III

A nation is a soul, a spiritual principle. Two things, which are really only one, go to make up this soul or spiritual principle. One of these things lies in the past, the other in the present. The one is the possession in common of a rich heritage of memories; and the other is actual agreement, the desire to live together, and the will to continue to make the most of the joint inheritance. Man, gentlemen, cannot be improvised. The nation, like the individual, is the fruit of a long past spent in toil, sacrifice and devotion. Ancestor-worship is of all forms the most justifiable, since our ancestors have made us what we are. A heroic past, great men and glory—I mean real glory—these should be the capital of our company when we come to found a national idea. To share the glories of the past, and a common will in the present; to have done great deeds together, and to desire to do more—these are the essential conditions of a people's being. Love is in proportion to the sacrifices one has made and the evils one has borne. We love the house that we have built and that we hand down to our successors. The Spartan song "We are what ye were, and we shall be what ye are," is, in its simplicity, the abridged version of every national anthem.

In the past, a heritage of glory and of grief to be shared; in the future, one common plan to be realized; to have suffered, rejoiced and hoped together; these are things of greater value than identity of custom-houses and frontiers in accordance with strategic notions. These are things which are understood, in spite of differences in race and language. I said just now "to have suffered together," for indeed common suffering unites more strongly than common rejoicing. Among national memories, sorrows have greater value than victories; for they impose duties and demand common effort.

Thus we see that a nation is a great solid unit, formed by the realization of sacrifices in the past, as well as of those one is prepared to make in the future. A nation implies a past; while, as regards the present, it is all contained in one tangible fact, viz., the agreement and clearly expressed desire to continue a life in common. The existence of a nation is (if you will forgive me the metaphor) a daily plebiscite, just as that of the individual is a continual affirmation of life. . . .

12. *DUTIES TOWARD YOUR COUNTRY** / *GIUSEPPE MAZZINI*

Your first duties—first as regards importance—are . . . towards Humanity. You are *men* before you are either citizens or fathers. If you do not embrace the whole human family in your affection, if you do not bear witness to your belief in the Unity of that family—consequent upon the Unity of God;—and in that fraternity among the peoples which is destined to reduce that Unity to action; if, wheresoever a fellow-creature suffers, or the dignity of human nature is violated by falsehood or tyranny—you are not ready, if able, to aid the unhappy, and do not feel called upon to combat, if able, for the redemption of the betrayed or oppressed—you violate your Law of life, you comprehend not that Religion which will be the guide and blessing of the future.

But what can each of you, singly, *do* for the moral improvement and progress of Humanity? You can from time to time give sterile utterance to your belief; you may, on some rare occasions, perform some act of *charity* towards a brother man not belonging to your own land;—no more. But charity is not the watchword of the Faith of the future. The watchword of the Faith of the future is *association* and fraternal co-operation of all towards a common aim, and this is as far superior to all charity, as the edifice which all of you should unite to raise would be superior to the humble hut each one of you might build alone or with the mere assistance of lending and borrowing stone, mortar, and tools.

But, you tell me, you cannot attempt united action, distinct and

* Giuseppe Mazzini, "Duties Toward Your Country," in *Introduction to Contemporary Civilization in the West*, 3rd ed. (New York: Columbia University Press, 1961), Vol. II, pp. 540–43. Reprinted by permission.

divided as you are in language, customs, tendencies, and capacity. The individual is too insignificant, and Humanity too vast. The mariner of Brittany prays to God as he puts to sea: *Help me, my God! my boat is so small and Thy ocean so wide!* And this prayer is the true expression of the condition of each one of you, until you find the means of infinitely multiplying your forces and powers of action.

This means was provided for you by God when he gave you a country; when, even as a wise overseer of labour distributes the various branches of employment according to the different capacities of the workmen, he divided Humanity into distinct groups or nuclei upon the face of the earth, thus creating the germ of Nationalities. Evil governments have disfigured the Divine design. Nevertheless you may still trace it, distinctly marked out—at least as far as Europe is concerned—by the course of the great rivers, the direction of the higher mountains, and other geographical conditions. They have disfigured it by their conquests, their greed, and their jealousy even of the righteous power of others; disfigured it so far that, if we except England and France—there is not perhaps a single country whose present boundaries correspond to that Design.

These governments did not, and do not, recognise any country save their own families or dynasty, the egotism of caste. But the Divine design will infallibly be realised. Natural divisions, and the spontaneous innate tendencies of the peoples, will take the place of the arbitrary divisions sanctioned by evil governments. The map of Europe will be re-drawn. The countries of the Peoples, defined by the vote of free men, will arise upon the ruins of the countries of kings and privileged castes, and between these countries harmony and fraternity will exist. And the common work of Humanity, of great amelioration, and the gradual discovery and application of its law of life, being distributed according to local and general capacities, will be wrought out in peaceful and progressive development and advance.

Then may each one of you, fortified by the power and the affection of many millions, all speaking the same language, gifted with the same tendencies, and educated by the same historical tradition, hope even by your own single effort to be able to benefit all Humanity.

O my brothers, love your Country! Our country is our Home, the House that God has given us, placing therein a numerous family that loves us, and whom we love; a family with whom we sympathize more readily, and whom we understand more quickly, than we do others; and which, from its being centred round a given spot, and from the homogeneous nature of its elements, is adapted to a special branch of activity.

Our Country is our common workshop, whence the products of our activity are sent forth for the benefit of the whole world; wherein the tools and implements of labour we can most usefully employ are gathered together; nor may we reject them without disobeying the play of the Almighty, and diminishing our own strength.

In labouring for our own country on the right principle, we labour for Humanity. Our country is the fulcrum of the lever we have to wield for the common good. In abandoning that fulcrum, we run the risk of rendering ourselves useless not only to humanity but to our country itself.

Before men can *associate* with the nations of which humanity is composed, they must have a National existence. There is no true association except among equals. It is only through our country that we can have a recognizeed *collective* existence.

Humanity is a vast army advancing to the conquest of lands unknown, against enemies both powerful and astute. The peoples are the different corps, the divisions of that army. Each of them has its post assigned to it, and its special operation to execute; and the common victory depends upon the exactitude with which those distinct operations shall be fulfilled. Disturb not the order of battle. Forsake not the banner given to you by God. Wheresoever you may be, in the centre of whatsoever people circumstances may have placed you, be ever ready to combat for the liberty of that people should it be necessary, but combat in such wise that the blood you shed may reflect glory, not on yourselves alone, but on your country. Say not *I*, but *we*. Let each man among you strive to incarnate his country in himself. Let each man among you regard himself as a guarantee, responsible for his fellow-countrymen, and learn so to govern his actions as to cause his country to be loved and respected through him.

Your country is the sign of the mission God has given you to fulfil towards humanity. The faculties and forces of *all* her sons should be associated in the accomplishment of that mission.

The true country is a community of free men and equals, bound together in fraternal concord to labour towards a common aim. You are bound to make it and to maintain it such.

The country is not an *aggregation*, but an *association*.

There is therefore no true country without an uniform Right. There is no true country where the uniformity of that Right is violated by the existence of castes, privilege, and inequality.

Where the activity of a portion of the powers and faculties of the individual is either cancelled or dormant; where there is not a common Principle, recognised, accepted, and developed by all, there is no true Nation, no People; but only a multitude, a fortuitous agglomeration of men whom circumstances have called together, and whom circumstances may again divide.

In the name of the love you bear your country you must peacefully but untiringly combat the existence of privilege and inequality in the land that gave you life.

There is but one sole legitimate privilege, the privilege of Genius when it reveals itself united with virtue. But this is a privilege given by God, and when you acknowledge it and follow its inspiration, you do so freely, exercising your own reason and your own choice.

Every privilege which demands submission from you in virtue of power, inheritance, or any other right than the Right common to all, is an usurpation and a tyranny which you are bound to resist and destroy.

Be your country your Temple. God at the summit; a people of equals at the base.

Accept no other formula, no other moral law, if you would not dishonour alike your country and yourselves. Let all secondary laws be but the gradual regulation of your existence by the progressive application of this supreme law.

And in order that they may be such, it is necessary that *all* of you should aid in framing them. Laws framed only by a single fraction of the citizens, can never, in the very nature of things, be other than the mere expression of the thoughts, aspirations, and desires of that fraction; the representation, not of the Country, but of a third or fourth part, of a class or zone of the Country.

The laws should be the expression of the *universal* aspiration, and promote the universal good. They should be a pulsation of the heart of the Nation. The entire Nation should, either directly or indirectly, legislate.

By yielding up this mission into the hands of a few, you substitute the egotism of one class for the Country, which is the Union of all classes.

Country is not a mere zone of territory. The true Country is the Idea to which it gives birth; it is the Thought of love, the sense of communion which unites in one all the sons of that territory.

So long as a single one amongst your brothers has no vote to represent him in the development of the National life, so long as there is one left to vegetate in ignorance where others are educated, so long as a single man, able and willing to work, languishes in poverty through want of work to do, you have no Country in the sense in which Country ought to exist—the Country of all and for all.

Education, labour, and the franchise, are the three main pillars of the Nation. Rest not until you have built them strongly up with your own labour and exertions.

Never deny your sister Nations. Be it yours to evolve the life of your Country in loveliness and strength; free from all servile fears or sceptical doubts; maintaining as its basis the People; as its guide the consequences of the principles of its Religious Faith, logically and energetically applied; its strength, the united strength of all; its aim the fulfilment of the mission given to it by God.

And so long as you are ready to die for Humanity, the Life of your Country will be immortal.

13. *THE GROWTH OF NATIONS* / KARL W. DEUTSCH*

. . . While peoples are found at almost any period in history, nationalism and nations have occurred during only a few periods. A nation is the result of the transformation of a people, or of several ethnic elements, in the process of social mobilization. Thus far, however, the processes of social mobilization and communication have at no time included all mankind. The "universal states" listed by A. J. Toynbee as stages in the disintegration of particular civilizations[4] were superficial short-cuts, rather than solutions to the problem of the unity of mankind.

* Karl W. Deutsch, "The Growth of Nations: Some Recurrent Patterns of Political and Social Integration," *World Politics*, Vol. 5, No. 2 (January 1953), pp. 169–72, 189–94. Reprinted by permission.

4 *A Study of History*, London, 1939, IV, pp. 2–3.

Periods of "universal states" have left behind them, however, a number of widespread languages, such as Latin, Greek, or Arabic; and a measure of cultural assimilation among certain social groups such as the nobility, town population, or the clergy of some "universal church."[5] The results have somewhat resembled a *layer-cake pattern,* with a high degree of cultural assimilation and participation in extended social communication among the top layers of society; a lesser degree on the intermediate levels; and little or no assimilation or participation among the mass of the population at the bottom.[6]

In several parts of the world, the cycle—from local isolation to "universal" empire and back to a new age of localism[7]—has been traversed more than once. Yet the cycle has usually shown a net gain, in the sense that there has been a gain in man's technological and scientific command over nature,[8] and that some of the most important cultural, intellectual, moral, and spiritual traditions of the earlier civilization have tended to survive that civilization in which they arose, and continue, often as a "universal church" or religion, to influence the development of new peoples and new regions.[9]

As a result, much of world history has consisted of recurrent "feudal ages" in various parts of the world, though such periods in most cases were "feudal" only in the loose sense of the word. They were characterized by intense localism and dispersion of agriculture and settlement, as well as of military and judicial power, and by sharp distinctions between the class of scattered power-holders and the mass of the peasant population. At the same time, these "feudal" periods were marked by a certain universalism of political and cultural traditions, by memories of a past universal state, or by the

[5] For examples of such limited assimilation during and after the expanding phase of certain civilizations or universal states, see *ibid.*, Vols. I–VI, *passim,* and the appendix on "Lingue Franche" in Vol. v, pp. 483–526. Cf. also A. C. Woolner, *Languages in History and Politics,* London, 1938; and H. A. Innis, *Empire and Communication,* Oxford, 1950, and *The Bias of Communications,* Toronto, 1952. On particular languages, see Woolner, *op. cit.*, pp. 109–48, 156–67; H. A. R. Gibb, *The Arabs,* Oxford, 1940; George Antonius, *The Arab Awakening,* Philadelphia, 1939, p. 16; P. K. Hitti, *History of Syria Including Lebanon and Palestine,* New York, 1951, pp. 483–89.

[6] Cf. Royal Institute of International Affairs, *Nationalism,* London, 1939, p. 9; A. P. Usher, *Economic History of England,* Boston, 1920, pp. 20–21.

[7] For a discussion of the chances of linguistic disintegration following upon the dissolution of a universal empire, see Ramón Menéndez Pidal, *Castilla, la tradición, el idioma,* Buenos Aires, 1945, pp. 191–94.

[8] For the Graeco-Roman and medieval civilizations, this point has been stressed by Gordon Childe, *What Happened in History,* Harmondsworth, Eng., Penguin Books, 1950, pp. 279–82.

[9] Toynbee, *op. cit.*, v, p. 79, and *passim.*

knowledge of a highly developed civilization in some other area.[10] Such unifying memories or traditions were no mere disembodied thoughts: they were carried and disseminated by the institutions of organized churches and monastic orders, by a thin but far-flung network of trade relations and routes of pilgrimage, and sometimes by the movement and resettlement of small numbers of persons with special skills, industrial or military, over considerable distances.

From the point of view of nationality, all these were variations of the common layer-cake pattern. Assimilation to a common standard among the upper classes might be feeble, as during the "dark ages" in Western Europe; it might be somewhat more strongly developed, as among the European nobility at the time of the Crusades; or it might be almost complete, as in a universal state, as it had been in that of Imperial Rome. In any case, it would touch the masses of the people in the villages only indirectly and slowly. And even where it did touch and assimilate them in the course of centuries, there their continued passivity and lack of direct participation in affairs of wider import seemed to make it irrelevant for long periods of time whether the underlying population in the villages had been assimilated at least imperfectly to a common standard as in Italy, or whether they had remained as sharply differentiated as Czechs and Germans in Bohemia, or as Malays and Chinese in Malaya.[11] Only when this relatively passive population was mobilized in the processes of economic growth and political organization, did its cultural and social characteristics acquire in each case a new and crucial importance in the process of nation-building.

The processes of partial social mobilization and of nation-building have been recurrent phenomena in history, at least in certain general characteristics. What uniformities can we find in this growth of nations in the past? And in what ways is our own age

[10] A Conference on Feudalism was held on October 31 and November 1, 1950, at Princeton University under the auspices of the Committee on Uniformities of the American Council of Learned Societies. For the point made in the text, see the papers submitted to the Conference and the abridged report on its proceedings issued by the Council (Washington, D.C., multigraphed). A volume on *Feudalism in History*, containing these papers, with an analytical essay by the editor, Professor Rushton Coulborn, is in process of publication.

[11] Cf. Elizabeth Wiskemann, *Czechs and Germans*, London, 1938; Victor Purcell, *The Chinese in Malaya*, London, 1948; Rupert Emerson, L. A. Mills, and V. Thompson, *Government and Nationalism in Southeast Asia*, New York, 1942; etc.

different in respect to the growth of nations from any age that has gone before?

Some Possible Specific Uniformities

Uniformities which have been found in the growth of nations include the following:

1. The shift from subsistence agriculture to *exchange economies.*

2. The social mobilization of rural populations in *core areas* of denser settlement and more intensive exchange.

3. The growth of *towns*, and the growth of social mobility within them, and between town and country.

4. The growth of *basic communication grids*, linking important rivers, towns, and trade routes in a flow of transport, travel, and migration.

5. The differential accumulation and *concentration of capital* and skills, and sometimes of social institutions, and their "*lift-pump*" *effect* on other areas and populations, with the successive entry of different social strata into the nationalistic phase.

6. The rise of the concept of "*interest*" for both individuals and groups in unequal but fluid situations, and the growth of *individual self-awareness* and awareness of one's predispositions to join a particular group united by language and communications habits.

7. The awakening of *ethnic awareness* and the acceptance of *national symbols*, intentional or unintentional. . . .

What does this process accomplish, and what does it aim at? When a nation has been built up, and when it has been reinforced finally by the full compulsive power of the state, then four things have been accomplished.

(1) A relatively large community of human beings has been brought into existence who can communicate effectively with each other, and who have command over sufficient economic resources to maintain themselves and to transmit this ability for mutual communication to their children as well. In other words, there has been brought into being a large, comprehensive, and very stable human network of communication, capable of maintaining, reproducing, and further developing its channels.

(2) There has been both an effective accumulation of eco-

nomic resources and a sufficient social mobilization of manpower to permit the social division of labor necessary for this process and to permit its continuation.

(3) There has been a social accumulation and integration of memories and symbols and of individual and social facilities for their preservation, transmission, and recombination, corresponding to the level of mobilization and integration of material and human resources, or even pointing beyond it.

(4) There has been at least some development of the capacity to redirect, re-allocate, or form a new combination of economic, social, and human resources as well as of symbols and items of knowledge, habit, or thought—that is to say, of the capacity to learn. Some of the social *learning capacity* is developed invisibly in the minds of individuals; some of it can be observed in the habits and patterns of culture prevailing among them; some of it finally is embodied in tangible facilities and specific institutions. Together, all these constitute the community's capacity to produce and accept new knowledge or new goals, and to take the corresponding action.

On all four counts, it should be evident, the nation represents a more effective organization than the supra-national but largely passive layer-cake society or the feudal or tribal localisms that preceded it.

On all these counts, there may be considerable contrasts between different nations. The social models accepted for imitation, the established institutions, the economic practices, and the methods of compulsion within each nation are all intimately connected with the cultural traditions and leading social classes currently prevailing there. Whether a leading class of businessmen or farmers or wage earners will prove more hospitable to accumulation of resources and to efficient dynamic innovation in their use may depend not merely on the general outlook to be found prevailing in each particular stratum, but also—and perhaps sometimes crucially—on the particular cultural goals and traditions which have become accepted by that particular class in that particular nation.[35] Yet, the

[35] For some problems of conservative aristocratic leadership in undeveloped nations, cf., for the Arabs, the writings of H. A. R. Gibb; for an example from Tibet, Nicholas Mansergh, "The Asian Conference, 1947," in *The Commonwealth and the Nations*, London, 1948, pp. 115–16; and for Southeast Asia, Cora Du Bois, *Social Forces in Southeast Asia*, Minneapolis, Minn., 1949, pp. 33–36, 59. On the contrast, e.g., between French and American business investment policies, cf. David S. Landes, "French Entrepreneurship and Industrial Growth in the Nineteenth Century," *Journal of Economic History*, IX (May 1949), pp. 45–61.

impression remains that even the worst-led nation represents, relative to its numbers of population, a greater amount of social communication facilities, of economic resources, and of social learning capacity than any pattern of ethnic or social organization preceding it.

Where does this process aim? The nation has been valued as a means of social advancement. In a world of extreme differences between living standards, men have tended to use the nation as an instrument to improve their own standards relative to those of their neighbors. The intrinsic bias of this process has been, where the opportunity offered itself, to produce in the temporarily most successful nation a sociological pattern reminiscent of a *mushroom cloud*. The stem of this social mushroom was formed by the "national solidarity" between the poorest and the lower-middle strata of the nation; the poorest strata, both rural and urban, however, tended to be somewhat less in relative numbers, and offered their members greater chances for "vertical mobility" than was the case in other less "successful" nations. The middle and upper strata, on the other hand, tended to form the crown of the mushroom; they tended to be somewhat larger in number than the corresponding group in other nations, with a greater propensity to spread out horizontally into new positions of privilege or control over new territories, populations, or capital resources, and correspondingly with at least somewhat greater opportunities to accept in their midst newcomers from the less favored strata of their own nation.

It is perhaps this sociological explosion into a mushroom cloud that has been at the heart of the transitory popularity of empire-building. Nationalism typically has led to attempts at empire or at least at establishing privileges over other peoples. The essence of this empire-building has been perhaps the attempt at ruling without sharing, just as the essence of nationalism has been the attempt at improving the position of one's "own" group without any sharing with "outsiders." To the extent that this process was successful it could only tend ultimately to transform the whole nation into a privileged class, a *Herrenvolk* lording it over servant peoples, as the Nazis dreamed of it, or a small, select population monopolizing vast natural resources or accumulations of technological equipment regardless of the fate of the rest of mankind. In reality, this state has probably never been achieved; and where it was even partially approximated, the results in the long-run were anything but lasting. Invariably, thus far, the same nation-building process which had permitted one nation to get temporarily on top of its neighbors subsequently raised up other nations to weaken or destroy it.

From this it might seem at first glance that the whole process of the rise and decline of nations has been cyclical, with only the names of the actors changing in an endlessly repeated drama. Closer scrutiny may show that this is not the case, and that some tentative inferences may be drawn from the events and processes surveyed.

The Uniqueness of the Present Period

Our survey offers no support for the belief of many nationalists that nations are the natural and universal form of social organization for mankind. But neither does it confirm entirely the opposite view held by many thoughtful and distinguished observers—the view that nations are exclusively the product of the modern period and of Western civilization.[36] Perhaps the impression that remains might be summed up by saying that the West has gone much farther on a road which all the world's great civilizations have traveled to some extent.

At this moment we might well pause to question the ease with which we accept the designation of our present-day civilization as exclusively "Western." By Western civilization we mean a civilization which arose from the mingling of the Graeco-Roman tradition with the Celtic, Teutonic, and Slavic barbarian cultures north of the Mediterranean; but this Western civilization was Semiticized and Orientalized by the twin influences of Judaism and Christianity, even if we allow for the very appreciable element of Greek tradition in the latter.[37]

Subsequently, this Hellenic-Barbarian-Judaeo-Christian civilization was partially Arabicized during more than five hundred years of culture contact from the seventh to the thirteenth century. During the thirteenth and fourteenth centuries, this Arabicized Western civilization was then Mongolized and Sinicized. The details of the origin and acquisition of almost all of these innovations offer room for controversy, but there should be little controversy about the cumulative picture. Nor should there be much controversy

[36] Cf. Toynbee, *op. cit., passim;* Hans Kohn, *The Idea of Nationalism,* New York, 1944, *passim;* Carlton H. Hayes, "Nationalism," *Encyclopedia of the Social Sciences;* etc.

[37] For this tradition of the poorest strata of the Hellenic world, see the intriguing case presented by Toynbee, "Christus Patiens," *op. cit.,* VI, pp. 376–539.

about the massive "Amerindianization" of that Western-Arabic-Mongolian world from the sixteenth century onward, once the Indian culture plants of corn and potatoes permitted an entirely new balance of populations on the land, and once the availability of plentiful sugar, cotton, and tobacco transformed man's food, clothing, and consumption habits. What we call today Western civilization is in a very real sense a World civilization, not merely in what it brought to other countries, but also very significantly in what it received from them. Perhaps its "Western" peculiarities lie, then, not only in its ability to originate, but also in its ability to innovate, that is, to learn actively from others.

All these traits of creativity and of the ability to learn are present in all great civilizations of the world, and the West here, too, has perhaps gone faster and farther on a road traveled to some extent by all. In a real sense, Western civilization is carrying on some—though certainly not all—of the traditions of all other civilizations, and its crisis in the world today is also their crisis, and not merely in externals.

It is this universal aspect that also characterizees the growth of nations in the present. During the last fifty years, there seems to have been growth in all the important regions of the world. Everywhere there has been growth in population, in gross economic wealth, and in national awareness. In no region has there been a decline to compensate for an advance elsewhere. Many of these advances in widely different areas have been the continuation of long-standing trends, which have been helped and speeded by the new resources and possibilities offered by the diffusion of science and technology during those last fifty years.

The result is that today all peoples are involved in the growth of national awareness, and that soon there will be no peoples left to play the role of submerged nationalities or underlying populations, or passive bystanders of history, or drawers of water and hewers of wood for their better organized neighbors.

The process has gone further. Within each people, all social strata have been mobilized, socially, economically, and politically, or are in the process of being so mobilized before our eyes. Wherever this social mobilization has progressed, it has undermined the patterns of authority and privilege inherited from an earlier day. The time can be envisioned now when the majority of all mankind will have shifted to non-agricultural occupations. There has never been a period like this in the history of the world. . . .

NATIONAL POWER

V

The measurement of a state's power or capability in international politics is both a very fundamental and a most complicated matter. The selections in this chapter deal with only a few of its aspects. The first selection is Machiavelli's view of the calculation of state power—Chapter 10 of his *The Prince*. His principal, but not exclusive, emphasis is on military factors.

The second selection is concerned with the influence of different governmental systems on national power. Can a democracy pursue a successful foreign policy? Alexis de Tocqueville (1805–59) gives a pessimistic answer to this question in his famous work *Democracy in America*.

The third selection is Stephen B. Jones' discussion of "Global Strategic Views." The author is Professor of Geography at Yale University. He has also written *Geography and World Affairs* and other works.

14. *HOW TO MEASURE THE POWER OF STATES**/ *NICCOLO MACHIAVELLI*

It is also important in the study of governments to examine whether the prince, in time of need, be powerful enough to defend himself by his own forces, without having recourse to the assistance of his allies. To place this point in the clearest view, I may observe that those only can so defend themselves who have men and money enough to bring an army into the field, and give battle to whoever shall attack them. But wretched indeed is the situation of that prince who is reduced to the necessity of shutting himself up in his native city, there to await the enemy's approach. I have already discussed the first point, and shall have occasion to return to it again.

As to the second, I cannot but warn princes of the necessity they are under to fortify and provision the place of their residence, without troubling themselves about the rest of the country; for it, as I have already observed, and shall again have occasion in the sequel to repeat, they have in addition to this precaution learned the art of gaining their people's affection, they will be secure from all danger. Men are naturally cautious of engaging in difficult enterprises without some appearance of success, and it is never prudent to attack a prince whose capital is in a good state of defense and who is on good terms with his subjects.

The cities of Germany enjoy a very extensive liberty; they possess a territory of inconsiderable extent, and obey the Emperor when they please, under no apprehension of being attacked either by him or by others, for the towns are defended by strong walls and deep ditches, and are provided with artillery and provisions for a year, so that the siege of these cities would be both long and painful. Added to this, they are always provided with the means of employing the people during the same space of time, so as to support them without the assistance of the public purse. Moreover, their troops are regularly exercised in military evolutions, and their regulations in that respect are wise and well observed.

A prince, therefore, who possesses a well fortified city, and is respected by his people, can hardly be attacked with advantage,

* Niccolo Machiavelli, *The Prince* (New York: The National Alumni, 1907), Chap. 10 (pp. 44–46).

because the affairs of this world are so liable to change that it would be almost impossible for an enemy to keep the field for a year before a place so defended.

It may perhaps be objected that the people who possess property in the country, and who see their lands ravaged, will lose their patience, and that their attachment to their prince will not long continue against the inconveniences of a long siege, and the desire of preserving their property. I answer, that a prudent and spirited prince will easily surmount these obstacles, by inspiring the people either with hopes that their sufferings will soon be over, or with a dread of the resentment and cruelty of the conqueror, or by taking other proper means to appease those that are clamorous.

To this may be added, that the enemy begins his ravage of the country as soon as he enters it, and at that time the besieged are most animated and disposed to defend themselves; in which case the prince has still less to apprehend, because, before their ardor has cooled, the inhabitants, perceiving that all the mischief has been accomplished, and the loss is irretrievable, will evince the more attachment to their prince in proportion as their sacrifices are greater. For such is the nature of mankind that they become as strongly attached to others by the benefits they render as by the favors they receive.

All these considerations persuade me that a wise and provident prince may, without difficulty, succeed in sustaining the courage of his people under the distress of a siege, if he take care that they are well provided with the means necessary for their sustenance and defense.

15. *DEMOCRACY AND FOREIGN POLICY**/ *ALEXIS DE TOCQUEVILLE*

. . . As the Union [the United States] takes no part in the affairs of Europe, it has, properly speaking, no foreign interests to discuss, since it has, as yet, no powerful neighbors on the American continent. The country is as much removed from the passions of the Old World by its position as by its wishes, and it is neither called upon

* Alexis de Tocqueville, *Democracy in America*, trans. Henry Reeve, rev. by Francis Bowen (Cambridge, Mass.: Sever and Francis, 1863), pp. 298–301.

to repudiate nor to espouse them; whilst the dissensions of the New World are still concealed within the bosom of the future.

The Union is free from all pre-existing obligations; it can profit by the experience of the old nations of Europe, without being obliged, as they are, to make the best of the past, and to adapt it to their present circumstances. It is not, like them, compelled to accept an immense inheritance bequeathed by their forefathers,—an inheritance of glory mingled with calamities, and of alliances conflicting with national antipathies. The foreign policy of the United States is eminently expectant; it consists more in abstaining than in acting.

It is therefore very difficult to ascertain, at present, what degree of sagacity the American democracy will display in the conduct of the foreign policy of the country; upon this point, its adversaries as well as its friends must suspend their judgment. As for myself, I do not hesitate to say that it is especially in the conduct of their foreign relations that democracies appear to me decidedly inferior to other governments. Experience, instruction, and habit almost always succeed in creating in a democracy a homely species of practical wisdom, and that science of the petty occurrences of life which is called good sense. Good sense may suffice to direct the ordinary course of society; and amongst a people whose education is completed, the advantages of democratic liberty in the internal affairs of the country may more than compensate for the evils inherent in a democratic government. But it is not always so in the relations with foreign nations.

Foreign politics demand scarcely any of those qualities which are peculiar to a democracy; they require, on the contrary, the perfect use of almost all those in which it is deficient. Democracy is favorable to the increase of the internal resources of a state; it diffuses wealth and comfort, promotes public spirit, and fortifies the respect for law in all classes of society: all these are advantages which have only an indirect influence over the relations which one people bears to another. But a democracy can only with great difficulty regulate the details of an important undertaking, persevere in a fixed design, and work out its execution in spite of serious obstacles. It cannot combine its measures with secrecy, or await their consequences with patience. These are qualities which more especially belong to an individual or an aristocracy; and they are precisely the qualities by which a nation, like an individual, attains a dominant position.

If, on the contrary, we observe the natural defects of aristocracy, we shall find that, comparatively speaking, they do not injure the direction of the external affairs of the state. The capital fault of which aristocracies may be accused is, that they work for themselves, and not for the people. In foreign politics, it is rare for the interest of the aristocracy to be distinct from that of the people.

The propensity which induces democracies to obey impulse rather than prudence, and to abandon a mature design for the gratification of a momentary passion, was clearly seen in America on the breaking out of the French Revolution. It was then as evident to the simplest capacity, as it is at the present time, that the interest of the Americans forbade them to take any part in the contest which was about to deluge Europe with blood, but which could not injure their own country. But the sympathies of the people declared themselves with so much violence in favor of France, that nothing but the inflexible character of Washington, and the immense popularity which he enjoyed, could have prevented the Americans from declaring war against England. And even then, the exertions which the austere reason of that great man made to repress the generous but imprudent passions of his fellow-citizens nearly deprived him of the sole recompense which he ever claimed,—that of his country's love. The majority reprobated his policy, but it was afterwards approved by the whole nation.*

If the Constitution and the favor of the public had not intrusted the direction of the foreign affairs of the country to Washington, it is certain that the American nation would at that time have adopted the very measures which it now condemns.

Almost all the nations which have exercised a powerful influence upon the destinies of the world, by conceiving, following out, and executing vast designs, from the Romans to the English, have

* See the fifth volume of Marshall's "Life of Washington." "In a government constituted like that of the United States," he says, "it is impossible for the chief magistrate, however firm he may be, to oppose for any length of time the torrent of popular opinion; and the prevalent opinion of that day seemed to incline to war. In fact, in the session of Congress held at the time, it was frequently seen that Washington had lost the majority in the House of Representatives." The violence of the language used against him in public was extreme, and, in a political meeting, they did not scruple to compare him indirectly with the traitor Arnold. "By the opposition," says Marshall, "the friends of the administration were declared to be an aristocratic and corrupt faction, who, from a desire to introduce monarchy, were hostile to France, and under the influence of Britain; that they were a paper nobility, whose extreme sensibility at every measure which threatened the funds induced a tame submission to injuries and insults which the interests and honor of the nation required them to resist."

been governed by aristocratic institutions. Nor will this be a subject of wonder, when we recollect that nothing in the world has so absolute a fixity of purpose as an aristocracy. The mass of the people may be led astray by ignorance or passion; the mind of a king may be biassed, and made to vacillate in his designs, and, besides, a king is not immortal. But an aristocratic body is too numerous to be led astray by intrigue; and yet not numerous enough to yield readily to the intoxication of unreflecting passion. An aristocracy is a firm and enlightened individual that never dies.

16. *GLOBAL STRATEGIC VIEWS** / *STEPHEN B. JONES*

. . . "Strategy" in the broad sense can be defined as the art of using power. "Global strategy" implies this art viewed in relation to the whole world. The "global strategic views" of our title are geographical patterns related to global strategic ideas. . . .

The focus is on certain major ideas about the world, their relationships and their consequences. We begin with one of the first men to write of strategy in global terms, Mahan.

Mahan's View

The name of Mahan immediately evokes images of gray ships and blue water. However, as all students of his works know, he was concerned not so much with naval operations (though he described many battles) as with sea power, and sea power is as much of the land as of the sea. In his most famous book[3] Mahan listed six fundamental factors affecting the development of sea power: geographical position, physical conformation, extent of territory, number of population, national character, and governmental character. Merely to read this list is to understand the importance of the land base.

Mahan devoted most of his attention to European and North Atlantic naval history, including offshoot campaigns in the Indian

* Stephen B. Jones, "Global Strategic Views," *The Geographical Review,* Vol. 45, No. 4 (October 1955), pp. 492–508. Reprinted by permission.

[3] A. T. Mahan: The Influence of Sea Power upon History, 1660–1783 (Boston, 1890), Chap. I.

Ocean. However, in one of his less well-known books we find a global view, somewhat crudely outlined, that adumbrates the views of Mackinder, Fairgrieve, and Spykman. Here Mahan describes Russia in terms that fit Mackinder's Heartland—a "vast, uninterrupted mass" whose "centre cannot be broken."[4] He emphasizes Russia's landlocked position and its dominance in Central Asia. He points to the latitudinal belt of 30° to 40° N. in Asia as the unstable zone between British sea power and Russian land power.[5] This resembles, roughly, the Asiatic part of Fairgrieve's "crush zone."[6] Mahan also adumbrates Fairgrieve's "northern belt of settlement and movement," pointing out that Suez and Panama would mark the southern limit of most active commerce and politics.[7]

Mahan thought that Russian expansion in Asia could be opposed by sea-transported power—a sort of containment policy. Somewhat surprisingly, he advocated giving Russia access to the sea through China[8]—a premonition of Yalta, one might say. He believed this would satisfy Russian aspirations for warm-water ports, though it is hard to see how that could be the case with the bulk of the Russian population in Europe.[9] Mahan also predicted that Britain, Germany, Japan, and the United States would find a common interest in containing Russia and controlling China.[10] This prediction is less startling in 1955 than it seemed 10 years ago, when the present writer first read it. Like Mackinder after him, Mahan probably overestimated the influence of navigable rivers. He refers repeatedly to the navigability of the Yangtze. During the years of China's weakness, when foreign gunboats patrolled the river, it did serve as an avenue for sea power. But adequate land or air forces could make the Yangtze untenable for foreign ships, as happened when the Japanese bombed the *Panay* and the Chinese Communists attacked the *Amethyst*.

Looking back, one may question whether "sea power" was a really happy phrase. It emphasized one medium of power transmission, rather than the whole picture of national power and the places and purposes of its use. A lingering effect of a too literal

[4] *Idem:* The Problem of Asia (Boston, 1900), pp. 24 and 26.

[5] *Ibid.*, pp. 21 ff.

[6] James Fairgrieve: Geography and World Power (8th edit., New York, 1941), p. 334.

[7] Mahan, The Problem of Asia, pp. 84–86.

[8] *Ibid.*, pp. 117–120.

[9] For an interesting related discussion, see J. A. Morrison: Russia and Warm Water, *U. S. Naval Inst. Proc.*, Vol. 78, 1952, pp. 1169–1179.

[10] Mahan, The Problem of Asia [see footnote 4 above], pp. 63–65.

interpretation of the sea-power doctrine is an American belief that might be called "naval isolationism." This is to be distinguished from "continental isolationism," which would defend America at its shores. Naval isolationism is the belief that superior sea power can keep an enemy off the oceans and hence that American shores are safe without sending armies to lands overseas. The basic thesis is doubtful in this age of the airplane and the submarine, and the need to maintain a balance of power in Eurasia is ignored. Mahan's own views on Asia do not support the naval isolationist position, and Mackinder and Spykman, to whom we now turn, regarded it as definitely unsound.

Mackinder's View

It is not surprising that the United States, painfully land-minded since the opening of the West and the decline of sailing ships, should have produced Mahan, while Britain, most maritime of great powers, should have produced Mackinder. Prophets traditionally are voices crying in the wilderness. However, as we have already indicated, the basic views of Mahan and Mackinder are not as far apart as is commonly believed. Mahan outlined in a rough way the Heartland concept. Both men understood that sea power is land-based and that the size, population, and productivity of the land base have much to do wtih the magnitude of the resulting sea power. Mahan recognized the peculiar virtues of Britain's position, a large island off the European shore, and one of Mackinder's most scholarly works is called "Britain and the British Seas."[11] It was in their forecasts that they drew apart. Mahan continued to believe in the greater capacity and flexibility of movement by sea; Mackinder thought the great improvements in land transportation put the shoe on the other foot.

In his famous paper of 1904,[12] Mackinder designated as the "Pivot Area" that part of Eurasia which has interior drainage or drains to the icebound Arctic. The word "heart-land" appears only once in this paper, but in the 1919 book[13] it is capitalized and

[11] H. J. Mackinder: Britain and the British Seas (Oxford, 1902).

[12] *Idem:* The Geographical Pivot of History, *Geogr. Journ.*, Vol. 23, 1904, pp. 421–444.

[13] *Idem:* Democratic Ideals and Reality (New York, 1919 and 1942).

dehyphenated and supersedes "Pivot Area." The rest of Eurasia was called by Mackinder in 1904 "the Inner or Marginal Crescent." In 1919 parts of this crescent were called Coastlands. (Spykman later coined the felicitous term "rimland" for the Inner Crescent.) The Americas, Africa south of the Sahara, Australia, and the large islands off the Eurasian shores, such as the British Isles and Japan, were called in 1904 "the Outer or Insular Crescent." In 1919, Eurasia and Africa together were named the "World Island," Africa south of the Sahara "the Southern Heartland," and the other lands of the Outer Crescent "satellites" of the World Island.[14]

Mackinder's recognition of central Eurasia as the source of powerful forces that have affected Europe, South Asia, and the Far East was of course soundly based and was a needed corrective to the egocentricity of maritime Europe. But the original definition of the Pivot Area was the extreme of hydrographic literalness. It assumed that maritime states could move their forces up rivers—though current would favor the continental power—but would be unable to cross divides, however low. Actually, most transport systems work both ways. This statement applies not only to rivers but to the modern means of land transport that Mackinder especially stressed. In 1940 the Germans pushed the British off the continent. In 1945 the armies of the maritime powers swept into Germany along *Autobahnen* built to serve German troops. It is really a question of which side has the most power and makes the best use of it. It is true that improvements in land and air transportation have increased the burdens of the maritime states. But their burdens are increased primarily because they can no longer put so many of their eggs in the naval basket and because they must advance their strategic frontier as deeply into the Rimland as possible, not because the rivers of central Eurasia fail to reach an open sea.

In "Democratic Ideals and Reality" Mackinder made some alterations in the boundaries of the Heartland. "The Heartland, for the purposes of strategical thinking, includes the Baltic Sea, the navigable Middle and Lower Danube, the Black Sea, Asia Minor, Armenia, Persia, Tibet, and Mongolia."[15] Thus Mackinder now thought that the Baltic and Black Seas were closed to the maritime powers, as they had been during the First World War. This again

[14] *Ibid.*, pp. 79–82 and 98–99 (1919 edit.).

[15] *Ibid.*, pp. 135–136 (1919 edit.). The headwaters of the great Indian and Chinese rivers were also included in the Heartland in 1919 (map on p. 94).

seems a highly literal view. If land-based forces can close the Danish and Turkish straits, they can also keep them open to friendly ships. It is a question of who has the power, the initiative, the speed, and of who is allied to whom.

On a small-scale map the central position of the Heartland, or of the Soviet Union, in Eurasia looks terrifying. The Rimland seems such a narrow margin that it might be overwhelmed in a night. It is true that the Soviet position is strong, and that improvements in land and air transportation make it easier to exploit its advantages. Mahan believed that the sea lanes around Eurasia were really the interior lines, strategically.[16] This may no longer be true. But the speed and size of ships have greatly increased since Mahan's day. A modern freighter can cover as great a distance in a day as a truck convoy, carrying far more cargo, and is fueled for thousands of miles. Fast ships are worthy rivals of railway trains. Only the airplane is clearly superior in speed. We shall see below that this does not necessarily give the Heartland an overwhelming positional advantage. The great advantages of the Soviet Union have been political, especially its ability to follow a planned strategy persistently. The shift of China from the non-Communist to the Communist side was not so much a victory of land power over sea power as of a persistent, planned strategy over an inconsistent and blundering one.

Haushofer and his school adopted the main features of the Mackinder global view as part of the mélange of Geopolitik. They hoped that the first term of the famous dictum could be brought about by a partnership of Germany and the Soviet Union,[17] a hope which proved as illusory as Hitler's belief that Britain would agree to his terms.

Spykman's View

Spykman adopted Mackinder's basic geography but gave it a different interpretation. He rejected the apparent fatalism of the land-power doctrine and offered his own formula: "Who controls the rimland rules Eurasia; who rules Eurasia controls the destinies of the

[16] Mahan, The Problem of Asia [see footnote 4 above], pp. 124 ff.

[17] Derwent Whittlesey: Haushofer: The Geopoliticians, *in* Makers of Modern Strategy, edited by E. M. Earle (Princeton, 1943), pp. 388–411, reference on p. 405.

world."[18] Spykman hoped that the Soviet Union, the United Kingdom, and the United States would realize their common stake in controlling the Rimland. He knew, however, that "it may be that the pressure of Russia outward toward the rimland will constitute one important aspect of the post-war settlement."[19]

Mackinder's view has often been twisted into a fatalistic doctrine of "Herzland über alles."[20] Spykman seems to imply such a doctrine when he says that Mackinder emphasized "an inevitable historical opposition between Russian land power and British sea power." But, says Spykman, "there has never really been a simple land power–sea power opposition. The historical alignment has always been in terms of some members of the rimland with Great Britain against some members of the rimland with Russia, or Great Britain and Russia together against a dominating rimland power."[21] Actually, Mackinder knew this, and said so. The Heartland, in its limited sense of the interior and Arctic drainage area, menaced the maritime states only in conjunction with part of the Rimland. In the 1904 paper Mackinder[22] spoke of the peril to the marginal lands if Germany were to ally itself with Russia and of the possibility that China, organized by Japan, might conquer the Russian Empire. In the 1919 book it was the domination of the Heartland by East Europe that would lead to command of the world.

Looked at broadly, the Mahan, Mackinder, and Spykman strategic geographies have much in common. They also have much in common with Kennan's containment policy,[23] which was conceived independently.[24] Containment primarily means preventing extensions of Soviet control in the Rimland. Kennan, it might be noted, does not speak of either land power or sea power, avoiding the confusion that those terms are likely to engender.

[18] N. J. Spykman: The Geography of the Peace (New York, 1944), p. 43.

[19] *Ibid.*, p. 53.

[20] J. D. Hayes discusses this in his comments on Miller's "Must We Live in Fear?" *U. S. Naval Inst. Proc.*, Vol. 79, 1953, pp. 759–766; in the *United States Naval Institute Proceedings*, Vol. 80, 1954, pp. 91–93.

[21] Spykman, *loc. cit.* [see footnote 18 above]. "Always," in this quotation, means considerably less than that.

[22] The Geographical Pivot of History [see footnote 12 above], pp. 436–437.

[23] X [G. F. Kennan]: The Sources of Soviet Conduct, *Foreign Affairs*, Vol. 25, 1946–1947, pp. 566–582. Reprinted in G. F. Kennan: American Diplomacy, 1900–1950 (Chicago, 1951), pp. 107–128.

[24] Personal communication from Mr. Kennan.

The Heartland Concept

Mackinder's first term for central Eurasia, the "Pivot Area," implies uniqueness as he uses it. "The Heartland," with the definite article, implies at least primacy among heartlands. In his 1919 book Mackinder[25] called Africa south of the Sahara the "Southern Heartland." Since then other regions have been nominated for heartland status. Cressey writes: "If there is anywhere a world citadel or Heartland, it may well lie in North America rather than in Eurasia. The American continent has adequate size, compact shape, internal accessibility, a central location, good boundaries, access to two oceans, favorable topography, rich minerals, excellent climate, and a dynamic spirit in its people."[26] The relative proximity of the Eurasian and North American heartlands, if there are two heartlands, across the Arctic has often been pointed out.[27] Renner goes on to say that, as a result of air transportation, "the natural world fortress, or heartland, has been expanded to include the interior parts of all the land masses which form a ring around the Arctic Mediterranean–Europe, Asia, and North America."[28] The United States Air Force has given still another meaning to "heartland." Every great power, perhaps every state, has one. "There are two broad aspects of air operations, heartland and peripheral actions. . . . Heartland actions involve attacks against the vital elements of a nation's war sustaining resources. . . ."[29] This definition, it will be noted, does not specifically require an interior location for heartlands.

This proliferation of heartlands suggests that we try to define "heartland" in terms of *what* it is rather than *where* it is. Cressey, we have just read, defines a heartland as "a world citadel" and lists a number of factors of power as criteria, including the unheartlandish one of access to the oceans. Mackinder thought of the Pivot Area as

25 Democratic Ideals and Reality [see footnote 13 above], p. 100 (1919 edit.). This is criticized by Spykman in "The Geography of the Peace" [see footnote 18 above], p. 41.

26 G. B. Cressey: The Basis of Soviet Strength (New York and London, 1945), p. 245.

27 For example, R. E. Harrison and H. W. Weigert: World View and Strategy, *in* Compass of the World, edited by H. W. Weigert and Vilhjalmur Stefansson (New York, 1944), pp. 74–88, reference on p. 79 (map).

28 G. T. Renner: Peace by the Map, *Collier's*, Vol. 113, 1944, pp. 44–47.

29 "Basic Doctrine," *U. S. Air Force Manual AFM 1–2*, April, 1954, p. 11.

primarily a region of mobility for land forces, impenetrable by sea power: "we have in this immense area all the conditions for the maintenance of a sparse, but in the aggregate considerable, population of horse-riding and camel-riding nomads"[30]—hardly the description of a great power base. In the 1919 book "Heartland" appears first as a synonym for "Pivot Area" but is extended, as we have seen, to include much of Eastern Europe. Mackinder used the word "citadel" for his Heartland, but he expected the citadel to be supplied and garrisoned chiefly from Eastern Europe, not from the original Pivot Area. By 1943, Mackinder had further shifted his definition. He wrote that "it is sufficiently accurate to say that the territory of the U.S.S.R. is equivalent to the Heartland, except in one direction." This exception is "Lenaland," or Siberia east of the Yenisei. "West of the Yenisei lies what I shall describe as Heartland Russia . . . It contains four and a quarter million square miles and a population of more than one hundred seventy millions."[31] The Heartland concept was thus shifted to conform to a national power base—one of the many things remodeled by the Five-Year Plans.

Renner's proposed transpolar heartland combines the interior power bases of Eurasia and North America with the region of aerial mobility in the high latitudes. Perhaps we might revive "pivot area" for an area where mobility is the chief strategic factor and confine "heartland" to interior power bases. Conceivably the Arctic region could play a role in the age of flight similar to that of central Eurasia in the age of nomadic horsemen. But such are the connotations of "pivot" and "heart" that it may be wiser to drop the terms altogether.[32]

The Wide Blue Yonder

When Mackinder's "The Geographical Pivot of History" was printed in the *Geographical Journal*, the comments made by members of the audience were, according to the usual practice, printed

[30] Mackinder, The Geographical Pivot of History [see footnote 12 above], p. 429.

[31] H. J. Mackinder: The Round World and the Winning of the Peace, *in* Compass of the World [see footnote 27 above], pp. 161–173, reference on pp. 164–165.

[32] Miller, in his "Must We Live in Fear?" [see footnote 20 above], p. 763, says that "the Mediterranean basin was the true heartland, the true power center of the ancient world." In the usage suggested above, the Mediterranean *Sea* might be called the pivot area of the ancient world.

also. Many readers have noted that one auditor, Amery, called attention to the airplane as possibly upsetting the assumptions on which Mackinder's theory was based[33]—this in 1904, only a few weeks after the Wright brothers had made their first flight.

Mackinder, we have seen, wrote of the seaman's and the landsman's points of view. The basic pattern of the physical world was of course the same for both, but the strategic forecast hinged on the belief that land transportation was overtaking sea transportation as a vehicle of power. We have also seen that putting, or seeming to put, seaman and landsman in strong contrast may have been a disservice to clear thinking. Now we have the airman. Must we add the airman's point of view? Or would that only increase the confusion?

For one thing, there is a wide range of thought about air power. Experience with air power is limited, and the pace of technological change has been extraordinary. We find variation from the "all-out" school, exemplified by such men as Douhet and Seversky, through moderate but firmly "air-first" men to the conservatives who hold that the main function of air power is to assist surface operations.

The conservative group holds that the surface battlefield remains the locus of decision. Sea power is vital to the supply of the battle front. Air power is vital to the security of sea routes, for observation and rapid transportation, and as long-range artillery to interdict enemy movements. Strategic bombardment, to this group, should be related to surface operations. Such a view of air power leads to no very new view of the globe. A third dimension has been added to the Mahan or Mackinder world, but its surface features have not been erased, and the travel-time scale has not been greatly altered, since surface movement dominates.

For an example of the air-first moderates, we may take Slessor, who holds that the strategic air force, with nuclear bombs, is "the Great Deterrent" which may prevent another general war.[34] But local wars are still possible, with ground forces bearing much of the load. Slessor sees a need for armies and navies and even for a special "semi-static" force or militia for local and civil defense. Slessor does not describe his global view, as we use that term here, but mani-

[33] Mackinder, The Geographical Pivot of History [see footnote 12 above], p. 441.

[34] John Slessor: Strategy for the West (New York, 1954), especially Chapters 3 and 4.

festly it must combine something like the Rimland—the locus of local wars—with a disbelief in heartlands. His views on heartlands seem like an echo of Amery's, amplified by half a century of aeronautical development:

> Meanwhile do not let us be distracted by geopolitical talk about heartlands, which was all very well in Mackinder's day but ceased to be relevant with the advent of the long-range bomber. Russia's central position has some tactical advantages, vis-à-vis her neighbours, but in a world air war she would be at a decisive disadvantage. Air power has turned the vast spaces that were her prime defence against Napoleon and Hindenburg and Hitler into a source of weakness. In these days of near-sonic speeds, the depth of penetration necessary to reach some of her vital centres is offset by the size of the area to be defended and the fact that it can be attacked from almost all round the compass.[35]

In Slessor's view, the virtues of the Heartland—size, centrality, and inaccessibility—have become either of no advantage or disadvantageous. Have *Raum und Lage* gone into reverse, so to speak, in the air age?

In order that the Soviet power base be penetrable "from almost all round the compass," it is essential that the non-Communist powers maintain a strong position in the Rimland and in what Spykman called the "off-shore islands" of Great Britain, Japan, Africa, and Australia.[36] If these areas come under Communist domination, it will be the Americas that are penetrable "from almost all round the compass."

Whether centrality in Eurasia gives the Soviet Union a commanding position or only a strong one has been discussed above. The relative value of land power and sea power in the Rimland was held undecided. What of air power? It is incomparably fast, of increasing capacity, and less and less restricted by weather and surface features. But the very speed of the airplane may offset some of the advantages of position. At near-sonic speeds, to fly, say, from Tashkent to Delhi would take less than two hours. But from Singapore to Delhi would take only four. Would the difference be critical? Would not what Whittlesey calls "pace"[37]—the average tempo of operations—and timing be more important than the velocity of flight, at such speeds? Fuel remains a great problem until

[35] *Ibid.*, p. 34.
[36] Spykman, *op. cit.* [see footnote 18 above], p. 38.
[37] Derwent Whittlesey: The Horizon of Geography, *Annals Assn. of Amer. Geogrs.*, Vol. 35, 1945, pp. 1–36; reference on p. 24.

atomic energy is adapted to aircraft, but could not Singapore be supplied as readily as Tashkent? If one is ready and resolute, need one be despondent over geographical position? For that matter, may not the Battle of the Rimland be decided by politics rather than by war? Was Vietminh lost by war, or by French delay in freeing and arming Vietnam and American unwillingness to enter the fray?

How do nuclear weapons affect these matters? One may readily agree that in an all-out nuclear war, with cities blasted from the face of the earth and even the countryside polluted with radioactive fall-out, "Heartland," "Rimland," "land power," and "sea power" are words with little significance. But we hear much of the tactical use of nuclear weapons. Just what "tactical use" means is not clear. Should it be stretched to include use against docks, bridges, and freight yards, it comes perilously close to "strategic bombardment," involving or inviting the destruction of cities. If, however, it is possible to confine nuclear weapons to tactical uses, it is not certain that either land power or sea power is favored or that the Heartland-Rimland relationship is altered. Much depends on the relative improvement in methods of attack and defense and on the alertness of the belligerents and the astuteness of their commanders.

Seversky's View

If there is a unique "airman's global view," it probably is essentially that of Seversky, and the azimuthal equidistant projection centered on the North Pole is its cartographic expression . . .[38] The popularity of North Polar projections has been a valuable corrective to the overuse of the Mercator. The equidistant form, however, has the serious defect of stretching the latitudinal scale in the Southern Hemisphere, and this in turn has the visual effect of greatly exaggerating the width of the southern oceans.

Seversky definitely subordinates the army and navy to the air force. He believes that virtually complete air supremacy, not just local or temporary air superiority, is possible. The side that obtains air supremacy holds the other at its mercy. He does not expect this to come without enormous effort and losses, but he feels that a country such as the United States, with advanced technology but limited manpower, can better pay the price of air supremacy than

[38] A. P. de Seversky: Air Power: Key to Survival (New York, 1950).

that of superiority in three media.[39] Since he wishes the United States to avoid surface, and particularly ground, combat, he regards overseas bases as undesirable, probably untenable, and, in an age of intercontinental flight, unnecessary. Besides the Soviet Union and the United States, Britain alone has the potentialities of great air power. Only in the vicinity of Bering Strait does orthodox warfare seem justified.[40] Latin America, within the circle of American air dominance, becomes the main reserve of American industry. Much of Africa and all of Southeast Asia are within the ellipse of Soviet air dominance. The overlap of the American circle and the Soviet ellipse is the "area of decision," where Seversky thinks the mastery of the air will be decided. Seversky's global view thus swings us back to the concept of Western Hemisphere defense, with a north-south rather than an east-west emphasis.

A number of American habits of mind favor acceptance of "the airman's view." A sort of "air isolationism" appears possible, the Western Hemisphere is revived, faith in machines and in American know-how is a string touched, the all-out air strategy seems economical in dollars and men. On the other hand, the conservatism of the Army and Navy and their civilian supporters is aroused. Dislike or disregard for "the frozen north" and habitual east-west thinking are strong. "The suggestive map" that speaks to most Americans is still likely to have the equator across the middle.

The choice among the conservative, moderate, and all-out air views is one of the most critical in the American future. The decision will determine the allocation of manpower and resources, the location of bases, policies toward Rimland countries and Latin America, and many other matters. It is beyond the reach of this paper to settle such weighty affairs. All we can do is to propound a few questions that bear on the evaluation of "the airman's view."

The first question concerns the reality of the Western Hemisphere and its self-sufficiency and defensibility. A report of a Senate subcommittee on strategic and critical materials says, as if it were axiomatic, "We belong in the Western Hemisphere."[41] The report demonstrates the present American dependence on sources of strategic and critical materials outside the Western Hemisphere but maintains that through stockpiling, exploration, subsidization, and

[39] *Ibid.*, p. 11.

[40] *Ibid.*, map facing p. 312.

[41] "Report of the Minerals, Materials, and Fuels Economic Subcommittee of the Committee on Interior and Insular Affairs," *83rd Congr., 2nd Sess., Senate Rept. No. 1627*, 1954, p. 12.

scientific research the Americas could be made self-sufficient for a period of war. It is held that sea lanes to South America could hug the shore and be protected from enemy aircraft or submarines. "In the last analysis land transportation can be improved."[42] If we grant, if only for the sake of the argument, that the Americas could be made self-sufficient for a period of war, we must still question their complete defensibility by the strategy envisioned. Soviet planes in Central or even East Africa, beyond the circle of American air dominance, would be approximately as near the most vital parts of South America as planes based on Florida. South American cities, and particularly the influential metropolises of Brazil and Argentina, would be vulnerable unless their defenses were virtually perfect. American ability to retaliate, or to "neutralize" African airfields after a blow had fallen, would offer little solace. If substantial parts of Africa should come under Soviet control, it is not certain that Latin America would remain steadfast in support of the United States. We may thus have to defend large parts of the Rimland in order to protect Latin America, which the Senate subcommittee, possibly influenced by the polar projection, calls "our own backyard."[43]

Another question is that of defense against intercontinental bombardment. Perfect defense on both sides would cancel out the offense. In that case, intercontinental bombardment would not even be "the Great Deterrent." True, perfect defense is improbable, but if defense is less than perfect, retaliation is to be expected, and thus to launch an intercontinental air attack entails great risks. Nevertheless, if a nation places all its defensive bets on this strategy, it must be prepared to use it.

The foregoing questions can be reduced to one: When, and under what circumstances, does a nation that adopts the all-out intercontinental strategy launch its aircraft? One choice would be preventive war, a choice that the United States is unlikely to make. Another would be to use the intercontinental air force in the event of any further aggression across the Iron Curtain. This would be containment by intercontinental means. It might succeed—even the threat might be enough—but it would require unlimited fortitude for an American commander in chief to stand ready to give the signal, risking retaliatory destruction of American cities, to halt, for example, Communist expansion in some country of southern Asia.

[42] *Ibid.*, p. 28.
[43] *Ibid.*, p. 23.

Third, there is "air isolationism." A defensive perimeter, to use that unhappy term, might be drawn around the Americas, perhaps including some overseas areas considered particularly important. Intercontinental air war would be used or threatened only if this perimeter were crossed. Such a stand would require as much fortitude as the other. In fact, we have seen that large parts of the Rimland might have to be included within the defensive perimeter if Latin America were to be secure. Thus "air isolationism" approaches "containment."

The nub of the matter is that strategy and foreign policy are complementary and inseparable. This is particularly true of the key question of when to resort to armed defense.[44] Moreover, they are continuing processes and cannot be redirected overnight. If a state adopts a rigid strategy keyed to a single kind of war, its foreign policy is made rigid in major ways. This is not necessarily evil if the rigid view is sound, but history does not encourage the belief that man can foresee the precise course of future events. Some flexibility in strategic view seems wise. "Flexibility" should be forward-looking, however, not patterned on the past.

Recipe for a Composite View

We have examined, in this and the preceding article, a series of global views of politics and strategy. None of them, taken singly, is an adequate picture of the world. None can unhesitatingly be called "the best" or even "the best yet." There is no simple system of political geography, no single thought filter through which to strain all geographical information. We need a series of filters, a composite or an eclectic global view.

Many of the men whose writings we have studied have in fact held composite views. For ease of analysis and comparison we have selected single items. Whittlesey's "exploitable world," though shrinking now, is a harmonious part of his historical approach. Taylor's maps and graphs show many environmental factors. Spykman discussed and mapped location, landforms, climate, economic production, and population before he proceeded to modify Mackinder's world.[45] There is, however, no virtue in the composite or

[44] Cf. W. W. Kaufmann: The Requirements of Deterrence, *Princeton Univ. Center of Internatl. Studies Memorandum No.* 7, 1954.

[45] Spykman, *op. cit.* [see footnote 18 above], pp. 19–34.

eclectic process per se. Haushofer's views were eclectic. Even if one chooses good ingredients, there is the problem of relative weight. Huntington, in his last book,[46] held climate, kith, and diet to be mainsprings of civilization, but, in a given case, which is the main spring?

There is no easy road out of these difficulties. The "recipe for a composite view" that we give here makes no pretense to completeness or finality, nor does it contain anything that a geographer does not already know. It is merely an attempt to list the elements of a global view based on the concept of national power. No map of it is presented. This may be cowardice, engendered by our own warning, in the first article, that mapping an idea is likely to reveal its fuzziness. But much of the material in our list is already on maps, and for other items data are incomplete.

National power, as has been elaborated elsewhere,[47] has two components that may be called "inventory" and "strategy." The former is what one has, the latter what one does with it. The inventory component can largely be subsumed, we believe, under Mackinder's old term "man settling," the strategic component largely under his "man travelling."[48]

I. Man Settling
- A. Population
- B. Culture
- C. Material Base

II. Man Traveling
- A. The Atmosphere
- B. Oceans and Islands
- C. Continental Interiors and Peripheries
- D. The Northern Region

This list probably needs little explanation. What is left out may be more surprising than what is included. For example, climate, landforms, and mineral resources are not specifically mentioned. They are, however, implied under other headings and would appear in the higher orders of subdivision.

No one is likely to question the place of population or material base in a global view of national power. Population has been mapped many times, and its elements have been carefully outlined by Trewartha.[49] Among the more significant subdivisions are trends, in

[46] Ellsworth Huntington: Mainsprings of Civilization (New York and London, 1945).

[47] S. B. Jones: The Power Inventory and National Strategy, *World Politics,* Vol. 6, 1953–1954, pp. 421–452.

[48] H. J. Mackinder: The Physical Basis of Political Geography, *Scottish Geogr. Mag.,* Vol. 6, 1890, pp. 78–84.

[49] G. T. Trewartha: A Case for Population Geography, *Annals Assn. of Amer. Geogrs.,* Vol. 43, 1953, pp. 71–97; reference on pp. 88–89.

relation to total numbers and age groups, and urbanization. Urbanization is an indication of the kind of economy and of the tempting targets for nuclear bombs. The material base of course includes sources of food, energy, and essential raw materials. Although maps of such items have been attempted, adequate and commensurable data for recent years are hard to find.[50]

The inclusion of culture as a major heading in a list based on the concept of national power may require some defense. But one element of culture is government, and the common political map is therefore a cultural map. The political interpretation of general culture is difficult and still in the experimental stage; thus it is perhaps faith that leads us to give culture so prominent a place. Culture has been placed between population and the material base because it is through culture that men make the material base economic, turn sources into resources, so to speak.

In subdividing "Man Traveling" our guiding principle has been that, for the immediate future at least, air, land, and sea movement are all of importance as means of projecting power. This is especially true because "projecting power" includes economic as well as military action. The relative importance of the three media varies for different kinds of action and in different parts of the world. The atmosphere, because of its global spread, its vertical extent, and the speed of the vehicles that use it, is of first and increasing importance. This is true whether or not "heartland operations" by strategic air forces are the pattern of future conflict. Every globe and relatively undistorted map gives an airman's view, but it takes imagination to see on them the useful and fearful canopy of air, so that emphasis is justified.

With the oceans we include the islands found in them. Every island is moated to a certain extent, and the defense of Britain in the Second World War and the delay the Formosa Strait imposed on

[50] M. K. Bennett, in his book "The World's Food" (New York, 1954, Chapters 12 and 13), subjects published data on national diets to considerable criticism. Excellent maps of energy production, consumption (1937, with estimates for 1948), and reserves accompany the study of "Energy Resources of the World" prepared under the direction of N. B. Guyol for the Department of State (*U. S. Dept. of State Publ. 3428*, 1949). The energy data in the *Statistical Yearbook* of the United Nations unfortunately do not include major Communist countries. The pending importance of atomic energy in industry further complicates the picture. Rapid strides in the beneficiation of lean iron ores make unreliable many published studies of the distribution of this basic metal.

the Chinese Communists show that the moating is still of some significance. But air power, and not just ships or water, is needed to make the moat effective. Not all islands or parts of the oceans are of equal importance. The islands and narrow seas off the Eurasian coast are of first importance today, those off the North American coast of second.

It is hardly news that the peripheries of continents differ from the interiors in ease of maritime access. In the age of nuclear weapons, peripheral location carries increased vulnerability from sabotage, ship- or submarine-launched missiles, and underwater explosion. It usually means a greater dependence on sea-borne supplies. But it also means wider economic contacts by the most capacious and economical of carriers. Only in Eurasia does the division into interior and periphery have great political significance, as Mackinder showed long ago. In the Americas the interior has been absorbed by the coastal states, with minor exceptions. Nearly all of Africa today is controlled from the shores, though its future political pattern is obscure.

The final item of our composite view is "the northern region," based on the nature of the Arctic Sea and the northern parts of North America and Eurasia and their relation to the great centers of power that are certain, for a long time at least, to lie in the Northern Hemisphere. In the northern region surface movement meets resistance for much or all of the year whereas air movement is relatively easy. The northern region may be, as we have said, an aerial "pivot area." There are other parts of the world where air movement is much easier than surface movement, such as the rain forests and the deserts, but these either are smaller than the northlands or offer less serious obstacles. The deserts, for instance, are traversed more easily than the northlands by conventional vehicles, and the Amazon and Congo basins have their immense, never-frozen rivers.

The global view just outlined is merely what the mythical German scientist is supposed to have written, *eine Einführung in das Leben des Elephanten*, though measurable in pages rather than in volumes. The whole elephant is too big for us to see in detail, but we are not blind, only myopic, and we can discern its outlines. And we can and do pursue it, though the path of our safari is beset by pitfalls. On one side is the flood of unfiltered information that rushes endlessly. On the other are the quicksands of oversimplification. To remain still is to be stung by the scholar's conscience. But hazards and discomforts are inevitable accompaniments of adventure, and the pursuit of the global view is the geographer's intellectual adventure.

DIPLOMACY

VI

DIPLOMACY IS OF CRUCIAL IMPORTANCE IN international affairs and several facets of it are highlighted in this chapter. The first selection is the account by Thucydides (471–400 B.C.) of the Melian Conference between the powerful Athenians and the much weaker Melians in 416 B.C. The description is taken from Thucydides' famous work *The Peloponnesian War*.

The second selection is Quincy Wright's discussion of the decline of "classic diplomacy." Quincy Wright, Professor Emeritus of International Law at the University of Chicago, is the author of *A Study of War* and *The Study of International Relations.*

The third selection discusses some of the often misunderstood peculiarities of diplomatic life and the reasons behind them. Michael H. Cardozo is Professor of Law at Cornell University and author of *Diplomats in International Cooperation.*

17. *THE MELIAN CONFERENCE* / THUCYDIDES*

. . . The Melians are a colony of Lacedæmon that would not submit to the Athenians like the other islanders, and at first remained neutral and took no part in the struggle, but afterwards upon the Athenians using violence and plundering their territory, assumed an attitude of open hostility. Cleomedes, son of Lycomedes, and Tisias, son of Tisimachus, the generals, encamping in their territory with the above armament, before doing any harm to their land, sent envoys to negotiate. These the Melians did not bring before the people, but bade them state the object of their mission to the magistrates and the few; upon which the Athenian envoys spoke as follows:—

Athenians.—'Since the negotiations are not to go on before the people, in order that we may not be able to speak straight on without interruption, and deceive the ears of the multitude by seductive arguments which would pass without refutation (for we know that this is the meaning of our being brought before the few), what if you who sit there were to pursue a method more cautious still! Make no set speech yourselves, but take us up at whatever you do not like, and settle that before going any farther. And first tell us if this proposition of ours suits you.'

The Melian commissioners answered:—

Melians.—'To the fairness of quietly instructing each other as you propose there is nothing to object; but your military preparations are too far advanced to agree with what you say, as we see you are come to be judges in your own cause, and that all we can reasonably expect from this negotiation is war, if we prove to have right on our side and refuse to submit, and in the contrary case, slavery.'

Athenians.—'If you have met to reason about presentiments of the future, or for anything else than to consult for the safety of your state upon the facts that you see before you, we will give over; otherwise we will go on.'

Melians.—'It is natural and excusable for men in our position to turn more ways than one both in thought and utterance. However,

* From the book *The History of the Peloponnesian War* by Thucydides, translated by Richard Crawley, pp. 330–37. Everyman's Library. Reprinted by permission of E. P. Dutton & Co. Inc. and J. M. Dent & Sons Ltd.

the question in this conference is, as you say, the safety of our country; and the discussion, if you please, can proceed in the way which you propose.'

Athenians.—'For ourselves, we shall not trouble you with specious pretences—either of how we have a right to our empire because we overthrew the Mede, or are now attacking you because of wrong that you have done us—and make a long speech which would not be believed; and in return we hope that you, instead of thinking to influence us by saying that you did not join the Lacedæmonians, although their colonists, or that you have done us no wrong, will aim at what is feasible, holding in view the real sentiments of us both; since you know as well as we do that right, as the world goes, is only in question between equals in power, while the strong do what they can and the weak suffer what they must.'

Melians.—'As we think, at any rate, it is expedient—we speak as we are obliged, since you enjoin us to let right alone and talk only of interest—that you should not destroy what is our common protection, the privilege of being allowed in danger to invoke what is fair and right, and even to profit by arguments not strictly valid if they can be got to pass current. And you are as much interested in this as any, as your fall would be a signal for the heaviest vengeance and an example for the world to meditate upon.'

Athenians.—'The end of our empire, if end it should, does not frighten us: a rival empire like Lacedæmon, even if Lacedæmon was our real antagonist, is not so terrible to the vanquished as subjects who by themselves attack and overpower their rulers. This, however, is a risk that we are content to take. We will now proceed to show you that we are come here in the interest of our empire, and that we shall say what we are now going to say, for the preservation of your country; as we would fain exercise that empire over you without trouble, and see you preserved for the good of us both.'

Melians.—'And how, pray, could it turn out as good for us to serve as for you to rule?'

Athenians.—'Because you would have the advantage of submitting before suffering the worst, and we should gain by not destroying you.'

Melians.—'So that you would not consent to our being neutral, friends instead of enemies, but allies of neither side.'

Athenians.—'No; for your hostility cannot so much hurt us as your friendship will be an argument to our subjects of our weakness, and your enmity of our power.'

Melians.—'Is that your subjects' idea of equity, to put those who have nothing to do with you in the same category with peoples that are most of them your own colonists, and some conquered rebels?'

Athenians.—'As far as right goes they think one has as much of it as the other, and that if any maintain their independence it is because they are strong, and that if we do not molest them it is because we are afraid; so that besides extending our empire we should gain in security by your subjection; the fact that you are islanders and weaker than others rendering it all the more important that you should not succeed in baffling the masters of the sea.'

Melians.—'But do you consider that there is no security in the policy which we indicate? For here again if you debar us from talking about justice and invite us to obey your interest, we also must explain ours, and try to persuade you, if the two happen to coincide. How can you avoid making enemies of all existing neutrals who shall look at our case and conclude from it that one day or another you will attack them? And what is this but to make greater the enemies that you have already, and to force others to become so who would otherwise have never thought of it?'

Athenians.—'Why, the fact is that continentals generally give us but little alarm; the liberty which they enjoy will long prevent their taking precautions against us; it is rather islanders like yourselves, outside our empire, and subjects smarting under the yoke, who would be the most likely to take a rash step and lead themselves and us into obvious danger.'

Melians.—'Well then, if you risk so much to retain your empire, and your subjects to get rid of it, it were surely great baseness and cowardice in us who are still free not to try everything that can be tried, before submitting to your yoke.'

Athenians.—'Not if you are well advised, the contest not being an equal one, with honour as the prize and shame as the penalty, but a question of self-preservation and of not resisting those who are far stronger than you are.'

Melians.—'But we know that the fortune of war is sometimes more impartial than the disproportion of numbers might lead one to suppose; to submit is to give ourselves over to despair, while action still preserves for us a hope that we may stand erect.'

Athenians.—'Hope, danger's comforter, may be indulged in by those who have abundant resources, if not without loss at all events without ruin; but its nature is to be extravagant, and those who go so far as to put their all upon the venture see it in its true colours only when they are ruined; but so long as the discovery would enable them to guard against it, it is never found wanting. Let not this be the case with you, who are weak and hang on a single turn of the scale; nor be like the vulgar, who, abandoning such security as human means may still afford, when visible hopes fail them in extremity, turn to invisible, to prophecies and oracles, and other such inventions that delude men with hopes to their destruction.'

Melians.—'You may be sure that we are as well aware as you of the difficulty of contending against your power and fortune, unless the terms be equal. But we trust that the gods may grant us fortune as good as yours, since we are just men fighting against unjust, and that what we want in power will be made up by the alliance of the Lacedæmonians, who are bound, if only for very shame, to come to the aid of their kindred. Our confidence, therefore, after all is not so utterly irrational.'

Athenians.—'When you speak of the favour of the gods, we may as fairly hope for that as yourselves; neither our pretensions nor our conduct being in any way contrary to what men believe of the gods, or practise among themselves. Of the gods we believe, and of men we know, that by a necessary law of their nature they rule wherever they can. And it is not as if we were the first to make this law, or to act upon it when made: we found it existing before us, and shall leave it to exist for ever after us; all we do is to make use of it, knowing that you and everybody else, having the same power as we have, would do the same as we do. Thus, as far as the gods are concerned, we have no fear and no reason to fear that we shall be at a disadvantage. But when we come to your notion about the Lacedæmonians, which leads you to believe that shame will make them help you, here we bless your simplicity but do not envy your folly. The Lacedæmonians, when their own interests or their country's laws are in question, are the worthiest men alive; of their conduct towards others much might be said, but no clearer idea of it could be given than by shortly saying that of all the men we know they are most conspicuous in considering what is agreeable honourable, and what is expedient just. Such a way of thinking does not promise much for the safety which you now unreasonably count upon.'

Melians.—'But it is for this very reason that we now trust to their respect for expediency to prevent them from betraying the

Melians, their colonists, and thereby losing the confidence of their friends in Hellas and helping their enemies.'

Athenians.—'Then you do not adopt the view that expediency goes with security, while justice and honour cannot be followed without danger; and danger the Lacedæmonians generally court as little as possible.'

Melians.—'But we believe that they would be more likely to face even danger for our sake, and with more confidence than for others, as our nearness to Peloponnese makes it easier for them to act, and our common blood insures our fidelity.'

Athenians.—'Yes, but what an intending ally trusts to, is not the goodwill of those who ask his aid, but a decided superiority of power for action; and the Lacedæmonians look to this even more than others. At least, such is their distrust of their home resources that it is only with numerous allies that they attack a neighbour; now is it likely that while we are masters of the sea they will cross over to an island?'

Melians.—'But they would have others to send. The Cretan sea is a wide one, and it is more difficult for those who command it to intercept others, than for those who wish to elude them to do so safely. And should the Lacedæmonians miscarry in this, they would fall upon your land, and upon those left of your allies whom Brasidas did not reach; and instead of places which are not yours, you will have to fight for your own country and your own confederacy.'

Athenians.—'Some diversion of the kind you speak of you may one day experience, only to learn, as others have done, that the Athenians never once yet withdrew from a siege for fear of any. But we are struck by the fact, that after saying you would consult for the safety of your country, in all this discussion you have mentioned nothing which men might trust in and think to be saved by. Your strongest arguments depend upon hope and the future, and your actual resources are too scanty, as compared with those arrayed against you, for you to come out victorious. You will therefore show great blindness of judgment, unless, after allowing us to retire, you can find some counsel more prudent than this. You will surely not be caught by that idea of disgrace, which in dangers that are disgraceful, and at the same time too plain to be mistaken, proves so fatal to mankind; since in too many cases the very men that have their eyes perfectly open to what they are rushing into, let the thing called disgrace, by the mere influence of a seductive name, lead them on to a point at which they become so enslaved by the phrase as in fact to fall wilfully into hopeless disaster, and incur disgrace more disgraceful as the companion of error, than when it comes as the result of misfortune. This, if you are well advised, you will guard against; and you will not think it dishonourable to submit to the greatest city in Hellas, when it makes you the moderate offer of becoming its tributary ally, without ceasing to enjoy the country that belongs to you; nor when you have the choice given you between war and security, will you be so blinded as to choose the worse. And it is certain that those who do not yield to their equals, who keep terms with their superiors, and are moderate towards their inferiors, on the whole succeed best. Think over the matter, therefore, after our withdrawal, and reflect once and again that it is for your country that you are consulting, that you have not more than one, and that upon this one deliberation depends its prosperity or ruin.'

The Athenians now withdrew from the conference; and the Melians, left to themselves, came to a decision corresponding with what they had maintained in the discussion, and answered, 'Our resolution, Athenians, is the same as it was at first. We will not in a moment deprive of freedom a city that has been inhabited these seven hundred years; but we put our trust in the fortune by which the gods have preserved it until now, and in the help of men, that is, of the Lacedæmonians; and so we will try and save ourselves. Meanwhile we invite you to allow us to be friends to you and foes to neither party, and to retire from our country after making such a treaty as shall seem fit to us both.'

Such was the answer of the Melians. The Athenians now departing from the conference said, 'Well, you alone, as it seems to us, judging from these resolutions, regard what is future as more certain than what is before your eyes, and what is out of sight, in your eagerness, as already coming to pass; and as you have staked most on, and trusted most in, the Lacedæmonians, your fortune, and your hopes, so will you be most completely deceived.'

The Athenian envoys now returned to the army; and the Melians showing no signs of yielding, the generals at once betook themselves to hostilities, and drew a line of circumvallation round the Melians, dividing the work among the different states. Subsequently the Athenians returned with most of their army, leaving behind them a certain number of their own citizens and of the allies to keep guard by land and sea. The force thus left stayed on and besieged the place.

. . . Reinforcements afterwards arriving from Athens in consequence, under the command of Philocrates, son of Demeas, the siege was now pressed vigorously; and some treachery taking place inside, the Melians surrendered at discretion to the Athenians, who put to death all the grown men whom they took, and sold the women and children for slaves, and subsequently sent out five hundred colonists and inhabited the place themselves.

18. *THE DECLINE OF CLASSIC DIPLOMACY** / *QUINCY WRIGHT*

Following the breakup of Medieval Christendom in the 15th century, classic diplomacy developed in Europe amid conditions of anarchy and continuous hostility among sovereign princes struggling for power by the methods advised by Niccolò Machiavelli early in the 16th century.

Origins of Classic Diplomacy

In the religious struggles of the 16th and 17th centuries which culminated in the Thirty-Years War, the territorial monarchs, having gained general recognition of their sovereignty, accepted the peace of Westphalia in 1648. Central Europe had lost a quarter of its population in a war which saw the Holy Roman Emperor, who had tried to restore the unity of Christendom, defeated by a combination of Protestant princes and Catholic France. The peace of Westphalia was based on the principle first suggested at the Augsburg Conference of 1555, *Cuius Regia Eius Religio* (whoever is the prince, that is the religion), thus relegating the religious struggle to the domestic jurisdiction of each prince. The relations of the princes came to be regulated *theoretically* by a law of nations set forth in 1625 by Hugo Grotius, and *practically* by their military

* Quincy Wright, "The Decline of Classic Diplomacy," *Journal of International Affairs,* Vol. 17, No. 1 (1963), pp. 18–28. Reprinted by permission.

rivalry which tended toward a balance of power maintained through diplomatic intercourse.

This "classic diplomacy" assumed the coexistence of many sovereign states each respecting the territorial integrity and political independence of the others. These states dealt bilaterally with controversies about territorial limits, maritime navigation, commercial intercourse, and other issues by means of the exchange of diplomatic representatives. Diplomats were guaranteed immunity from the jurisdiction of the local sovereign, thus enabling them to conclude treaties under the sole instruction of the prince they represented. Through these treaties, a network of obligations arose which confirmed the sovereignty of states, the immunity of diplomats, the freedom of the seas, the sanctity of treaties, and the rights of belligerents and neutrals in time of war. The system recognized that the rights of princes to initiate war, the *ultima ratio regem*, was implicit in their sovereignty, as was their right to keep out of the wars of others so long as they observed an impartial neutrality. This conception of war as a duel of princes superseded the medieval concept that the right to make war depended on the justice of the cause and that non-belligerents should not be neutral, but should help, or at least not hinder, the just cause and should hinder, or at least not help, the unjust.

The Balance of Power

Although the diplomacy which operated under this concept was basically bilateral, power rivalries and the right to initiate war nevertheless made it clear that if a state conquered a neighbor, it would be likely to attack another neighbor. Thus all states were interested in maintaining the "balance of power" by ganging up against any one who was becoming too powerful. The reconciliation of the precepts of power politics, which urged attack on the overly-powerful prince, and the precepts of international law, which required a non-belligerent to be neutral unless one side violated its own rights under international law, was considered by international jurists such as Gentili and Vattel. They concluded that maintenance of the balance of power was essential to the stability and security of all, but in deference to international law, a threatened state should not attack an overly-powerful state until the latter had violated that law. This contingency, they thought, would occur because the overly-powerful state would soon commit aggression.[1,2]

In times of great emergency, especially after major wars, it was not possible to maintain the bilateralism of international relations, so that, following the precedent of Westphalia, multilateral congresses met to consider the general interests of Europe. But the treaties which emerged were more likely to be bilateral than multilateral. The Treaty of Utrecht in 1713 was based explicitly on the principle of the balance of power. The treaties of Paris in 1763, Vienna in 1815, Paris in 1856, Berlin in 1878 and 1885, Peking in 1901, and Washington in 1922, though less explicit, also sought to maintain the existing balance. The 19th century conferences were products of the Concert of Europe which originated in the post-Napoleonic conferences and which induced the five, later six, great powers to harmonize their efforts to settle European problems such as those which developed from the separation of Belgium from the Netherlands, the independence of the Balkan states from the Ottoman Empire, the colonization of Africa, and rivalries for spheres of interest in China.[3] However, classic diplomacy assumed (a) that the dominant interest of states was the preservation of their independence and territorial integrity, (b) that bilateral diplomatic negotiations or war were the means of maintaining rights or promoting interests, (c) that international law and treaties would be respected, at least verbally, but (d) that wars would recur and threats, subversion, and duplicity would be used within an atmosphere of secrecy. It also assumed, somewhat inconsistently, that stability, peace, and plenty were desirable and possible for considerable periods of time if the balance of power were maintained.[4]

Such maintenance was facilitated by the existence of a balancing state, itself relatively invulnerable and able to shift its support to the weaker side in a crisis, thus preventing the most powerful state from establishing a new Roman empire, the possibility of which was in the mind of each statesman, whether his immediate object was to build such an empire for his prince or to prevent its building by another. Great Britain served as such a balancer after it had aban-

[1] Alberico Gentili, *De Jure Belli* (1585) (London: Milford, 1933), chap. xiv, p. 66.

[2] Emerich Vattel, *Le Droit des Gens* (1758) (Washington: Carnegie Institution, 1916), Bk. III, chap. iii, pp. 248–249.

[3] Sir Charles K. Webster, *The Art and Practice of Diplomacy* (London: Chatto, 1961), pp. 55ff.

[4] Hans J. Morgenthau, *Politics Among Nations* (3d ed. rev.; New York: Knopf, 1960), pp. 178ff.

doned continental conquests and devoted attention to overseas colonization, trade, and the defeat of any power which threatened to unite Western Europe. Britain followed this policy for its own security and was successful for several centuries, because seapower and geography made it relatively safe from invasion, and it could rely on the cooperation of many continental states, equally anxious to frustrate the overly powerful in a given emergency.

Diplomacy in the 20th Century

The late 19th century witnessed changes no less momentous than those of the 15th and 16th centuries. These changes have greatly modified, if not displaced, the practice of classic diplomacy in the 20th century.[5,6] Science and technology have greatly augmented industrial production, transportation, commerce, and the dependence of most states on international trade for raw materials and markets. The range, speed, and destructiveness of weapons have made nations vulnerable to sudden and unbearably destructive attack from the most distant parts of the world. The airplane destroyed the security of Britain, and the missile that of the United States. The speed and destructiveness of a nuclear attack promises to leave no time to mobilize traditional alliances, resources, and counterattacks which in the past assured the eventual defeat of the aggressor even though he was usually better prepared on the opening of hostilities and won the first battles. No state could any longer be an invulnerable and effective diplomatic balancer, and war was not likely to restore a shattered balance.

Science and technology, in addition to shrinking the world and making war suicidal, have accelerated the rate of change, making custom and tradition less useful guides to action, reducing the predictability of the intentions—and the calculability of the offensive, defensive, and deterrent capability—of the powers, and therefore increasing the difficulty of maintaining a stable balance of power.

In the past, power relations have been more stable when there has been a large number of states with relatively equal power. There has, however, always been a tendency for more powerful states to

[5] Webster, *op. cit.*, pp. 13ff.

[6] Quincy Wright, *A Study of War* (Chicago: University of Chicago Press, 1942), pp. 647ff, 760ff.

absorb their weaker neighbors, for permanent alliances to be formed, and for the balance of power to become bipolarized and unstable. Formerly, these tendencies have led to war, as illustrated in the situation before the two World Wars. Once power became bipolarized, each side regarded eventual war as inevitable, and if the course of events seemed to favor one side, the other was likely to start war immediately rather than wait until its relative power position deteriorated further. In a multi-polar balance of power, on the other hand, uncommitted states rapidly shifted their positions by opposing the most powerful state, thus making it possible to maintain the equilibrium by diplomacy for some time. Because of this tendency, the balance of power has usually broken down at intervals of roughly fifty years into general wars, such as those against France in the times of Louis XIV and Napoleon, and against Germany under the Kaiser and Hitler, with lesser wars midway between. However, in the experience of Europe during the past three centuries, equilibrium has been re-established after such wars. The new military, political, and economic conditions arising from the new technology have, however, rendered the balance of power system chronically unstable.

Other factors militating against a stable balance of power have been the rise of great powers outside of Europe, such the United States, Japan, and China, and the break up of empires by defeat in war or by independence of their former colonies. The dismemberment of the Ottoman and Hapsburg Empires in the Near East and in Europe, and of the British, Spanish, Portuguese, French, German, American, Japanese, Dutch, and Belgian Empires overseas, have proceeded since 1776 and at an accelerated rate since World War II. The behavior in times of crisis of non-European states, unfamiliar with the European diplomatic system, is difficult to calculate. The new states of Asia and Africa continue to be suspicious of an international law based on European ethical standards which allowed these states to become victims of European colonialism.[7,8,9]

Finally, the spirit of Westphalia, calling for the coexistence of

[7] R. P. Anand, "Role of the New Asian-African Countries in the Present International Legal Order," *American Journal of International Law (AJIL)*, Vol. LVI (April 1962), pp. 387ff.

[8] Quincy Wright, "The Goa Incident," *AJIL*, Vol. LVI (July 1962), pp. 629ff.

[9] Quincy Wright, "Asian Experience and International Law," *International Studies* (New Delhi: Indian School of International Studies), Vol. I (July 1959), pp. 71ff.

territorial states, each unified by an absolute monarch, was affected by democratic ideals springing from the British, American, and French Revolutions and set forth in the writings of Locke, Jefferson, and Rousseau. The philosophy of free trade, free enterprise, and free communication springing from the British liberalism expounded by Adam Smith and John Stuart Mill was also rooted in these revolutions. Freedom of the nation, however, was never reconciled with freedom of the individual. The ideology of communism, initiated by Marx (who was familiar with the ideas of the British economists, French revolutionists, and German Hegelian philosophers) and developed into a strategy of action by Lenin, was emphasized by the Russian and Chinese Revolutions of the 20th century. These philosophies and ideologies, creating missionary zeal to convert peoples, to emancipate colonies, or to remake boundaries raised serious doubts about the Westphalian principle of coexistence of independent states, each competent to regulate its own political philosophy, economy, and government.

Diplomacy and International Organization

The consequences of these changes have been the incapacity of bilateral diplomacy to maintain a stable balance of power or general respect for international law, the occurrence of two world wars of unparalleled destructiveness, and the emergence of a Cold War in a world tending toward bipolarization where the precipitation of a nuclear holocaust might destroy the human race.

The emergence of these forces was dimly foreseen in the late 19th century when efforts were made to build a new international system. Public international unions were established to administer common interests of all states in such matters as communication, transport, trade, and health. The Hague Conferences of 1899 and 1907 met to prevent war, promote disarmament, codify international law, and establish institutions facilitating arbitration and conciliation of disputes. The League of Nations was established after World War I to promote international cooperation and to prevent hasty resort to war by putting teeth into the Hague System. The Kellogg-Briand Pact of 1929 was initiated by the United States, ratified by nearly all nations, and enforced against individuals by the Nuremburg and other war crimes tribunals. The Pact outlawed war as an instrument of national policy and required the settlement of all international disputes and conflicts by peaceful means. The United Nations was established after World War II to fulfill the purposes of the League and the Pact more effectively.

These instruments and organizations were not designed to supersede classic diplomacy, but to supplement it with permanent multilateral obligations and institutions for collective security and cooperative betterment of human welfare. They were not designed to supersede traditional international law, but to supplement it with principles outlawing war and recognizing the rights of man and of the organized international community. The scope of state sovereignty was, therefore, to be limited by requiring each state to settle its international disputes by peaceful means, to abstain from the threat or use of force in its international relations, to assist the United Nations in ending hostilities, to cooperate in general and regional agencies for social and economic progress, to promote the protection of human rights, and to accept the status and the operative authority of the United Nations and the Specialized Agencies.

These efforts have been only partially successful because of the prevailing sentiment demanding the complete sovereignty of the nation-state and because of the influence of zealous ideologies. The conflict between democracy and communism has led, since World War II, to a situation similar to that of the century of religious wars before Westphalia. The principle of coexistence of sovereign states which ended that period has not been fully re-established among adherents of the new "religions." (It is worth noting that the militancy of these new "religions" appears roughly proportionate to the recency of the national revolutions from which they stemmed.) In spite of the assertion in the Charter of the United Nations of the sovereign equality of states, of the assertion by the Soviet Union of the principle of peaceful coexistence of sovereign states of different ideologies,[10] and of the affirmation by the United States of the right of every state to enjoy security and self-determination within its domestic jurisdiction,[11] each side in the East-West conflict has been convinced that the other is less interested in stabilizing peaceful

[10] Nikita S. Khrushchev, "Peaceful Coexistence," *Foreign Affairs*, Vol. XXXVIII (October 1959), pp. 1–18.

[11] Quincy Wright, "Maintaining Peaceful Coexistence," *Preventing World War III*, ed. Quincy Wright, William M. Evan, and Morton Deutsch (New York: Simon & Schuster, 1962), pp. 414ff.

coexistence in accord with United Nations principles than in establishing its own ideology throughout the world by using deceptive propaganda, subversion, or even military force, if debate in the forum of world opinion proves unsuccessful.

Classic diplomacy cannot deal adequately with the problems of a world with more than 110 states of diverse culture and ideology, militarily dominated by two great alliances competing for superior nuclear power in an unstable balance of terror, and for support of the militarily weak but heavily populated uncommitted half of the world. The complexity of the situation is compounded by small wars erupting sporadically in areas such as China, Vietnam, Korea, Germany, Berlin, Kashmir, Israel, and the Caribbean. Peace is threatened by accident, miscalculation, or escalation, if not by design. All states are militarily vulnerable, most are economically dependent on each other, many have extensive political and military commitments, and few are inapprehensive that border hostilities may escalate into global thermonuclear war.

If there is to be stability under such conditions, the vision of major decision-makers must not be limited to the parties to a conflict or a negotiation; it must not be limited to the parties to a defensive alliance, a regional arrangement, or an ideology; it must be world-wide. Decision-makers must be aware that the security and progress of each state is dependent upon the security and progress of all states. Such decision-makers require contacts and information beyond that which classic diplomacy can provide. They must be able to initiate action for collective security and international cooperation by agencies of more extensive competence than diplomatic negotiation. They must be prepared to subordinate regional and defense organizations and a considerable measure of sovereign initiative to universal institutions guided by international law. Such a world was formally accepted by all United Nations members when they ratified the Charter.

Whether the world will actually develop in accord with the needs of the 20th century cannot be predicted, but if general war can be avoided, it seems probable that technologies will spread, that tensions will be reduced, and that ideologies will converge.[12] While in the past, the immediate effect of increased contact among divergent cultures has been conflict, the long-run effect has been

[12] Pitirim A. Sorokin, *Mutual Convergence of the United States and USSR to the New Mixed Socio-Cultural Type* (Mexico City, 1961).

peaceful competitive coexistence, with increasing cooperation as common values and interests were perceived.[13,14]

The progress toward such a realization should not be minimized. The United Nations has promoted cooperation in many fields and has helped to stop incipient wars in Greece, Indonesia, Kashmir, Palestine, Korea, Suez, Lebanon, and Cuba. Its action in the Congo appears promising at this writing. It has organized United Nations forces and has mediated or otherwise settled more than a score of disputes. Since World War II it has, on the whole, been more successful than has classic diplomacy which has attempted to deal with the problems of Vietnam, China, and Germany. This progress gives hope that classic diplomacy, while operative with considerable success under the conditions of the 17th, 18th, and 19th centuries, will subordinate itself to universal institutions better adapted to the conditions of the 20th century.

Diplomacy and Democracy

Classic diplomacy faces particular difficulties in democracies because of their inherent incapacity to adapt themselves to the secrecy, rapidity of maneuver, and freedom from public opinion regarded as essential for its operation. All governments in the age of absolute monarchy could, and totalitarian dictatorships in the present period can, operate with more secrecy, freedom, and dispatch than can constitutional democracies. For this reason, Alexis de Tocqueville[15] was convinced that the American democracy of which he wrote in the 1830's could not play the game of power politics successfully.

Secret diplomacy was regarded by many as a contributing cause of World War I. President Wilson called for its termination in his Fourteen Points. The League of Nations Covenant and the United Nations Charter called for the publication of treaties. The practice of recent diplomatic conferences, such as that at San Francisco, has been to give much greater facilities to newsmen to

[13] Malcomb M. Willey and Stuart A. Rice, "The Agencies of Communications," *Recent Social Trends in the United States*, ed. William F. Ogburn (New York: McGraw-Hill, 1933), Vol. I, p. 217.

[14] Harold D. Lasswell, *World Politics and Personal Insecurity* (New York: McGraw-Hill, 1935), pp. 203ff.

[15] *Democracy in America* (1834) (New York: A. S. Barnes, 1862), Vol. I, p. 254.

broadcast the proceedings than was usual in earlier history. Statesmen have frequently practiced "diplomacy of the housetops," publishing diplomatic communications to the world simultaneously with their delivery to the government addressed.

There has been vigorous criticism of these practices. Walter Lippmann[16] asserted that President Kennedy should have communicated his information about missile bases in Cuba to Soviet Foreign Minister Gromyko, and entered into bilateral diplomatic negotiations before establishing a unilateral quarantine of Cuba on October 22, 1962. There can be no doubt that classic diplomacy still has a role to play. Conflicts can sometimes be resolved at private negotiations in which neither side loses face. Publicity may arouse public opinion within the disputing states, preventing either side from making the concessions necessary for peaceful settlement. Private negotiation is important among party leaders in parliaments and nominating conventions if the processes of election and legislation are to proceed within democratic states. Such negotiation can be no less important in international relations.

It seems unlikely, however, that people who have a voice in the selection of major officials and the processes of domestic government will, unless faced by military necessity, abandon that voice in the making of a foreign policy which involves problems of war and peace more vital to them than domestic legislation. It is true that in England during the 19th century the public understood tacitly that foreign policy should be left to the government and should not become a subject of public agitation in parliament and elections. The concept that politics should end at the water's edge in times of crisis and that the nation should support the government "whether right or wrong" expressed this idea. These prescriptions have never been entirely carried out: in England this concept could not withstand the rise of the Labour Party and of a more egalitarian democracy in the 20th century. The governments of democratic countries have found it necessary to inform and, to some extent, be guided by public opinion in foreign policy. Even modern dictators have found it necessary to gain the support of public opinion, although their control of communications allows them to mold public opinion in support of their policies more easily than can leaders of democracies who must face a free press and free radio and television.

16 "Blockade Proclaimed," *New York Herald Tribune*, October 25, 1962, p. 20.

All genuine democracies impose constitutional limitations upon the freedom of the executive to conduct foreign policy, usually requiring that major international commitments and major uses of force have the consent of one or both houses of the legislature. Also, consent is required for appropriations which today are a vital element in military preparations, alliance commitments, economic assistance programs, and participation in international organizations.

Noting the frequent misinformation and prejudice of public opinion and legislative bodies, the limitations which obedience to public opinion imposes on the flexibility of governmental response to foreign attitudes and conditions, and governmental inability to initiate action, some students of international relations have urged an abandonment of democratic methods in the conduct of foreign relations and a return to a system of government that would be free to employ secrecy, to act rapidly, to make threats, to utilize deception, and to retreat if necessary without loss of face.[17] However, if governments abandon democracy in making foreign policy decisions, they are likely to abandon it also in other decisions. They will find it necessary to support threats with espionage and military action, to develop defense forces by rapid coordination of national arms, economy, and morale, and to gain allies and foreign bases by concessions and bribery, all by secret executive action.

These tendencies of democracy are to be observed in periods of war and crisis. All democracies in such situations tend to abandon democratic methods, to curb civil liberties, and to exercise wide authority not only in recruiting the population for war but also in controlling the economy and opinion. In times of prolonged international crisis, all states tend to become "garrison" or "warfare" states embracing certain totalitarian principles. Such states have an advantage under the conditions of classic diplomacy as Machiavelli and de Tocqueville observed. The prince, according to Machiavelli, must pay major attention to his arms, must practice duplicity, and must keep his movements secret.[18, 19] For these reasons democracy has developed only in countries which for long periods have felt relatively secure from invasion, as did England and the United States when sheltered by seas and navies, and states of Western

[17] Fred. J. Cook, "The Radical Right," *The Warfare State* (New York: Macmillan, 1962), pp. 260ff, 318.

[18] Niccolò Machiavelli, *The Prince* (1513) (New York: Dutton, 1948), chap. xv.

[19] Harold D. Lasswell, "The Garrison State," *American Journal of Sociology*, Vol. XLVI (January 1941), pp. 455–469.

Europe when protected, as in the 19th century, by a relatively stable multilateral balance of power and a viable international law.

While the functioning of democracy through classic diplomacy may be assisted by better education of the public on the realities of international politics, on the precepts of international law, and on the need for secrecy and freedom of action by governments in many circumstances, its survival in the long run may depend not only on such education but on the creation of conditions in the international community favorable to democracy.

These conditions include publicity for all basic decisions in the international field, universal forums in which representatives of all interested parties can participate in such decisions, elimination of war and threat of war making possible the deliberation and publicity basic to democracy, development of basic rules of order and principles of justice adapted to changing conditions of technology and ideology, and maintenance of these conditions by a world public opinion operating through universal institutions able to organize collective security and enforcement of international court decisions.

Conclusion

Classic diplomacy faces great difficulties because of the instability of the balance of power, because of the vital interests of many states in major decisions, because of the rapidity and pervasiveness of change, because of the enlarged and possibly catastrophic consequences of single decisions,[20, 21, 22] and because of the zeal of crusading ideologies. While useful in limited circumstances, classic diplomacy cannot establish conditions suitable for the functioning of democracy in a world in which the use of force may become an instrument of suicide rather than of policy. Such conditions can spring only from successful efforts to reduce tensions, to eliminate the threat or use of force as an instrument of national policy, to achieve a spirit of tolerance among diverse ideologies, to develop among states a modicum of mutual trust and confidence in agreements, and to develop in the minds of men everywhere the image of a world of peacefully coexisting states, each confident that its terri-

[20] John von Neumann, "Can We Survive Technology?," *Fortune*, Vol. LI (June 1955), pp. 106ff.

[21] Adlai E. Stevenson, "My Faith in Democratic Capitalism," *Fortune*, Vol. LII (October 1955), pp. 126ff.

[22] Quincy Wright, "The Human Spirit in the Atomic Age," *Contributors to Synthetic Jurisprudence*, ed. Minocher J. Sethna (Bombay: Tripath, 1962), pp. 69ff.

torial integrity and political independence will be respected and that it will be free to experiment with its system of economy, culture, and politics within its own borders.

The changed conditions of today's world call for less emphasis on classic diplomacy and more on international law and on international institutions able to deal with problems not only of nations, but also of Mankind.

19. *DIPLOMATIC IMMUNITIES, PROTOCOL, AND THE PUBLIC* / MICHAEL H. CARDOZO*

A diplomat is a success when he can influence the nation where he is assigned to see world affairs as his country sees them and to follow policies that his government espouses. In part, of course, his influence depends on the strength of his own nation and the image it projects abroad. His own personality and behavior, however, may prove to be major factors in the success of his mission. Consequently, he is well advised to give attention to the impression his conduct makes, not only on his colleagues in the foreign office, but also on the non-official populace.

In his effort to maintain a favorable image in the eyes of the public, however, the diplomat starts with a serious handicap. It is a widely held popular misconception that a foreign envoy may draw on his diplomatic immunity to let him casually disregard the laws of the host country, and that he wastes much of his time worrying about the rules of protocol at fancy teas, cocktail parties, and banquets. There is little awareness that the public laws do apply to him and that at the teas and the parties he gets most of his work done.

Diplomatic Immunity

All nations acknowledge the principle of international law called "diplomatic immunity." The effect of this immunity, however, is not to free an envoy from the general obligation to obey the law,

* Michael H. Cardozo, "Diplomatic Immunities, Protocol, and the Public," *Journal of International Affairs,* Vol. 17, No. 1 (1963), pp. 61–69. Reprinted by permission.

but to clothe him during his term of duty with a cloak of untouchability. If a robber flees across the nation's border with his loot, no one would say that he is free from the law's restraints just because the police may not, without permission, follow him onto foreign soil and bring him back. Once permission has been granted by the country of refuge, he may be apprehended by the pursuers, generally through extradition procedures, carried back across the border, and tried and punished for his offence.

The diplomat is in a comparable position. While he is in a foreign country as the accredited representative of his government, he is treated as though he is standing on his native soil. This is what is meant by the term "extraterritoriality." He may not be molested or arrested unless he loses his immunity through waiver, resignation, or removal. During World War II, for example, the United States waived the immunity of Tyler Kent, an embassy clerk in England who was accused of spying for the Germans. He was duly tried and convicted in the British courts, and served his sentence.

When a long limousine with diplomatic license plates is parked beside a sign saying "No Parking at Any Time," the law is being violated just as much as if the car belonged to the irate ordinary motorist whose access to his destination is blocked. While it is somewhat cumbersome to bring the diplomat to account, it is entirely proper for the transgression to be reported to the State Department and for the Department to complain to the government whose representative has offended. Repeated violations even of traffic laws can justify a request for recall of the envoy, and such a request cannot be denied. A single serious offence against the law may result in immediate recall. In recent years this has been the result after a first secretary of the Haitian Embassy in Washington was accused of shooting the Minister-Counsellor of the same Embassy, and when the son of the Irish Ambassador was involved in an automobile fatality in Washington. The son of an American diplomat in Ireland was similarly shipped home after a girl reported she had been attacked. A Guatemalan diplomat in New York was stripped of his immunity by his own government and exposed to trial when he was caught by United States officials in the act of smuggling a large amount of heroin into the country.

These instances clearly demonstrate the responsibility of diplomats to respect the laws of the host country. Their immunity is only from jurisdiction, which means the exercise of governmental power. When the Constitution states that all persons born in the

United States "and subject to the jurisdiction thereof" are citizens of the United States, diplomats are thereby excluded. A child born in Washington to a foreign diplomat and his wife is not a citizen by birth. This is true whether the birth occurs in a hospital or in the foreign embassy. The latter is not foreign territory; an alien mother will not win United States citizenship for her child by gaining admittance to an American embassy abroad at the crucial moment. The embassy building is within the host country's territory and is subject to all the local laws, such as those respecting sanitation and the use of real property. Its diplomatic immunity means that, for some purposes, it is *treated* as though on foreign territory. The local police, for example, may not enter it without permission, since they may not exercise their powers in places devoted to diplomatic purposes.

These immunities have their roots in the same soil as their parent, sovereign immunity. From earliest times, a host sovereign has refrained from trying to impose his local laws and customs on a visiting sovereign and his entourage. The purpose of this self-restraint was primarily to show friendship. Even today the reciprocal demonstration of the comity between two nations is of primary significance in diplomatic immunity.

There has always been, however, a highly practical justification for the immunity of diplomatic emissaries from local jurisdiction in the host country. Like the legislative representative of a local community sent to the capital to speak for his constituents, the diplomat must be able to reach his destination, deliver his message, and report back to those who sent him without the hindrance of local rules, customs, and police. In a foreign country he may encounter strange and exotic practices to which he cannot conform without years of habituation. There may be fundamental religious differences, calling for observances that would be impossible for a believer in another faith. Gastronomic tastes may vary so widely that the visitor must carry his own victuals and beverages with him, some of which may, in turn, be highly distasteful to the people of the receiving state. Even local traffic regulations might unduly interfere with a diplomat's access to the head of the host nation or to other high officials. The importance of extending the immunity even to the chauffeur of the visiting emissary can also be easily perceived. Naturally it covers the subordinate officers of an embassy who are needed to assist the chief of mission. Indeed, the logic behind the basic concept of immunity—that it makes possible the accomplishment of the diplomatic mission—leads inexorably to the inclusion in its ambit of clerks and messengers in the embassy, the families of the ambassador and his entire staff, their household servants, and their living and working quarters.

There may seem to be less justification today for the full range of immunities for diplomats sent to the United States than in earlier times when life here was more primitive. For representatives from some countries, however, the high-speed, mechanized, urban civilization here may be the very reason why they must be excused from meticulous observance of all our laws and customs. Endless difficulties would be presented if degrees of immunity, depending on local conditions, were adopted.

Some special conditions, however, are often accepted when local situations require them. It is normal practice, for example, for diplomats today to have their automobiles covered by liability insurance. This removes the need for the plea of diplomatic immunity in case of suit arising from an accident, and the custom is to waive the immunity. In New York City the Fire Department, with the concurrence of the State Department in Washington, has notified the various diplomatic missions to the United Nations that even cars bearing diplomatic license plates will be towed away when parked so close to fire hydrants that the public safety is endangered. Neither law nor comity requires that the activities of diplomats create serious hazards to the public safety.

Espionage cases inevitably touch very sensitive nerves. Some irreverent observers have characterized all diplomatic service as a great program of spying for one's country. Admittedly the line between improper spying and legitimate observing is often blurred, especially when the diplomat in question is a military or naval attaché reporting to the intelligence sections of the service department. Nonetheless there can be clear-cut instances of spying by diplomats, such as the seeking and reporting of information that the host government has classified as secret and for the eyes only of its own designated officials.

The advent of representatives of the Soviet Union in the diplomatic world has greatly increased the number of cases of alleged spying by diplomats and quasi-diplomats. The Kremlin has a habit of using such charges as a means of reciprocating for various forms of asserted offences against any of their interests. Every now and then an officer or member of the staff of the embassy of a Western power will be charged with espionage in Moscow or some other Soviet city. The charges are, of course, duly denied. In these cases, after the first apprehension, the Russians appear to have been scrupulous to observe the demands of diplomatic immunity, merely demanding the prompt recall of the named culprit. There is no alternative to complying, whether or not the diplomat's government believes the charges.

On our own side of the Iron Curtain, however, the problem has been more complicated. In the first place, the charges are not likely to be made unless there has been real evidence of improper activity in the nature of espionage. Certainly Russian diplomats have been convincingly shown more often than ours to have engaged in spying. When the charge is against an accredited diplomat, we follow the traditional practice and demand his recall. Frequently, however, the accused is in a kind of twilight zone of diplomatic status. With the United Nations Headquarters in this country, a large number of people working with and for the Organization have some kind of immunity, ranging from full diplomatic immunity for the chief officers of permanent delegations from member countries to the limited immunity related to the official duties of officers and employees of the Organization itself. A member of the latter group would not be immune from prosecution for espionage, an activity clearly outside the scope of his official duties. The Russians, however, often nominate to positions in this category members of their regular foreign service and send them over with diplomatic passports. When such a person is apprehended on charges of spying, the Soviet Government promptly claims diplomatic immunity. While the United States has not agreed to the claim, it has also found it expedient to refrain from subjecting the accused to a jail sentence. The courts have quite properly acceded to State Department representations that the interests of the nation's foreign relations required release of the defendant, treating him as though entitled to diplomatic immunity but without formally expanding its scope. Such releases are not likely to be very popular in the public's eye, but sometimes the release of one or two American aviators from Soviet custody will occur at about the same time. Reciprocity in restraint may be the greater wisdom when government agents are involved with the law.

Another area calling for judicious restraint appeared during the years of Prohibition in the United States, when it was illegal for anyone to transport liquor within the country. Without violating this law, how was a diplomat to entertain in the manner required by the customs of the general international community where wines are as indispensable to a meal as salt? Acceptable compromises were soon developed by enforcement officers, and the beverages were available for the receptions, banquets, and parties of the *corps diplomatique*.

Protocol

Compromises by law enforcement agencies are necessary where the social affairs of a diplomat are concerned simply because they are such an essential part of his work. At a party a diplomat is not off duty; he is representing his government. When Congressional committees roughly cut down the funds requested for "representation allowances" for the United States Foreign Service, it is as though an industrial concern was being denied money for its advertising program. A Congressman representing a typical U.S. constituency finds it hard to be generous with "whiskey money." But could a Senator do his work if he were not permitted to attend committee meetings? The analogy is fair.

The diplomat abroad has two major functions that require him to mingle as much as possible with the officials of the government to which he is accredited and with other diplomats. One of these functions may be called "negotiation." He is expected to convey to the other officials and diplomats his government's views and to seek to convince them of the correctness of those views. Some of this can, of course, be accomplished in formal sessions in the austere setting of government buildings. Far more, however, will be accomplished in the lighter, more informal conversation of social events. In an atmosphere of friendly intercourse the official strain is removed, and unofficial views can be exchanged. As the diplomats and the officials get better acquainted, more trust and confidence can flourish in a way that is most unlikely when contact is limited to office calls.

Social affairs are perhaps even more important to the accomplishment of the diplomat's other vital function, that of reporting to his government the general views of the foreign officials and their attitude toward all the problems of concern to his country. Far more than the officially expressed and publicly announced position is needed. The personal reactions of government officials are much more valuable. These can be learned only with difficulty in the cold atmosphere of the typical office or meeting room, but in the warmth of a comfortable residence, with fine food and wine to foster a companionable feeling, the sought-for opinions will more likely reveal themselves. Any diplomat whose government parsimoniously denies him the means of playing his reciprocal part to maintain this social intercourse is being deprived of an essential tool of his trade. An American Foreign Service officer who is unable to afford to serve bourbon whiskey and dry martinis to his opposite numbers in the foreign office and other embassies will be like a politician denied funds for travel, radio, and television during an election campaign. If he cannot communicate with the right people, he cannot accomplish his mission effectively.

Related to doubts about the importance of the diplomatic reception, cocktail party, or banquet in the skeptical mind of the general public is the whole subject of protocol. The average American is likely to be contemptuous of people who pay close attention to who shakes hands first with a dignitary at an official reception, who sits closest to the host at a lunch or dinner, and who has "DPL 1" or "2" on his car's license plate.

The significance of who has the lowest license number, however, is a matter that the man in the street can understand. He has seen the magic effect of a distinguished plate on the local police. This, however, should give him a clue to the reason for the diplomat's insistence on the proper place in the handshaking line or at the banquet table: these are the indicia of rank, not just of the man, but of the country he represents.

Before the statesmen who gathered at the Congress of Vienna in 1815 agreed that precedence among diplomats sent to a nation's capital would depend on the date of their arrival at the post, each ambassador had to elbow his way to the front of the line at diplomatic gatherings in order to maintain the dignity of his country. It would be unseemly for the representative of a great power to follow behind an envoy from a less significant nation. As a result, there were instances of physical violence among diplomats, each trying to prevent an affront to his country. Sometimes this concern is still expressed in diplomatic correspondence. At one capital, during World War II, there was a shortage of ladies in the diplomatic set because wartime conditions required many diplomats to leave their families at home. At a certain party given by the foreign minister, there was seen an attractive young lady without diplomatic rank. She was the secretary of one of the ambassadors, one of the few ladies available for such a gathering. The next day the foreign minister received a formal note from the government of another country, protesting the presence of a "clerk" from one embassy at a party to which "the Counsellor of our embassy was not invited." This was a violation of protocol.

Diplomats with New Functions

While there is now a generally accepted and very rigid protocol for determining precedence among those performing the normal functions of the diplomatic corps, there are still some serious problems to be solved. The growing number of people concerned with multilateral diplomacy, in international organizations, and in the diplomacy of international cooperation, through which various mutual aid programs are operated, has called for new rules respecting immunities and new solutions from the chiefs of protocol. Many of these people are outside the ranks of the traditional foreign service. The United States, for example, now sends to Brussels and to Paris envoys with the top rank of ambassador who are not part of our embassies in those capitals. They head the missions to the international organizations whose headquarters are also in those cities. Which ambassador in Brussels, under the rules of protocol, has the higher rank: the new Chief of the United States Mission to the European Communities or the holder of the venerable title of United States Ambassador to Belgium?

Before World War II the State Department seldom had to cope with the problem of ranking people who were not in the regular order of the Foreign Service. During the war, however, representatives of all kinds of unusual agencies were scattered about the world, and suddenly the question of their status and rank began to press for an answer. Lend-lease and economic warfare specialists needed as much access to officials of the other governments as did the regular embassy officers, but how could they be included in diplomatic functions if they were not in the foreign service and so not really diplomats? Furthermore, how could they be considered diplomats by the host government if they did not even carry diplomatic passports, which were the exclusive privilege of employees of the Department of State?

One of the greatest huddles the State Department had to cross before it could place these new emissaries in their proper slots was the passport question. It was common for the chief lend-lease representative, with responsibilities commensurate with a multi-billion dollar program, to carry a passport that connoted a non-diplomatic status, while a code clerk or stenographer sent to work in the same embassy would carry the magic diplomatic passport. This distinction can be crucial in the success of a special envoy's mission. If the officials in the other countries see that his own government ranks him below the salt and gives him credentials importing minor stature, why should they give much heed to his pleas for prompt acquiescence in his proposals?

During the long period while the functional diplomacy of international cooperation has been maturing as a fixed part of United States foreign relations, the passport question has arisen recurrently as a symbol of the conflict between traditional foreign service and the special missions required for modern programs such as relief and rehabilitation, economic recovery, technical assistance, and military aid. It has been as hard for a specialist in these areas to gain admittance to the diplomatic club house as for the camel to pass through the needle's eye. The march of events, however, has eroded some of the resistance. Missions to NATO and the OEEC from the beginning were almost always headed by persons of such eminence that their stature was not dependent on their title or passport. When Averell Harriman acted as lend-lease representative in London early in the war, Winston Churchill did not have to hear him addressed by subordinates as "Your Excellency" to know that he was the man to listen and talk to. His pipeline to the White House was known to be better than the holder of the formal title of United States Ambassador to the Court of St. James. Harriman carried the same weight when he headed the first European mission in the Marshall Plan, with headquarters in Paris.

Heads of lesser special missions and the officers on their staffs, however, need the support of recognized rank to assure them the power to function effectively. This means the assignment by their own government of titles and other indicia commensurate with their responsibilities. In diplomatic circles, as we have seen, protocol is likely to be inexorable, and insufficient rank can be a serious obstacle to success. A special envoy sent abroad to negotiate on an important subject will fume in vain as he sits at the foot of a table while the people he is supposed to be convincing converse gaily at the head with higher ranked Foreign Service officers who have none of the special knowledge required under the circumstances. No matter how unseemly and undignified it may appear to insist, before departure on a mission, that the necessary rank, immunities, and passport be assigned, the specialist from outside the Department of State is wise if he raises the issue before he encounters the frustrations of the innocent official abroad.

During the past decade there has been a gradual return to the State Department of various responsibilities in the field of international cooperation that started out under separate administration. While this development calls for a vigor and imagination that has not always characterized that venerable department, it is nonetheless highly desirable because it concentrates under one authority the various aspects of foreign relations. Today even the miscellaneous aid programs, although administered by separate staffs, are still within the State Department and under the Secretary of State. A similar trend has appeared abroad where the special missions are being placed under embassy control. Even in Paris, the United States Mission to the European Regional Organization—NATO and OECD—is in the State Department, unlike its predecessor, the Special Representative for Europe, which was part of the independent Economic Cooperation Administration and its renamed successors.

While this concentration within the foreign affairs department removes one of the problems that has created protocol difficulties, the way is not yet all smooth sailing. Suspicion still exists that functional specialists sent abroad to work on the programs in international cooperation are not really considered diplomats, entitled to all the privileges, immunities, and recognition that go with that characterization. Perhaps, as in the case of the United Nations staff, there will have to be degrees of immunities so as not to create too large a body of people who can claim the special treatment that is needed for diplomatic service. The distinction, however, should not be based on the identity of the government agency or bureau that employs the emissary, but the importance of his mission. With responsibility should go whatever rank, passport, and immunities are required by the traditions and demands of diplomatic service.

INTERNATIONAL CONFLICT

part III

CAUSES OF CONFLICT

VII

In one form or another, war is an almost permanent condition of the world. It is therefore of great importance to diagnose its causes. Professor Kenneth N. Waltz of Swarthmore College does a masterful job of classifying and analyzing the various origins to which war has been attributed, in his book *Man, the State and War*. The first chapter of this book is reprinted here.

Waltz distinguishes three "images" of international relations and the origin of conflict. The first image which locates the source of war in man himself, is exemplified by the second and third selections in this chapter. Plato (427–347 B.C.) ascribes war to a first-image cause in his *The Republic*. A different form of the first-image concept of war is the UNESCO approach, criticized by Frederick S. Dunn in his book *War and the Minds of Men*. Dunn was Professor of Politics at Princeton University and founder of the journal *World Politics.*

Examples of the second and third images of the origins of war may be found in other chapters. For instance, Lenin is a second-image theorist (selection 24) and the discussions of sovereignty in Chapter III are directly relevant to the third image.

20. *MAN, THE STATE, AND WAR*/ KENNETH N. WALTZ*

Asking who won a given war, someone has said, is like asking who won the San Francisco earthquake. That in wars there is no victory but only varying degrees of defeat is a proposition that has gained increasing acceptance in the twentieth century. But are wars also akin to earthquakes in being natural occurrences whose control or elimination is beyond the wit of man? Few would admit that they are, yet attempts to eliminate war, however nobly inspired and assiduously pursued, have brought little more than fleeting moments of peace among states. There is an apparent disproportion between effort and product, between desire and result. The peace wish, we are told, runs strong and deep among the Russian people; and we are convinced that the same can be said of Americans. From these statements there is some comfort to be derived, but in the light of history and of current events as well it is difficult to believe that the wish will father the condition desired.

Social scientists, realizing from their studies how firmly the present is tied to the past and how intimately the parts of a system depend upon each other, are inclined to be conservative in estimating the possibilities of achieving a radically better world. If one asks whether we can now have peace where in the past there has been war, the answers are most often pessimistic. Perhaps this is the wrong question. And indeed the answers will be somewhat less discouraging if instead the following questions are put: Are there ways of decreasing the incidence of war, of increasing the chances

* Kenneth N. Waltz, *Man, the State and War: A Theoretical Analysis* (New York and London: Columbia University Press, 1959), Chap. 1. Copyright © 1954, 1959 Columbia University Press. Reprinted by permission.

of peace? Can we have peace more often in the future than in the past?

Peace is one among a number of ends simultaneously entertained. The means by which peace can be sought are many. The end is pursued and the means are applied under varying conditions. Even though one may find it hard to believe that there are ways to peace not yet tried by statesmen or advocated by publicists, the very complexity of the problem suggests the possibility of combining activities in different ways in the hope that some combination will lead us closer to the goal. Is one then led to conclude that the wisdom of the statesman lies in trying first one policy and then another, in doing what the moment seems to require? An affirmative reply would suggest that the hope for improvement lies in policy divorced from analysis, in action removed from thought. Yet each attempt to alleviate a condition implies some idea of its causes: to explain how peace can be more readily achieved requires an understanding of the causes of war. . . .

Why does God, if he is all-knowing and all-powerful, permit the existence of evil? So asks the simple Huron in Voltaire's tale, and thereby confounds the learned men of the church. The theodicy problem in its secular version—man's explanation to himself of the existence of evil—is as intriguing and as perplexing. Disease and pestilence, bigotry and rape, theft and murder, pillage and war, appear as constants in world history. Why is this so? Can one explain war and malevolence in the same way? Is war simply mass malevolence, and thus an explanation of malevolence an explanation of the evils to which men in society are prey? Many have thought so.

> For though it were granted us by divine indulgence to be exempt from all that can be harmful to us from without [writes John Milton], yet the perverseness of our folly is so bent, that we should never cease hammering out of our own hearts, as it were out of a flint, the seeds and sparkles of new misery to ourselves, till all were in a blaze again.[1]

Our miseries are ineluctably the product of our natures. The root of all evil is man, and thus he is himself the root of the specific evil, war. This estimate of cause, widespread and firmly held by many as an article of faith, has been immensely influential. It is the conviction of St. Augustine and Luther, of Malthus and Jonathan Swift, of Dean Inge and Reinhold Niebuhr. In secular terms, with men defined as beings of intermixed reason and passion in whom passion

[1] Milton, "The Doctrine and Discipline of Divorce," in *Works*, III, 180.

repeatedly triumphs, the belief has informed the philosophy, including the political philosophy, of Spinoza. One might argue that it was as influential in the activities of Bismarck, with his low opinion of his fellow man, as it was in the rigorous and austere writings of Spinoza. If one's beliefs condition his expectations and his expectations condition his acts, acceptance or rejection of Milton's statement becomes important in the affairs of men. And, of course, Milton might be right even if no one believed him. If so, attempts to explain the recurrence of war in terms of, let us say, economic factors, might still be interesting games, but they would be games of little consequence. If it is true, as Dean Swift once said, that "the very same principle that influences a bully to break the windows of a whore who has jilted him, naturally stirs up a great prince to raise mighty armies, and dream of nothing but sieges, battles, and victories,"[2] then the reasons given by princes for the wars they have waged are mere rationalizations covering a motivation they may not themselves have perceived and could not afford to state openly if they had. It would follow as well that the schemes of the statesman Sully, if seriously intended to produce a greater peace in the world, were as idle as the dreams of the French monk Crucé–idle, that is, unless one can strike at the roots, the pride and petulance that have produced the wars as they have the other ills that plague mankind.

There are many who have agreed with Milton that men must look to man in order to understand social and political events, but who differ on what man's nature is, or can become. There are many others who, in effect, quarrel with the major premise. Does man make society in his image or does his society make him? It was to be expected, in a time when philosophy was little more than a branch of theology, that the theologian-philosophers would attribute to human agency what many philosophers before and since have described as the effects of the polity itself. Rousseau, among many who could be mentioned, makes a clean break with the view that, man being a social animal, one can explain his behavior in society by pointing to his animal passion and/or his human reason. Man is born and in his natural condition remains neither good nor bad. It is society that is the degrading force in men's lives, but it is the moralizing agency as well. And this latter effect Rousseau was unwilling to surrender even had he thought it possible for men to retreat to the state of nature. This is his position, consistently reflected in his various works, though the myth persists that he

[2] Swift, *A Tale of a Tub*.

believed the savage noble and lamented the advent of society.[3] Man's behavior, his very nature, which some have taken as cause, is, according to Rousseau, in great part a product of the society in which he lives. And society, he avers, is inseparable from political organization. In the absence of an organized power, which as a minimum must serve as the adjudicating authority, it is impossible for men to live together with even a modicum of peace. The study of society cannot be separated from the study of government, or the study of man from either. Rousseau, like Plato, believes that a bad polity makes men bad, and a good polity makes them good. This is not to say that the state is the potter and man a lump of clay posing no resistance to the shape the artist would impart. There are, as Rousseau recognized, similarities among men wherever they may live. There are also differences, and the search for causes is an attempt to explain these differences. The explanation of consequence—whether one is worried about the recurrence of theft or of war—is to be found in studying the varying social relations of men, and this in turn requires the study of politics.

Can man in society best be understood by studying man or by studying society? The most satisfactory reply would seem to be given by striking the word "or" and answering "both." But where one begins his explanation of events makes a difference. The Reverend Thomas Malthus once wrote that, "though human institutions appear to be the obvious and obtrusive causes of much mischief to mankind; yet, in reality, they are light and superficial, they are mere feathers that float on the surface, in comparison with those deeper seated causes of impurity that corrupt the springs, and render turbid the whole stream of human life."[4] Rousseau looked at the same world, the same range of events, but found the locus of major causes in a different ambit.

Following Rousseau's lead in turn raises questions. As men live in states, so states exist in a world of states. If we now confine our attention to the question of why wars occur, shall we emphasize the role of the state, with its social and economic content as well as its political form, or shall we concentrate primarily on what is sometimes called the society of states? Again one may say strike the word "or" and worry about both, but many have emphasized either

[3] For further discussion of Rousseau, see ch. vi, of *Man, the State and War*.

[4] Malthus, *An Essay on the Principle of Population*, pp. 47–48 (ch. x of the 1798 ed.).

the first or the second, which helps to explain the discrepant conclusions reached. Those who emphasize the first in a sense run parallel to Milton. He explains the ills of the world by the evil in man; they explain the great ill of war by the evil qualities of some or of all states. The statement is then often reversed: If bad states make wars, good states would live at peace with one another. With varying degrees of justification this view can be attributed to Plato and Kant, to nineteenth-century liberals and revisionist socialists. They agree on the principle involved, though they differ in their descriptions of good states as well as on the problem of bringing about their existence.

Where Marxists throw the liberals' picture of the world into partial eclipse, others blot it out entirely. Rousseau himself finds the major causes of war neither in men nor in states but in the state system itself. Of men in a state of nature, he had pointed out that one man cannot begin to behave decently unless he has some assurance that others will not be able to ruin him. This thought Rousseau develops and applies to states existing in a condition of anarchy in his fragmentary essay on "The State of War" and in his commentaries on the works of the Abbé de Saint-Pierre. Though a state may want to remain at peace, it may have to consider undertaking a preventive war; for if it does not strike when the moment is favorable it may be struck later when the advantage has shifted to the other side. This view forms the analytic basis for many balance-of-power approaches to international relations and for the world-federalist program as well. Implicit in Thucydides and Alexander Hamilton, made explicit by Machiavelli, Hobbes, and Rousseau, it is at once a generalized explanation of states' behavior and a critical *point d'appui* against those who look to the internal structure of states to explain their external behavior. While some believe that peace will follow from the improvement of states, others assert that what the state will be like depends on its relation to others. The latter thesis Leopold Ranke derived from, or applied to, the history of the states of modern Europe. It has been used to explain the internal ordering of other states as well.[5]

Statesmen, as well as philosophers and historians, have attempted to account for the behavior of states in peace and in war. Woodrow Wilson, in the draft of a note written in November of

[5] Ranke, "The Great Powers," tr. H. H. Von Laue, in Theodore H. Von Laue, *Leopold Ranke*. And see, e.g., Homo, *Roman Political Institutions*, tr. Dobie, especially pp. 146, 364–69.

1916, remarked that the causes of the war then being fought were obscure, that neutral nations did not know why it had begun and, if drawn in, would not know for what ends they would be fighting.[6] But often to act we must convince ourselves that we do know the answers to such questions. Wilson, to his own satisfaction, soon did. He appears in history as one of the many who, drawing a sharp distinction between peaceful and aggressive states, have assigned to democracies all the attributes of the first, to authoritarian states all the attributes of the second. To an extent that varies with the author considered, the incidence of war is then thought to depend upon the type of national government. Thus Cobden in a speech at Leeds in December of 1849:

> Where do we look for the black gathering cloud of war? Where do we see it rising? Why, from the despotism of the north, where one man wields the destinies of 40,000,000 of serfs. If we want to know where is the second danger of war and disturbance, it is in that province of Russia—that miserable and degraded country, Austria—next in the stage of despotism and barbarism, and there you see again the greatest danger of war; but in proportion as you find the population governing themselves—as in England, in France, or in America—there you will find that war is not the disposition of the people, and that if Government desire it, the people would put a check upon it.[7]

The constant interest of the people is in peace; no government controlled by the people will fight unless set upon. But only a few years later, England, though not set upon, did fight against Russia; and Cobden lost his seat in 1857 as a result of his opposition to the war. The experience is shattering, but not fatal to the belief; for it relives in the words of Wilson, for example, and again in those of the late Senator Robert Taft. In the manner of Cobden but in the year 1951, Taft writes: "History shows that when the people have the opportunity to speak they as a rule decide for peace if possible. It shows that arbitrary rulers are more inclined to favor war than are the people at any time."[8] Is it true, one wonders, that there is a uniquely peaceful form of the state? If it were true, how much would it matter? Would it enable some states to know which other states they could trust? Should the states that are already good seek ways of making other states better, and thus make it possible for all

[6] Link, *Woodrow Wilson and the Progressive Era,* p. 257n.
[7] Cobden, *Speeches,* ed. Bright and Rogers, I, 432–33.
[8] Robert A. Taft, *A Foreign Policy for Americans,* p. 23.

men to enjoy the pleasures of peace? Wilson believed it morally imperative to aid in the political regeneration of others; Cobden thought it not even justifiable. Agreeing on where the causes are to be found, they differ in their policy conclusions.

But what of those who incline to a different estimate of major causes? "Now people," President Dwight Eisenhower has said, "don't want conflict—people in general. It is only, I think, mistaken leaders that grow too belligerent and believe that people really want to fight."[9] Though apparently not all people want peace badly enough, for, on a different occasion, he had this to say: "If the mothers in every land could teach their children to understand the homes and hopes of children in every other land—in America, in Europe, in the Near East, in Asia—the cause of peace in the world would indeed be nobly served."[10] Here the President seems to agree with Milton on where cause is to be found, but without Milton's pessimism—or realism, depending on one's preconceptions. Aggressive tendencies may be inherent, but is their misdirection inevitable? War begins in the minds and emotions of men, as all acts do; but can minds and emotions be changed? And, if one agrees that they can be, how much and how fast can whose minds and feelings be changed? And, if other factors are relevant as well, how much difference would the changes make? The answers to these questions and to those of the preceding paragraph are not obvious, but they are important. How can they best be sought?

Some would suggest taking possible answers as hypotheses to be investigated and tested empirically. This is difficult. Most English liberals at the time of the First World War argued, as did Wilson, that the militarist and authoritarian character of the German state prompted Germany to seek the war that soon spread to most of the world. At the same time some liberals, most notably G. Lowes Dickinson, argued that no single state could be held guilty. Only by understanding the international system, or lack of system, by which the leaders of states were often forced to act with slight regard for conventional morality, could one understand and justly assess the processes by which the war was produced.[11] Dickinson was blasted by liberals and socialists alike for reversing the dominant inside-out explanation. Acceptance or rejection of explanatory theses in

[9] Quoted by Robert J. Donovan, "Eisenhower Will Cable Secret Geneva Reports," in New York *Herald Tribune,* July 13, 1955, p. 1.

[10] Eisenhower, address to a meeting of the National Council of Catholic Women. Text in New York *Times,* November 9, 1954, p. 14.

[11] Dickinson, *The European Anarchy, passim.*

matters such as this most often depends on the skill of the pleaders and the mood of the audience. These are obviously not fit criteria, yet it would be foolish to argue that simply by taking a more intensive look at the data a compelling case could be built for one or the other explanatory theory. Staring at the same set of data, the parties to the debate came to sharply different conclusions, for the images they entertained led them to select and interpret the data in different ways. In order to make sense of the liberals' hypothesis we need somehow to acquire an idea of the interrelation of many possibly relevant factors, and these interrelations are not given in the data we study. We establish or, rather, assert them ourselves. To say "establish" would be dangerous; for, whether or not we label them as such, we cannot escape from philosophic assumptions. The idea we entertain becomes a filter through which we pass our data. If the data are selected carefully, they will pass like milk through cheesecloth. The recalcitrance of the data may cause us to change one filter for another, to modify or scrap the theory we hold—or it may produce ever more ingenious selection and interpretation of data, as has happened with many Marxists trying to salvage the thesis that with the development of capitalism the masses become increasingly impoverished.

If empirical investigations vary in incidence and in result with the ideas the empiricists entertain, it is worth asking ourselves if the ideas themselves can be subjected to scrutiny. Obviously they can be. The study of politics is distinguished from other social studies by concentration upon the institutions and processes of government. This focuses the political scientists' concern without constituting a self-denying ordinance against the use of materials and techniques of other social scientists.[12] On the latter point there is no difficulty for the student of international relations; there is considerable difficulty on the former, for international relations are characterized by the absence of truly governmental institutions, which in turn gives a radically different twist to the relevant processes. Yet there is a large and important sense in which traditional political philosophy, concentrating as it does upon domestic politics, is relevant for the student of international relations. Peace, it is often said, is the problem of the twentieth century. It is also one of the continuing concerns of political philosophers. In times of relative quiescence

[12] Cf. David B. Truman, "The Impact on Political Science of the Revolution in the Behavioral Sciences," in Bailey *et al.*, *Research Frontiers in Politics and Government*, pp. 202–31.

the question men put is likely to be: What good is life without justice and freedom? Better to die than live a slave. In times of domestic troubles, of hunger and civil war, of pressing insecurity, however, many will ask: Of what use is freedom without a power sufficient to establish and maintain conditions of security? That life takes priority over justice and freedom is taken to be a self-evident truth by St. Augustine and Luther, by Machiavelli, Bodin, and Hobbes. If the alternative to tyranny is chaos and if chaos means a war of all against all, then the willingness to endure tyranny becomes understandable. In the absence of order there can be no enjoyment of liberty. The problem of identifying and achieving the conditions of peace, a problem that plagues man and bedevils the student of international relations, has, especially in periods of crisis, bedeviled political philosophers as well.

R. G. Collingwood once suggested that the best way to understand the writings of philosophers is to seek out the questions they were attempting to answer. It is here suggested that the best way to examine the problems of international political theory is to pose a central question and identify the answers that can be given to it. One may seek in political philosophy answers to the question: Where are the major causes of war to be found? The answers are bewildering in their variety and in their contradictory qualities. To make this variety manageable, the answers can be ordered under the following three headings: within man, within the structure of the separate states, within the state system. The basis of this ordering, as well as its relevance in the world of affairs, is suggested in the preceding pages. These three estimates of cause will subsequently be referred to as images of international relations, numbered in the order given, with each image defined according to where one locates the nexus of important causes.

Previous comments indicate that the views comprised by any one image may in some senses by as contradictory as are the different images *inter se*. The argument that war is inevitable because men are irrevocably bad, and the argument that wars can be ended because men can be changed, are contradictory; but since in each of them individuals are taken to be the locus of cause, both are included in the first image. Similarly, acceptance of a third-image analysis may lead to the false optimism of the world federalists or to the often falsely defined pessimism of a *Realpolitik* position. Since in all respects but one there may be variety of opinion within images and since prescription is related to goal as well as to analysis, there is no one prescription for each image. There are, however, in relation to each image-goal pairing, logical and illogical prescriptions.

One can say that a prescription is wrong if he can show that following it does not bring about the predicted result. But can one ever show that a prescription was actually followed? One often hears statements like this: "The League of Nations didn't fail; it was never tried." And such statements are irrefutable. But even if empirical disproof were possible, the problem of proving a prescription valid would remain to be solved. A patient who in one period of illness tries ten different medications may wonder just which pill produced thc cure. The apportioning of credit is often more difficult than the assigning of blame. If a historical study were to show that in country A increases in national prosperity always followed increases in tariffs, to some observers this might seem to prove that high tariffs are a cause of prosperity; to others, that both of these factors are dependent on a third; and to still others, nothing at all. The empirical approach, though necessary, is not sufficient. The correlation of events means nothing, or at least should not be taken to mean anything, apart from the analysis that accompanies it.

If there is no empirical solution to the problem of prescription verification, what solution is there? Prescription is logically impossible apart from analysis. Every prescription for greater peace in the world is then related to one of our three images of international relations, or to some combination of them. An understanding of the analytical terms of each of the images will open up two additional possibilities for accepting or rejecting prescriptions. (1) A prescription based on a faulty analysis would be unlikely to produce the desired consequences. The assumption that to improve men in a prescribed way will serve to promote peace rests on the further assumption that in some form the first image of international relations is valid. The latter assumption should be examined before the former is made. (2) A prescription would be unacceptable if it were not logically related to its analysis. One who suffers from infected tonsils profits little from a skillfully performed appendectomy. If violence among states is caused by the evilness of man, to aim at the internal reform of states will not do much good. And if violence among states is the product of international anarchy, to aim at the conversion of individuals can accomplish little. One man's prognosis confounds the other man's prescription. If the validity of the images themselves can be ascertained, the critical relating of prescription to image becomes a check on the validity of prescriptions. There is, however, an additional complicating factor. Some combination of our three images, rather than any one of them, may be required for an accurate understanding of international relations. We may not be in a situation where one can consider just the patient's tonsils or his appendix. Both may be infected but removing either may kill the patient. In other words, understanding the likely consequences of any one cause may depend on understanding its relation to other causes. The possible interrelation of causes makes the problem of estimating the merit of various prescriptions more difficult still.

What are the criteria of merit? Suppose we consider again the person who argues that "bad" states produce war, that "good" states would live peacefully together, that therefore we must bring states into accord with a prescribed pattern. To estimate the merit of such a series of propositions requires asking the following questions: (1) Can the final proposition be implemented, and if so, how? (2) Is there a logical relation between prescription and image? In other words, does the prescription attack the assigned causes? (3) Is the image adequate, or has the analyst simply seized upon the most spectacular cause or the one he thinks most susceptible to manipulation and ignored other causes of equal or greater importance? (4) How will attempts to fill the prescription affect other goals? This last question is necessary since peace is not the only goal of even the most peacefully inclined men or states. One may, for example, believe that world government and perpetual peace are synonymous, but one may also be convinced that a world state would be a world tyranny and therefore prefer a system of nation-states with a perpetual danger of war to a world state with a promise of perpetual peace. . . .

21. *THE ORIGIN OF WAR*/ PLATO*

A State, I said, arises, as I conceive, out of the needs of mankind; no one is self-sufficing, but all of us have many wants. Can any other origin of a State be imagined?

There can be no other.

* Plato, *The Republic,* trans. Benjamin Jowett, rev. ed. (New York: Willey Book Co., 1901), pp. 47–53.

Then, as we have many wants, and many persons are needed to supply them, one takes a helper for one purpose and another for another; and when these partners and helpers are gathered together in one habitation the body of inhabitants is termed a State.

True, he said.

And they exchange with one another, and one gives, and another receives, under the idea that the exchange will be for their good.

Very true.

Then, I said, let us begin and create in idea a State; and yet the true creator is necessity, who is the mother of our invention.

Of course, he replied.

Now the first and greatest of necessities is food, which is the condition of life and existence.

Certainly.

The second is a dwelling, and the third clothing and the like.

True.

And now let us see how our city will be able to supply this great demand: We may suppose that one man is a husbandman, another a builder, someone else a weaver—shall we add to them a shoemaker, or perhaps some other purveyor to our bodily wants?

Quite right.

The barest notion of a State must include four or five men.

Clearly.

And how will they proceed? Will each bring the result of his labors into a common stock?—the individual husbandman, for example, producing for four, and laboring four times as long and as much as he need in the provision of food with which he supplies others as well as himself; or will he have nothing to do with others and not be at the trouble of producing for them, but provide for himself alone a fourth of the food in a fourth of the time, and in the remaining three-fourths of his time be employed in making a house or a coat or a pair of shoes, having no partnership with others, but supplying himself all his own wants?

Adeimantus thought that he should aim at producing food only and not at producing everything.

Probably, I replied, that would be the better way; and when I hear you say this, I am myself reminded that we are not all alike; there are diversities of natures among us which are adapted to different occupations.

Very true.

And will you have a work better done when the workman has many occupations, or when he has only one?

When he has only one.

Further, there can be no doubt that a work is spoilt when not done at the right time?

No doubt.

For business is not disposed to wait until the doer of the business is at leisure; but the doer must follow up what he is doing, and make the business his first object.

He must.

And if so, we must infer that all things are produced more plentifully and easily and of a better quality when one man does one thing which is natural to him and does it at the right time, and leaves other things.

Undoubtedly.

Then more than four citizens will be required; for the husbandman will not make his own plough or mattock, or other implements of agriculture, if they are to be good for anything. Neither will the builder make his tools—and he, too, needs many; and in like manner the weaver and shoemaker.

True.

Then carpenters and smiths and many other artisans will be sharers in our little State, which is already beginning to grow?

True.

Yet even if we add neatherds, shepherds, and other herdsmen, in order that our husbandmen may have oxen to plough with, and builders as well as husbandmen may have draught cattle, and curriers and weavers fleeces and hides—still our State will not be very large.

That is true; yet neither will it be a very small State which contains all these.

Then, again, there is the situation of the city—to find a place where nothing need be imported is well-nigh impossible.

Impossible.

Then there must be another class of citizens who will bring the required supply from another city?

There must.

But if the trader goes empty-handed, having nothing which they require who would supply his need, he will come back empty-handed.

That is certain.

And therefore what they produce at home must be not only enough for themselves, but such both in quantity and quality as to accommodate those from whom their wants are supplied.

Very true.

Then more husbandmen and more artisans will be required?

They will.

Not to mention the importers and exporters, who are called merchants?

Yes.

Then we shall want merchants?

We shall.

And if merchandise is to be carried over the sea, skilful sailors will also be needed, and in considerable numbers?

Yes, in considerable numbers.

Then, again, within the city, how will they exchange their productions? To secure such an exchange was, as you will remember, one of our principal objects when we formed them into a society and constituted a State.

Clearly they will buy and sell.

Then they will need a market-place, and a money-token for purposes of exchange.

Certainly.

Suppose now that a husbandman or an artisan brings some production to market, and he comes at a time when there is no one to exchange with him—is he to leave his calling and sit idle in the market-place?

Not at all; he will find people there who, seeing the want, undertake the office of salesmen. In well-ordered States they are commonly those who are the weakest in bodily strength, and therefore of little use for any other purpose; their duty is to be in the market, and to give money in exchange for goods to those who desire to sell, and to take money from those who desire to buy.

This want, then, creates a class of retail-traders in our State. Is not "retailer" the term which is applied to those who sit in the market-place engaged in buying and selling, while those who wander from one city to another are called merchants?

Yes, he said.

And there is another class of servants, who are intellectually hardly on the level of companionship; still they have plenty of bodily strength for labor, which accordingly they sell, and are called, if I do not mistake, hirelings, "hire" being the name which is given to the price of their labor.

True.

Then hirelings will help to make up our population?

Yes.

And now, Adeimantus, is our State matured and perfected?

I think so.

Where, then, is justice, and where is injustice, and in what part of the State did they spring up?

Probably in the dealings of these citizens with one another. I cannot imagine that they are more likely to be found anywhere else.

I dare say that you are right in your suggestion, I said; we had better think the matter out, and not shrink from the inquiry.

Let us then consider, first of all, what will be their way of life, now that we have thus established them. Will they not produce corn and wine and clothes and shoes, and build houses for themselves? And when they are housed, they will work, in summer, commonly, stripped and barefoot, but in winter substantially clothed and shod. They will feed on barley-meal and flour of wheat, baking and kneading them, making noble cakes and loaves; these they will serve up on a mat of reeds or on clean leaves, themselves reclining the while upon beds strewn with yew or myrtle. And they and their children will feast, drinking of the wine which they have made, wearing garlands on their heads, and hymning the praises of the gods, in happy converse with one another. And they will take care that their families do not exceed their means; having an eye to poverty or war.

But, said Glaucon, interposing, you have not given them a relish to their meal.

True, I replied, I had forgotten; of course they must have a relish—salt and olives and cheese—and they will boil roots and herbs such as country people prepare; for a dessert we shall give them figs and peas and beans; and they will roast myrtle-berries and acorns at the fire, drinking in moderation. And with such a diet they may be expected to live in peace and health to a good old age, and bequeath a similar life to their children after them.

Yes, Socrates, he said, and if you were providing for a city of pigs, how else would you feed the beasts?

But what would you have, Glaucon? I replied.

Why, he said, you should give them the ordinary conveniences of life. People who are to be comfortable are accustomed to lie on sofas, and dine off tables, and they should have sauces and sweets in the modern style.

Yes, I said, now I understand: the question which you would have me consider is, not only how a State, but how a luxurious State is created; and possibly there is no harm in this, for in such a State we shall be more likely to see how justice and injustice originate. In my opinion the true and healthy constitution of the State is the one which I have described. But if you wish also to see a State at fever-heat, I have no objection. For I suspect that many will not be satisfied with the simpler way of life. They will be for adding sofas and tables and other furniture; also dainties and perfumes and incense and courtesans and cakes, all these not of one sort only, but in every variety. We must go beyond the necessaries of which I was at first speaking, such as houses and clothes and shoes; the arts of the painter and the embroiderer will have to be set in motion, and gold and ivory and all sorts of materials must be procured.

True, he said.

Then we must enlarge our borders; for the original healthy State is no longer sufficient. Now will the city have to fill and swell with a multitude of callings which are not required by any natural want; such as the whole tribe of hunters and actors, of whom one large class have to do with forms and colors; another will be the votaries of music—poets and their attendant train of rhapsodists, players, dancers, contractors; also makers of divers kinds of articles, including women's dresses. And we shall want more servants. Will not tutors be also in request, and nurses wet and dry, tirewomen and barbers, as well as confectioners and cooks; and swineherds, too, who were not needed and therefore had no place in the former edition of our State, but are needed now? They must not be forgotten: and there will be animals of many other kinds, if people eat them.

Certainly.

And living in this way we shall have much greater need of physicians than before?

Much greater.

And the country which was enough to support the original inhabitants will be too small now, and not enough?

Quite true.

Then a slice of our neighbors' land will be wanted by us for pasture and tillage, and they will want a slice of ours, if, like ourselves, they exceed the limit of necessity, and give themselves up to the unlimited accumulation of wealth?

That, Socrates, will be inevitable.

And so we shall go to war, Glaucon. Shall we not?

Most certainly, he replied.

Then, without determining as yet whether war does good or harm, thus much we may affirm, that now we have discovered war to be derived from causes which are also the causes of almost all the evils in States, private as well as public.

Undoubtedly.

22. *POLITICS, CULTURE, AND PEACE*/ FREDERICK S. DUNN*

Most government documents make deplorably dull reading and only on rare occasions are they illumined by new ideas or a fresh turn of phrase. An exception is to be found in the opening lines of the Constitution of the United Nations Educational, Scientific and Cultural Organization (UNESCO). With disarming candor and an easy poetic rhythm, the preamble discusses the eternal problem of war and peace in terms somewhat different from those which governments normally use in their relations with each other. It suggests that the origin of wars is to be found not, as had generally been supposed, in the formal acts of sovereign states, but rather in the minds of the masses of men, and it is accordingly in the minds of men that the defenses of peace must be constructed. The preamble further argues that ignorance among nations of each other's ways and lives leads to suspicion and mistrust which in turn lead to war, and hence the way to peace is to remove such ignorance. On the whole, it takes a distinctly skeptical view of the durability of a peace based principally upon the usual political and economic arrangements of governments, and places its faith instead on the removal from men's minds of the attitudes and predispositions that lead them to entertain the idea of war with each other.

* Frederick S. Dunn, *War and the Minds of Men* (New York: Harper & Brothers, for the Council on Foreign Relations, 1950), Chap. 1. Reprinted by permission.

The deceptive simplicity of this statement might give the impression that it is intended merely as melodious preamble music, to be repeated on solemn public occasions but not to be taken seriously as an expression of empirical truth about the source of political conflicts. There is in fact some reason to suppose that the drafters themselves were not in full agreement as to the precise significance of the theory they were offering as the basis for the operations of UNESCO. But whatever may have been the original intention, there can be no doubt that the phrase about the "minds of men" has caught hold of the imagination of a great many people in a number of countries and has come to symbolize a distinctive and somewhat optimistic approach to the whole problem of how to lessen the threat of war in the present age.

1. Peace by Changing Men's Attitudes

There are some obvious reasons why this idea of constructing the defenses of peace in the minds of men should have attracted so much attention.

In the first place, it is quite clear that there has been a general loss of confidence in existing notions about how to avoid war in the current world crisis. While most governments are proceeding on traditional assumptions about the sources of war and are endeavoring to construct the defenses of peace in an expanded national strength and in useful alliances, there is a strong undercurrent of despair arising from the belief that in the end this method is just not going to work. The ancient dilemma of trying to achieve security in a world of sovereign states seems to have become vastly more baffling in an atomic age. The prospect of maintaining a lasting equilibrium in a bipolar world appears more doubtful than ever.

Now the threat of the hydrogen bomb, with its fantastic capacity for destruction, has come along to sharpen the dilemma a hundredfold. At the moment, it does not appear that armed forces of any size could insure the great industrial centers from instant incineration at the hands of a determined enemy possessing even a small supply of these bombs. Mighty ships and well-equipped divisions can no longer provide even a minimum of that comfortable feeling of safety which they used to be able to give. A trial by battle involving the use of all the newest weapons of mass destruction can appear only as the final madness of men. Hence great numbers of people have anxiously turned to this doctrine which seems to open up a whole new method of attack on the problem of war and peace.

A second reason why the minds-of-men theory has attracted so much attention is the realization that the masses of men are now exerting a great and apparently expanding influence on the making of policy decisions in international affairs. As the interests of people have spread outward, a greater concern with the way in which those interests are fostered has likewise begun to penetrate the international level. Everywhere outside the Soviet orbit there has been a definite tendency toward wider popular control of foreign policy. In the colonial empires of the world, the native populations have surged forward to enforce their demands for a direct voice in the determination of their status in the international community. In all save the dictator countries, legislative bodies seem to have won an increased share in the making of foreign policy. Hence, a theory which proposes to construct the defenses of peace in the minds of men appears to make much more sense today than it would have made when the management of foreign affairs was the exclusive province of a small group of officials.

A third reason why the minds-of-men doctrine has seemed to offer a ray of hope in the current crisis is the growing belief that we are at last coming into the possession of knowledge and techniques that will enable us to influence men's political behavior in desired directions and so exercise a greater control over international events. We seem to be traveling along the edge of a new and engrossing experience in the long and difficult enterprise of learning about the forces that influence social action. There is excitement in the air and a feeling that we are breaking out into new and fertile territory in the understanding of social behavior. Spectacular improvements in the technical means of communication with the masses of men have added to the hope that we are acquiring new power as well as new insights in the control of international events.

For these reasons, there has been a ready audience for the theory that the conflicts of nations arise in the minds of men and might be controlled by changing men's attitudes. On the surface there seems to be much in favor of the idea. It is easy enough to see that widespread feelings of hostility and misunderstanding provide fertile soil for the seeds of war. It is also obvious that conflicts among nations can grow fat on a diet of ignorance and bias. Presumably a state of peace and order is what nearly everybody wants, and if its achievement is really a matter of influencing men's minds, one would be hard pressed to say why massive efforts should not be made in this field.

2. *Large Hopes and Small Results*

However, when it comes to the actual effort to put this doctrine into effect, the difficulties seem mountainous. . . .

Everyone knows in general what is meant by "mutual understanding" and everyone approves of it as a sentiment, but little effort seems to have been made to translate it into categories of observable data about which hypotheses can be made and tested by objective methods. The result is that no two people who use the term can ever be sure that they are talking about the same thing or that what they say has any basis in reality. The language and the conceptual systems used in the halls of UNESCO are for the most part of a traditional character, and reveal little appreciation of what has been taking place recently in the way of systematic analysis of social action.

Some people who are genuinely convinced of the essential validity of the minds-of-men doctrine have nevertheless raised serious questions about the premises on which this doctrine is being put into effect. Thus the belief that men go to war because they are ignorant of each other's ways of life or have incorrect views of each other's motives has been strongly challenged on the basis of past history. It is pointed out that the nations which go to war most frequently are not those in which ignorance of other people is most common, but are instead the more advanced nations with the highest educational standards. For example, the people of France and Germany have had abundant opportunity to get to know each other well; yet this has not prevented them from engaging in wars of spectacular dimensions.

Even in everyday human affairs, the connection between knowledge of others and peaceful relations with them is not always evident. Thus on the family level the bitterest of controversies frequently take place between the closest of relatives. Civil wars, which are between peoples of the same civilization who presumably possess a good understanding of each other, are notoriously sharp and cruel. On the other hand, isolated nations have managed to live both in ignorance of, and in harmony with, other nations for long periods of time.

It is persistently asked whether the differences between Soviet Russia and the United States today are really due to a lack of understanding of their respective positions, or whether these differences do not in fact arise out of a clear realization that the two countries have fundamental goals which are to a large extent incompatible. One recalls the case of the European monarch who, when urged by his advisers to settle a boundary war with a neighboring sovereign, replied that there was really no dispute at all between them—they both wanted the same thing. Their mutual understanding was perfect.

Will full knowledge of what nations want in fact bring peace among them, or is it not more likely that, under certain circumstances, such knowledge might even increase the tendency to go to war? Those who raise this question are quite ready to concede that, where means can be found for giving both contestants substantially what they desire, a full exploration of the possible alternatives would undoubtedly contribute to the avoidance of hostilities. But when such inquiry reveals that the goals of the two sides are incompatible and there is no way in which they can be harmonized, it is a serious question whether public revelation of that fact would increase the chances for peace.

Past experience affords some ground for skepticism as to whether extensive cultural interchange has had much effect upon the underlying causes of wars. Does freedom of communication across national boundaries necessarily lead to the development of common conceptions of justice among nations? Is it even true that nations possessing similar conceptions of justice will therefore refrain from going to war against each other? Cultural interchange is freely conceded to be a good thing in itself. But some scholars have asked whether, in the light of historical instances, one can expect such interchange to have much effect in preventing wars.[1]

Finally, there is little reason, it is said, for supposing that governments are really serious in wanting to take action that would reduce the nationalistic attitudes of their citizens. Such attitudes may be a useful source of support for a government that is engaged in a power competition with a rival nation. Under such circum-

[1] See Hans J. Morgenthau, *Politics Among Nations,* New York, Alfred A. Knopf, 1948, pp. 407–412; also Reinhold Niebuhr, "The Theory and Practice of UNESCO," *International Organization,* February 1950, pp. 3–11.

stances, it would be too much to expect that any government would seriously want its own citizens to become more internationally minded. Thus in the present contest between the Soviet Union and the United States, a program of education for international understanding on one side of the line but not on the other would merely strengthen the side that relies on the fostering of nationalistic attitudes among its people.

The upshot of all these criticisms is that a good many people who would normally be well disposed toward the idea that the defenses of peace should be built in the minds of men nevertheless feel that the doctrine really has no particular relevancy to the present world crisis. They believe that UNESCO's activities in improving standards of education, science and culture in various countries may be excellent in themselves, but that aside from the infinitely slow building up of the tissues of a world community, there is little that UNESCO can contribute to the maintenance of peace in the years ahead.

It would be difficult to deny the strength of many of the points made above. However, they could all be admitted, and it might still be a perfectly good working proposition that wars begin in the minds of men and that the defenses of peace must be constructed there. What is valid in these criticisms is directed not so much at the idea itself as at the way in which people have sought to apply it.

Where else, one might ask, could wars begin save in the minds of men? Even the greenest tyro in the halls of world politics is now aware that, although we talk about states acting and making decisions, only human beings can act. The state, being an abstraction of thought, cannot have a will of its own apart from human wills. It is in one sense just a name to describe the process whereby politically organized people arrive at decisions and take action which is accepted as the action of the collectivity.

But having said this, one is still a long way from knowing what to do about it, or even whether anything can be done about it at all. Having identified the source of our troubles, it is still a highly perplexing business to discover reliable ways of freeing men's minds from the impulses and attitudes that lead to wars. Yet it is obvious that, if there is a grain of truth in the minds-of-men doctrine, one must examine it with sympathetic care to see what guidance it can offer for more intelligent policy-making in the future.

In order to do this with any hope of success, it will be necessary to break out of the traditional framework of thinking about foreign affairs and to use a new focus for our analysis. This is always a difficult thing to do, but there is no other way of getting a fresh view of the problem and of arriving at an objective evaluation of the steps that are being taken to solve it.

At any rate it is time that the case for approaching the problem of war and peace through the minds-of-men doctrine should be placed on some other ground than that of stirring appeals to the sentiments. If the phrase has any useful meaning as a signpost to effective action, that meaning will be discovered only by a realistic analysis that will reveal its connection with the actual world of events and suggest hypotheses which can be tested by observation and concrete experience.

To a crusader in a cause, a realistic appraisal of the premises on which his beliefs are founded can appear only as rank heresy. Many people today have a sacred-cow attitude toward UNESCO that prevents them from looking at it with a detached eye. But if a movement or doctrine cannot stand up under a realistic examination, then it does not deserve the support of intelligent men; if it can, it is doubly strong.

3. A Problem of Communication

The most important thing to be observed about the minds-of-men theory is that it is primarily a theory of communication and learning. It asserts that, if only the right things are communicated by some people to some other people, a change can be effected in the attitudes of nations toward each other that will make a durable peace possible. This is a technical proposition which rests upon our knowledge of the processes of using ideas or symbols to modify the behavior of men. . . .

In the present state of the world, this is a very complicated business indeed. Because of the prodigious revolutionary changes taking place in various parts of the world, it is no easy matter to identify either the proper communicators or the appropriate audiences, or even the correct aims of communication policies. One cannot simply say that the purpose of such policies is to avoid open warfare, since that kind of peace might be purchased, at least temporarily, by making men submissive to tyrants. One would have to assume that the purpose is to achieve a peace based on those attitudes which make for the full development of the capacities of free men in a free society. Instead of merely seeking to deprive men of the will to resist those whose aim is to enslave them, the goal of the minds-of-men theory might even be to strengthen their resistance in the face of threats of violence. Certainly a peace of subservience based on the deterioration of human society and the breakdown of individual personality is not what is desired by those who embrace the theory. Such a peace could end finally only in the jungle warfare of barbarians. In the complex society of today, no enduring peace is possible that is not based on the continuing development of human potentialities. . . .

IMPERIALISM AND COLONIALISM

VIII

WHY DO SOME STATES SEEK TO EXPAND BEyond their own boundaries? What is their justification? And what are the effects of expansionism? In the first selection, Theodore Roosevelt (1858–1919), 26th President of the United States, presents an enthusiastic defense of American empire building. He delivered his speech "The Strenuous Life" before the Hamilton Club in Chicago on April 10, 1899.

The second selection consists of excerpts from V. I. Lenin's *Imperialism.* Lenin (1870–1924), the leader of the Bolshevik Revolution of 1917 and the first ruler of the Soviet Union, argued that imperialism was a product of specific economic forces. In one form or another, this economic explanation of imperialism has had great appeal in the twentieth century in spite of its obvious shortcomings.

The third selection is by William L. Langer, who is eminently qualified to review the history of imperialism. He is Professor of Modern History at Harvard University and author of *The Diplomacy of Imperialism.*

23. *THE STRENUOUS LIFE* / THEODORE ROOSEVELT*

In speaking to you, men of the greatest city of the West, men of the State which gave to the country Lincoln and Grant, men who preëminently and distinctly embody all that is most American in the American character, I wish to preach, not the doctrine of ignoble ease, but the doctrine of the strenuous life, the life of toil and effort, of labor and strife; to preach that highest form of success which comes, not to the man who desires mere easy peace, but to the man who does not shrink from danger, from hardship, or from bitter toil, and who out of these wins the splendid ultimate triumph.

A life of slothful ease, a life of that peace which springs merely from lack either of desire or of power to strive after great things, is as little worthy of a nation as of an individual. I ask only that what every self-respecting American demands from himself and from his sons shall be demanded of the American nation as a whole. Who among you would teach your boys that ease, that peace, is to be the first consideration in their eyes—to be the ultimate goal after which they strive? You men of Chicago have made this city great, you men of Illinois have done your share, and more than your share, in making America great, because you neither preach nor practise such a doctrine. You work yourselves, and you bring up your sons to work. If you are rich and are worth your salt, you will teach your sons that though they may have leisure, it is not to be spent in idleness; for wisely used leisure merely means that those who possess it, being free from the necessity of working for their livelihood, are all the more bound to carry on some kind of non-remunerative work in science, in letters, in art, in exploration, in historical research—work of the type we most need in this country, the successful carrying out of which reflects most honor upon the nation. We do not admire the man of timid peace. We admire the man

* Theodore Roosevelt, *The Strenuous Life: Essays and Addresses* (New York: The Century Co., 1905), pp. 1–10, 16–21.

who embodies victorious effort; the man who never wrongs his neighbor, who is prompt to help a friend, but who has those virile qualities necessary to win in the stern strife of actual life. It is hard to fail, but it is worse never to have tried to succeed. In this life we get nothing save by effort. Freedom from effort in the present merely means that there has been stored up effort in the past. A man can be freed from the necessity of work only by the fact that he or his fathers before him have worked to good purpose. If the freedom thus purchased is used aright, and the man still does actual work, though of a different kind, whether as a writer or a general, whether in the field of politics or in the field of exploration and adventure, he shows he deserves his good fortune. But if he treats this period of freedom from the need of actual labor as a period, not of preparation, but of mere enjoyment, even though perhaps not of vicious enjoyment, he shows that he is simply a cumberer of the earth's surface, and he surely unfits himself to hold his own with his fellows if the need to do so should again arise. A mere life of ease is not in the end a very satisfactory life, and, above all, it is a life which ultimately unfits those who follow it for serious work in the world.

In the last analysis a healthy state can exist only when the men and women who make it up lead clean, vigorous, healthy lives; when the children are so trained that they shall endeavor, not to shirk difficulties, but to overcome them; not to seek ease, but to know how to wrest triumph from toil and risk. The man must be glad to do a man's work, to dare and endure and to labor; to keep himself, and to keep those dependent upon him. The woman must be the housewife, the helpmeet of the homemaker, the wise and fearless mother of many healthy children. In one of Daudet's powerful and melancholy books he speaks of "the fear of maternity, the haunting terror of the young wife of the present day." When such words can be truthfully written of a nation, that nation is rotten to the heart's core. When men fear work or fear righteous war, when women fear motherhood, they tremble on the brink of doom; and well it is that they should vanish from the earth, where they are fit subjects for the scorn of all men and women who are themselves strong and brave and high-minded.

As it is with the individual, so it is with the nation. It is a base untruth to say that happy is the nation that has no history. Thrice happy is the nation that has a glorious history. Far better it is to dare mighty things, to win glorious triumphs, even though checkered by failure, than to take rank with those poor spirits who neither enjoy much nor suffer much, because they live in the gray twilight that knows not victory nor defeat. If in 1861 the men who loved the Union had believed that peace was the end of all things, and war and strife the worst of all things, and had acted up to their belief, we would have saved hundreds of thousands of lives, we would have saved hundreds of millions of dollars. Moreover, besides saving all the blood and treasure we then lavished, we would have prevented the heartbreak of many women, the dissolution of many homes, and we would have spared the country those months of gloom and shame when it seemed as if our armies marched only to defeat. We could have avoided all this suffering simply by shrinking from strife. And if we had thus avoided it, we would have shown that we were weaklings, and that we were unfit to stand among the great nations of the earth. Thank God for the iron in the blood of our fathers, the men who upheld the wisdom of Lincoln, and bore sword or rifle in the armies of Grant! Let us, the children of the men who proved themselves equal to the mighty days, let us, the children of the men who carried the great Civil War to a triumphant conclusion, praise the God of our fathers that the ignoble counsels of peace were rejected; that the suffering and loss, the blackness of sorrow and despair, were unflinchingly faced, and the years of strife endured; for in the end the slave was freed, the Union restored, and the mighty American republic placed once more as a helmeted queen among nations.

We of this generation do not have to face a task such as that our fathers faced, but we have our tasks, and woe to us if we fail to perform them! We cannot, if we would, play the part of China, and be content to rot by inches in ignoble ease within our borders, taking no interest in what goes on beyond them, sunk in a scrambling commercialism; heedless of the higher life, the life of aspiration, of toil and risk, busying ourselves only with the wants of our bodies for the day, until suddenly we should find, beyond a shadow of question, what China has already found, that in this world the nation that has trained itself to a career of unwarlike and isolated ease is bound, in the end, to go down before other nations which have not lost the manly and adventurous qualities. If we are to be a really great people, we must strive in good faith to play a great part in the world. We cannot avoid meeting great issues. All that we can determine for ourselves is whether we shall meet them well or ill. In

1898 we could not help being brought face to face with the problem of war with Spain. All we could decide was whether we should shrink like cowards from the contest, or enter into it as beseemed a brave and high-spirited people; and, once in, whether failure or success should crown our banners. So it is now. We cannot avoid the responsibilities that confront us in Hawaii, Cuba, Porto Rico, and the Philippines. All we can decide is whether we shall meet them in a way that will redound to the national credit, or whether we shall make of our dealings with these new problems a dark and shameful page in our history. To refuse to deal with them at all merely amounts to dealing with them badly. We have a given problem to solve. If we undertake the solution, there is, of course, always danger that we may not solve it aright; but to refuse to undertake the solution simply renders it certain that we cannot possibly solve it aright. The timid man, the lazy man, the man who distrusts his country, the over-civilized man, who has lost the great fighting, masterful virtues, the ignorant man, and the man of dull mind, whose soul is incapable of feeling the mighty lift that thrills "stern men with empires in their brains"—all these, of course, shrink from seeing the nation undertake its new duties; shrink from seeing us build a navy and an army adequate to our needs; shrink from seeing us do our share of the world's work, by bringing order out of chaos in the great, fair tropic islands from which the valor of our soldiers and sailors has driven the Spanish flag. These are the men who fear the strenuous life, who fear the only national life which is really worth leading. They believe in that cloistered life which saps the hardy virtues in a nation, as it saps them in the individual; or else they are wedded to that base spirit of gain and greed which recognizes in commercialism the be-all and end-all of national life, instead of realizing that, though an indispensable element, it is, after all, but one of the many elements that go to make up true national greatness. No country can long endure if its foundations are not laid deep in the material prosperity which comes from thrift, from business energy and enterprise, from hard, unsparing effort in the fields of industrial activity; but neither was any nation ever yet truly great if it relied upon material prosperity alone. All honor must be paid to the architects of our material prosperity, to the great captains of industry who have built our factories and our railroads, to the strong men who toil for wealth with brain or hand; for great is the debt of the nation to these and their kind. But our debt is yet greater to the men whose highest type is to be found in a statesman like Lincoln, a soldier like Grant. They showed by their lives that they recognized the law of work, the law of strife; they toiled to win a competence for themselves and those dependent upon them; but they recognized that there were yet other and even loftier duties—duties to the nation and duties to the race.

We cannot sit huddled within our own borders and avow ourselves merely an assemblage of well-to-do hucksters who care nothing for what happens beyond. Such a policy would defeat even its own end; for as the nations grow to have ever wider and wider interests, and are brought into closer and closer contact, if we are to hold our own in the struggle for naval and commercial supremacy, we must build up our power without our own borders. We must build the isthmian canal, and we must grasp the points of vantage which will enable us to have our say in deciding the destiny of the oceans of the East and the West.

So much for the commercial side. From the standpoint of international honor the argument is even stronger. The guns that thundered off Manila and Santiago left us echoes of glory, but they also left us a legacy of duty. If we drove out a medieval tyranny only to make room for savage anarchy, we had better not have begun the task at all. It is worse than idle to say that we have no duty to perform, and can leave to their fates the islands we have conquered. Such a course would be the course of infamy. It would be followed at once by utter chaos in the wretched islands themselves. Some stronger, manlier power would have to step in and do the work, and we would have shown ourselves weaklings, unable to carry to successful completion the labors that great and high-spirited nations are eager to undertake. . . .

In the West Indies and the Philippines alike we are confronted by most difficult problems. It is cowardly to shrink from solving them in the proper way; for solved they must be, if not by us, then by some stronger and more manful race. If we are too weak, too selfish, or too foolish to solve them, some bolder and abler people must undertake the solution. Personally, I am far too firm a believer in the greatness of my country and the power of my countrymen to admit for one moment that we shall ever be driven to the ignoble alternative.

The problems are different for the different islands. Porto Rico is not large enough to stand alone. We must govern it wisely and well, primarily in the interest of its own people. Cuba is, in my judgment, entitled ultimately to settle for itself whether it shall be an independent state or an integral portion of the mightiest of republics. But until order and stable liberty are secured, we must remain in the island to insure them, and infinite tact, judgment, moderation, and courage must be shown by our military and civil representatives in keeping the island pacified, in relentlessly stamping out brigandage, in protecting all alike, and yet in showing proper recognition to the men who have fought for Cuban liberty. The Philippines offer a yet graver problem. Their population includes half-caste and native Christians, warlike Moslems, and wild pagans. Many of their people are utterly unfit for self-government, and show no signs of becoming fit. Others may in time become fit but at present can only take part in self-government under a wise supervision, at once firm and beneficent. We have driven Spanish tyranny from the islands. If we now let it be replaced by savage anarchy, our work has been for harm and not for good. I have scant patience with those who fear to undertake the task of governing the Philippines, and who openly avow that they do fear to undertake it, or that they shrink from it because of the expense and trouble; but I have even scanter patience with those who make a pretense of humanitarianism to hide and cover their timidity, and who cant about "liberty" and the "consent of the governed," in order to excuse themselves for their unwillingness to play the part of men. Their doctrines, if carried out, would make it incumbent upon us to leave the Apaches of Arizona to work out their own salvation, and to decline to interfere in a single Indian reservation. Their doctrines condemn your forefathers and mine for ever having settled in these United States.

England's rule in India and Egypt has been of great benefit to England, for it has trained up generations of men accustomed to look at the larger and loftier side of public life. It has been of even greater benefit to India and Egypt. And finally, and most of all, it has advanced the cause of civilization. So, if we do our duty aright in the Philippines, we will add to that national renown which is the highest and finest part of national life, will greatly benefit the people of the Philippine Islands, and, above all, we will play our part well in the great work of uplifting mankind. But to do this work, keep ever in mind that we must show in a very high degree the qualities of courage, of honesty, and of good judgment. Resistance must be stamped out. The first and all-important work to be done is to establish the supremacy of our flag. We must put down armed resistance before we can accomplish anything else, and there should be no parleying, no faltering, in dealing with our foe. As for those in our own country who encourage the foe, we can afford contemptuously to disregard them; but it must be remembered that their utterances are not saved from being treasonable merely by the fact that they are despicable.

When once we have put down armed resistance, when once our rule is acknowledged, then an even more difficult task will begin, for then we must see to it that the islands are administered with absolute honesty and with good judgment. If we let the public service of the islands be turned into the prey of the spoils politician, we shall have begun to tread the path which Spain trod to her own destruction. We must send out there only good and able men, chosen for their fitness, and not because of their partisan service, and these men must not only administer impartial justice to the natives and serve their own government with honesty and fidelity, but must show the utmost tact and firmness, remembering that, with such people as those with whom we are to deal, weakness is the greatest of crimes, and that next to weakness comes lack of consideration for their principles and prejudices.

I preach to you, then, my countrymen, that our country calls not for the life of ease but for the life of strenuous endeavor. The twentieth century looms before us big with the fate of many nations. If we stand idly by, if we seek merely swollen, slothful ease and ignoble peace, if we shrink from the hard contests where men must win at hazard of their lives and at the risk of all they hold dear, then the bolder and stronger peoples will pass us by, and will win for themselves the domination of the world. Let us therefore boldly face the life of strife, resolute to do our duty well and manfully; resolute to uphold righteousness by deed and by word; resolute to be both honest and brave, to serve high ideals, yet to use practical methods. Above all, let us shrink from no strife, moral or physical, within or without the nation, provided we are certain that the strife is justified, for it is only through strife, through hard and dangerous endeavor, that we shall ultimately win the goal of true national greatness.

24. *IMPERIALISM: THE HIGHEST STAGE OF CAPITALISM* / V. I. LENIN*

Under the old capitalism, when free competition prevailed, the export of *goods* was the most typical feature. Under modern capitalism, when monopolies prevail, the export of *capital* has become the typical feature.

Capitalism is commodity production at the highest stage of development, when labour power itself becomes a commodity. The growth of internal exchange, and particularly of international exchange, is the characteristic distinguishing feature of capitalism. The uneven and spasmodic character of the development of individual enterprises, of individual branches of industry and individual countries, is inevitable under the capitalist system. England became a capitalist country before any other, and in the middle of the nineteenth century, having adopted free trade, claimed to be the "workshop of the world," the great purveyor of manufactured goods to all countries, which in exchange were to keep her supplied with raw materials. But in the last quarter of the nineteenth century, *this* monopoly was already undermined. Other countries, protecting themselves by tariff walls, had developed into independent capitalist states. On the threshold of the twentieth century, we see a new type of monopoly coming into existence. Firstly, there are monopolist capitalist combines in all advanced capitalist countries; secondly, a few rich countries, in which the accumulation of capital reaches gigantic proportions, occupy a monopolist position. An enormous "superabundance of capital" has accumulated in the advanced countries.

It goes without saying that if capitalism could develop agriculture, which today lags far behind industry everywhere, if it could raise the standard of living of the masses, who are everywhere still poverty-stricken and underfed, in spite of the amazing advance in technical knowledge, there could be no talk of a superabundance of capital. This "argument" the petty-bourgeois critics of capitalism advance on every occasion. But if capitalism did these things it

* V. I. Lenin, *Imperialism: The Highest Stage of Capitalism* (New York: International Publishers, 1939), Chap. 4, 7, 10. By permission of International Publishers Co., Inc.

would not be capitalism; for uneven development and wretched conditions of the masses are fundamental and inevitable conditions and premises of this mode of production. As long as capitalism remains what it is, surplus capital will never be utilised for the purpose of raising the standard of living of the masses in a given country, for this would mean a decline in profits for the capitalists; it will be used for the purpose of increasing those profits by exporting capital abroad to the backward countries. In these backward countries profits are usually high, for capital is scarce, the price of land is relatively low, wages are low, raw materials are cheap. The possibility of exporting capital is created by the fact that numerous backward countries have been drawn into international capitalist intercourse; main railways have either been built or are being built there; the elementary conditions for industrial development have been created, etc. The necessity for exporting capital arises from the fact that in a few countries capitalism has become "over-ripe" and (owing to the backward state of agriculture and the impoverished state of the masses) capital cannot find "profitable" investment. . . .

We must now try to sum up and put together what has been said above on the subject of imperialism. Imperialism emerged as the development and direct continuation of the fundamental attributes of capitalism in general. But capitalism only became capitalist imperialism at a definite and very high stage of its development, when certain of its fundamental attributes began to be transformed into their opposites, when the features of a period of transition from capitalism to a higher social and economic system began to take shape and reveal themselves all along the line. Economically, the main thing in this process is the substitution of capitalist monopolies for capitalist free competition. Free competition is the fundamental attribute of capitalism, and of commodity production generally. Monopoly is exactly the opposite of free competition; but we have seen the latter being transformed into monopoly before our very eyes, creating large-scale industry and eliminating small industry, replacing large-scale industry by still larger-scale industry, finally leading to such a concentration of production and capital that monopoly has been and is the result: cartels, syndicates and trusts, and merging with them, the capital of a dozen or so banks manipulating thousands of millions. At the same time monopoly, which has grown out of free competition, does not abolish the latter, but exists over it and alongside of it, and thereby gives rise to a number of very acute, intense antagonisms, friction and conflicts. Monopoly is the transition from capitalism to a higher system.

If it were necessary to give the briefest possible definition of imperialism we should have to say that imperialism is the monopoly stage of capitalism. Such a definition would include what is most important, for, on the one hand, finance capital is the bank capital of a few big monopolist banks, merged with the capital of the monopolist combines of manufacturers; and, on the other hand, the division of the world is the transition from a colonial policy which has extended without hindrance to territories unoccupied by any capitalist power, to a colonial policy of monopolistic possession of the territory of the world which has been completely divided up.

But very brief definitions, although convenient, for they sum up the main points, are nevertheless inadequate, because very important features of the phenomenon that has to be defined have to be especially deduced. And so, without forgetting the conditional and relative value of all definitions, which can never include all the concatenations of a phenomenon in its complete development, we must give a definition of imperialism that will embrace the following five essential features:

1) The concentration of production and capital developed to such a high stage that it created monopolies which play a decisive role in economic life.

2) The merging of bank capital with industrial capital, and the creation, on the basis of this "finance capital," of a "financial oligarchy."

3) The export of capital, which has become extremely important, as distinguished from the export of commodities.

4) The formation of international capitalist monopolies which share the world among themselves.

5) The territorial division of the whole world among the greatest capitalist powers is completed.

Imperialism is capitalism in that stage of development in which the dominance of monopolies and finance capital has established itself; in which the export of capital has acquired pronounced importance; in which the division of the world among the international trusts has begun; in which the division of all territories of the globe among the great capitalist powers has been completed.

. . . We have seen that the economic quintessence of imperialism is monopoly capitalism. This very fact determines its place in history, for monopoly that grew up on the basis of free competition, and precisely out of free competition, is the transition from the capitalist system to a higher social-economic order. We must take special note of the four principal forms of monopoly, or the four principal manifestations of monopoly capitalism, which are characteristic of the epoch under review.

Firstly, monopoly arose out of the concentration of production at a very advanced stage of development. This refers to the monopolist capitalist combines, cartels, syndicates and trusts. We have seen the important part that these play in modern economic life. At the beginning of the twentieth century, monopolies acquired complete supremacy in the advanced countries. And although the first steps towards the formation of the cartels were first taken by countries enjoying the protection of high tariffs (Germany, America), Great Britain, with her system of free trade, was not far behind in revealing the same basic phenomenon, namely, the birth of monopoly out of the concentration of production.

Secondly, monopolies have accelerated the capture of the most important sources of raw materials, especially for the coal and iron industries, which are the basic and most highly cartelised industries in capitalist society. The monopoly of the most important sources of raw materials has enormously increased the power of big capital, and has sharpened the antagonism between cartelised and non-cartelised industry.

Thirdly, monopoly has sprung from the banks. The banks have developed from modest intermediary enterprises into the monopolists of finance capital. Some three or five of the biggest banks in each of the foremost capitalist countries have achieved the "personal union" of industrial and bank capital, and have concentrated in their hands the disposal of thousands upon thousands of millions which form the greater part of the capital and income of entire countries. A financial oligarchy, which throws a close net of relations of dependence over all the economic and political institutions of contemporary bourgeois society without exception—such is the most striking manifestation of this monopoly.

Fourthly, monopoly has grown out of colonial policy. To the numerous "old" motives of colonial policy, finance capital has added the struggle for the sources of raw materials, for the export of capital, for "spheres of influence," *i.e.*, for spheres for profitable deals, concessions, monopolist profits and so on; in fine, for economic territory in general. When the colonies of the European powers in Africa, for instance, comprised only one-tenth of that territory (as was the case in 1876), colonial policy was able to develop by methods other than those of monopoly—by the "free grabbing" of territories, so to speak. But when nine-tenths of Africa had been seized (approximately by 1900), when the whole world had been divided up, there was inevitably ushered in a period of colonial monopoly and, consequently, a period of particularly intense struggle for the division and the redivision of the world.

The extent to which monopolist capital has intensified all the contradictions of capitalism is generally known. It is sufficient to mention the high cost of living and the oppression of the cartels. This intensification of contradictions constitutes the most powerful driving force of the transitional period of history, which began from the time of the definite victory of world finance capital.

Monopolies, oligarchy, the striving for domination instead of the striving for liberty, the exploitation of an increasing number of small or weak nations by an extremely small group of the richest or most powerful nations—all these have given birth to those distinctive characteristics of imperialism which compel us to define it as parasitic or decaying capitalism. More and more prominently there emerges, as one of the tendencies of imperialism, the creation of the "bondholding" (rentier) state, the usurer state, in which the bourgeoisie lives on the proceeds of capital exports and by "clipping coupons." It would be a mistake to believe that this tendency to decay precludes the possibility of the rapid growth of capitalism. It does not. In the epoch of imperialism, certain branches of industry, certain strata of the bourgeoisie and certain countries betray, to a more or less degree, one or other of these tendencies. On the whole, capitalism is growing far more rapidly than before. But this growth is not only becoming more and more uneven in general; its unevenness also manifests itself, in particular, in the decay of the countries which are richest in capital (such as England). . . .

From all that has been said in this book on the economic nature of imperialism, it follows that we must define it as capitalism in transition, or, more precisely, as moribund capitalism. It is very instructive in this respect to note that the bourgeois economists, in describing modern capitalism, frequently employ terms like "interlocking," "absence of isolation," etc.; "in conformity with their functions and course of development," banks are "not purely private business enterprises; they are more and more outgrowing the sphere of purely private business regulation." And this very Riesser, who uttered the words just quoted, declares with all seriousness that the "prophecy" of the Marxists concerning "socialisation" has "not come true"!

What then does this word "interlocking" express? It merely expresses the most striking feature of the process going on before our eyes. It shows that the observer counts the separate trees, but cannot see the wood. It slavishly copies the superficial, the fortuitous, the chaotic. It reveals the observer as one who is overwhelmed by the mass of raw material and is utterly incapable of appreciating its meaning and importance. Ownership of shares and relations between owners of private property "interlock in a haphazard way." But the underlying factor of this interlocking, its very base, is the changing social relations of production. When a big enterprise assumes gigantic proportions, and, on the basis of exact computation of mass data, organises according to plan the supply of primary raw materials to the extent of two-thirds, or three-fourths of all that is necessary for tens of millions of people; when the raw materials are transported to the most suitable place of production, sometimes hundreds or thousands of miles away, in a systematic and organised manner; when a single centre directs all the successive stages of work right up to the manufacture of numerous varieties of finished articles; when these products are distributed according to a single plan among tens and hundreds of millions of consumers (as in the case of the distribution of oil in America and Germany by the American "oil trust")—then it becomes evident that we have socialisation of production, and not mere "interlocking"; that private economic relations and private property relations constitute a shell which is no longer suitable for its contents, a shell which must inevitably begin to decay if its destruction be delayed by artificial means; a shell which may continue in a state of decay for a fairly long period (particularly if the cure of the opportunist abscess is protracted), but which will inevitably be removed. . . .

25. *FAREWELL TO EMPIRE** / *WILLIAM L. LANGER*

Now that the liquidation of Europe's overseas empires is all but complete, the world is in travail, beset by problems of readjustment and groping for new relationships that may make possible the peace-

*William L. Langer, "Farewell to Empire," *Foreign Affairs*, Vol. 41, No. 1 (October 1962), pp. 115–30. Copyright by the Council on Foreign Relations, Inc., New York. Reprinted by permission.

ful and prosperous coexistence of more than a hundred states of widely differing characters and needs. The age-old expansion of Europe in terms of military power, settlement, trade, proselytism, territorial rule and, finally, social dominance has come to an abrupt end. Thoughtful people, particularly in the Western world, are bound to reflect on this epochal upheaval, and to realize that one of the very great revolutions in human affairs has taken place. They must be impressed, not to say awed, by the thought that the political and social structure of our planet has undergone such fundamental alterations at the very time when science and technology are opening to view the vast possibilities as well as the dangers of the space age.

Historians and political scientists have for some time been grappling with the problems of expansion, without, however, having come to anything like generally accepted conclusions. Political controversy has seriously beclouded the meaning of the terms *imperialism* and *colonialism,* while scholarly analysis has revealed ever more clearly how loose and unmanageable these words and concepts really are. I take it that, in its broadest sense, imperialism means domination or control of one nation or people over another, recognizing that there may be many forms and degrees of control. But there is probably no hope of ever constructing a generalized theory of imperialism. Indeed, the most violent differences of opinion persist with regard to the causes and character even of modern European expansion, with little if any prospect of reconciling the Communist doctrine, so positively formulated by Lenin, with the manifold theories advanced by Western "bourgeois" writers.

However, among non-Communist critics and students substantial progress is being made in the evaluation of European imperialism. The initial phase of expansion, consequent to the great discoveries of the fifteenth and sixteenth centuries, involved large-scale settlement of Europeans in sparsely populated areas of the world. This in turn led to the gradual conquest of vast territories, along with complete subjection and at least partial extermination of the natives. But this earlier stage of imperialism, while it certainly remade much of the globe in the European image, had relatively little bearing on recent and contemporary problems of expansion. For in the late eighteenth and early nineteenth centuries most of the American colonies of Britain, Spain and Portugal attained their complete independence of European rule. In the sequel Canada,

Australia, New Zealand and eventually South Africa became British dominions, independent of the mother country in all but name. Meanwhile Siberia, which was overrun and partially settled by Russians in the seventeenth century, became an integral part of the contiguous Tsarist state.

This process of settlement and territorial extension occasionally brought in its train the destruction of highly developed cultures like those of the Inca, Maya and Javanese. But in general it touched only primitive, thinly populated regions, which previously had been outside the main stream of history. Such was the case also with the trading posts and military establishments acquired in the East by the Portuguese, Dutch, British and French in the seventeenth and eighteenth centuries. Only with the military victories of the British over local potentates and the repeated extension of their territorial domination in India did modern imperialism, in the sense of the rule or control of one state or nation over an alien people or culture, become a reality. Even so, India remained a rather special case, an almost unique instance of a private company over a long period of time ruling a huge area of highly developed cultures and constantly expanding its territorial control even at times when the home government was opposed to any extension of its responsibilities. For the European powers had, by the early nineteenth century, become highly skeptical about overseas commitments. It is true that both the British and the French made substantial territorial acquisitions in these years, but they resulted largely from the efforts of local officials to safeguard existing establishments and further trade. Only in Russia, where the government engaged in systematic encroachment and eventually in the conquest of the Transcaucasian principalities, was there anything like purposeful expansionism, though on this side of the Atlantic the war against Mexico was certainly a comparable demonstration of imperial acquisitiveness.

Imperialism revived only in the period after 1870 when, however, it developed to such a degree that most of Africa was quickly partitioned among a few European powers and some form of domination or control was established over many Asian peoples. Concurrently Russia, operating against adjoining countries, imposed its rule upon most of Central Asia and, having earlier acquired the Maritime Province on the Pacific, inaugurated a policy of peaceful penetration of Manchuria and Korea.

To account for this phenomenal spread of European authority is certainly a fascinating and challenging assignment for the historian. Innumerable theories, both general and special, have been advanced in the search for an adequate explanation. They run the gamut from the hard-hitting, straightforward propaganda of Lenin's "Imperialism, the Highest Stage of Capitalism" to the highly sophisticated and daringly original speculation of Schumpeter's "Sociology of Imperialism." But the one conclusion to be safely drawn from all this ratiocination is that modern imperialism constituted a most complicated episode of recent history, that it was the expression of many and varied forces and motives, and that the economic explanation, so cogently argued by Hobson in his "Imperialism: A Study" (1902), and so fondly cherished by Lenin, is as inadequate as it is popular. Humanitarian, religious and psychological factors were clearly important, to say nothing of considerations of national power and pride. It should never be forgotten that the present condemnation and rejection of imperialism by the Western world is a very recent development. Prior to 1920, if not even later, European rule of overseas colonies was considered honorable and altruistic—definitely in the best interest of the "backward" peoples. It has been pointed out with complete justice that the campaign against the slave trade and the effort to propagate Christianity were among the prime motive forces behind modern expansion, and that the imperial powers as well as their agents were moved, with some exceptions, by a desire to play a beneficent role in the world, to fulfill a noble, national mission.

Recent monographic studies of various aspects of modern imperialism suggest also that certain elusive, not to say irrational, forces contributed to the dynamism of expansion. Schumpeter, and indeed both Kautsky and Hobson before him, gave emphasis to the atavistic feature of imperialism. That is to say, they saw it as a survival in modern society of an outworn, feudal-militaristic mentality, devoted to conquest for its own sake, without specific objective or limit. One might underline also the importance of basic human traits such as aggressiveness and acquisitiveness, along with the urge to dominate, as fundamental to any analysis of imperialism. To do so would leave open, however, many instances in which powerful states with dynamic populations showed no inclination to express these drives in terms of expansion and domination. The American people's rejection of imperialism almost as soon as it was tried, in the wake of the war with Spain, would be a case in point.

Yet it does seem that there was something feudal or at least aristocratic about imperialism, even in its modern phase. It was, in fact, frequently criticized on this score. Colonies, it was said, were desired by the ruling classes in order to provide for their "clamorous and needy dependents." They were, according to James Mill, "a vast system of outdoor relief for the upper classes," and, in the words of Richard Cobden, a "costly appendage of an aristocratic government."[1] And much later, in 1903, Henry Labouchere referred to imperialists as magpies: "They steal for the love of stealing." Certainly the men who made the decisions for expansion were, in England, peers and great landowners, and on the Continent aristocrats, notables and soldiers. Bismarck, than whom no statesman of modern times had a keener sense of the requirements of power politics, reckoned at all times with the dynamism of the traditional military castes. He encouraged Russian expansion in Central Asia on the theory that it was better to have the military engaged there than on the European front. In the same spirit he attempted to divert the attention of the French from the blue line of the Vosges by supporting their activities in North Africa. And a particularly clear demonstration of the operation of feudal-military forces is provided by the history of modern Japan. The Genyosha Society, which was the driving power behind Japan's expansion, represented primarily the samurai elements which had been eclipsed by the Restoration.[2]

It may be argued that the above theory is at least in part invalidated by the fact that imperialism enjoyed great popular acclaim. But actually this proves very little, for it was more true of England than of other countries, and in England, it will be conceded, the lower classes were traditionally interested in the doings of the aristocracy and readily applauded its achievements. Actually the common man, in England as elsewhere, knew little of the issues and policies involved in imperialism. Colonial affairs, like foreign affairs, remained the preserve of the ruling class. As for continental countries, it is perfectly clear that popular interest in and support for colonial enterprise were never widespread or sustained. Explorers, missionaries, publicists, professors and certain business interests were the prime movers in the cause of overseas undertakings.

With further reference to the economic interpretation of imperialism, I would say that recent studies of specific cases reinforce the proposition that business interests were much less important

[1] Klaus Knorr, "British Colonial Theories, 1570–1850." Toronto: University of Toronto Press, 1944, p. 356 ff.

[2] E. H. Norman, "The Genyosha: A Study in the Origins of Japanese Imperialism," *Pacific Affairs*, XVII, 1944, p. 261–284.

than considerations of national power and prestige, to say nothing of national security. A new analysis of the partition of Africa[3] contends convincingly that Britain, concerned by the disturbance of the European balance of power by the German victories of 1870–1871, was driven primarily by concern for its communications with India to assume control of Egypt, and that this move in turn had such repercussions on international relations as to precipitate the "scramble for Africa." It certainly becomes increasingly clear that much of modern imperialism reflected problems of power in Europe itself during a period when the alliance systems had produced a temporary deadlock.

The competition for markets and for sources of raw materials as well as the search for new fields for capital investment were much talked of in the heyday of imperialism and underlay the argumentation of a host of writers on economic imperialism. But it is well known now that in actual fact the colonies played a distinctly subordinate role in the foreign economic activities of the major imperial powers. These powers at all times remained each others' best customers. At the height of the colonial age, in the early twentieth century, less than a third of Britain's exports went to the dominions and colonies, and less than one-half of British foreign investment was in the Empire. The major European investments in this period were in the United States, Russia, the Ottoman Empire and Latin America, where there could hardly be any question of true imperial domination.

If in fact the European governments in the 1880s and 1890s plunged headlong into the scramble for colonies, they were evidently acting in panic. Confronted with the entirely novel problems arising from progressive industrialization, and alarmed by the depression that set in in 1873, as well as by the strong tendency on the Continent to abandon free trade in favor of protection, they sought to safeguard their overseas economic interests by acquiring actual control of as much territory as possible. They hoped thereby to ensure themselves against unknown eventualities. Failure to act seemed improvident and dangerous. I would call this "preclusive imperialism," and would describe it as obviously a concomitant of the onrushing industrial revolution. A misguided effort, this reaction to hypothetical dangers, as we can now recognize; but in the late

[3] Ronald Robinson and John Gallagher, "Africa and the Victorians." New York: St. Martin's, 1961.

nineteenth century it evidently was so compelling that most statesmen, even the skeptical Bismarck, were carried away by it.

III

The final accounting suggests that the colonies brought their masters but indifferent returns. It has been frequently argued that even though the European governments may have spent more on their overseas possessions—especially in terms of defense, police, administration and public health—than they ever received in return, private interests made huge profits through the ruthless exploitation of native labor and natural resources. Bookkeeping in these matters is extremely difficult, because it is impossible to isolate and allocate specific items of expense. The best recent studies indicate that the governments, and so the home countries, did in fact make large and continuing outlays, in many ways anticipating more recent policies of aid to underdeveloped nations. An admirable analysis of the finances of the Congo[4] arrives at the conclusion that that colony, unusually rich in raw materials such as ivory, rubber and copper, was indeed a source of considerable enrichment for Belgium as a country, but that between 1908 (when the Belgian government took over the colony from King Leopold II) and 1950 the Brussels government spent 260 million gold francs on the Congo in return for only 25 million francs in taxes and other income. In like manner an eminent French authority[5] has estimated that even in the period prior to 1914 the Paris government spent two billion gold francs on the French colonial empire.

In the large, the profits taken by private interests seem to have been anything but exorbitant—indeed, little above the average returns of home investments. Of course there were instances of huge profits made through forced labor and other forms of ruthless exploitation, as in the Congo of King Leopold, in German Southwest Africa and in British South Africa. No one would excuse or condone such practices, but again it is important to retain a proper sense of proportion. The mercantilist idea that colonies existed solely for the purpose of enriching the mother country persisted for

[4] Jean Stengers, "Combien le Congo a-t-il coûté à la Belgique?" Brussels: Académie royale des sciences coloniales, 1957.

[5] Henri Brunschwig, "Mythes et réalités de l'impérialisme colonial français." Paris: A. Colin, 1960.

a long time. Leopold II of Belgium, for example, was an ardent admirer of the Dutch "culture system" as enforced in the East Indies, and was interested in the Congo exclusively for the revenue it might bring. As for the treatment of the natives, it may be doubted whether it was any worse than that meted out to Russian serfs and American Negro slaves until past the middle of the nineteenth century. Sad though it may be, the fact is that the human race became sensitive to suffering only at a very late date. When one considers the heartless attitude taken toward the miseries of the early factory workers or even toward the Irish peasantry in the days before the great famine, one is bound to marvel at the callousness of human nature, obviously not restricted to the brutalities of Hitler's Nazi régime.

Students of the problem have of late devoted much attention to the advantages which accrued to the colonies from European rule. They included defense and public order, suppression of tribal warfare and restriction of patriarchal tyranny, the establishment of adequate administration and justice, the furtherance of public health and, in many cases, substantial contributions to the development of communications.

No doubt the price paid by the colonies was a high one: the subversion of traditional institutions and social forms, not necessarily intentionally, but none the less effectively. To some Europeans as well as to many natives this has been a matter of real regret. But if in fact European expansion was the ineluctable expression of a dynamism generated by the economic and social revolution of the nineteenth century, then it follows that the progressive destruction of static, traditional societies was inevitable under the impact of outside forces. Thinkers and statesmen of the Ottoman Empire, of Japan and of China recognized this feature of the situation at an early date. They saw that the only hope of survival lay in the adoption of Western technology and institutions, however distasteful they might be. The remaking of the world in the Western image began long before the tide of imperialism came to the flood.

IV

The South African War (1899–1902) not only drained imperialism of much of its emotional content but also induced the British and other imperial governments to reconsider their relations to the colonies. Far more thought was given to the welfare of the colonial peoples, and far more effort was made in the direction of development and improvement. The more liberal régimes encouraged the education of the natives and their participation at the lower levels of the administration. Thereby they fostered the growth of the native élite, members of which presently began to apply the lessons learned from the West to the task of getting rid of Western control. The imperial powers, having themselves inculcated the ideas of equality, self-determination, independence and nationalism, thereby prepared the way for the destruction of their own dominion. For it would hardly seem possible, in historical retrospect, that Western rule could have long withstood the weight of the arguments drawn from its own intellectual armory. Imperialism was bound to lose its moral basis as soon as the principle of equality was recognized and the notions of responsibility and trusteeship were generally accepted. The reaction of British liberals, radicals and socialists to the war in South Africa was in itself irrefutable proof of the incompatibility of democracy and imperialism. Without doubt the anti-colonialist movement that developed in Europe and in the United States following the war with Spain contributed heavily to the growth of nationalism in various colonies during the early twentieth century. So also did the defeat of the Russians by Japan in 1904–1905, for that defeat broke the spell of European superiority and invincibility.

The First World War then set the stage for the actual breakdown of imperialism. The fratricidal conflict within the European master race deflated whatever prestige the ruling nations may still have had, while the employment of hundreds of thousands of colonial troops and laborers in the great war opened the eyes of multitudes of natives to conditions in the more advanced countries of the world. It is generally recognized that in 1919, while the victorious powers were busily applying the principle of self-determination to European peoples and as consistently ignoring it as regards the colonial peoples, imperialism had already received the mortal blow. The subsequent inter-war period then witnessed the rapid development of nationalist movements in many additional areas, despite the drastic measures of repression employed by some of the imperial governments. It took only the Second World War, fought as it was in many of the most remote places of the world, to loose the impounded flood-waters of colonial nationalism. The European nations were now so weakened and discredited that they could no longer offer effective resistance. Those which, like France, attempted to hold their possessions found themselves involved in long and costly wars, ending invariably in colonial triumph. In less than 20 years, millions of subject peoples attained their independence and more than 50 new states appeared on the international scene.

V

Ever since its advent to power in Russia, the Soviet Government has proclaimed the right of self-determination and has given all possible encouragement and support to the national movements aimed at liberation of the European overseas colonies from imperial rule. Soviet propaganda has to a large extent succeeded in restricting the definition of "imperialism" and "colonialism" to these overseas territories and in fostering the idea that Russia, having no such colonies, has had no part in imperial domination. Actually, it is impossible to draw a valid distinction between the expansion of Russia and that of other European states. The conquest of Central Asia was basically equivalent to the extension of British power in India. It began with trade interests, followed by conquest and annexation for reasons for security and prestige. And at the end of the nineteenth century Russian penetration of Manchuria and Korea was an integral part of the European effort to "partition" the Celestial Empire. Eminent Russian historians like Kliuchevski and Miliukov were just as bitterly critical of Russian expansion as were the anti-colonialists of the West with reference to the overseas empires.

The Russian-Japanese War put an early end to Tsarist aspirations in China, while the First World War, by precipitating the revolution in Russia, brought on a premature struggle for independence or autonomy on the part of almost all the subject peoples of the old empire. In this extremity Lenin and Stalin proclaimed the most conciliatory policy, even going so far as to recognize the right of any people to cast off all ties to Russia. It soon turned out, however, that these moves were purely tactical. Self-determination was to be restricted to the "workers" of the subject nations, which were warned by Stalin that if they seceded, they would surely fall victim to world imperialism. It was inconceivable, he added, that these peoples should abandon the Soviet Union, which was so dependent on them for food and raw materials. They clearly had an important contribution to make to the victory of socialism. In order to forestall "treason" on their part, the Soviet Government proceeded to suppress liberation movements, by force if necessary, carrying on a protracted war against even the avowedly Communist leaders of the various Turkic peoples.

For geographical reasons it is much easier for Soviet Russia to hold adjacent peoples in subjection than it was for countries like Britain and France to maintain their hold on distant overseas possessions. For a time following Hitler's attack in 1941, Soviet rule was, nevertheless, again seriously jeopardized. In revenge, the Kremlin in its hour of victory meted out the most ferocious treatment to the disaffected peoples and furthermore set up on its western borders a system of satellites reminiscent of the client system through which the great Napoleon controlled so much of the Continent. Whether for ideological or for security reasons, the Soviet Government now exercises effective control over adjoining states all the way from Finland in the north to Bulgaria in the south. To safeguard that control it will, if necessary, resort to military force, as was demonstrated so clearly in the case of Hungary.

In short, the Soviet Government has taken advantage of its contiguity to hold in subjection not only the ancient states of Eastern Europe, but also Armenians, Georgians and other Caucasian peoples, as well as some millions of Turkic peoples in Central Asia. Under the old régime, spasmodic attempts were made at Russification and at forced conversion to orthodoxy. In Central Asia much of the best land was appropriated by the conquerors, while the natives were subjected to heavy taxation. On the other hand, the nomadic tribes were left largely to themselves and the well-developed khanates of Khiva and Bokhara enjoyed a large measure of autonomy. The Soviet Government, especially in Stalin's time, was much more repressive. The status of the subject nationalities as federated republics was altogether misleading, for all important political and economic posts were held by Russians or by carefully selected native Communists. Besides, the economic life of these puppet republics was regulated entirely by the needs of the Kremlin. For a time the Soviet Government carried on propaganda directed even at the language, religion and culture of the subject peoples.

In some respects this policy is still in effect. In any event, the subject nationalities have been deprived of all hope of freedom. Their leaders disappear before they can become dangerous. Unobtrusively, Russians are being settled among the native populations, so that by now some six or seven million Europeans are established in Central Asia. In Kazakhstan it has been reported that fully half of the population is now European. Furthermore, the Russian language is an obligatory subject in all schools and a Cyrillic-type alphabet has been introduced for the Turkic languages. While there is no concerted attack on non-Russian cultures, it has been made abundantly clear that the chances of success in life depend largely on identification with Russianism as well as with Communism.

In view of the realities of Russian imperialism, it is surprising that the Soviets have been so successful in their efforts at concealment and have managed so well to exploit the issue of "colonialism" to the detriment of the West. It is likely, however, that the effectiveness of their propaganda has already passed its peak. After all, the world cannot ignore the fact that the overseas empires have now been largely liquidated. Besides, the experience of some of the new states with Soviet guidance and aid has been disillusioning and disquieting. Already at the Bandung Conference (1955) there were round denunciations of Soviet imperialism, accompanied by pointed warnings against Communist designs on the freedom of colonial peoples.

It is unrealistic to suppose that either the European satellites or the subject nationalities of the Soviet Union can obtain their independence so long as the Soviet Government remains what it is and its objectives are unaltered. How long that may be is certainly a debatable question. The Soviet régime, having itself become outspokenly nationalistic and having systematically supported nationalist movements in the overseas colonies, can no longer condemn nationalism among its own subjects as a reactionary deviation. Furthermore, Soviet society is steadily evolving along lines familiar to us from Western history. It is at least not inconceivable that its transformation under the impact of industrialization may become accelerated and that, with the growth of representative institutions and the development of a more democratic mentality, there will come a change of attitude toward the imperialism that is now so basic to Russian policy. At the same time the economic evolution of the satellites and subject nationalities is speeding their westernization and strengthening forces which in the long run the Kremlin may find it difficult to hold in check.

The Soviet Government, with its prodigious military and economic power, can for the present certainly hold in subjection the adjacent nationalities of Europe and Asia. It may, indeed, succeed in exploiting the nationalist theme to the point of luring some of the newly liberated peoples into the Communist camp and thereby bending the anti-colonialist sentiment of the entire world to the purposes of the world revolution. But the subjection of weaker peoples by the stronger runs counter to the democratic sentiments characteristic of modern industrial societies. There may be serious lapses, such as the Nazi interlude in Germany. But the example of Western nations suggests that industrial populations are basically peace-loving and definitely averse to the subjugation and exploitation of other peoples. In the later nineteenth century the imperial aspirations of the French Government met their strongest obstacle in the opposition of democratic and socialist elements. It is most unlikely, therefore, that the Soviet Union, simply by denying its imperialism, will be able, in the long term, to shield itself from the forces inherent in modern society.

In this context, some reference to the forces of Chinese Communist expansion and indeed to the entire problem of world Communist domination is perhaps unavoidable. Communist China's imperialist aspirations permit of no doubt. They appear, however, to derive from traditional notions of universal or at least Asian empire as well as from more immediate considerations of national security or ideological zeal. The Chinese thus interpret their efforts to establish control over Korea, Taiwan and the countries of southeastern Asia as a gathering-in of the *membra disjecta* of the millenary Celestial Empire, less as the conquest of new than the recovery of ancient domains.

As for the world revolution and the new world of Communism, it would seem that whatever validity this program might have would depend on its ideological content. If neither Napoleon nor Hitler could dominate Europe, it can hardly be supposed that Soviet leaders—on the whole a sober and realistic lot—imagine it possible for the U.S.S.R. to control the entire world. The developments of recent years must suggest to them the difficulties of managing even the present Communist domain. No doubt the Soviet Union would feel more secure in an all-Communist world, just as the United States would in a world made safe for democracy. But as the Soviet Union grows in strength this consideration is bound to lose some of its importance. It is quite possible, in fact, that Marxism, already so largely overtaken by events, may in time lose not only its revolutionary fervor but also its incentive to world domination.

VI

The end of European political domination in Africa and Asia does not alter the fact that the stamp of European ideas and institutions has now been put upon the whole world. Even the Soviet and Chinese Communists rely for their power upon Western technology and to a considerable extent upon the imitation of Western institutions. As for the newly liberated peoples, they have set themselves the same course. No doubt there are in all of them conservative and even reactionary elements which would like, if possible, to return to their traditional society. But in most countries the ruling group consists of men educated in Western schools and convinced that the future lies with the adoption of Western techniques. They have no intention whatever of reverting to pre-imperialist days. On the contrary, they want more and more of what imperialism brought them: great productivity and a higher standard of living through industrialization; social improvements of every kind, and especially more and better education as a basis for democracy.

Their problems are many, and by no means exclusively economic. The transformation of assorted tribes into modern nations is in itself a stupendous undertaking. Besides, these new states are for the most part too weak militarily as well as economically to stand on their own feet. Their political independence therefore does not by any means imply complete independence. Because of their almost unlimited need for economic and technical assistance they are certainly in some danger of falling again under the influence if not the control of powerful advanced nations, be they Western or Communist.

They can find some insurance against such threats in the antagonism between the free world and Communism, which enables their leaders to play off one side against the other. They are bound to derive some protection also from the strong anti-imperialism that has come to pervade the entire free world and will probably become ever more deeply enrooted. Indeed, the new underdeveloped states will be fortunate if Western disillusionment with empire does not reach the point where it will obstruct seriously the aid programs without which many of the former colonies cannot hope to survive. Happily some progress is being made in the coördination of the economic efforts of the free world through the Organization for

Economic Coöperation and Development. The Western world has so much greater an aid potential that it should be possible, with even a modicum of statesmanship, to maintain the connection of Europe and the United States with the erstwhile colonial world.

It is truly noteworthy that, for all the heat and rancor generated by anti-colonialism, so many liberated colonies have chosen to remain members of the British Commonwealth or the French Community. The enthusiastic reception accorded to Queen Elizabeth in India and Ghana provided occasions for the expression, on the part of their governments, of appreciation for the important contribution made by imperial rule. No doubt considerations of security have a significant bearing on the attitude of the former colonies, but it would seem that in the world at large the old—shall we say atavistic, aristocratic?—notion of domination and exploitation has given way to the concept of association and collaboration. Even in the Communist world it has become fashionable to speak of the "Socialist Commonwealth."

VII

In bidding farewell to empire we cannot and must not suppose that human nature has undergone a sudden, radical change—that basic aggressive urges will disappear completely and that sweetness and light will soon prevail. The argument of this essay has been that fundamental drives lay behind imperial expansion; that European dynamism, combined with technological superiority, enabled the European nations to settle the largely unoccupied continents and to found European communities all over the globe. It permitted them also, in the sequel, to impose their rule over many peoples of old and highly developed, as well as of primitive, cultures. So marked was Europe's material power and so alluring its political and economic institutions that within a comparatively short span of time the stamp of European civilization was put upon the whole earth.

Europe's political domination is gone. Its cultural influence remains, and there is no likelihood that it will be supplanted in the foreseeable future. The new states, while still vociferously denouncing "colonialism," may genuinely fear that cultural influence will eventually change to economic control and so to some new form of political domination. The Soviet Government is already accusing the Common Market of being a new device by which the Western powers will attempt to keep the colonial world in an economically subordinate and undeveloped state. In this connection the importance of the erstwhile colonial areas as sources of raw materials for the industrialized nations remains a prominent consideration. But imperialism provided no real solution for this problem, while for the future more, it would seem, is to be hoped from coöperation than from domination and exploitation.

It is highly unlikely that the modern world will revert to the imperialism of the past. History has shown that the nameless fears which in the late nineteenth century led to the most violent outburst of expansionism were largely unwarranted. The Scandinavian states and Germany since Versailles have demonstrated that economic prosperity and social well-being are not dependent on the exploitation of other peoples, while better distribution of wealth in the advanced countries has reduced if not obviated whatever need there may have been to seek abroad a safety-valve for the pressures building up at home. Even in the field of defense, the old need for overseas bases or for the control of adjacent territories is rapidly being outrun.

It is often said that human nature does not change, but it is none the less true that it does undergo changes of attitude. With reference to imperialism it is certainly true that there has been over the past century a marked alteration of mood, reflecting greater sensitivity to human suffering and a greater readiness to assume responsibility for the weak and helpless. In our day, anti-imperialism runs as strong in the West as did imperialism a couple of generations ago. Domination and exploitation of weaker peoples by the stronger, which seemed altogether natural in the past, is now felt to be incompatible with the principles of freedom, equality and self-determination so generally accepted in modern societies. Imperialism has been on its way out since the beginning of the century and particularly since the First World War. Writing on imperialism in this very journal in the days when Mussolini was embarking on the conquest of Ethiopia, I ventured to disparage his undertaking and to describe him as being behind the times. The world, I opined, had outgrown the mentality of imperialism. I could not, of course, foresee that the edifice of colonialism would collapse so suddenly and so completely after the Second World War, but I suggested that if the tide of native resistance continued to rise, the abandonment of the colonies would soon become inevitable. To make this forecast did not require any particular prescience, but only recognition of the forces at work in modern society. At the present day the Soviet Union may still pose as the doughty opponent of a system that is already done for, but by maintaining its own imperial sway it is appearing more and more in the role of champion of an outworn and discredited system.

Imperialism's one great achievement was to open up all parts of the world and to set all humanity on the high road to eventual association and collaboration. In the process much has been lost of cultural value, but much also has been gained in the suppression of abuses, in the alleviation of suffering, and above all in the raising of the standard of living. The seamy sides of industrial society are familiar to us all, but it should never be overlooked that the machine age for the first time in history provided the common man with more than the requirements of the barest subsistence. This in itself has given human life a new dimension. It was perhaps the greatest of Europe's contributions to the world. Without the imperialist interlude it is difficult to see how the static, secluded, backward peoples of the globe could possibly have come to share in it. So much at least seems certain: without the period of European rule none of these peoples or states, not even India, would today be embarked on the course leading to a better and richer life.

WAR

IX

THE CLASSIC DEFINITION OF WAR IS THAT OF Carl von Clausewitz. It is most appropriate therefore that we begin this chapter with an excerpt from his principal work, *On War*. Von Clausewitz (1780–1831) wrote it during the 1820's, and it was published after his death. Although the book is nearly a century and a half old, his forceful observations on war and particularly on the relationship between war and politics are still very relevant today.

The second selection, on guerilla war, is an address by W. W. Rostow at the graduation ceremonies of the U.S. Army Special Warfare School in Fort Bragg, N.C., on June 28, 1961. Rostow, Chairman of the Policy Planning Council of the State Department, is a former Professor of Economic History at the Massachusetts Institute of Technology. He has written *The United*

States in the World Arena, The Stages of Economic Growth, and many other works.

The third selection is also a commencement address. It was delivered by Robert S. McNamara, Secretary of Defense in the Kennedy and Johnson Administrations, at the University of Michigan in Ann Arbor on June 16, 1962. The speech achieved instant fame as an incisive analysis of nuclear strategy for the NATO alliance.

What is the nature of total war in the nuclear era? General Douglas MacArthur, who needs no introduction as a military expert, reaches some provocative conclusions on this subject. He delivered his speech at a civic banquet sponsored by the Los Angeles County Council of the American Legion on the dedication of a monument to General MacArthur on January 26, 1955.

26. *WHAT IS WAR?* / CARL VON CLAUSEWITZ*

Definition

We do not want to give a ponderous and tedious definition of war, but concentrate on its basic element: the duel. War is nothing but an expanded duel. To conceive as a unit the countless number of separate duels of which a war consists, we should envisage two wrestlers. By means of physical force each attempts to bring his opponent completely under his control. His aim is to overpower his opponent and thus render him incapable of any further resistance.

War is, therefore, an act of violence to compel our opponent to do our will.

Violence arms itself with the inventions of art and science in order to contend against violence. The restrictions imposed by international law and custom are insignificant and hardly worth mentioning, and do not really weaken its power. Violence, that is to say, physical force (for there is no moral force apart from the conception of state and law), is therefore the *means;* the *end* is to

* Carl von Clausewitz, *Vom Kriege* (Potsdam, 1832), Book I, Chap. 1, par. 2, 3, 11, 23, 24. Translated by Eva Tamm Lijphart and Arend Lijphart.

impose our will on the enemy. In order to ensure the achievement of this goal, we must render the enemy defenseless. This is the real purpose of the war act. It takes the place of the final object, and to a certain extent pushes it aside as something not belonging to war itself.

Utmost Use of Violence

A humanitarian might easily imagine the existence of a skillful way of disarming or defeating the enemy without causing too many wounds, and that this is the proper function of the art of warfare. No matter how good this may appear, it is an error and must be extirpated. Because war is such a dangerous enterprise, the mistakes arising from kindness and compassion are exactly the worst. Because the utmost use of physical force in no way excludes the cooperation of the intelligence, it follows that he who uses this force ruthlessly and without regard to the bloodshed involved must gain the upper hand if his opponent does not do the same. Thereby the former forces the latter's hand, and they push each other to extremes only limited by each side's counter-acting power.

That is how one must look at the matter, and it is to no avail and completely wrong to disregard its real nature because of one's aversion to its horrors. . . .

We therefore repeat our statement: War is an act of violence and there are no limits to its use. Each party forces its opponent's hand, and a reciprocal action arises which logically must lead to an extreme. . . .

The Political Object of War

Now *the political object of war* again enters the picture. . . . The smaller the sacrifice we demand from our opponent, the smaller may we expect his efforts to be to resist us. But the smaller his efforts, the smaller need our own be. Furthermore, the smaller our political object is, the less will be the value we attach to it and the sooner shall we be ready to give it up altogether. Likewise, the smaller will our efforts be.

Hence, the political object, as the original motive for war, will be the standard both for the goal of the military action and for the efforts required. However, it will not be an absolute standard but a standard relative to the two belligerent states, since we are dealing with realities rather than abstract concepts. One and the same political object may produce entirely different effects on different peoples or even on the same people at different times. We can only use the political object as the standard, therefore, if we take into consideration its influence on the masses. Hence the nature of these masses must also be considered. It is easy to realize that the result varies according to the strengthening or weakening of the action by the feelings of the masses. In two peoples and states such tensions and such animosities may exist that a very minor motive for war may produce an effect completely out of proportion—a veritable explosion.

This applies to the efforts that the political object calls forth in both states, and to the aim it prescribes for the military action. At times it may itself become this aim, for instance, in the case of the conquest of a certain province. At other times the political object itself will not be suited to provide the aim for military action. In that case, an equivalent aim must be found to substitute for it in the conclusion of peace. But here also due attention to the special characteristics of the states involved is always assumed. There are circumstances where the equivalent must be much greater than the political object if this object is to be attained. The more indifferent the attitude of the masses and the less the tensions stemming from other causes in both states and their relations, the more will the political object be the dominant and decisive standard. There are also cases where the political object almost alone will be the decisive factor.

Now if the aim of the military action is an equivalent of the political object, they will usually decrease together, especially the more the political object dominates. That is why, without self-contradiction, there may be wars of all degrees of importance and energy, ranging from a war of annihilation to mere armed observation. . . .

War Is a Serious Means to a Serious End

. . . war is no pastime, no mere delight in daring and winning, no work of a free enthusiasm. It is a serious means to a serious end. All the glamor of fortune, passion, courage, imagination, and enthusiasm, are only the special characteristics of this means.

The war of a community—of whole nations and particularly of civilized nations—always stems from a political condition and is called forth by a political motive. Hence it is a political act. If it were a complete, unrestrained, and absolute expression of violence, as we had to deduce from its mere conception, it would, from the moment it is called forth by policy, take the place of policy as a quite independent factor, push it aside and only follow its own laws, just as an exploding mine can take no other direction than the one originally prepared for it. This is how the matter has really been viewed up to now, whenever a lack of harmony between policy and the conduct of war has led to such theoretical distinctions. But this is not so, and this idea is basically false. War in the real world, as we have seen, is not of such an extreme nature that its tension is released in a single explosion; it is the operation of powers which do not develop exactly in the same way and to the same extent, but which sometimes expand enough to overcome the resistance caused by inertia and friction, while at another moment they are too weak to have any effect. Hence, war is, to a certain extent, a pulsation of violence more or less vehement, and consequently releasing its tensions and exhausting its powers more or less quickly. In other words, it leads more or less quickly to its goal, but it always lasts long enough to be influenced in this or that direction. In short, it remains subject to a guiding intelligence. Now if we keep in mind that war arises from a political object, then it follows that this first motive which called it into being also remains the first and foremost consideration in its conduct. But the political object is no despotic lawgiver; it must adapt itself to the nature of the means which may even change it completely, but it always has to be considered first. Policy, therefore, will permeate the entire military action, and exert a continuous influence on it to the extent its inherent explosive powers will permit.

War Is a Mere Continuation of Policy by Other Means

So we see that war is not merely a political act but a real political instrument, a continuation of political relations, a carrying out of the same by other means. What remains peculiar to war is only the peculiar nature of its means. The art of war in general and the commander in each particular case can demand that the directions and intentions of policy do not conflict with these means, and this claim is certainly no minor one. But no matter how strongly this may affect the political intentions in isolated cases, it always has to be regarded as only a modification of the intentions. For the political aim is the end, while war is the means, and the means can never be considered apart from the end.

27. *GUERRILLA WARFARE IN THE UNDERDEVELOPED AREAS* / W. W. ROSTOW*

. . . What is happening throughout Latin America, Africa, the Middle East, and Asia is this: Old societies are changing their ways in order to create and maintain a national personality on the world scene and to bring to their peoples the benefits modern technology can offer. This process is truly revolutionary. It touches every aspect of the traditional life–economic, social, and political. The introduction of modern technology brings about not merely new methods of production but a new style of family life, new links between the villages and the cities, the beginnings of national politics, and a new relationship to the world outside.

Like all revolutions, the revolution of modernization is disturbing. Individual men are torn between the commitment to the old familiar way of life and the attractions of a modern way of life. The power of old social groups–notably the landlord, who usually dominates the traditional society–is reduced. Power moves toward those who can command the tools of modern technology, including modern weapons. Men and women in the villages and the cities, feeling that the old ways of life are shaken and that new possibilities are open to them, express old resentments and new hopes.

This is the grand arena of revolutionary change which the Communists are exploiting with great energy. They believe that their techniques of organization–based on small disciplined cadres of conspirators–are ideally suited to grasp and to hold power in these turbulent settings. They believe that the weak transitional governments that one is likely to find during this modernization process are highly vulnerable to subversion and to guerrilla warfare. And whatever Communist doctrines of historical inevitability may

* W. W. Rostow, "Guerrilla Warfare in the Underdeveloped Areas," *The Department of State Bulletin,* Vol. 45, No. 1154 (August 7, 1961), pp. 234–38.

be, Communists know that their time to seize power in the underdeveloped areas is limited. They know that, as momentum takes hold in an underdeveloped area—and the fundamental social problems inherited from the traditional society are solved—their chances to seize power decline.

It is on the weakest nations, facing their most difficult transitional moments, that the Communists concentrate their attention. They are the scavengers of the modernization process. They believe that the techniques of political centralization under dictatorial control—and the projected image of Soviet and Chinese Communist economic progress—will persuade hesitant men, faced by great transitional problems, that the Communist model should be adopted for modernization, even at the cost of surrendering human liberty. They believe that they can exploit effectively the resentments built up in many of these areas against colonial rule and that they can associate themselves effectively with the desire of the emerging nations for independence, for status on the world scene, and for material progress.

This is a formidable program; for the history of this century teaches us that communism is not the longrun wave of the future toward which societies are naturally drawn. On the contrary. But it is one particular form of modern society to which a nation may fall prey during the transitional process. Communism is best understood as a disease of the transition to modernization.

America's Purpose and Strategy

What is our reply to this historical conception and strategy? What is the American purpose and the American strategy? We, too, recognize that a revolutionary process is under way. We are dedicated to the proposition that this revolutionary process of modernization shall be permitted to go forward in independence, with increasing degrees of human freedom. We seek two results: first, that truly independent nations shall emerge on the world scene; and, second, that each nation will be permitted to fashion, out of its own culture and its own ambitions, the kind of modern society it wants. The same religious and philosophical beliefs which decree that we respect the uniqueness of each individual make it natural that we repect the uniqueness of each national society. Moreover, we Americans are confident that, if the independence of this process can be maintained over the coming years and decades, these societies will choose their own version of what we would recognize as a democratic, open society.

These are our commitments of policy and of faith. The United States has no interest in political satellites. Where we have military pacts we have them because governments feel directly endangered by outside military action and we are prepared to help protect their independence against such military action. But, to use Mao Tse-tung's famous phrase, we do not seek nations which "lean to one side." We seek nations which shall stand up straight. And we do so for a reason: because we are deeply confident that nations which stand up straight will protect their independence and move in their own ways and in their own time toward human freedom and political democracy.

Protecting Independence of Revolutionary Process

Thus our central task in the underdeveloped areas, as we see it, is to protect the independence of the revolutionary process now going forward. This is our mission, and it is our ultimate strength. For this is not—and cannot be—the mission of communism. And in time, through the fog of propaganda and the honest confusions of men caught up in the business of making new nations, this fundamental difference will become increasingly clear in the southern half of the world. The American interest will be served if our children live in an environment of strong, assertive, independent nations, capable, because they are strong, of assuming collective responsibility for the peace.

The diffusion of power is the basis for freedom within our own society, and we have no reason to fear it on the world scene. But this outcome would be a defeat for communism—not for Russia as a national state, but for communism. Despite all the Communist talk of aiding movements of national independence, they are driven in the end, by the nature of their system, to violate the independence of nations. Despite all the Communist talk of American imperialism, we are committed, by the nature of our system, to support the cause of national independence. And the truth will out.

The victory we seek will see no ticker tape parades down Broadway, no climactic battles, nor great American celebrations of victory. It is a victory which will take many years and decades of hard work and dedication—by many peoples—to bring about. This will not be a victory of the United States over the Soviet Union. It will not be a victory of capitalism over socialism. It will be a victory of men and nations which aim to stand up straight, over the forces which wish to entrap and to exploit their revolutionary aspirations of modernization. What this victory involves, in the end, is the assertion by nations of their right to independence and by men and women of their right to freedom as they understand it. And we deeply believe this victory will come—on both sides of the Iron Curtain.

If Americans do not seek victory in the usual sense, what do we seek? What is the national interest of the United States? Why do we Americans expend our treasure and assume the risks of modern war in this global struggle? For Americans the reward of victory will be, simply, this: It will permit American society to continue to develop along the old humane lines which go back to our birth as a nation—and which reach deeper into history than that—back to the Mediterranean roots of Western life. We are struggling to maintain an environment on the world scene which will permit our open society to survive and to flourish.

U.S. Responsibilities

To make this vision come true places a great burden on the United States at this phase of history. The preservation of independence has many dimensions.

The United States has the primary responsibility for deterring the use of nuclear weapons in the pursuit of Communist ambitions. The United States has a major responsibility to deter the kind of overt aggression with conventional forces which was launched in June 1950 in Korea.

The United States has the primary responsibility for assisting the economies of those hard-pressed states on the periphery of the Communist bloc, which are under acute military or quasi-military pressure which they cannot bear from their own resources; for example, south Korea, Viet-Nam, Taiwan, Pakistan, Iran. The United States has a special responsibility of leadership in bringing not merely its own resources but the resources of all the free world to bear in aiding the longrun development of those nations which are serious about modernizing their economy and their social life.

And, as President Kennedy has made clear, he regards no program of his administration as more important than his program for long-term economic development, dramatized, for example, by the Alliance for Progress in Latin America. Independence cannot be maintained by military measures alone. Modern societies must be built, and we are prepared to help build them.

Finally, the United States has a role to play—symbolized by your presence here and by mine—in learning to deter guerrilla warfare, if possible, and to deal with it, if necessary.

Local and International Responsibilities

I do not need to tell you that the primary responsibility for dealing with guerrilla warfare in the underdeveloped areas cannot be American. There are many ways in which we can help—and we are searching our minds and our imaginations to learn better how to help; but a guerrilla war must be fought primarily by those on the spot. This is so for a quite particular reason. A guerrilla war is an intimate affair, fought not merely with weapons but fought in the minds of the men who live in the villages and in the hills, fought by the spirit and policy of those who run the local government. An outsider cannot, by himself, win a guerrilla war. He can help create conditions in which it can be won, and he can directly assist those prepared to fight for their independence. We are determined to help destroy this international disease; that is, guerrilla war designed, initiated, supplied, and led from outside an independent nation.

Although as leader of the free world the United States has special responsibilities which it accepts in this common venture of deterrence, it is important that the whole international community begin to accept its responsibility for dealing with this form of aggression. It is important that the world become clear in mind, for example, that the operation run from Hanoi against Viet-Nam is as clear a form of aggression as the violation of the 38th parallel by the north Korean armies in June 1950.

In my conversations with representatives of foreign governments, I am sometimes lectured that this or that government within the free world is not popular; they tell me that guerrilla warfare cannot be won unless the peoples are dissatisfied. These are, at best, half-truths. The truth is that guerrilla warfare, mounted from external bases—with rights of sanctuary—is a terrible burden to carry for any government in a society making its way toward modernization. As you know, it takes somewhere between 10 and 20 soldiers to control 1 guerrilla in an organized operation. Moreover, the guerrilla force has this advantage: its task is merely to destroy, while the government must build and protect what it is building. A guerrilla war mounted from outside a transitional nation is a crude act of international vandalism. There will be no peace in the world if the international community accepts the outcome of a guerrilla war, mounted from outside a nation, as tantamount to a free election.

The sending of men and arms across international boundaries and the direction of guerrilla war from outside a sovereign nation is aggression; and this is a fact which the whole international community must confront and whose consequent responsibilities it must accept. Without such international action those against whom aggression is mounted will be driven inevitably to seek out and engage the ultimate source of the aggression they confront. . . .

Learning To Prevent Guerrilla Wars

In facing the problem of guerrilla war, I have one observation to make as a historian. It is now fashionable—and I daresay for you it was compulsory—to read the learned works of Mao Tse-tung and Che Guevara on guerrilla warfare. This is, indeed, proper. One should read with care and without passion into the minds of one's enemies. But it is historically inaccurate and psychologically dangerous to think that these men created the strategy and tactics of guerrilla war to which we are now responding. Guerrilla warfare is not a form of military and psychological magic created by the Communists. There is no rule or parable in the Communist texts which was not known at an earlier time in history. The operation of Marion's men in relation to the Battle of Cowpens in the American Revolution was, for example, governed by rules which Mao merely echoes. Che Guevara knows nothing of this business that T. E. Lawrence did not know or was not practiced, for example, in the Peninsular Campaign during the Napoleonic wars, a century earlier. The orchestration of professional troops, militia, and guerrilla fighters is an old game whose rules can be studied and learned.

My point is that we are up against a form of warfare which is powerful and effective only when we do not put our minds clearly to work on how to deal with it. I, for one, believe that with purposeful efforts most nations which might now be susceptible to guerrilla warfare could handle their border areas in ways which would make them very unattractive to the initiation of this ugly game. We can learn to prevent the emergence of the famous sea in which Mao Tse-tung taught his men to swim. This requires, of course, not merely a proper military program of deterrence but programs of village development, communications, and indoctrination. The best way to fight a guerrilla war is to prevent it from happening. And this can be done.

Similarly, I am confident that we can deal with the kind of operation now under way in Viet-Nam. It is an extremely dangerous operation, and it could overwhelm Viet-Nam if the Vietnamese —aided by the free world—do not deal with it. But it is an unsubtle operation, by the book, based more on murder than on political or psychological appeal.

When Communists speak of wars of national liberation and of their support for "progressive forces," I think of the systematic program of assassination now going forward in which the principal victims are the health, agriculture, and education officers in the Viet-Nam villages. The Viet Cong are not trying to persuade the peasants of Viet-Nam that communism is good; they are trying to persuade them that their lives are insecure unless they cooperate with them. With resolution and confidence on all sides and with the assumption of international responsibility for the frontier problem, I believe we are going to bring this threat to the independence of Viet-Nam under control.

My view is, then, that we confront in guerrilla warfare in the underdeveloped areas a systematic attempt by the Communists to impose a serious disease on those societies attempting the transition to modernization. This attempt is a present danger in southeast Asia. It could quickly become a major danger in Africa and Latin America. I salute in particular those among you whose duty it is—along with others—to prevent that disease, if possible, and to eliminate it where it is imposed.

As I understand the course you are now completing, it is designed to impress on you this truth: You are not merely soldiers in the old sense. Your job is not merely to accept the risks of war and to master its skills. Your job is to work with understanding with your fellow citizens in the whole creative process of modernization. From our perspective in Washington you take your place side by side with those others who are committed to help fashion independent, modern societies out of the revolutionary process now going forward. I salute you as I would a group of doctors, teachers, economic planners, agricultural experts, civil servants, or those others who are now leading the way in the whole southern half of the globe in fashioning new nations and societies that will stand up straight and assume in time their rightful place of dignity and responsibility in the world community; for this is our common mission.

Each of us must carry into his day-to-day work an equal understanding of the military and the creative dimensions of the job. I can tell you that those with whom I have the privilege to work are dedicated to that mission with every resource of mind and spirit at our command.

28. *THE UNITED STATES AND WESTERN EUROPE**/ *ROBERT S. McNAMARA*

. . . A central military issue facing NATO today is the role of nuclear strategy. Four facts seem to us to dominate consideration of that role. All of them point in the direction of increased integration to achieve our common defense. First, the Alliance has over-all nuclear strength adequate to any challenge confronting it. Second, this strength not only minimizes the likelihood of major nuclear war, but it makes possible a strategy designed to preserve the fabric of our societies if war should occur. Third, damage to the civil societies of the Alliance resulting from nuclear warfare could be very grave. Fourth, improved non-nuclear forces, well within Alliance resources, could enhance deterrence of any aggressive moves short of direct, all-out attack on Western Europe.

Let us look at the situation today. First, given the current balance of nuclear power, which we confidently expect to maintain in the years ahead, a surprise nuclear attack is simply not a rational act for any enemy. Nor would it be rational for an enemy to take the initiative in the use of nuclear weapons as an outgrowth of a

* Robert S. McNamara, "The United States and Western Europe: Concrete Problems of Maintaining a Free Community," *Vital Speeches of the Day*, Vol. 28, No. 20 (August 1, 1962), pp. 627–29. Reprinted by permission.

limited engagement in Europe or elsewhere. I think we are entitled to conclude that either of these actions has been made highly unlikely.

Second, and equally important, the mere fact that no nation could rationally take steps leading to a nuclear war does not guarantee that a nuclear war cannot take place. Not only do nations sometimes act in ways that are hard to explain on a rational basis, but even when acting in a "rational" way they sometimes, indeed disturbingly often, act on the basis of misunderstandings of the true facts of a situation. They misjudge the way others will react, and the way others will interpret what they are doing. We must hope, indeed I think we have good reason to hope, that all sides will understand this danger, and will refrain from steps that even raise the possibility of such a mutually disastrous misunderstanding. We have taken unilateral steps to reduce the likelihood of such an occurrence. We look forward to the prospect that through arms control, the actual use of these terrible weapons may be completely avoided. It is a problem not just for us in the West, but for all nations that are involved in this struggle we call the Cold War.

For our part, we feel we and our NATO allies must frame our strategy with this terrible contingency, however remote, in mind. Simply ignoring the problem is not going to make it go away.

The U. S. has come to the conclusion that to the extent feasible, basic military strategy in a possible general nuclear war should be approached in much the same way that more conventional military operations have been regarded in the past. That is to say, principal military objectives, in the event of a nuclear war stemming from a major attack on the Alliance, should be the destruction of the enemy's military forces, not of his civilian population.

The very strength and nature of the Alliance forces make it possible for us to retain, even in the face of a massive surprise attack, sufficient reserve striking power to destroy an enemy society if driven to it. In other words, we are giving a possible opponent the strongest imaginable incentive to refrain from striking our own cities.

The strength that makes these contributions to deterrence and to the hope of deterring attack upon civil societies even in wartime does not come cheap. We are confident that our current nuclear programs are adequate and will continue to be adequate for as far into the future as we can reasonably foresee. During the coming fiscal year, the United States plans to spend close to $15 billion on its nuclear weapons to assure their adequacy. For what this money buys, there is no substitute.

In particular, relatively weak national nuclear forces with enemy cities as their targets are not likely to be sufficient to perform even the function of deterrence. If they are small, and perhaps vulnerable on the ground or in the air, or inaccurate, a major antagonist can take a variety of measures to counter them. Indeed, if a major antagonist came to believe there was a substantial likelihood of it being used independently, this force would be inviting a pre-emptive first strike against it. In the event of war, the use of such a force against the cities of a major nuclear power would be tantamount to suicide, whereas its employment against significant military targets would have a negligible effect on the outcome of the conflict. Meanwhile, the creation of a single additional national nuclear force encourages the proliferation of nuclear power with all of its attendant dangers.

In short, then, limited nuclear capabilities, operating independently, are dangerous, expensive, prone to obsolescence, and lacking in credibility as a deterrent. Clearly, the United States nuclear contribution to the Alliance is neither obsolete nor dispensable.

At the same time, the general strategy I have summarized magnifies the importance of unity of planning, concentration of executive authority, and central direction. There must not be competing and conflicting strategies to meet the contingency of nuclear war. We are convinced that a general nuclear war target system is indivisible, and if, despite all our efforts, nuclear war should occur, our best hope lies in conducting a centrally controlled campaign against all of the enemy's vital nuclear capabilities, while retaining reserve forces, all centrally controlled.

We know that the same forces which are targeted on ourselves are also targeted on our allies. Our own strategic retaliatory forces are prepared to respond against these forces, wherever they are and whatever their targets. This mission is assigned not only in fulfillment of our treaty commitments but also because the character of nuclear war compels it. More specifically, the U. S. is as much concerned with that portion of Soviet nuclear striking power that can reach Western Europe as with that portion that also can reach the United States. In short, we have undertaken the nuclear defense of NATO on a global basis. This will continue to be our objective. In the execution of this mission, the weapons in the European theater are only one resource among many.

There is, for example, the POLARIS force, which we have been substantially increasing, and which, because of its specially invulnerable nature, is peculiarly well suited to serve as a strategic reserve force. We have already announced the commitment of five of these ships, fully operational, to the NATO Command.

This sort of commitment has a corollary for the Alliance as a whole. We want and need a greater degree of Alliance participation in formulating nuclear weapons policy to the greatest extent possible. We would all find it intolerable to contemplate having only a part of the strategic force launched in isolation from our main striking power.

We shall continue to maintain powerful nuclear forces for the Alliance as a whole. As the President has said, "Only through such strength can we be certain of deterring a nuclear strike, or an overwhelming ground attack, on our forces and allies."

But let us be quite clear about what we are saying and what we would have to face if the deterrent should fail. This is the almost certain prospect that, despite our nuclear strength, all of us would suffer deeply in the event of major nuclear war.

We accept our share of this responsibility within the Alliance. And we believe that the combination of our nuclear strength and a strategy of controlled response gives us some hope of minimizing damage in the event that we have to fulfill our pledge. But I must point out that we do not regard this as a desirable prospect, nor do we believe that the Alliance should depend solely on our nuclear power to deter actions not involving a massive commitment of any hostile force. Surely an Alliance with the wealth, talent, and experience that we possess can find a better way than extreme reliance on nuclear weapons to meet our common threat. We do not believe that if the formula, $e = mc^2$, had not been discovered, we should all be Communist slaves. On this question, I can see no valid reason for a fundamental difference of view on the two sides of the Atlantic.

With the Alliance possessing the strength and the strategy I have described, it is most unlikely that any power will launch a nuclear attack on NATO. For the kinds of conflicts, both political and military, most likely to arise in the NATO area, our capabilities for response must not be limited to nuclear weapons alone. The Soviets have superiority in non-nuclear forces in Europe today. But that superiority is by no means overwhelming. Collectively, the Alliance has the potential for a successful defense against such forces. In manpower alone, NATO has more men under arms than the Soviet Union and its European satellites. We have already shown our willingness to contribute through our divisions now in place on European soil. In order to defend the populations of the NATO countries and to meet our treaty obligations, we have put in hand a series of measures to strengthen our non-nuclear power. We have added $10 billion for this purpose to the previously planned level of expenditures for fiscal years 1962 and 1963. To tide us over while new permanent strength was being created, we called up 158,000 reservists. We will be releasing them this summer, but only because in the meantime we have built up on an enduring basis more added strength than the call-up temporarily gave us. The number of U. S. combat-ready divisions has been increased from 11 to 16. Stockpiled in Europe now are full sets of equipment for two additional divisions; the men of these divisions can be rapidly moved to Europe by air.

We expect that our allies will also undertake to strengthen further their non-nuclear forces, and to improve the quality and staying power of these forces. These achievements will complement our deterrent strength. With improvements in Alliance ground force strength and staying power, improved non-nuclear air capabilities, and better equipped and trained reserve forces, we can be assured that no deficiency exists in the NATO defense of this vital region, and that no aggression, small or large, can succeed.

I have described very briefly the United States' views on the role of nuclear forces in the strategy of the Alliance. I have pointed out that the Alliance necessarily depends, for the deterrence of general nuclear war, on the powerful and well protected nuclear forces of the United States, which are necessarily committed to respond to enemy nuclear strikes wherever they may be made. At the same time, I have indicated the need for substantial non-nuclear forces within the Alliance to deal with situations where a nuclear response may be inappropriate or simply not believable. Throughout I have emphasized that we in the Alliance all need each other.

I want to remind you also that the security provided by military strength is a necessary, but not sufficient, condition for the achievement of our foreign policy goals, including our goals in the field of arms control and disarmament. Military security provides a base on which we can build Free World strength through the economic advances and political reforms which are the object of the President's programs, like the Alliance for Progress and the Trade Expansion legislation. Only in a peaceful world can we give full scope to the individual potential, which is for us the ultimate value.

A distinguished European visited the United States last month as a guest of the President. Andre Malraux, French Minister of State for Cultural Affairs, is an eminent novelist and critic. He led an archaeological expedition to Cambodia and fought in the Spanish Civil War and the French Resistance Movement. Malraux paid a moving tribute to our nation when he said: "The only nation that has waged war but not worshipped it, that has won the greatest power in the world but not sought it, that has wrought the greatest weapon of death but has not wished to wield it . . . May it inspire men with dreams worthy of its action."

The community of learning to which you have been admitted carries with it great privileges. It also carries great responsibilities. And perhaps the greatest of these is to help ensure the wise use of our national power. Let me paraphrase Malraux: May your dreams be worthy of action and your actions be shaped by your dreams.

29. *THE ABOLITION OF WAR*/ DOUGLAS MACARTHUR*

War's History

. . . Many in this brilliant audience were my comrades-in-arms in the days of used-to-be. They have known war in all its horror and, as veterans, hope against its recurrence. How, we ask ourselves, did such an institution become so integrated with man's life and civilization? How has it grown to be the most vital factor in our existence? It started in a modest enough way as a sort of gladiatorial method of settling disputes between conflicting tribes. One of the oldest and most classical examples is the biblical story of David and Goliath. Each of the two contesting groups selected its champion. They fought and based upon the outcome an agreement resulted. Then, as time went on, small professional groups . . . known as armies replaced the individual champions. And these groups fought in some

* Douglas MacArthur, "The Abolition of War: Triumph of Scientific Annihilation," *Vital Speeches of the Day*, Vol. 21, No. 9 (February 15, 1955), pp. 1041–43. Reprinted by permission.

obscure corner of the world and victory or defeat was accepted as the basis of an ensuing peace. And from then on, down through the ages, the constant record is an increase in the character and strength of the forces with the rate of increase always accelerating. From a small percentage of the populace it finally engulfed all. It is now the nation in arms.

Within the span of my own life I have witnessed this evolution. At the turn of the century, when I entered the Army, the target was one enemy casualty at the end of a rifle or bayonet or sword. Then came the machine gun designed to kill by the dozens. After that, the heavy artillery raining death upon hundreds. Then the aerial bomb to strike by the thousands—followed by the atom explosion to reach the hundreds of thousands. Now electronics and other processes of science have raised the destructive potential to encompass millions. And with restless hands we work feverishly in dark laboratories to find the means to destroy all at one blow.

But, this very triumph of scientific annihilation—this very success of invention—has destroyed the possibility of war being a medium of practical settlement of international differences. The enormous destruction to both sides of closely matched opponents makes it impossible for the winner to translate it into anything but his own disaster.

The second World War, even with the now antiquated armaments, clearly demonstrated that the victor had to bear in large part the very injuries inflicted on his foe. Our own country spent billions of dollars and untold energies to heal the wounds of Germany and Japan. War has become a Frankenstein to destroy both sides. No longer is it the weapon of adventure whereby a short cut to international power and wealth—a place in the sun—can be gained. If you lose, you are annihilated. If you win, you stand only to lose. No longer does it possess the chance of the winner of duel—it contains rather the germs of double suicide. Science has clearly outmoded it as a feasible arbiter. The great question is—does this mean that war can now be outlawed from the world? If so, it would mark the greatest advance in civilization since the Sermon on the Mount. It would lift at one stroke the darkest shadow which has engulfed mankind from the beginning. It would not only remove fear and bring security—it would not only create new moral and spiritual values—it would produce an economic wave of prosperity that would raise the world's standard of living beyond anything ever dreamed of by man. The hundreds of billions of dollars now spent in mutual preparedness could conceivably abolish poverty from the face of the globe. It would accomplish even more than this; it would at one stroke reduce the international tensions that seem so insurmountable now to matters of more probable solution. For instance, the complex problems of German rearmament, of preventive war, of satellite dominance by major powers, of Universal Military Service, of unconscionable taxation, of nuclear development for industry, of freer exchange of goods and people, of foreign aid and indeed of all issues involving the application of armed force. It would have equally potent political effects. It would reduce immeasurably the power of leaders of Government and thus render more precarious totalitarian or autocratic rule. The growing and dangerous control by an individual over the masses—the socialistic and paternal trends resulting therefrom—is largely by virtue of his influence to induce war or to maintain peace. Abolish this threat and the position of chief magistrate falls into a more proper civic perspective.

Abolition Possible

You will say at once that although the abolition of war has been the dream of man for centuries every proposition to that end has been promptly discarded as impossible and fantastic. Every cynic, every pessimist, every adventurer, every swashbuckler in the world has always disclaimed its feasibility. But that was before the science of the past decade made mass destruction a reality. The argument then was that human character has never reached a theological development which would permit the application of pure idealism. In the last two thousand years its rate of change has been deplorably slow, compared to that of the arts and sciences. But now the tremendous and present evolution of nuclear and other potentials of destruction has suddenly taken the problem away from its primary consideration as a moral and spiritual question and brought it abreast of scientific realism. It is no longer an ethical equation to be pondered solely by learned philosophers and ecclesiastics but a hard core one for the decision of the masses whose survival is the issue. This is as true of the Soviet side of the world as of the free side—as true behind the Iron Curtain as in front of it. The ordinary people of the world, whether free or slave, are all in agreement on this solution; and this perhaps is the only thing in the world they do agree upon.

But it is the most vital and determinate of all. The leaders are the laggards. The disease of power seems to confuse and befuddle them. They have not even approached the basic problem, much less evolved a working formula to implement this public demand. They debate and turmoil over a hundred issues—they bring us to the verge of despair or raise our hopes to Utopian heights over the corollary misunderstandings that stem from the threat of war—but never in the chancelleries of the world or the halls of the United Nations is the real problem raised. Never do they dare to state the bald truth, that the next great advance in the evolution of civilization cannot take place until war is abolished. It may take another cataclysm of destruction to prove to them this simple truth. But, strange as it may seem, it is known now by all common men. It is the one issue upon which both sides can agree, for it is the one issue upon which both sides will profit equally. It is the one issue—and the only decisive one—in which the interests of both are completely parallel. It is the one issue which, if settled, might settle all others.

Both Must Profit

Time has shown that agreements between modern nations are generally no longer honored as valid unless both profit therefrom. But both sides can be trusted when both do profit. It becomes then no longer a problem based upon relative integrity. It is now no longer convincing to argue, whether true or not, that we cannot trust the other side—that one maverick can destroy the herd. It would no longer be a matter depending upon trust—the self-interest of each nation outlawing war would keep it true to itself. And there is no influence so potent and powerful as self-interest. It would not necessarily require international inspection of relative armaments—the public opinion of every part of the world would be the great denominator which would insure the issue—each nation would so profit that it could not fail eventually to comply. This would not, of course, mean the abandonment of all armed forces, but it would reduce them to the simpler problems of internal order and international police. It would not mean utopia at one fell stroke, but it would mean that the great roadblock now existing to development of the human race would have been cleared.

The present tensions with their threat of national annihilation are kept alive by two great illusions. The one, a complete belief on the part of the Soviet world that the capitalist countries are preparing to attack them; that sooner or later we intend to strike. And the other, a complete belief on the part of the capitalistic countries that the Soviets are preparing to attack us; that sooner or later they intend to strike. Both are wrong. Each side, so far as masses are concerned, is equally desirous of peace. For either side war with the other would mean nothing but disaster. Both equally dread it. But the constant acceleration of preparation may well, without specific intent, ultimately produce a spontaneous combustion.

I am sure that every pundit in the world, every cynic and hypocrite, every paid brainwasher, every egotist, every troublemaker, and many other of entirely different mold will tell you with mockery and ridicule that this can be only a dream—that it is but the vague imaginings of a visionary. But, as David Lloyd George once said in Commons at the crisis of the First World War, "We must go on or all will go under." And the great criticism we can make of the world's leaders is their lack of a plan which will enable us "to go on." All they propose merely gravitates around but dares not face the real problem. They increase preparedness by alliances, by distributing resources throughout the world, by feverish activity in developing new and deadlier weapons, by applying conscription in times of peace—all of which is instantly matched by the prospective opponent. We are told that this increases the chances of peace—which is doubtful—and increases the chances of victory if war comes—which would be incontestable if the other side did not increase in like proportion. Actually, the truth is that the relative strengths of the two change little with the years. Action by one is promptly matched by reaction from the other.

Dangerous Doctrines

We are told we must go on indefinitely as at present—some say fifty years or more. With what at the end? None say—there is no definite objective. They but pass along to those that follow the search for a final solution. And, at the end, the problem will be exactly the same, as that which we face now. Must we live for generations under the killing punishment of accelerating preparedness without an announced final purpose or, as an alternative, suicidal war; and trifle in the meanwhile with corollary and indeterminate theses—such as limitation of armament, restriction on the use of nuclear power, adoption of new legal standards as propounded at Nuremberg—all of which are but palliatives and all of which in varying form have been tried in the past with negligible results? Dangerous doctrines, too, appear—doctrines which might result in actual defeat; such doctrines as a limited war, of enemy sanctuary, of failure to protect our fighting men when captured, of national subversive and sabotage agencies, of a substitute for victory on the battlefield—all in the name of peace. Peace, indeed, can be obtained at least temporarily by any nation if it is prepared to yield its freedom principles. But peace at any price—peace with appeasement—peace which passes the dreadful finality to future generations—is a peace of sham and shame which can end only in war or slavery.

I recall so vividly this problem when it faced the Japanese in their new Constitution. They are realists; and they are the only ones that know by dread experience the fearful effect of mass annihilation. They realize in their limited geographical area, caught up as a sort of no man's land between two great ideologies, that to engage in another war, whether on the winning or the losing side, would spell the probable doom of their race. And their wise old Prime Minister, Shidehara, came to me and urged that to save themselves they should abolish war as an international instrument. When I agreed, he turned to me and said, "The world will laugh and mock us as impractical visionaries, but a hundred years from now we will be called prophets."

Sooner or later the world, if it is to survive, must reach this decision. The only question is, when? Must we fight again before we learn? When will some great figure in power have sufficient imagination and moral courage to translate this universal wish—which is rapidly becoming a universal necessity—into actuality? We are in a new era. The old methods and solutions no longer suffice. We must have new thoughts, new ideas, new concepts, just as did our venerated forefathers when they faced a new world. We must break out of the straitjacket of the past. There must always be one to lead, and we should be that one. We should now proclaim our readiness to abolish war in concert with the great powers of the world. The result would be magical. . . .

THE SEARCH FOR ORDER AND PEACE

part IV

BALANCE OF POWER

X

THE BALANCE OF POWER IS OF VITAL IMPORtance in contemporary international relations and a central analytical concept in the study of world affairs, in spite of all its weaknesses and ambiguities. One of the earliest thorough discussions of the balance of power is the famous essay by David Hume (1711–76), which is included here as the first selection.

The second selection is Ernst B. Haas' careful analysis of the various meanings of the term "balance of power." Haas is Professor of Political Science at the University of California at Berkeley. He has written *The Uniting of Europe*, *Beyond the Nation-State*, and many other books and articles.

The balance of power in the age of nuclear weapons and ballistic missiles is discussed by Glenn H. Snyder of the University of Buffalo, an expert on military strategy and security policy. He has written *Deterrence by Denial and Punishment*, *Deterrence and Defense*, and other works.

30. *OF THE BALANCE OF POWER** / *DAVID HUME*

It is a question, whether the *idea* of the balance of power be owing entirely to modern policy, or whether the *phrase* only has been invented in the later ages? It is certain that Xenophon[a], in his Institution of Cyrus, represents the combination of the Asiatic powers to have arisen from a jealousy of the increasing force of the Medes and Persians; and though that elegant composition should be supposed altogether a romance, this sentiment, ascribed by the author to the Eastern princes, is at least a proof of the prevailing notion of ancient times.

In all the politics of Greece, the anxiety, with regard to the balance of power, is apparent, and is expressly pointed out to us, even by the ancient historians. Thucydides[b] represents the league which was formed against Athens, and which produced the Peloponnesian war, as entirely owing to this principle. And after the decline of Athens, when the Thebans and Lacedemonians disputed for sovereignty, we find that the Athenians (as well as many other republics) always threw themselves into the lighter scale, and endeavoured to preserve the balance. They supported Thebes against Sparta, till the great victory gained by Epaminondas at Leuctra; after which they immediately went over to the conquered, from generosity, as they pretended, but in reality from their jealousy of the conquerors[c].

Whoever will read Demosthenes's oration for the Megalopolitans, may see the utmost refinements on this principle that ever entered into the head of a Venetian or English speculatist. And upon the first rise of the Macedonian power, this orator immediately discovered the danger, sounded the alarm throughout all Greece,

* David Hume, *Essays and Treatises on Several Subjects* (Edinburgh: Bell & Bradfute, and W. Blackwood, 1825), Vol. I, pp. 331–39.

[a] Lib. i.

[b] Lib. i.

[c] Xenoph. Hist. Græc. lib. vi. and vii.

and at last assembled that confederacy under the banners of Athens which fought the great and decisive battle of Chaeronea.

It is true, the Grecian wars are regarded by historians as wars of emulation rather than of politics; and each state seems to have had more in view the honour of leading the rest, than any well-grounded hopes of authority and dominion. If we consider, indeed, the small number of inhabitants in any one republic, compared to the whole, the great difficulty of forming sieges in those times, and the extraordinary bravery and discipline of every freeman among that noble people; we shall conclude, that the balance of power was, of itself, sufficiently secured in Greece, and need not to have been guarded with that caution which may be requisite in other ages. But whether we ascribe the shifting of sides in all the Grecian republics to *jealous emulation* or *cautious politics*, the effects were alike, and every prevailing power was sure to meet with a confederacy against it, and that often composed of its former friends and allies.

The same principle, call it envy or prudence, which produced the *Ostracism* of Athens, and *Petalism* of Syracuse, and expelled every citizen whose fame or power over-topped the rest; the same principle, I say, naturally discovered itself to foreign politics, and soon raised enemies to the leading state, however moderate in the exercise of its authority.

The Persian monarch was really, in his force, a petty prince compared to the Grecian republics; and therefore, it behoved him, from views of safety more than from emulation, to interest himself in their quarrels, and to support the weaker side in every contest. This was the advice given by Alcibiades to Tissaphernes[a], and it prolonged, near a century, the date of the Persian empire; till the neglect of it for a moment, after the first appearance of the aspiring genius of Philip, brought that lofty and frail edifice to the ground, with a rapidity of which there are few instances in the history of mankind.

The successors of Alexander showed great jealousy of the balance of power; a jealousy founded on true politics and prudence, and which preserved distinct for several ages the partition made after the death of that famous conqueror. The fortune and ambition of Antigonus[b] threatened them anew with a universal monarchy; but their combination, and their victory at Ipsus, saved them. And in subsequent times, we find, that, as the Eastern princes considered

[a] Thucyd. lib. viii.
[b] Diod. Sic. lib. xx.

the Greeks and Macedonians as the only real military force with whom they had any intercourse, they kept always a watchful eye over that part of the world. The Ptolemies, in particular, supported first Aratus and the Achæans, and then Cleomenes king of Sparta, from no other view than as a counterbalance to the Macedonian monarchs. For this is the account which Polybius gives of the Egyptian politics[a].

The reason why it is supposed that the ancients were entirely ignorant of the *balance of power*, seems to be drawn from the Roman history more than the Grecian; and as the transactions of the former are generally more familiar to us, we have thence formed all our conclusions. It must be owned, that the Romans never met with any such general combination or confederacy against them, as might naturally have been expected for their rapid conquests and declared ambition, but were allowed peaceably to subdue their neighbours, one after another, till they extended their dominion over the whole known world. Not to mention the fabulous history of the Italic wars, there was, upon Hannibal's invasion of the Roman state, a remarkable crisis, which ought to have called up the attention of all civilized nations. It appeared afterwards (nor was it difficult to be observed at the time)[b] that this was a contest for universal empire; yet no prince or state seems to have been in the least alarmed about the event or issue of the quarrel. Philip of Macedon remained neuter, till he saw the victories of Hannibal; and then most imprudently formed an alliance with the conqueror, upon terms still more imprudent. He stipulated, that he was to assist the Carthaginian state in their conquest of Italy; after which they engaged to send over forces into Greece, to assist him in subduing the Grecian commonwealth[c].

The Rhodian and Achæan republics are much celebrated by ancient historians for their wisdom and sound policy; yet both of them assisted the Romans in their wars against Philip and Antiochus. And what may be esteemed still a stronger proof, that this maxim was not generally known in those ages, no ancient author has remarked the imprudence of these measures, nor has even blamed that absurd treaty above mentioned, made by Philip with the Carthaginians. Princes and statesmen, in all ages, may, beforehand,

[a] Lib. ii. cap. 51.

[b] It was observed by some, as appears by the speech of Agesilaus of Naupactum, in the general congress of Greece. See Polyb. lib. v. cap. 104.

[c] Tit. Livii, lib. xxiii. cap. 33.

be blinded in their reasonings with regard to events: But it is somewhat extraordinary, that historians, afterwards, should not form a sounder judgment of them.

Massinissa, Attalus, Prusias, in gratifying their private passions, were all of them the instruments of the Roman greatness, and never seem to have suspected, that they were forging their own chains, while they advanced the conquests of their ally. A simple treaty and agreement between Massinissa and the Carthaginians, so much required by mutual interest, barred the Romans from all entrance into Africa, and preserved liberty to mankind.

The only prince we meet with in the Roman history, who seems to have understood the balance of power, is Hiero, king of Syracuse. Though the ally of Rome, he sent assistance to the Carthaginians during the war of the auxiliaries; "Esteeming it requisite," says Polybius[a], "both in order to retain his dominions in Sicily, and to preserve the Roman friendship, that Carthage should be safe; lest by its fall the remaining power should be able, without control or opposition, to execute every purpose and undertaking. And here he acted with great wisdom and prudence: For that is never, on any account, to be overlooked; nor ought such a force ever to be thrown into one hand, as to incapacitate the neighbouring states from defending their rights against it." Here is the aim of modern politics pointed out in express terms.

In short, the maxim of preserving the balance of power is founded so much on common sense and obvious reasoning, that it is impossible it could altogether have escaped antiquity, where we find, in other particulars, so many marks of deep penetration and discernment. If it was not so generally known and acknowledged as at present, it had at least an influence on all the wiser and more experienced princes and politicians. And indeed, even at present, however generally known and acknowledged among speculative reasoners, it has not, in practice, an authority much more extensive among those who govern the world.

After the fall of the Roman empire, the form of government, established by the northern conquerors, incapacitated them, in a great measure, for farther conquests, and long maintained each state in its proper boundaries. But when vassalage and the feudal militia were abolished, mankind were anew alarmed by the danger of universal monarchy, from the union of so many kingdoms and principalities in the person of the Emperor Charles. But the power

[a] Lib. i. cap. 83.

of the house of Austria, founded on extensive but divided dominions; and their riches, derived chiefly from mines of gold and silver, were more likely to decay, of themselves, from internal defects, than to overthrow all the bulwarks raised against them. In less than a century, the force of that violent and haughty race was shattered, their opulence dissipated, their splendour eclipsed. A new power succeeded, more formidable to the liberties of Europe, possessing all the advantages of the former, and labouring under none of its defects, except a share of that spirit of bigotry and persecution, with which the house of Austria was so long, and still is so much infatuated.

In the general wars maintained against this ambitious power, Great Britain has stood foremost, and she still maintains her station. Beside her advantages of riches and situation, her people are animated with such a national spirit, and are so fully sensible of the blessings of their government, that we may hope their vigour never will languish in so necessary and so just a cause. On the contrary, if we may judge by the past, their passionate ardour seems rather to require some moderation; and they have oftener erred from a laudable excess than from a blameable deficiency.

In the *first* place, we seem to have been more possessed with the ancient Greek spirit of jealous emulation, than actuated by the prudent views of modern politics. Our wars with France have been begun with justice, and even perhaps from necessity, but have always been too far pushed, from obstinacy and passion. The same peace, which was afterwards made at Ryswick in 1697, was offered so early as the year ninety-two; that concluded at Utrecht in 1712 might have been finished on as good conditions at Gertruytenberg in the year eight; and we might have given at Frankfort, in 1743, the same terms which we were glad to accept of at Aix-la-Chapelle in the year forty-eight. Here then we see, that above half of our wars with France, and all our public debts, are owing more to our own imprudent vehemence, than to the ambition of our neighbours.

In the *second* place, we are so declared in our opposition to French power, and so alert in defence of our allies, that they always reckon upon our force as upon their own; and expecting to carry on war at our expence, refuse all reasonable terms of accommodation. *Habent subjectos, tanquam suos; viles, ut alienos.* All the world knows, that the factious vote of the House of Commons, in the beginning of the last parliament, with the professed humour of the nation, made the Queen of Hungary inflexible in her terms, and prevented that agreement with Prussia, which would immediately have restored the general tranquillity of Europe.

In the *third* place, we are such true combatants, that, when once engaged, we lose all concern for ourselves and our posterity, and consider only how we may best annoy the enemy. To mortgage our revenues at so deep a rate in wars where we were only accessaries, was surely the most fatal delusion that a nation, which had any pretensions to politics and prudence, has ever yet been guilty of. That remedy of funding, if it be a remedy, and not rather a poison, ought, in all reason, to be reserved to the last extremity; and no evil, but the greatest and most urgent, should ever induce us to embrace so dangerous an expedient.

These excesses, to which we have been carried, are prejudicial, and may, perhaps, in time, become still more prejudicial another way, by begetting, as is usual, the opposite extreme, and rendering us totally careless and supine with regard to the fate of Europe. The Athenians, from the most bustling, intriguing, warlike, people of Greece, finding their error in thrusting themselves into every quarrel, abandoned all attention to foreign affairs; and in no contest ever took part on either side, except by their flatteries and complaisance to the victor.

Enormous monarchies are probably destructive to human nature in their progress, in their continuance[a], and even in their downfall, which never can be very distant from their establishment. The military genius, which aggrandized the monarchy, soon leaves the court, the capital, and the centre of such a government, while the wars are carried on at a great distance, and interest so small a part of the state. The ancient nobility, whose affections attach them to their sovereign, live all at court, and never will accept of military employments, which would carry them to remote and barbarous frontiers, where they are distant both from their pleasures and their fortune. The arms of the state must therefore be entrusted to mercenary strangers, without zeal, without attachment, without honour, ready on every occasion to turn them against the prince, and join each desperate malcontent who offers pay and plunder. This is the necessary progress of human affairs. Thus human nature checks itself in its airy elevation; thus ambition blindly labours for the destruction of the conqueror, of his family, and of every thing

[a] If the Roman empire was of advantage, it could only proceed from this, that mankind were generally in a very disorderly, uncivilized condition, before its establishment.

near and dear to him. The Bourbons, trusting to the support of their brave, faithful, and affectionate nobility, would push their advantage without reserve or limitation. These, while fired with glory and emulation, can bear the fatigues and dangers of war; but never would submit to languish in the garrisons of Hungary or Lithuania, forgot at court, and sacrificed to the intrigues of every minion or mistress who approaches the prince. The troops are filled with Cravates and Tartars, Hussars and Cossacs, intermingled, perhaps, with a few soldiers of fortune from the better provinces; and the melancholy fate of the Roman emperors, from the same cause, is renewed over and over again, till the final dissolution of the monarchy.

31. *THE BALANCE OF POWER: PRESCRIPTION, CONCEPT, OR PROPAGANDA?* / ERNST B. HAAS*

Balance of Power as Description

Forswearing any theoretical or analytical purpose, writers commonly have recourse to the term "balance of power" in discussing international affairs. Current references to the balance of power by journalists and radio commentators most frequently fall into this category. And in most instances the meaning to be conveyed to the audience merely implies "distribution" of power, rather than "balance" in anything like the literal sense. . . .

On other occasions, however, the descriptive use of the term implies more than a mere distribution of power. It may then come to mean "equilibrium" or even "hegemony" or "preponderance" of power, still without implying more than a descriptive intent. It is quite possible that the political motivations of the particular user may make their entrance at this point. Thus Lisola, writing in the seventeenth century, saw in the balance of power the equilibrium between Habsburg and Bourbon interests. But he used his description to counsel war on France in order to maintain that very

* Ernst B. Haas, "The Balance of Power: Prescription, Concept, or Propaganda?" *World Politics*, Vol. 5, No. 4 (July 1953), pp. 459–74. Reprinted by permission. Footnotes follow original sequence.

equilibrium. Austrian writers again invoked the balance of power principle during the wars of the Polish and Austrian Succession in order to secure allies against France and Prussia, represented as seeking hegemony. During the preceding century, French writers had used the equilibrium connotation of the term to demand war on Austria. And it might be pointed out parenthetically that during the Seven Years' War British officials frowned on the use of balance of power terms to justify British aid to Prussia, since it was Frederick II who had "disturbed the balance" with his attack on Austria.[41] In all these writings and statements the term "balance of power" is used and abused as a descriptive phrase, connoting the existence or non-existence of equilibrium and the actual or threatened hegemony of some state or alliance. The same easy transition in meaning from "distribution" to "equilibrium" and finally to "hegemony" can sometimes be detected in contemporary references to the balance of power. These usages are rarely kept in their separate compartments. And, when the users' intentions go beyond that of mere description, clarity of thought and purpose may be seriously jeopardized.

Balance of Power as Propaganda and "Ideology"

A precise understanding of the verbal meaning of the term "balance of power" becomes especially important when it is used as a propagandistic slogan or as an ideological phrase, in the Mannheimian sense. The meanings of "balance" as being identical with either "peace" or "war" fall into this category. Obviously, while it might be correct to speak of a state of balance or imbalance *implying* or *engendering* either war or peace, the balance as such cannot logically be equated with conditions which might arise as a consequence of the balance, i.e., war or peace. In the cases in which the authors employed it to mean "peace" or "war," "balance of power" then became no more than a convenient catchword to focus individual aspirations into a generally acceptable mold; and there can be no doubt that at certain times the concept of balance was an extremely popular one, whether it was used for policy-making or not. If used in a patently forced manner, the term becomes indistin-

[41] For examples, see E. Kaeber, *Die Idee des Europäischen Gleichgewichts in der publizistischen Literatur vom 16. bis zur Mitte des 18. Jahrhunderts*, Berlin, 1906, pp. 44–47.

guishable from plain propaganda. Of this particular usage some striking examples may be cited.

Thus, the anonymous author of the *Relative State of Great Britain in 1813* saw fit to make the phrase cover the total complex of his social, economic, moral, and political predilections:

> The French revolution being founded in the principle of depraving and reversing the human heart and feeling (as the American Republic is built upon frigid indifference and calculation of gain), it is not difficult to perceive how everything which tended to preserve the bond of sacredness of national contracts, and the reciprocity of benefits and engagements—how history, and memory itself, became objects of hatred and jealousy, and organized assault and hostility—and how the balance of power, in particular, opposed and threatened the views of France, which were to ruin and destroy everything, and the views of America to make profit and percentage upon the ruin and destruction of everything. Nor is it easy to pronounce a juster or more happy panegyric upon that system, than what evidently and immediately results from the forced and unnatural coalition of such powers as these (the very worst extremes of democracy and despotism), and the common interest their leaders conceive themselves to have discovered in extinguishing it.

The depraved ideology of France and the United States seemed here to be identified with the upsetting of the balance of power. And the re-establishment of the balance would be the means to end this deplorable state of morality:

> For my part, I shall never blush to confess, that I am able to form no conception of any security in any peace that shall have no guarantees—any effectual guarantee, without a distribution and partition of force, adjusted by political alliance and combination—of any defense or protection for that distribution without a permanent and recognized system of public law, and a real or reputed balance of power amongst the several states it embraces.[42]

This treatment, then, identifies the balance of power with the kind of world conditions, in their totality, which the author desires. The fact that domestic, moral, and ideological factors are haphazardly mixed up with considerations of pure power seems not to have made any difference.

This invocation of the balance of power was no more propagandistic, however, than the use made of it by Friedrich Wilhelm II

[42] Anon., *Considerations on the Relative State of Great Britain in 1813*, London, 1813, pp. 3–4.

in the Declaration of Pillnitz, June 25, 1792, which constituted the manifesto of the allied monarchs attacking France:

> There was no power interested in maintaining the European balance which could be indifferent when the Kingdom of France, which formed such a considerable weight in that great balance, was delivered for long periods of time to internal agitation and to the horrors of disorder and anarchy, which, so to speak, have nullified its political existence.[43]

But the era of the Revolution and the Empire by no means provided the only examples of this type of application. It enjoyed a renaissance during World War I. Then F. J. Schmidt, for instance, asserted that "Germany has the historical call to realize the idea of the balance of power in all its territorial and maritime consequences."[44] And as detached a scholar as Friedrich Meinecke argued that the peace treaty should establish a "new balance of power" instead of depriving Germany of all her conquests.[45] Nor was the invocation of the balance by Louis XIV much different when he used it to justify the accession of his grandson to the throne of Spain, nor Fleury's use of it when he called upon its absolving force to explain France's attack on the Pragmatic Sanction in 1740.[46]

It is apparent that in all these cases the balance of power was invoked in such a way as to serve as the justification for policies not *ipso facto* related to balancing anything. In some instances it was used to cloak ideological conflicts, in others to sanctify the search for hegemony over Europe, and in still others to "justify" the continued strength and size of a defeated state. The significance of this invocation, then, lies not in any theoretical belief but in the fact that the users of the term felt so convinced of its popularity as to

[43] Cited in A. de Stieglitz, *De l'équilibre politique, du légitimisme et du principe des nationalités*, Paris, 1893–1897, I, p. 51. See also the facile use of the doctrine made by Bonald in (1) justifying Napoleonic expansion and (2) asking for a lenient peace in 1815 (Moulinié, *De Bonald*, Paris, 1915, pp. 390–97).

[44] F. J. Schmidt, in *Preussische Jahrbücher*, CLVIII (1914), pp. 1–15; also H. Oncken, *Das alte und das neue Mitteleuropa*, Gotha, 1917, passim.

[45] F. Meinecke, *Probleme des Weltkriegs*, Munich, 1917, p. 134. In his important *Die Idee der Staatsräson in der neueren Geschichte*, in which he claims to be analyzing the doctrine and philosophical meaning of the *raison d'état* idea completely dispassionately, the same argument shows up rather prominently in the last chapter dressed up in terms of historical necessity.

[46] K. Jacob, "Die Chimäre des Gleichgewichts," *Archiv für Urkundenforschung*, VI (1918), pp. 349, 351, 354–55.

make its conversion into a symbol of proper policy propagandistically profitable.

Propaganda assumes the dishonest use of facts and the distortion of concepts devised on intellectually sincere grounds. It implies conscious and deliberate falsification.[47] Ideology, as defined by Mannheim, however, postulates belief in a set of symbols which, even though they may be "false" objectively, still characterize the total myth system of social groups and are essential to the spiritual cohesion of a ruling group which would lose its sense of control if it were conscious of the "real" state of affairs. It is therefore possible to raise the hypothesis that the balance of power may have served such "ideological" purposes. It may have been used to explain policies in terms of natural laws, in terms of moral rightness, or in terms of historical necessity if the symbol chosen to "put it over" was a sufficiently widely accepted one; indeed, if it was a symbol—even a metaphorical one—which the ruling groups themselves tended to accept. In this sense, the term "balance of power" would not serve a strictly propagandistic purpose, since the element of falsification yields to the element of self-deception.[48]

In a remarkable eighteenth-century essay the whole concept of the balance of power was criticized in these very terms. In his *Die Chimäre des Gleichgewichts von Europa*, Justi concluded that the balance of power theory is nothing but the ideological justification adopted by statesmen eager to hide their real motives, motives usually described by the term "aggression." As he put it:

> We regard the dependence of a free state upon another and more powerful state, the latter trying to prevent the former from adopting the proper measures for its happiness, as the greatest misfor-

[47] My conception of propaganda may be expressed in Leonard W. Doob's definition: "Intentional propaganda is a systematic attempt by an interested individual (or individuals) to control the attitudes of groups of individuals through the use of suggestion and, consequently, to control their actions" (*Propaganda*, New York, 1935, p. 89). It is clear that this postulation does not assume that the propagandist himself accepts the material or shares the attitudes he attempts to disseminate. I cannot accept the definition of propaganda offered by Doob in *Public Opinion and Propaganda* (New York, 1948, p. 240), since it seems almost indistinguishable from the more general concept of ideology.

[48] For a masterful analysis of this aspect of the balance of power, see Alfred Vagts, "The Balance of Power: Growth of an Idea," *World Politics*, I (October 1948), pp. 88–89, 100 ff. I have explored the ideological significance of the concept with respect to European diplomacy in the 1830's in my doctoral dissertation, *Belgium and the Balance of Power*, Columbia University Library.

> tune of a people, which should be avoided through the system of the balance of power. Yet such a coarse idea of universal monarchy which aims at reducing all states to provinces of its own state can scarcely ever be realized; however, the means proposed to avoid it are far more to be feared than the evil itself. If a balance of power were to exist in actuality then no slavery would be as hard, since each state would oppose every other state. Upon each new domestic arrangement, each internal improvement, the other states would be compelled to protest and interfere in order to prevent the first state from growing too powerful because of its domestic perfection. And the mutual dependence of such states would be far worse slavery than dependence upon one powerful neighbor. One state would object to one feature and the second to another feature of the internal improvement, and each state would concern itself more with the domestic business of its neighbors than with its own perfection.

All this, Justi argues, means that the whole concept is impossible.[49] And again, he urges what he considers the real *raison d'être* of the usage, thus, incidentally, coming perilously close to characterizing the balance of power as a purely propagandistic device:

> When a state which has grown more powerful internally is attacked . . . in order to weaken it, such action is motivated least of all by the balance of power. This would be a war which is waged by the several states against the strong state for specific interests, and the rules of the balance of power will only be camouflage under which these interests are hidden. . . . States, like private persons, are guided by nothing but their private interests, real or imaginary, and they are far from being guided by a chimerical balance of power. Name one state which has participated in a war contrary to its interests or without a specific interest, only to maintain the balance of power.[50]

The distinction between the propagandistic and ideological uses is thus a tenuous one. The "camouflage" is ideological only if the actors on the international stage are themselves convinced, to some extent, of the identity of "private interest" with a general need for balancing power *qua* power.

[49] J. H. G. von Justi, *Die Chimäre des Gleichgewichts von Europa*, Altona, 1758, p. 60.

[50] *Ibid.*, p. 65. Albert Sorel's estimate of the invocation of balancing terminology by statesmen is a similar one. Since he denies that balancing policies are deliberately chosen by diplomats and since he urges that only the search for unilateral hegemony motivates policy, he argues in fact that the use of the term by statesmen implies a disguised hankering for superiority and no more (*L'Europe et la Révolution francaise*, Paris, 1908, I, p. 34).

Balance of Power as Analytical Concept

At the opposite pole of the propaganda-oriented application of the term "balance of power" lies the user's intention to employ the term as a tool of analysis. It is in this area of intentions that the term rose to the status of a theory of international relations during the eighteenth and nineteenth centuries, no less than it has in our own era. It is also truc, however, that in this area as well as in the other fields of intentions analyzed so far not one but several of the verbal meanings of the term find application. Even as a tool of scholarly analysis the term has been used to mean "power politics," "equilibrium," "hegemony" and, finally, a "universal law" of state conduct.

"The basic principle of the balance of power," wrote Réal de Curban, "is incontestable: the power of one ruler, in the last analysis, is nothing but the ruin and diminution of that of his neighbors, and his power is nothing but the weakness of the others."[51] And in a Hobbesian state of nature which was presupposed to exist among sovereign states no other conclusion seemed possible. This reasoning has led numerous writers to equate the balance of power with power politics or *Realpolitik* generally. The struggle for self-preservation in the state of nature implies the formation of alliances and mutually antagonistic blocs which in turn make negotiations in "good faith" a contradiction in terms. Power politics are the only discernible pattern in which balancing is an inherent process. As such, it is not separate from but identical with competitive power struggles. Consequently, in dispassionate analyses of international affairs the "balance" of power carries no significance other than that usually associated with "power politics," unrefined by any conception of equilibrium or deliberate balancing measures.[52]

Furthermore, the concept of evenly balanced power, or "equilibrium," finds frequent application as a tool of analysis. In the preceding discussion the equilibrium concept found application merely as a descriptive phrase implying no generalized behavior pattern in international relations. In the present context the reverse

[51] Réal de Curban, *La science du gouvernement*, Paris, 1764, VI, p. 442.

[52] See, e.g., H. N. Brailsford and G. Lowes Dickinson, as quoted in Georg Schwarzenberger, *Power Politics*, London, 1940, p. 123, and also the author's own comments, which also tend to equate power politics with power balance.

is true. Lasswell, in speaking of the "balancing process," for instance, assumes that under conditions of expected future violence—domestic as well as international—any increase in the coercion potential of one power unit will lead to a compensatory increase in the competing unit or units. Further increases on the part of one side will always bring corresponding increases on the part of its competitors, so that in effect a rough equality of power potential will always prevail, a factor which may make for either open conflict or induce fear of refraining from hostilities, depending on circumstances, the nature of the elites in question, and the accuracy of intelligence reports concerning the degree of "balancing." The analytical application of the equilibrium-meaning of the balance of power, in short, generalizes the basic assumption of the absence of international consensus and the consequent inherent presence of conflict into a pattern of balancing.

Carrying the equilibrium-meaning one step further results in the application of the balance of power concept as implying the search for hegemony. This application again finds its counterpart in the intentions of detached analysts striving for a generalized understanding of phenomena rather than for description. Spykman, as demonstrated above, clearly sets forth the assumptions of this approach. His argument is that the search for power by sovereign states is an end in itself, since conflict—actual or potential—is the only consistent pattern in relations between state units. While the search for power originally implied the desire for self-preservation, a generalized desire for power-seeking over a long period of time converts this process into an end in itself. On this level, the discussion of the balance of power is identical with power politics generally. As in the case of Lasswell's balancing process, however, the generalized process of competitive power-seeking must result in equilibrium if war is avoided—temporarily. But statesmen, as indicated above, seek a margin of safety in superiority of power and not in equality of power. Hence the search for equilibrium in effect is the search for hegemony, and the balance of power as an analytical concept becomes another term for the simultaneous search for preponderance of power by all the sovereign participants. No wonder Spykman exclaims that

> He who plays the balance of power can have no permanent friends. His devotion can be to no specific state but only to balanced power. The ally of today is the enemy of tomorrow. One of the charms of power politics is that it offers no opportunity to grow weary of one's friends. England's reputation as *perfide Albion* is

> the inevitable result of her preoccupation with the balance of power.[53]

In this refined analysis, the balance of power comes to be considered as a special case—either in its equilibrium or its hegemony connotation—in the general pattern of power politics, though Spykman in the passage just cited again tends to use the two terms interchangeably.

The supreme attempt to use the balance of power as an analytical concept arises in the case of those writers who make the balance the essence of a theory of international relations. It is here that the balance attains the quality of a "law of history," as indeed Rousseau and Donnadieu implied by their very choice of words, and many contemporary writers by their emphasis on the "naturalness" of state behavior in accordance with the dictates of balanced power. The universal law connotation of the balance of power presupposes state conduct in no way different from the assumptions of Spykman and Lasswell. But Professors Morgenthau and Schuman, for instance, in giving the balance of power this extended meaning, go beyond the characterization of equilibrium and hegemony. They develop the thesis that it is inherent in the nature of a multi-state system based on sovereignty to engage in mutually hostile policies, for whatever motives. In this process the search for balanced power, the need to form blocs and counterblocs to prevent the feared attainment of hegemony by one or the other of the participants in the conflict is a natural, if not instinctive, choice of policy. A group of revisionist states always lines up against a group of states devoted to the maintenance of the status quo in such a way that approximate balance results. So general is this pattern that it attains the quality of a historical law. And the characteristic feature of this law is that it does not necessarily assume a conscious intention on the part of statesmen to "balance power with power" in a sense which would imply the official acceptance of a balance of power theory by governments. Statesmen, to be sure, may be consciously motivated by balancing notions. But, if they are not, the policies which they would most logically adopt would be those consistent with the balance of power. As Professor Morgenthau indicates, if they fail to do so, they do not make "logical" policy and thereby violate historically proven and generalized modes of conduct. The distinc-

[53] N. Spykman, *America's Strategy in World Politics*, New York, 1942, pp. 1–21, 103–4.

tive feature about the balance of power applied as a tool of analysis, then, is its possible separation from the motivations of governments.

Balance of Power as Prescription

While the analytical application of the term does not imply conscious acceptance of balancing rules by governments, there is a large body of thought—historical and contemporary—which does insist that the balance of power is—or should be—a guiding principle for decision-making on the part of governments. It is this application of the term which makes use of the meaning defined above as "guide-and-system." Once more international relations are pictured, in one version, as being in the Hobbesian state of nature, so that survival dictates the formation of alliances among those states committed to "preserving the balance" against the onslaught of the state(s) allegedly seeking world or regional domination or, as the eighteenth-century writers put it, "universal monarchy." In this sense, the balance is a conscious guide dictating the rules of survival. In another sense, however, the world (or Europe, in the earlier writing) is represented as a "system" of states tied together by mutual interdependence, common institutions, and a common system of law (the law of nations), and the search for hegemony of a single member of this "system" was then represented as an attack upon the whole organic unit.[54] The system was based on the continued independence of all members and their common will to resist the search for hegemony by any one of their number. The balance of power was inherent in the very system itself and also acted as a body of rules dictating the proper policies for preventing the attainment of hegemony, i.e., it acted as a "guide."

That Metternich subscribed in principle and in considerable detail to the theory of the balance of power as a guide to foreign policy-making is beyond any doubt. Consistent with his overall political philosophy of the value of historically sanctioned social and political traditions, of the need for preserving what the historical process had created and for protecting it against the fanaticism and stupidity of misguided men, i.e., the liberals, Metternich considered

[54] The extreme example of this body of thought is represented by Wolff with his concept of the *civitas maxima* and the role of the balance of power in preventing its destruction (*Ius Gentium Methoda Scientifica Pertractantum*, pars. 642–43, 646, 651. *Classics of International Law*, no. 13, 1934). Also Pufendorf, *Ius Naturae et Gentium*. Book viii, ch. 6, *ibid.*, no. 17, 1934.

the balance of power as another of these time-hallowed doctrines, and as an international institution vital to the preservation of the total institutional status quo which he so cherished. As he wrote:

> Politics is the science of the life of the state, on its highest level. Since isolated states no longer exist . . . it is the society of states, this important condition of the contemporary world, which has to be watched carefully. Thus each state, in addition to its particular interests, has certain common interests, either with the totality of the other states or with certain groups among them. The great axioms of political science derive from the understanding of real political interests, of all states; the guarantee for their existence rests in these general interests, whereas particular interests . . . only possess a relative and secondary value. History teaches that whenever the particular interests of one state are in contradiction with the general interest and whenever the latter is neglected or misunderstood, this condition . . . is to be regarded as exceptional and pathological. . . . The modern world is characterized, in distinction to the old world, by a tendency of states to approach one another and to enter into the bonds of society in some manner; so that the resulting bond rests on the same foundations as the great society which developed in the shadow of Christianity. This foundation consists of the command of the Book of Books: "Do not do unto others what you would not have others do unto you." Applying this basic rule of all human associations to the state, the result is reciprocity, politically speaking, and its effect is. . . : mutual respect and honest conduct. In the ancient world, politics sought pure isolation and practiced absolute egoism, without any control save common sense. . . . Modern history, however, shows us the application of the principle of solidarity and the balance of power offers us the drama of the unified efforts of several states in restraining the hegemony of a single state and limiting the expansion of its influence, and thus forcing it to return to public law.[55]

This formulation of international relations in general as necessary and close rapport between the states of Europe, which he regarded in the then customary manner as so many atoms in a universe held together by Christian moral rules and the dictates of international law, and of the balance of power as the *ad hoc* regulating mechanism of this system, is in almost all respects identical with the formulation of Ancillon, of Castlereagh, of Brougham, and of Gentz. Thus Ancillon, Prussian court chaplain in the 1820's, tutor to Frederick William IV, and State Secretary for Foreign Affairs from 1832 until 1835, argued:

[55] Metternich, *Aus Metternichs Nachgelassenen Papieren*, Vienna, 1882, I, pp. 32ff., a section entitled, "Maxims on Which the Actions of My Political Career Have Been Based."

> All forces are similar to the nature of expanding bodies; thus, in the society of large states in which law does not enjoy an external guarantee, we take as our point of departure the possible or even probable misuse of force. What will be the result? Mutual distrust, fear and restlessness, always recurring and always effective. Each state can have no other maxims in its external relations than these: whoever can do us damage through an excessive balance of power in his favor, or through his geographical position, is our natural enemy, but whoever in view of his position and forces is able to harm our enemy, is our natural friend. These simple maxims which the need for self-preservation has given to man, are and have been at all times the anchors on which all of politics rests.[56]

Nor was Castlereagh's understanding of the balance of power much different, even though he indicated that "my real and only object was to create a permanent counterpoise to the power of France in peace as well as in war." The Concert of Europe through its regular conferences was merely to be the consultative mechanism whereby the *ad hoc* balance could be maintained through timely negotiations.[57] However, the likelihood of the guide-and-system version of the balance implying different "rules" for different states is here betrayed.

Gentz's theory of the balance of power was stated in his *Fragmente aus der neusten Geschichte des politischen Gleichgewichts in Europa* (1806), the purpose of which was to give the Austrian and British governments an excuse for unleashing a new war on Napoleon without having been attacked first. Gentz, it might be added, was in the pay of the British cabinet to produce writings of this type. He rejected the arguments that an exact equilibrium is impossible and that power cannot be measured as irrelevant to the system, since all the system requires is eternal vigilance that no state acquires enough power to overawe all of Europe.[58] Also, he thought that the certainty of a strong counterforce being mustered against the hegemony-seeker was a sufficient deterrent and that actual war would usually be unnecessary. And

[56] Paul Haake, *J. P. F. Ancillon and Kronprinz Friedrich Wilhelm IV. von Preussen*, Munich, 1920, p. 40. Of Ancillon's own works, see his *Ueber den Geist der Staatsverfassungen und dessen Einfluss auf die Gesetzgebung*, Berlin, 1825, pp. 16–19, 313–14, 317–31, and *Tableau des révolutions du système de l'Europe*, Paris, 1806, iv, pp. 5–19.

[57] Sir Charles Webster, *British Diplomacy, 1813–1815*, London, 1921, pp. 62, 218; and Castlereagh's memorandum of October 30, 1814, for Alexander I, cited in Angeberg, *Les traités de Vienne*, Paris, 1864, pp. 399–401.

[58] Gentz, *Fragmente aus der neutsten Geschichte des politischen Gleichgewichts in Europa*, St. Petersburg, 1806, pp. 1–8.

> Only when one or the other state, with open violence, invented pretexts, or artificially concocted legal titles, undertakes enterprises which, directly or in their inevitable consequences, lead to the enslavement of its weaker neighbors, or to the constant endangering, gradual weakening and eventual demise of its stronger neighbors, only then there will come about a breach of the balance, according to the sound conceptions of the collective interest of a system of states; only then will the several states combine in order to prevent the hegemony of a single state, through a timely contrived counterweight.[59]

Yet Gentz opposed policies of partition and compensation as violating the true conservative character of the theory. Moreover, there could be no such thing as indifference to a given issue, since under the power rules all issues had to be of equal interest to all states in the system.[60] His comments on the right to intervene in the domestic affairs of other states are of the highest interest. Gentz urged that ideological distastes for internal changes elsewhere did not in themselves constitute a ground for balance of power intervention and war. But as soon as such changes had the necessary consequence of upsetting the balance of power, i.e., as soon as the new ideology seemed to suggest the search for hegemony, then the right to intervene existed, as in 1793.[61]

The case of Lord Brougham is a fascinating one for the study of the theory of the balance of power. In his essay on "The Balance of Power," written in 1803, he urged that the balance was the only tenable theory of international relations. He defined it in the same terms as Gentz and Ancillon and added:

> Had it not been for that wholesome jealousy of rival neighbors, which modern politicians have learned to cherish, how many conquests and changes of dominion would have taken place, instead of wars, in which some lives were lost, not perhaps the most valuable in the community, and some superfluous million were squandered! How many fair portions of the globe might have been deluged in blood, instead of some hundreds of sailors fighting harmlessly on the barren plains of the ocean, and some thousands of soldiers carrying on a scientific and regular and quiet system of warfare in countries set apart for the purpose, and resorted to as the arena where the disputes of nations might be determined.

The old argument of the tacit federation of Europe, the common system of law and morals, and the need for the regulating mechanism of the balance to keep one of the "federated" states from

59 *Ibid.*, pp. 10–14.
60 *Ibid.*, ch. ii.
61 *Ibid.*, ch. iv.

absorbing the others is restated in full.[62] The principle, as well as the detailed application of the theory in its guide-and-system form, were stated by the young Brougham in the classical manner, and with unsurpassed and brief lucidity:

> It is not then in the mere plan for forming offensive or defensive alliances; or in the principles of attacking a neighbor in order to weaken his power, before he has betrayed hostile views; or in the policy of defending a rival, in order to stay, in proper time, the progress of a common enemy; it is not in these simple maxims that the modern system consists. These are indeed the elements, the great and leading parts of the theory; they are the maxims dictated by the plainest and coarsest views of political expediency: but they do not form the whole system; nor does the knowledge of them . . . comprehend an acquaintance with the profounder and more subtile parts of modern policy. The grand and distinguishing feature of the balancing theory, is the systematic form to which it reduces those plain and obvious principles of national conduct; the perpetual attention to foreign affairs which it inculcates; the constant watchfulness which it prescribes over every movement in all parts of the system; the subjection in which it tends to place all national passions and antipathies to the views of remote expediency; the unceasing care which it dictates of national concerns most remotely situated, and apparently unconnected with ourselves; the general union, which it has effected, of all the European powers in one connecting system–obeying certain laws and actuated, for the most part, by a common principle; in fine, as a consequence of the whole, the right of mutual inspection, now universally recognized among civilized states, in the appointment of public envoys and residents [sic]. This is the balancing theory.[63]

Intervention in domestic developments of other states, of course, is legal if the balance of power is really and truly threatened by these changes. The superiority of the balance to all ideological considerations, so plainly stated here, is especially striking. This principle he repeated in his "General Principles of Foreign Policy" (1843) in most emphatic terms:

> But the mere circumstance of our preferring a democratic to an aristocratic or a monarchical to a republican scheme of government, can never afford any good ground for uniting with others who have the same preference, against a community or a league of states, whose views of national polity are of a contrary description.[64]

[62] Brougham, *Works*, London, 1872, viii, pp. 4–12.
[63] *Ibid.*, pp. 12–13, 33–38.
[64] *Ibid.*, pp. 70–71, 77, 79–80, 80–83.

Hence the Holy Alliance—or the Western bloc against it after 1832—was not consistent with the rules of the balance. Not only is ideological intervention condemned, but Brougham urged that

> it is the bounden duty of all rulers to discourage sentiments in their subjects leading to national enmities; and when a popular cry arises against any foreign people, a general clamor for war, there is no more sacred duty on the part of the government than to resist such a clamor and keep the peace in spite of it.[65]

In short, any manifestations of public opinion had to be rigorously excluded from policy-making under balancing rules, a sentiment heard more and more frequently in our present epoch.

Whether the balance of power is regarded merely as a set of rules to be applied to the preservation of the state or whether it is expanded into the defensive mechanism of some "system"—and by analogy the United Nations system might today be considered the successor to the European system postulated by the earlier writers—the rules laid down by Gentz and Brougham remain the same. The statesman who is anxious to preserve his state must have recourse to balancing principles in averting the hegemony of his rival. The perusal of the contemporary literature on this subject confirms this conclusion. George F. Kennan's *American Diplomacy* is merely the latest and best-known example of the continuing importance ascribed to balancing rules in international relations. And the fact that the examples cited concerned statesmen conscious of the balance as a motivating force underlines the possible importance of the concept as prescription. . . .

32. *BALANCE OF POWER IN THE MISSILE AGE* / GLENN H. SNYDER*

The idea of "balance of power" is still the central theoretical concept in international relations. However, its meaning is now undergoing fundamental change because of the development of nuclear weapons and long-range ballistic missiles. This article at-

[65] *Ibid.*, pp. 91–93, 100–2.

* Glenn H. Snyder, "Balance of Power in the Missile Age," *Journal of International Affairs*, Vol. 14, No. 1 (1960), pp. 21–34. Reprinted by permission.

tempts to explore the impact of these developments and to suggest some changes in the traditional concept to take account of them.[1]

The "power" that was balanced in the pre-nuclear balancing process was essentially the military power to take or hold territory. Moreover, territory, and the human and material resources on it, was the predominant source of power. The motive for engaging in the balancing process was to prevent any single state or bloc from becoming so powerful that it could make territorial conquests with impunity and eventually achieve a hegemony over the other states in the system. The objectives were, first, to *deter* the potential disturber from initiating war by forming alliances and building up armaments sufficient to defeat him, and secondly, if deterrence failed, to *defend* or restore the balance by engaging in war.

Nuclear weapons, long-range aircraft and missiles have superimposed a new balancing process over the old. The new balance, which we might call the "balance of terror" (to borrow Churchill's striking phrase), centers on a different form of power—not the power to contest control of territory but the power to inflict severe punishment and to deter by the threat of such punishment. One might say that the new technology has tended to split apart the twin objectives of deterrence and defense by making it possible to deter simply by the threat to inflict terrible costs, quite regardless of the relative balance of capabilities to take or hold territory. Moreover, the capabilities to punish may have little value for defense in the traditional sense, and their actual use may generate costs for both sides which are far beyond the value of most conceivable objectives. Calculations of probable cost have become at least as important as calculations of the probability of winning.

Thus nuclear weapons and long-range delivery systems have done much more than simply add higher levels of potential destructiveness to the balance of power. They have changed the very nature and meaning of "balance." Two balancing systems—the strategic balance of terror and a truncated tactical balance of power[2]—now operate simultaneously, each according to somewhat different criteria.

[1] For an earlier treatment of this subject, see Arthur Lee Burns, "From Balance to Deterrence," *World Politics*, Vol. IX, No. 4 (July, 1957), pp. 494–530.

[2] The term "tactical balance of power" refers chiefly to the balance of conventional capabilities, but it may also be taken to include tactical nuclear forces. The word "tactical" also preserves a distinction between the "balance of power" conceived as the overall combination of the two systems discussed here, and the narrower balance of power for non-strategic action.

The Balance of Terror

In its "pure" form, the balance of terror would have to do only with the deterrence of, and defense against, all-out nuclear attack. However, the threat of nuclear retaliation may also deter lesser contingencies. To simplify, we may assume that each nuclear power is interested in deterring two types of attack against itself—all-out strategic nuclear attack and a major conventional attack. We may postulate a "minimum" and a "maximum" deterrent for each of these contingencies. Thus we have four salient levels of "balance" in the balance of terror, although these do not exhaust the possibilities.

SECOND-STRIKE DETERRENCE OF NUCLEAR ATTACK

A country has a *minimum second-strike deterrent* when it has just enough nuclear striking power—*after* subtracting the forces which the potential aggressor would be able to eliminate in a surprise attack and by his air defenses—to cause damage to the opponent's economy and population thereby more than offsetting the value which the opponent places on his objective.

If both sides have at least this capability, they are in the familiar condition of "nuclear parity" or "stalemate"—neither side can prevent unacceptable damage to itself by striking first at the other side's nuclear forces. To consider this condition an automatic corollary of nuclear armament, as we have been somewhat prone to do in the recent past, seems ill-advised in the light of recent thinking.[3] Whether, even now, the United States and the Soviet Union are in nuclear stalemate is a matter of conjecture. The balance may shift against the United States in the years immediately ahead if the Soviets develop the substantial lead in ICBM production which is officially conceded as possible. If such a "missile gap" develops, a minimum second-strike capability for the United States may have to depend, for a time at least, on keeping a certain portion of the SAC long-range bomber force in the air at all times—a difficult and costly measure.

One hesitates to make even qualified predictions in the face of the technological revolution now taking place, but it seems likely that achievement of "balance" in this sense will become progres-

[3] See Albert Wohlstetter, "The Delicate Balance of Terror," *Foreign Affairs*, Vol. 37, No. 2 (January, 1959), pp. 211–35.

sively easier as long-range missiles begin to make up a considerable portion of the striking forces on both sides—perhaps by 1965. If appropriate protective measures are taken, such as "hardening," concealment, mobility and deployment of missiles on submarines, the balance of terror should become quite stable, at least as compared to the present and the three or four years immediately ahead when the fear of a surprise counter-force attack will still be an important factor in strategic calculations. Of course, we should not forget that an unexpected technological breakthrough—such as the development of a near-perfect defense against missiles or a method of accurate peacetime tracking and near-simultaneous destruction of a nation's fleet of missile-firing submarines—would give one side a temporarily decisive advantage, but there is no evidence that such a development is likely.

A minimum second-strike deterrent should provide high confidence of deterring a deliberate nuclear attack. It might be irrational, after the attack, for the deterrer actually to use such a force as threatened—*i.e.*, "all-out" against the enemy's cities. He would not be able to defeat the aggressor, he probably would insure that more of his own cities would be destroyed than otherwise, and he would be throwing away whatever bargaining power remained to him. But for the aggressor to expect his victim to act rationally in the wake of a massive nuclear attack would itself be a form of irrationality. However, there is always the possibility of accidents, lunacy in the aggressor's leadership and miscalculation—for example, miscalculation by the aggressor in estimating his counter-force capability, or by the deterrer in estimating the level of potential retaliatory damage necessary to deter. Considering these possibilities, the deterrer may be bothered by the fact that, should deterrence fail, he could not hope to "win" with a minimum second-strike force. He might wish to have the nuclear wherewithal to defeat the attacker—*i.e.*, to force the latter to capitulate, or to destroy his economy and war-making capacity, including his unused strategic nuclear forces—or (more reasonably, perhaps) to persuade the attacker to terminate the war on the basis of the territorial *status quo*, after a series of limited retaliatory strikes. He might want, in other words, a *maximum second-strike deterrent.* Such an objective would require a much larger number of bombs and delivery vehicles than a minimum deterrent designed to produce just barely unacceptable costs for the enemy.

FIRST-STRIKE DETERRENCE OF GROUND ATTACK

For the deterrence of conventional ground attack, unaccompanied by a surprise nuclear strike, the relevant nuclear capability is of course the "first-strike" variety. Conceivably, deterrence of ground invasion might be effective with a *minimum first-strike* force—just enough to cause sufficient damage to the attacker to offset the value he places on conquest of the country attacked.

For a small country such as Holland, an ability to wipe out perhaps only one or two Russian cities would probably meet this criterion. For a larger country such as West Germany, the requirement might be a little higher. But to retaliate with such a minimum force would be irrational, it seems, since conquest could not be prevented and severe nuclear counter-retaliation would very likely follow. If a country wished to vindicate its honor (a "rational" aim perhaps) there are less costly ways. But the prospective aggressor—*e.g.*, the Soviet Union—cannot be sure how rational the prospective victim is, and it must consider that under the stress of war, reason can easily become unhinged, or the victim may retaliate more or less by reflex action because of a previous commitment to retaliation for deterrent purposes. It seems clear that a major Soviet surface attack on a West Germany able to "take out" five or six large Russian cities would pose a grave risk for the Soviet Union, even without considering West Germany's possible alliance connections with other nuclear powers such as the United States. The more the victim's damage-producing capacity exceeds the minimum the aggressor can accept, the more reluctant will he be to undertake the risk of attack.

But for a completely credible nuclear deterrent against ground attack, a *maximum first-strike* force is necessary. This is a strategic nuclear force able not only to inflict unacceptable costs on the aggressor after he has launched a ground attack, but also to defeat him (or at least force him to accept the *status quo ante*) *and* in the process—by attrition of the enemy's nuclear forces and by passive and active defense measures—to limit one's own costs to a level which makes all-out nuclear war preferable to subjugation.

It seems quite obvious that such a force is beyond the reach of any small country against a superpower opponent, and it may become unattainable even for the latter *vis-à-vis* each other. Not only is the quantitative requirement very high, but the qualitative requirements are more stringent than for a minimum force. A good part of the maximum force must be composed of very accurate and very powerful weapons—such as piloted aircraft carrying high-yield bombs, and missiles based relatively close to the enemy—weapons suitable for destroying small and highly-protected military installations such as missile sites, bomb stockpiles, deep-sheltered aircraft, and communications centers. A minimum capability—either the first or the second-strike variety—requires only enough accuracy to hit cities. The maximum first-strike force and the minimum second-strike force are, in a sense, reciprocal; if one side has the former, its opponent, by definition, cannot have the latter.

If a nuclear power wishes to deter either conventional or nuclear attack on other countries, its maximum first-strike requirement is considerably higher than for deterrence of attack on itself. Since all countries naturally value their neighbors' independence somewhat less than their own, they will defend others by strategic nuclear means only at the prospect of less costs to themselves.

These categories are intended as benchmarks for discussion rather than as an exhaustive listing of the various levels of capability which a country might wish to have for deterrence. A small country might want to have somewhat more than the bare minimum for a first strike, even though it did not attempt to achieve a minimum second-strike force. The extra forces would not increase the credibility of its deterrent threat, but they would insure against underestimation of the aggressor's civil and air defenses and his level of unacceptable damage. The threat of greater costs to the enemy might also offset the latter's doubts about the deterrer's willingness to use his forces. Of course, if the deterrer's forces are highly invulnerable, the quantitative requirement for a second-strike minimum might not be much beyond that for a first-strike minimum.

A country with a minimum second-strike capability might want to have some additional forces for the reasons just mentioned, and also to hedge against underestimation of the aggressor's first-strike force. If the extra forces were of a counter-force nature (even though the total did not approach the maximum first-strike requirement) they might increase to some extent the country's ability to deter tactical ground attack or a strategic attack on its allies. Or they might provide the means to make a credible threat of limited retaliation in these contingencies.

In none of the categories mentioned above does "balance" mean *matching* the enemy in offensive striking forces or having a slight margin of superiority over the enemy in such forces, as in the traditional concept of balance of power. Both of the minimums probably require less than the enemy's forces, and both of the maximums require more. In the balance of terror, the striking forces do not exist primarily to fight each other for the control of territorial objects, but rather to pose for the opponent the prospect of unacceptable costs. "Balancing" means introducing into the enemy's risk calculus a prospect of cost which will be sufficient to offset his prospect of gain, *after* discounting the costs by some factor representing the enemy's doubts about one's willingness to inflict them.

An important characteristic of any balancing system is its degree of stability—*i.e.*, the strength of tendencies for the system to remain in balance once an equilibrium has been reached. The most dangerous form of instability is that which tends to move the system in the direction of war. In general, the stability of the balance of terror at any particular time depends on three prime factors: the vulnerability of striking forces, the accuracy of striking forces, and the number of such forces on each side.

Instability is greatest when the forces on both sides are both highly vulnerable and highly accurate, so that with roughly equal numbers of forces on each side, one side could practically eliminate the forces of the other in a single blow. Even if both sides wished fervently to avoid war, each would be forced to consider that the opponent had both the capability and the incentive for a knock-out blow, the incentive arising from the opponent's desire to forestall such a strike against himself. From such considerations, the "first" side would develop an incentive for a first strike, and the second side, knowing this, would have his own incentives reinforced. Clearly, this is an explosive situation.

Maximum stability would be obtained when both sides, by virtue of the invulnerability of their forces, have something approaching maximum second-strike capabilities—*i.e.*, a capacity virtually to destroy the opponent's economy and society even after the opponent has had the advantage of the first strike. Stability would be fairly great even if one side had only a little more than a *minimum* invulnerable second-strike force, because the other side would then not have to fear being the recipient of a surprise attack. Only a small increase in the capability of the latter side, however, (possibly because of some secret scientific development) might give it a maximum first-strike force—*i.e.*, deprive the opponent of its minimum second-strike capability—and thereby make a deliberate attack rational.

Differences and Interaction Between Balance of Terror and Balance of Power

The traditional "tactical" balance of power continues to operate in conflict situations in which strategic nuclear retaliation cannot be credibly threatened or rationally employed. In modern strategic theory it survives chiefly in the concept of "limited war." Before considering the interaction between the balance of terror and the tactical balance of power, it may be useful to note certain important differences between the two systems in their "pure" form.

One difference has already been noted: the irrelevance of quantitatively matching the opponent's military capabilities in the balance of terror. Another concerns the strategic value of territory and of territorial boundaries. In the tactical balance, the strategic value of territory, and the human and material assets associated with territory, continues to be high. The traditional "elements of national power," such as manpower, natural resources, industrial strength, space, geographic separation, command of the seas and so on, continue to be the primary sources of power and they are important criteria for determining the existence or non-existence of a tactical "balance."

These territorially-based elements are also a source of power in the balance of terror, but their significance is less and considerably different than in the tactical balance. Strategic nuclear weapons have reduced the importance of geographical separation between opponents in the balance of terror, since ICBM's can reach from continent to continent.

However, distance still retains some significance in the strategic balance of terror. An aggressor can reduce the required range and hence increase the accuracy and possible payload of his missiles by obtaining control of territory between himself and his prospective nuclear opponent. He may also increase the points of the compass from which he can attack, thus complicating the opponent's warning and air defense problem. He may increase the space available for dispersal of his striking forces, and he may obtain useful staging bases and post-attack landing points for his long-range aircraft.

The acquisition of industrial and resource assets by conquest may increase a nuclear power's capability to produce additional strategic weapons. While "raw" manpower is not a significant source of power in the balance of terror, an aggressor may turn to his own uses the scientific brainpower of a conquered nation. On balance, however, the strategic value of territory and its associated assets is probably smaller in the balance of terror than in the tactical balance.

"War potential" is a source of power in the tactical balance not only prior to war but also after the war has begun. Stockpiles of raw materials, standby war production plants and the like can be translated into actual military power during the progress of the war, provided of course that the forces ready in advance of the attack can hold off the enemy until the additional power is mobilized. But in the balance of terror, industrial potential provides only pre-attack power, not post-attack power. Once the war has started, if it is not destroyed, its usefulness probably would be limited to survival and reconstruction.

In the tactical balance, alliances are useful for both deterrence and defense, in roughly equal proportion; if deterrence fails, the costs of war are low enough and the incentives to prevent the conquest of an ally are high enough that allies are likely to see a balance of advantage in coming to each other's aid. Nuclear powers may also find it advantageous to ally themselves for deterrent purposes in the balance of terror, but the alliance's value for defense is likely to be low. For example, two countries which cannot separately muster a minimum second-strike force against the prospective aggressor may be able to do so by combining. But it would be irrational for either to retaliate when the other is attacked unless its own forces plus the undamaged forces of the attacked ally were sufficient to reduce the residual forces of the aggressor to a level which was tolerable for the supporting ally.

However, even if this condition did not hold (in which case the allies would not intend to carry out their obligation) the alliance would still have deterrent value because of the aggressor's uncertainties, and because deterrence does not depend on absolute credibility. A nuclear attack on a single country would be a very momentous act which might stimulate enough emotional reaction and irrationality among the victims' allies to trigger their retaliation. The aggressor would have to realize that the *possible* damage he might suffer at the hands of the whole alliance would be very much higher than the value he placed on conquest of the single victim. The magnitude of the possible retaliatory damage might very well offset in his mind the low credibility of an alliance response. If so, he would have to consider striking simultaneously at all the alliance members; "presumably" he would be deterred from this move if the alliance could muster a minimum second-strike force with respect to such a simultaneous attack.

A country with a minimum second-strike force might have little interest in alliances even for deterrent purposes if it was confident of being able to maintain such a capability at bearable cost in the face of an aggressor's expansion. But if it lacked such confidence, it might wish to make a deterrent pledge to aid friendly nuclear powers, even though it did not intend to carry out the pledge for lack of an adequate first-strike, counter-force capability.[4]

The Choice Between Strategic Deterrence and Tactical Defense

The great dilemma which faces nuclear powers and alliances concerns the degree to which deterrence by threats of nuclear punishment can substitute for a capacity to defend territory with conventional or tactical forces. Or, to put it another way, to what exent can the scope of the balance of terror be enlarged to reduce the burden of maintaining a position in the tactical balance of power?

Since the end of World War II, the United States has used its dominant position in the balance of terror to deter a considerably wider range of contingencies than direct nuclear attack on itself. The *means* of the balance of terror, in other words, have been applied to the furtherance of certain *ends* in the tactical balance of power, notably the deterrence of a large-scale Soviet ground attack in Western Europe. Consequently, in US and Western policy, the scope of the tactical balancing process has shrunk to the deterrence and defense of "limited" aggression, primarily outside Western Europe. The validity of this concept became increasingly questionable after 1953 and 1954, when the Russians exploded a hydrogen bomb and then demonstrated that they had a modern, long-range delivery capability. Disclosures since 1957 have underlined the fact that the Soviets have achieved or are near to achieving a substantial second-strike capability. The logical consequence of these disclosures is to reduce the plausibility of the strategic nuclear threat, for contingencies other than direct nuclear attack on the United States,

[4] The question of the degree to which democratic countries can credibly practice such bluffing is beyond the scope of this paper.

and to reinstate the tactical balancing process in something approaching its pre-nuclear dimensions.

However, it is a commonplace that world politics do not turn entirely on logic. The balance of terror may not be narrowed to its "pure" form—the deterrence of strategic nuclear war between nuclear powers—when both sides lack a maximum first-strike force. This would be the case only if both sides were omniscient with respect to each other's risk calculations and degree of rationality, and if both actually *were* rational. Since the aggressor can never be sure how the deterrer estimates and costs the consequences of war, or how prone he is to emotionalism and lapses of reason, there may still be some range of major tactical aggressions which can be deterred with fairly high confidence by strategic nuclear threats, even though the deterrer's nuclear forces fall short of a maximum first-strike capability. But what is the limit of this range? Major ground invasion of a country possessing strategic nuclear forces of at least minimum first-strike dimensions probably falls within the range, especially if this country is allied with other nuclear powers. Perhaps security against conventional ground attack against an area, such as Western Europe, which one or more nuclear powers considers "vital," could safely be left to the strategic deterrent. This would mean that tactical forces must be provided for the defense of all countries considered important but not "vital" by the nuclear powers.

The range of enemy moves on the ground which can be left to nuclear deterrence depends on how *effective* the nuclear threat is judged to be, and *how costly* the consequences of the failure of deterrence would be, with respect to each move. The cost would be counted in terms of the expected cost of war if the nuclear forces can defend successfully at acceptable cost; if they cannot (*i.e.*, if the threat is a bluff) the cost would be in the currency of territorial and other values lost in not carrying out the threat. More precisely, the balancing power or alliance must, in some sense, calculate a *product* of the probability of war and the cost of war (appropriately modified to take account of uncertainties and the disutility of gambling at high stakes) and compare this product with a similar product for the alternative of ground defense, after adding to each product the peacetime cost of providing the forces for each alternative. Nuclear deterrence rather than ground defense would be relied on for those contingencies for which the nuclear alternative promised the lesser aggregate of peacetime preparedness cost and "expected cost"[5] in war. The factors involved in such a calculation are highly intangible and immeasurable but some sort of intuitive judgment along these lines is basic.

Interaction Between the Strategic and Tactical Balances

If we assume that the strategic nuclear threat may still deter certain major tactical moves by the enemy, certain interactions between the balance of terror and the tactical balancing process within this "intermediate" area are worth noting.

A prominent idea in current NATO strategic doctrine is that although the ground force "shield" in West Germany is insufficient to block a determined Soviet push, it may be considered adequate to make any Soviet gains dependent on a decision to initiate war at a level of violence high enough to implicate the Big Deterrent with significant credibility. The validity of this concept is greater, the larger the strategic counter-force capability available to the West. When strategic forces are large enough, and of such a kind, that they *might* be used in a first strike, the aggressor will be aware of some critical level of violence in the lower-case balance of power which will either signal an objective large enough, or stimulate a sufficient degree of emotion or irrationality in the leadership of the West, to produce an intolerable probability of all-out war.

It would seem that there is an upper limit to the size of ground forces necessary to produce this "trip-wire" or "triggering" effect—a limit which is considerably below the level of tactical forces necessary to hold or defeat the Red Army. Once the shield is at the level at which it produces maximum support for the retaliatory threat (it may be there now) and the West does not have and cannot muster sufficient strategic first-strike capability to make its retaliatory threat plausible, there is little point in further *small* increases in the shield; it must become large enough, at least when supplemented by well-trained ready reserves, to block a full-scale Soviet ground attack. Under these conditions, the utility of tactical means for complementing the strategic threat drops to zero. The security of Western Europe then can no longer be left to the balance of terror, and becomes dependent on the achievement of a tactical balance of power in Europe.

[5] The term "expected cost" is used here in its technical sense, meaning the product of the probability of war and the estimated cost of war.

It should be noted that there may be other means, within the context of the balance of terror, which may be substituted in part for a US all-out retaliatory threat which has lost its credibility—notably the creation of nuclear deterrents controlled by the European countries themselves, either independently or on a group basis, and the development of a strategy of limited retaliation by the United States. These alternatives may turn out to be useful or necessary to counter Soviet attempts at nuclear blackmail, even if the Soviets are balanced tactically.

Within this intermediate range of contingencies, where both types of balancing are operative, the balance of terror may also complement the tactical balance. Thus, the US threat to respond with nuclear weapons outside the immediate battle theater in case of new outbreaks of war in Korea and Indochina may operate in Asia to discourage aggressions so blatant that they would raise an uncomfortable probability of the threat being carried out. They might contribute to holding the enemy's force commitment to a level which could be dealt with effectively with the limited conventional forces available.

There is an important interaction to be noted between the stability of the strategic balance and the stability of the tactical balance. When the strategic balance is unstable—*i.e.*, when both sides have a substantial first-strike counter-force capability—the tactical balance tends toward stability. Limited aggression will be undertaken with reluctance, and once started, will be carried out and defended against with caution because of the danger that at some point one side or the other will be provoked into striking first at the strategic level. But when the strategic balance is stable—when both sides have the capacity to strike back powerfully after absorbing a first strike—the tactical balance tends to become unstable because limited attacks can be undertaken and limited wars can be carried to fairly high levels of intensity without serious danger that either side will decide to initiate all-out strategic warfare.[6]

I have rather simplified the "real world" in assuming only two balancing systems. It would be more realistic to speak of several systems, each centering on a rather well-defined type of conflict. Ranging from low to high cost, the categories might be non-mili-

[6] Thomas C. Schelling has pointed out that when both sides have invulnerable second-strike forces, the limitations and inhibitions in limited war are likely to be weakened. See his "Surprise Attack and Disarmament," in Klaus Knorr (ed.), *NATO and American Security*, Princeton: Princeton University Press, 1959, p. 207.

tary "cold war," violent revolutionary conflict within a state in which outside powers participated only with material aid, civil war participated in by "volunteers" from the outside, limited inter-state conventional conflict between organized military forces, "tactical" nuclear warfare in a limited geographical area, limited strategic warfare involving the territories of the superpowers, and finally all-out war or the ultimate balance of terror. Each major contending power would then have in mind several "critical points," each representing the intensity of action at each level which would pose an unacceptable probability that the opponent would cross the boundary into the next or higher levels. The incipient aggressor would then be "balanced" if he could not win his objective at any level without crossing the critical threshold into another balancing system in which he would either lose or suffer unbearable costs. He would not be balanced if there were one or more weak links—*i.e.*, levels of conflict at which he could achieve his goal at acceptable cost without crossing the point of critical risk.

Speaking very generally, the defender can balance at each level in either of two ways: by providing a capacity for effective defense, or by posing a credible prospect to the enemy that in committing enough forces to win he would exceed his critical risk of moving to higher levels. The first method would be the safer, but the more costly in peacetime preparation. To illustrate the second or deterrent method, NATO might provide only enough conventional forces to insure that an attack would trigger tactical nuclear war. The Soviets might still be able to win at the tactical nuclear level, but foresee a high probability that if the conflict reached this stage, it would in turn spiral into limited strategic warfare, which they would consider too costly or too liable to expand to the all-out level. In order for such spiralling to seem reasonably possible to the Soviets, the US (or NATO jointly) would have to have somewhat more than a minimum, second-strike deterrent—*i.e.*, somewhat more than the basic requirement for its own security against all-out nuclear attack—but not necessarily a maximum, first-strike force.

Intentions and Capabilities

Nuclear technology has increased the importance of *intentions*, relative to *capabilities*, in the balancing process. Intentions have always been important, of course. In the pre-nuclear balance, the balancing process was set in motion by the perception of the disturber's aggressive intent, as well as by his military capabilities and war potential. And the adequacy of balance as a deterrent rested in part on the aggressor being clear about the intentions of the states which would eventually oppose him. But both sides could be fairly sure that once the conflict was joined, all states which did participate would do so to the full extent of their military power. An important calculation for each side, therefore, concerned the balance of total capabilities.

The relation between total capabilities is still important at the level of the balance of terror—*i.e.*, in the deterrence and fighting of all-out war. But for conflicts beginning at lower levels, the balance between overall capabilities is less important, and a new dimension had been added to the factor of intentions—namely, each side's assessment of the other's intent regarding what portion of its destructive power will be used. Each knows that the other can inflict costs far outweighing the value of any political objective if it cares to do so. Total capabilities establish the bounds of what is possible, but what is probable depends on a reciprocal assessment of wills, which in turn depends on each side's appraisal of the opponent's values at stake in each particular issue, his gambling propensities, his tendencies toward irrationality, his ideological or organizational commitments to certain responses, and his image of one's own characteristics in these respects.

Such estimates are of course highly subjective and uncertain, and the pervasive uncertainty adds an important element of stability to the overall balance of power. Each side is driven to think in terms of probabilities, and when even the smallest military action *may* eventuate in nuclear war and totally unacceptable costs, small probabilities are likely to be important. Consequently, there is considerable deterrent value in making threats which the threatener knows, and the threatened party suspects, would be irrational to carry out; if the threat increases the probability of unacceptable costs to the other side by only a few percentage points, it may be sufficient to deter.

This is to say that the existence of a "balance of power," or the capabilities requirements for balancing, can hardly be determined without attempting to look into the "mind" of the enemy. One might say that a subjective "balance of intentions" has become at least as important as the more objectively calculable "balance of capabilities."

A Concluding Comment

This article has attempted only to touch the high spots of a subject which sorely needs further theoretical analysis. International relations theory must come to terms with the weapons revolution and the logical place to start is with the balance of power concept. I have tried to show that the classical formulation is outmoded as a framework for analysis; that the modern balance of power is a multi-dimensional thing, with each dimension having different characteristics. I have been able to deal with only two broad dimensions here, but I should at least mention a third—the "balance of persuasion" or balance of capabilities to influence the internal politics of other countries—a dimension which Sigmund Neumann has picturesquely described as the "international civil war." Just as the balance of terror is the product of the revolution in weapons, the balance of persuasion is the product of the nationalist revolutions in Asia and Africa and the Soviet attempts to exploit these revolutions for its own ends. There are both supporting and competing interactions between this balance and the two military balances. It is misleading to think of the "balance of power" between the West and the Soviet bloc as a simple one-dimensional relationship in the traditional sense. To do so leads to such errors as believing that nuclear weapons have made industrial potential obsolete as a source of power, or that the criterion for security in the balance of terror is to have as many missiles as the Russians have, or that military forces and alliances are adequate responses to Russian initiative in the "balance of persuasion."

COLLECTIVE SECURITY

XI

Collective security is the key element of the peace and security systems contained in both the League of Nations Covenant and the United Nations Charter. Based on the idea of "all for one and one for all," it seeks to counter or, better yet, deter any breach of the peace by marshaling overwhelming strength against any aggressor.

The first selection is the second of the three Definitive Articles for a Perpetual Peace proposed by Immanuel Kant (1724–1804) in his essay *Perpetual Peace*. Although Kant uses such terms as "federation" and "state of nations," he does not propose the establishment of a single world-state. Instead he proposes a less far-reaching arrangement that is yet superior to the anarchy of unrestrained sovereignties: an "alliance of peace" or an "alliance for the prevention of war."

The name most prominently associated with collective security is that of Woodrow Wilson (1856–1924), 28th President of the United States. Though the idea of using collective force to maintain or achieve peace can be traced far back, it was not fully elaborated and envisaged on a worldwide scale until the early years of the twentieth century. During the First World War, the establishment of a collective security system following the war's end was advocated by an international association with headquarters in neutral The Hague. In the United States, the League to Enforce Peace was in the forefront of the propaganda effort. The second selection is President Wilson's speech to the first annual meeting of this League to Enforce Peace in Washington, D.C., on May 27, 1916. It embodies his first endorsement of the collective security approach to peace.

The theory of collective security seems appealingly simple and foolproof, but it has not been very successful in practice. What is wrong with the idea? And what is right? The second selection is a slightly abridged version of the trenchant analysis of collective security by Kenneth W. Thompson. The author taught at the University of Chicago and Northwestern University, and is now Vice-President of the Rockefeller Foundation.

33. *SECOND DEFINITIVE ARTICLE OF PERPETUAL PEACE* / IMMANUEL KANT*

The law of nations must be founded on a federation of free states.

Nations, as states, may be judged like single individuals, who in their natural condition (that is, independent of external laws) injure each other merely because they live side by side. For his own safety's sake, each can and ought to enter into a constitution with his neighbor by which everyone's rights are guaranteed. This would be an alliance of nations, but not necessarily a state of nations. A "state of nations" would be self-contradictory, because a state entails a relationship of a sovereign lawgiver to the subject people

* Immanuel Kant, *Zum ewigen Frieden: Ein philosophischer Entwurf*, 9th ed. (Königsberg, 1796). Translated by Eva Tamm Lijphart and Arend Lijphart.

and many nations in one state would constitute only one nation. This contradicts our premise, since we are considering the rights of nations in their mutual relations insofar as they remain separate states and will not merge into one.

We despise and regard as crude, barbaric, and a brutal degradation of humanity the attachment of savages to their lawless freedom and their preference for constant fighting rather than for submission to a legal constraint to be established by themselves, that is, their preference for chaotic freedom rather than reasonable liberty. Likewise one might imagine that civilized nations (each constituting a state by itself) would hasten to emerge from such a depraved condition as soon as possible. But instead each state thinks that its majesty (the term "majesty" applied to a nation is ridiculous) means precisely that it is not subject to any external force and that the glory of its ruler is based on the fact that thousands of people are at his command, ready to sacrifice themselves for a cause which does not even concern them without any risk to the ruler's own safety. The difference between the European savages and those in America lies mainly in this, that whereas several tribes among the latter have been completely devoured by their enemies, the former know a better way of using their captives: they prefer to add them to their subjects, and thus also increase the number of tools available to them for even more widespread wars.

The vicious element in human nature appears openly in the unrestrained relations among nations, whereas much of it remains hidden within the state as a result of governmental compulsion. It is therefore remarkable that the term "right" has not yet been completely banished from the politics of war as pedantic, and that no state has yet dared to declare itself publicly in support of this opinion. For Hugo Grotius, Puffendorf, Vattel, and others (all poor comforters) are still faithfully quoted in justification of a military attack, even though their code is no more than a philosophical or diplomatic one, and does not and cannot have the slightest legal force, because states as such are not subject to a common external authority. No example can be given of a state being moved to refrain from its intention by arguments supported by the testimony of such eminent men. This homage rendered to the concept of justice by each state, at least in words, does prove the existence of a higher, although at times dormant, moral tendency in man which will one day overcome his undeniably evil inclinations. And this hope he also holds for others. Otherwise, states wishing to fight against each other would not make use of the word "right," except in derision like the Gallic prince who stated: "The prerogative nature has given to the stronger is that the weaker should obey him."

The means by which states pursue their rights can never be a legal process as in an external court of justice, but only war. But the question of right is not settled by war and victory. A peace treaty may put an end to a particular war, but not to the conditions of war for which new pretexts can always be found; one cannot even dismiss this as completely unjust, as each one is his own judge under these circumstances. The law of nature charges individuals living in a lawless condition to "emerge from this condition." But according to the law of nations, not quite the same rule holds good for states. The reason is that, as states, they already have a legal constitution established within themselves, and consequently cannot be forced by others, according to their sense of right, to enter into an expanded legal constitution. Nevertheless, reason from the throne of the highest moral lawgiving power absolutely condemns war as a rightful procedure and makes a state of peace an immediate duty. But this peace cannot be established or guaranteed without a treaty among nations. A special kind of alliance must be formed which we may call an alliance of peace (*foedus pacificum*) different from a peace treaty (*pactum pacis*) in that the latter only seeks to end one war whereas the alliance of peace seeks to end all wars forever. This alliance does not seek to deprive the state of any of its power, but merely strives to maintain and secure the freedom of the state and of all other allied states, without compelling them to submit, like men in a state of nature, to public laws and coercion. The practicability (objective reality) of this idea of a federation which will gradually extend to all states and so lead to perpetual peace, can be demonstrated. If fortune directs that a powerful and enlightened people should form a republic (which is by nature inclined to perpetual peace), this state would serve as a center for the federal union. Other states would join it and thus the freedom of all states would be secured in accordance with the idea of the law of nations. And the alliance would gradually extend further and further.

If a people should say: "There shall be no war among us, for we shall organize ourselves into a state, that is, set up a supreme legislative, administrative, and judicial power which shall settle our differences peaceably," their decision is a logical one. But if this state says: "There shall be no war between me and other states although I recognize no supreme lawgiving power which shall guarantee my rights and whose rights I shall guarantee," then it is not clear at all on what it bases its confidence in having its rights guaranteed. The only solid basis for such a confidence would be an alliance of societies, namely a free federation, which reason must necessarily link with the idea of the law of nations, if that idea is to have any meaning at all.

The idea of the law of nations as giving the right to make war is really meaningless, for this right can only be a power of deciding what is just not according to universally valid external laws limiting the freedom of each individual, but according to one-sided application of force. Unless it means that people so inclined get their just reward when they exterminate each other, and thus find perpetual peace in the wide grave which covers them together with their atrocities. It stands to reason that there is no other remedy for the lawless and warlike condition of international relations than that states give up their wild, lawless freedom, just like individuals within the state, and accept the compulsion of public laws. Thus they can form a continually growing state of nations (*civitas gentium*) which would eventually include all the peoples of the earth. But states, according to their idea of international law, are absolutely opposed to this, and therefore reject in practice what is correct in theory. Hence, instead of the positive idea of a world-republic, if all is not to be lost, only a negative substitute may be feasible: a permanent and ever expanding alliance for the prevention of war. This alliance may stem the tide of lawless and warlike propensities, although there will always be the risk of war breaking out.

34. *A LEAGUE TO ENFORCE PEACE**/ *WOODROW WILSON*

When the invitation to be here to-night came to me, I was glad to accept it,—not because it offered me an opportunity to discuss the program of the League,—that you will, I am sure, not expect of

* James Brown Scott, ed., *President Wilson's Foreign Policy: Messages, Addresses, Papers* (New York: Oxford University Press, 1918), pp. 189–95.

me,—but because the desire of the whole world now turns eagerly, more and more eagerly, towards the hope of peace, and there is just reason why we should take our part in counsel upon this great theme. It is right that I, as spokesman of our Government, should attempt to give expression to what I believe to be the thought and purpose of the people of the United States in this vital matter.

This great war that broke so suddenly upon the world two years ago, and which has swept within its flame so great a part of the civilized world, has affected us very profoundly, and we are not only at liberty, it is perhaps our duty, to speak very frankly of it and of the great interests of civilization which it affects.

With its causes and its objects we are not concerned. The obscure fountains from which its stupendous flood has burst forth we are not interested to search for or explore. But so great a flood, spread far and wide to every quarter of the globe, has of necessity engulfed many a fair province of right that lies very near to us. Our own rights as a Nation, the liberties, the privileges, and the property of our people have been profoundly affected. We are not mere disconnected lookers-on. The longer the war lasts, the more deeply do we become concerned that it should be brought to an end and the world be permitted to resume its normal life and course again. And when it does come to an end we shall be as much concerned as the nations at war to see peace assume an aspect of permanence, give promise of days from which the anxiety of uncertainty shall be lifted, bring some assurance that peace and war shall always hereafter be reckoned part of the common interest of mankind. We are participants, whether we would or not, in the life of the world. The interests of all nations are our own also. We are partners with the rest. What affects mankind is inevitably our affair as well as the affair of the nations of Europe and of Asia.

One observation on the causes of the present war we are at liberty to make, and to make it may throw some light forward upon the future, as well as backward upon the past. It is plain that this war could have come only as it did, suddenly and out of secret counsels, without warning to the world, without discussion, without any of the deliberate movements of counsel with which it would seem natural to approach so stupendous a contest. It is probable that if it had been foreseen just what would happen, just what alliances would be formed, just what forces arrayed against one another, those who brought the great contest on would have been glad to substitute conference for force. If we ourselves had been afforded some opportunity to apprise the belligerents of the attitude which it would be our duty to take, of the policies and practices against which we would feel bound to use all our moral and economic strength, and in certain circumstances even our physical strength also, our own contribution to the counsel which might have averted the struggle would have been considered worth weighing and regarding.

And the lesson which the shock of being taken by surprise in a matter so deeply vital to all the nations of the world has made poignantly clear is, that the peace of the world must henceforth depend upon a new and more wholesome diplomacy. Only when the great nations of the world have reached some sort of agreement as to what they hold to be fundamental to their common interest, and as to some feasible method of acting in concert when any nation or group of nations seeks to disturb those fundamental things, can we feel that civilization is at last in a way of justifying its existence and claiming to be finally established. It is clear that nations must in the future be governed by the same high code of honor that we demand of individuals.

We must, indeed, in the very same breath with which we avow this conviction admit that we have ourselves upon occasion in the past been offenders against the law of diplomacy which we thus forecast; but our conviction is not the less clear, but rather the more clear, on that account. If this war has accomplished nothing else for the benefit of the world, it has at least disclosed a great moral necessity and set forward the thinking of the statesmen of the world by a whole age. Repeated utterances of the leading statesmen of most of the great nations now engaged in war have made it plain that their thought has come to this, that the principle of public right must henceforth take precedence over the individual interests of particular nations, and that the nations of the world must in some way band themselves together to see that that right prevails as against any sort of selfish aggression; that henceforth alliance must not be set up against alliance, understanding against understanding, but that there must be a common agreement for a common object, and that at the heart of that common object must lie the inviolable rights of peoples and of mankind. The nations of the world have become each other's neighbors. It is to their interest that they should understand each other. In order that they may understand each other, it is imperative that they should agree to co-operate in a common cause, and that they should so act that the guiding principle of that common cause shall be even-handed and impartial justice.

This is undoubtedly the thought of America. This is what we ourselves will say when there comes proper occasion to say it. In the dealings of nations with one another arbitrary force must be rejected and we must move forward to the thought of the modern world, the thought of which peace is the very atmosphere. That thought constitutes a chief part of the passionate conviction of America.

We believe these fundamental things: First, that every people has a right to choose the sovereignty under which they shall live. Like other nations, we have ourselves no doubt once and again offended against that principle when for a little while controlled by selfish passion, as our franker historians have been honorable enough to admit; but it has become more and more our rule of life and action. Second, that the small states of the world have a right to enjoy the same respect for their sovereignty and for their territorial integrity that great and powerful nations expect and insist upon. And, third, that the world has a right to be free from every disturbance of its peace that has its origin in aggression and disregard of the rights of peoples and nations.

So sincerely do we believe in these things that I am sure that I speak the mind and wish of the people of America when I say that the United States is willing to become a partner in any feasible association of nations formed in order to realize these objects and make them secure against violation.

There is nothing that the United States wants for itself that any other nation has. We are willing, on the contrary, to limit ourselves along with them to a prescribed course of duty and respect for the rights of others which will check any selfish passion of our own, as it will check any aggressive impulse of theirs.

If it should ever be our privilege to suggest or initiate a movement for peace among the nations now at war, I am sure that the people of the United States would wish their Government to move along these lines: First, such a settlement with regard to their own immediate interests as the belligerents may agree upon. We have nothing material of any kind to ask for ourselves, and are quite aware that we are in no sense or degree parties to the present quarrel. Our interest is only in peace and its future guarantees. Second, a universal association of the nations to maintain the inviolate security of the highway of the seas for the common and unhindered use of all the nations of the world, and to prevent any war begun either contrary to treaty covenants or without warning and full submission of the causes to the opinion of the world,—a virtual guarantee of territorial integrity and political independence.

But I did not come here, let me repeat, to discuss a program. I came only to avow a creed and give expression to the confidence I feel that the world is even now upon the eve of a great consummation, when some common force will be brought into existence which shall safeguard right as the first and most fundamental interest of all peoples and all governments, when coercion shall be summoned not to the service of political ambition or selfish hostility, but to the service of a common order, a common justice, and a common peace. God grant that the dawn of that day of frank dealing and of settled peace, concord, and co-operation may be near at hand!

35. *COLLECTIVE SECURITY REEXAMINED** / *KENNETH W. THOMPSON*

. . . What is collective security in theory? What are its precepts and main tenets? What, in simplest terms, is the philosophy of collective security? The rock bottom principle upon which collective security is founded provides that an attack on any one state will be regarded as an attack on all states. It finds its measure in the simple doctrine of one for all and all for one. War anywhere, in the context of Article 11 of the League of Nations, is the concern of every state.

Self-help and neutrality, it should be obvious, are the exact antithesis of such a theory. States under an order of neutrality are impartial when conflict breaks out, give their blessings to combatants to fight it out, and defer judgment regarding the justice or injustice of the cause involved. Self-help in the past was often "help yourself" so far as the great powers were concerned; they enforced their own rights and more besides. In the eighteenth and nineteenth centuries this system was fashionable and wars, although not elimi-

* Kenneth W. Thompson, "Collective Security Reexamined," *The American Political Science Review,* Vol. 47, No. 3 (September 1953), pp. 754–55, 757–63, 766–72. Reprinted by permission.

nated, were localized whenever possible. In a more integrated world environment, a conflict anywhere has some effect on conditions of peace everywhere. A disturbance at one point upsets the equilibrium at all other points, and the adjustment of a single conflict restores the foundations of harmony at other points throughout the world.

This idea of collective security is simple, challenging and novel. It would do for the international society what police action does for the domestic community. If the individual is threatened or endangered in municipal society, he turns to the legitimate agents of law enforcement, the police. The comparatively successful operation of this system has meant relative peace and tolerable harmony for most local communities. Through the action of police or "fire brigades" on a world scale, collective security has as its goal two comparable objectives. It would *prevent* war by providing a deterrent to aggression. It would *defend* the interests of peace-loving states in war if it came, by concentrating a preponderance of power against the aggressor. These two ends have been the goals of both the League and the United Nations. Through power and persuasion, a collective system would seek to deter aggression, as in the case of the Soviet imperialist threat to Titoist Yugoslavia. A potential aggressor must know that Yugoslavia and other United Nations powers stand together under the same protective umbrella. If war comes, the security system by pooling resources defends its interests against any nation which threatens to undermine it by swallowing up one of its members. . . .

This simple picture of the idea of collective security hardly furnishes a useful and realistic perspective on the way such a system operates in practice today. Nor are we helped by comparing the structure of the two historic experiments in collective security. The formal agencies for collective security after World War I were in several important respects unimpressive. Article 16 of the Covenant provided that any member resorting to war contrary to the Covenant had committed *ipso facto* an act of aggression against all other members. It was intended that first economic measures and then overt force should be applied against any offender. But although the international obligations of members were less ambiguous than in the Charter, there was no clear provision for their implementation or organization by a central enforcement agency. Each nation had full freedom to provide what troops it saw fit. The Council could then advise on additional measures. In contrast, Article 39 of the

Charter of the United Nations commissions the Security Council to determine the existence of a threat to the peace or act of aggression and Articles 43–47 obligate the members, upon the completion of agreements, to supply troops to the Military Staff Committee. The agencies for partial collective security, as found in the constitutional provisions of the North Atlantic Pact and the practical steps undertaken under NATO, are even more impressive and formidable today.

From the beginning, however, the real issue concerning collective security has had little to do with charters or compacts. The real issue has been the question of why the implementation of a system logically so flawless, and enjoying such impressive official devotion and popular support, should have been accompanied by a period of virtually unprecedented collective insecurity. It is a sobering fact that the nineteenth century was perhaps the most peaceful of modern centuries; the twentieth, by contrast, has been an epoch of unparalleled bloodshed. From 1815 to 1914 a system of old-fashioned balance of power contributed to the achievement of nearly a full century of uninterrupted peace. The past forty years have witnessed in rapid succession two great wars which the historian Arnold J. Toynbee compares to the double wars of the Romans and the Carthaginians and the two struggles of the Peloponnesian War which wrecked Hellenic Civilization. He has observed that quite possibly we have dealt ourselves the same "knockout blows" that these wars represented for the older civilizations. There were only eighteen months in the nineteenth century when France, Russia, Austria, Prussia, England and Spain found themselves at war with one another (excluding the Crimean War as a colonial struggle). By contrast, our experience thus far with the novel machinery of collective security has hardly warranted the unqualified postwar optimism of men like Mr. Hull that, with the new international organization, power politics and war were being left far behind in our progress toward utopia.

Instead the recent decades have been years of unceasing war or threats of war. What are the causes of this state of affairs? What are the reasons for the enormous gap between the theory and practice, the promise and performance of collective security? The most popular and reassuring answer has been that the radical doctrines of National Socialism and Communism have undermined the ideal system, and that modern technology has shattered the earlier limitations on conflict. Yet an equally dynamic creed challenged peace and order in the nineteenth century and provided a fighting faith for imperialist France.

The serious observer must look more deeply at the substance of political reality. In so doing he will find that collective security yesterday and today has been viewed unrealistically, and that its executors have been asked to perform tasks which could be performed with complete success only if certain objective conditions were realized. The most vital questions regarding collective security have seldom been asked; the real problems have often been evaded. The fundamental issues and problems which should have been boldly and realistically confronted have been concealed and obscured in constitutional verbiage and formal legalistic arguments. The four basic problems responsible for the tragic predicament of collective security include the problem of its basic preconditions, the political problem, the psychological problem and the problem of peaceful change. The first is from one standpoint most basic, for the preconditions of collective security, being frequently misunderstood, have presented the most stubborn obstacle to the maintenance of international peace.

Preconditions of Collective Security. Manifestly, collective enforcement is unattainable in the absence of appropriate international machinery and binding obligations clearly set forth in recognized legal instruments. Yet every informed citizen knows from experience that a legal arrangement imposed upon political and social conditions incompatible with its fulfillment makes successful political action difficult. Therefore it is essential in considering the reality of collective security that we understand fully its assumptions and requirements.

First, collective enforcement assumes a status quo, or situation of peace, on which the nations with predominant strength agree. In practical terms, the peace which a collective system must defend is the territorial status quo existing at the time the system is brought into being. There is nothing in past experience to indicate that all nations, or even a combination sufficiently powerful to defy the rest, will agree on the meaning of a particular status quo. Following every war, the defeated powers who feel they have suffered most by the terms of peace come to oppose the established status quo. In the aftermath of World War II, however, the question of satisfaction or dissatisfaction with the status quo has largely been superseded by an earlier and prior question. Up to the present time, no practical arrangement has been worked out acceptable to the major powers, who in this case are primarily the Soviet Union and the United States, on which the postwar status quo could be founded. The unresolved conflict between East and West has prevented the establishment of peace. Consequently, the latest experiment in collective security presents us with the anomalous picture of a system created to defend a status quo which has not yet been brought into being. . . .

Second, collective security demands that nations subscribing to the status quo be willing and able at all times to muster overwhelming strength for collective defense at successive points of conflict. In theory, the supporters of the status quo might be capable in particular emergencies of mobilizing effective and decisive power against the single aggressor who sought to defy them. Or, by pooling the resources of all the nations in a permanently organized international force, collective enforcement could be made automatic, instantaneous, and preponderant. The former condition, however, is practically impossible of fulfillment, inasmuch as the threat to the status quo comes historically from more than one dissatisfied power or aggressor. The second condition would call for the unprecedented practice of international contingents operating under an international agency empowered to decide conclusively when and how they should be used.

The United Nations Charter seems to take a long step toward this objective by providing that all members are "to make available to the Security Council, on its call and in accordance with a special agreement or agreements, armed forces, assistance and facilities. . . ." (Article 43, Paragraph 1.) Through this provision, the incurable weakness of decentralized enforcement by which past international systems have been rendered impotent is ostensibly rectified. For the Achilles' heel of the earlier experiments was the decentralized character of the enforcement process; separate nations retained the right to determine whether or not military forces would be made available to meet particular crises. In 1942, Cordell Hull had urged that "some international agency must be created which can—by force, if necessary—keep the peace. . . ."[15] Yet Mr. Hull's proposition and Articles 43ff of the Charter, by which this historic difficulty apparently had been surmounted, in practice have remained a dead letter. No special agreements have been concluded by Members with the Security Council; talks in the Military Staff Committee soon reached an impasse. The Soviet Union has opposed proportionate contributions to an international air and naval force,

[15] 7 Department of State *Bulletin* (1942), p. 645.

which would leave it particularly vulnerable to forces overwhelmingly more powerful than its own. The United States has been concerned to make the United Nations Armed Force as strong as possible against the military preponderance of the Soviet Army in Europe and Asia, while the Russians have sought to keep it as weak as possible.[16] The stalemate in the Military Staff Committee is fundamentally a symptom of the struggle between the two great powers and between supporters and opponents of the undefined status quo. In practice, the realization of the second condition of overwhelming strength for collective enforcement has constantly run afoul of special national demands for military security and supremacy.

There is a *third* and final prerequisite of collective security, however, to which we now turn, that was widely assumed to be in existence at the time preparations for the United Nations were first being made. It is essential to collective security in a world of unequal powers that at least the major powers enjoy a minimum of political solidarity and moral community. On October 13, 1944, Premier Stalin asked himself, in an article appearing in the Soviet *Information Bulletin*, if the world organization could be effective. He predicted that it would "be effective if the Great Powers, which have borne the brunt of the war against Hitler-Germany continue to act in a spirit of unanimity and accord."[17]

The effectiveness of the United Nations and of the Security Council in particular was predicated upon the unanimity of the five great powers. It was an article of political faith in the Roosevelt Administration that trustworthiness and good will on the part of Americans would inspire the same qualities among the Russians. In a particularly revealing memorandum for President Harry S. Truman dated September 11, 1945, Mr. Stimson explained: "The chief lesson I have learned in a long life is that the only way you can make a man trustworthy is to trust him; and the surest way to make him

[16] It should be noted that the Russians have no monopoly on opposition to a powerful world police force. Senator Vandenberg declares in his Memoirs: "I am opposed to what is generally understood by the term 'international police force.' So, I believe, are the President, Secretary Hull and most realistic students of this problem. To be adequate, an international police force would have to be larger than the regular army and navy of any other power on earth. I think it is fantastic to believe that the people would long consent to the maintenance of any such enormous concentration of power in the postwar peace; and I also think that the temptation to reach for its ultimate control could become the greatest possible threat to peace in years to come." Vandenberg, *Private Papers*, pp. 120–21.

[17] USSR *Information Bulletin*, Oct. 13, 1944.

untrustworthy is to distrust him and show your distrust."[18] Unanimity among the great powers which alien ideologies and conflicting interests might otherwise undermine would be secured through the application of a code of social ethics that had in general been effective within the United States.[19]

By October of 1947, Mr. Stimson, writing in *Foreign Affairs*, had cause to reformulate his proposition and to say: "I have often said that the surest way to make a man trustworthy is to trust him. But I must add that this does not always apply to a man who is determined to make you his dupe. Before we can make friends with the Russians, their leaders will have to be convinced that they have nothing to gain, and everything to lose, by acting on the assumption that our society is dying and that our principles are outworn."[20] Thus the preconditions of collective security under the United Nations have either been wanting from the beginning, or have been corroded and destroyed by the all-consuming forces of the "cold war."

The Political Problem. The chief practical obstacle to collective security is the political problem deriving from the conflict of independent foreign policies. The loyalties and interests of nations participating in international organizations and collective security systems are of a different order from those of individuals taking part in the more intimate communities of the family and nation.[21] Both individuals and nations pursue their own interests, but in some areas

[18] Stimson, *On Active Service*, p. 644.

[19] It remained, however, for Premier Stalin in conversation with Harry Hopkins to furnish unwittingly the key to the success or failure of this endeavor. He declared that trust and confidence in international as in national relations is dependent upon the existence of ". . . a minimum moral standard between all nations and without such a minimum moral standard nations could not exist." Premier Stalin continued that the leaders of Nazi Germany "knew no such minimum moral standard [but] . . . without a second's thought would sign a treaty today, break it tomorrow and sign a second one the following day. Nations must fulfill their treaty obligations, he said, or international society could not exist." Nor, it might be added, could collective security survive. Sherwood, *Roosevelt and Hopkins*, Vol. 1, pp. 399–400.

[20] Stimson, *On Active Service*, pp. 649–50.

[21] Some years ago Monsieur Paul Henri Spaak in an address before the Foreign Press Union declared: "There must be a hierarchy in international obligations. The nations of the continent cannot be asked to consider with the same realism and sincerity of judgment affairs which directly concern them and events which are taking place thousands of kilometres away in regions where they have neither interests nor influence. Indivisible peace, mutual assistance, and even collective security are general ideas whose practical effect must be clearly explained and clearly limited." Quoted in *Survey of International Affairs, 1936* (London, 1937), pp. 354–55.

and on certain occasions the individual may forsake his egotistic motives for loyalty to some higher institution or nobler cause. There are institutions in integrated societies which provide common standards under which the individual can realize his aspirations. There need be no inherent conflict between an individual's private interests and his national loyalties, for the latter can often promote the realization of the former. On the other hand, conflicts are often inevitable between national and supranational loyalties, and when the projected policy of an international organization conflicts with that of a particular nation, at all times and in all places the national interest prevails. . . .

The Psychological Problem. Collective security founders on other shoals. It sometimes breaks down because of collective resentments or hatreds and reactions which express certain features of a particular national character. In 1931, the Japanese spilled over into Manchuria. Why was it that more positive action was not taken? To be sure there were legal, economic, and political obstacles existing. "War" in international relations is a weaselword, and debates which surround it easily become legal quagmires. Japan said it had not declared war, China had not done so, and therefore the bombs were a mere illusion. Behind this legal smokescreen the struggle went on and men were as dead as if they had fought in a legally more respectable war. Economically, the world was deep in a painful depression; politically, Manchuria seemed far away and of little immediate interest of Western nations. There was in addition, however, a psychological factor. Certain groups in the West harbored deep resentments against the victims of Japanese imperialism. In particular, certain elements within the British trading community remembered private scores that had not been settled and the recent ingratitude of the Chinese toward the West. This sector of Western public opinion took a kind of vicarious pleasure in the punishment the Japanese were inflicting upon China which, with India, became a symbol of the heavy toll being taken economically and psychologically in Europe by Asia's revolt. The Japanese action was unconsciously viewed as a retaliation against the whole anti-foreign movement that was sweeping Asia.

Another psychological factor was the attitude of responsible naval and military experts in Britain. One major result of the Washington Treaties of 1921–22 had been to leave Japan supreme on all fronts in the Far East. Its strategic position made it virtually immune from any serious attack. This confronted the newborn collective system with a military and naval problem which was made more acute by the prospects of joint operations by British and American naval forces. To British naval experts, American admirals and naval leaders were a boisterous and unproven lot. They had emerged overnight as the one irresistible threat to British naval supremacy. As youngsters in naval warfare, they would as likely as not prove erratic and unreliable under fire. Therefore, for Britain to commit herself unqualifiedly to a policy of military and naval intervention in an area where the newly acquired American naval supremacy would prevail would be risky and hazardous to British national interests. The disdain in which British naval leaders held their American opposite numbers was a psychological factor of great importance in 1931.[30]

In 1950–51, a new psychological obstacle appeared to block effective universal collective security. The British have had a Far Eastern policy for nearly a century-and-a-half. To them the policy of the United Nations, as influenced by the United States and especially by its spectacular and outspoken general, was from the first based on false assumptions. When General MacArthur's abortive thrust toward the Yalu River was turned back and the one action which all Western policy had sought to forestall—the intervention of the Chinese Communists—followed, the British reaction, however restrained, was clearly inevitable. Given the policy, the outcome was inescapable.

Peaceful Change. Collective security, as we have seen, depends upon agreed concepts of justice in international society shared by all or most of its members. In domestic societies this consensus is arrived at by public opinion's availing itself of the instruments of government in registering the majority will. If societies were characterized by ideal justice and perfect equilibrium among contending social groups, the problems of social change would perhaps disappear. Since the demands for social change are continuously asserted in the market place and resolved in legislative and electoral debates, the pursuit of abstract justice assumes less urgency than the claims for justice of particular social groups.

In every society two social forces inevitably exist in basic tension with one another. The one force comprises the groups

[30] The psychological turn of mind among certain professional Western soldiers before the Second World War offers a further illustration of this point. Admiration and respect for Germany's amazing rearmament program inspired the opinion that the conquest of England by Germany would prove the inevitable superiority of ground and air over sea power.

supporting the status quo as stabilized and perpetuated in the political and legal order of the day. Another force made up of the groups sharing common opposition to the status quo seeks to change or overturn it. In the light of this conflict, the basic problem of government is to provide ways by which continuity is achieved and social change not prevented. Within organized and integrated societies, the courts historically have contributed continuity whereas legislatures have been the faithful agents of change. As Congress was the forum in which the claims and grievances of distressed groups were alleviated by New Deal laws and decrees in the 1930's, the British Parliament in the nineteenth century was the agency in which the middle-class revolt against feudalism was expressed and achieved.

It should be apparent, however, that the process of change in society is made possible by other agencies as well. The executive has provided an instrument through which opinion can be channeled and transformed into effective policy. Peaceful change thus involves the whole of society with its orderly machinery through which social groups seek support for their claims elevated into principles of justice that must be compatible with the society's fundamental values. It is the whole of domestic society, therefore, and not the legislature in isolation, that brings about social change. For while the making of new laws is the formal act of social change, the role of legislatures is essentially the ratification of the choices at which unorganized society has already arrived. This is made possible by the generally accepted framework of justice within which disputes can be settled.

It is obvious that the conditions and institutions which exist within domestic societies are absent or greatly weakened in international society. Legislative bodies with law-making powers capable of fulfilling the functions that Congress or any other legislature performs are conspicuously absent on the international scene. The General Assembly has the power to "make recommendations" on matters prescribed in the Charter; the Security Council may "decide" on measures to be taken and "call upon" members to act. While these powers appear to mark an advance, in practice they have hardly resulted in any especially decisive step toward international law-making. The basic defects in the structure of international society are nowhere more apparent than in connection with peaceful change. . . .

In the face of the problems we have outlined and discussed, two approaches to the idea and the reality of collective security have vied with one another in recent years. The one demands in the name of a principle that all nations at all times resist aggression. Its adherents maintain that only in this way can the national interests of independent states be protected and served. This approach takes its stand on the abstract and uncorruptible ideal of collective security.

Another approach, based primarily on what we have denoted the reality of collective security, reaches other conclusions on the basis of opposing concepts and principles. In the present state of world affairs, we are told, a policy of collective security leads inevitably down the road of general war and universal catastrophe. The Founding Fathers of this Republic knew more clearly than their present day heirs the futility of seeking to coerce sovereign states. At the Constitutional Convention of 1787, it was argued that unless states were united in one sovereign government (which both approaches agree is absent from the international scene today), they could be coerced only through civil war. Alexander Hamilton declared to the New York State Convention, met to ratify the new Constitution: "to coerce the states is one of the maddest projects that was ever devised. A failure of compliance will never be confined to a single state. This being the case can we suppose it wise to hazard a civil war."[34] Writing in the same tradition, Hans J. Morgenthau has maintained: "Under a system of collective security operating under less than ideal conditions, war between A and B or between any other two nations anywhere in the world is of necessity tantamount to war among all or at best most nations of the world."[35] Since ideal conditions are not presently in sight, collective security is tantamount to war.

Thus the West is presented, in theory at least, with a choice between almost equally hopeless and catastrophic alternatives. Through the fact of membership in the United Nations, Western nations are committed to a system of collective security embodied in the Charter. Confronted with reality, however, the staunchest champions of collective security are driven to invoke a dual standard as a guide for action. On the one hand, they must firmly resolve

[34] Quoted in Harrop Freeman and Theodore Paullin, *Coercion of States in Federal Unions* (Philadelphia, 1943), p. 14. The late Professor Edwin Borchard warned: "There is no element of the proposal of punishing aggressors which is not contested by history and disproved by experience." "The Impracticability of Enforcing Peace," *The Yale Law Journal*, Vol. 55, p. 968 (Aug., 1946).

[35] Hans J. Morgenthau, *Politics Among Nations* (New York, 1948), p. 335.

on principle to intervene to arrest aggression at its source. On the other hand, while unable to disavow the principle, in concrete actions they are required to apply it judiciously with immense self-restraint.

The gulf between principles and actions in 1935–36 and again in 1950 illustrates the irony of collective security in the real world for, under its dispensation, Mussolini's aggression in Ethiopia and the North Korean invasion of South Korea made intervention a foregone conclusion. Once aggression is identified, the duty of the nations espousing collective security is unequivocal. Yet since Britain and France were unprepared in 1935, it was doubtful that more could be accomplished than to drive Italy into the camp of Germany. Notwithstanding, the viewpoint prevailed that if the champions of collective security did nothing, other more dangerous acts of aggression would follow.

The perils in pursuing the idea of collective security to its logical conclusion are matched only by the hazards involved in abandoning it. It is tempting to say that since collective security against a great power is unworkable, since psychological and political obstacles exist, and since the requirements for peaceful change are quite frequently at odds with enforcement, the system should be scrapped and replaced. Yet the coalition of the Western nations has been aroused to the threat confronting it by the resolute stand that was taken in Korea, and the whole free world has been animated and inspired by our boldness, courage and, lately, our patience and restraint. In the struggle against Soviet imperialism, it is vital that we have firm friends and willing allies who recognize mutual interests. We can best assure their cooperation by preserving and strengthening the tenuous ties by which all are bound together within the United Nations.

Perhaps the supreme paradox of American foreign policy today is the necessity placed upon us to seize and employ the essentially utopian instruments of collective security in a brutally realistic power struggle. Its agencies furnish a political framework through which the broad coalition of the free world can be strengthened and a more stable equilibrium of world power be restored. Britain and France and the free powers of Asia are more likely to play their part and contribute to the restoration of a balance of power in Europe and Asia if we assure them of support through mutual guarantees and create confidence by discussions in the halls and anterooms of the United Nations.

Collective security, with its present foundations weakened

and enfeebled, can contribute to peace and order if wisely and moderately employed. It has become clear in Korea that policies undertaken in the name of collective security are not necessarily tantamount to world war. Localized struggles are still possible if major powers are not confounded by the ideal or misled by a too absolute interpretation of the meaning of collective enforcement. Moreover, the influence of other nations more skilled in historic diplomacy has served within the United Nations as a kind of built-in restraint on the impulses of American foreign policy. Our partners in utopia have nudged us in the direction of what would appear to be a more realistic foreign policy. Beyond this, with the recent breakup of the simple bi-polar balance of power in the world, the practical uses for collective agencies may be multiplied indefinitely as the prospect of action by coalitions of members against independent if minor centers of power becomes a reality.

The uses of collective security are more modest and limited than its more ardent advocates appreciate. Yet if participants base their policies on enduring political principles and judge and measure each action by the interests and power involved, it need not be an inevitable blind alley. Between the scylla of blind acceptance and the charybdis of logical rejection we must aim to establish the intellectual foundations required for an empirical and pragmatic approach to the modern concept of collective security.

INTERNATIONAL ORGANIZATION

XII

THIS CHAPTER WILL BE DEVOTED TO THE TWO universal multi-purpose international organizations: the League of Nations and the United Nations. Regional and functional organizations will be considered in the next chapter.

An early blueprint for a U.N.-type organization—complete with a charter, an assembly, rules of financing the organization, provisions for voting and charter revision, a collective security agreement, etc.—was outlined by Jean Jacques Rousseau (1712–78) in his *A Lasting Peace.* The essay is a summary and commentary on a similar work by the Abbé de Saint Pierre written in the early eighteenth century, and the proposals are partly those of the Abbé de Saint Pierre and partly Rousseau's.

The League and the United Nations are compared in the second selection by

U Thant, the third U.N. Secretary General. Thant delivered this speech at the University of California in Berkeley on April 2, 1964.

The third selection is by Thant's predecessor, Dag Hammarskjöld, Secretary General from 1953 until 1961. Hammarskjöld's analysis of the two concepts of the U.N.'s proper role were incorporated in his introduction to the last annual report to the General Assembly that he prepared. The introduction is dated August 17, 1961, a short time before his tragic death in Africa.

The final selection in this chapter is by one of the most prominent and outspoken critics of the United Nations: General Charles de Gaulle, first President of the Fifth French Republic. De Gaulle made these remarks at a press conference in the Elysée Palace on April 11, 1961.

36. *SKETCH OF A PROJECT FOR PERMANENT PEACE*/ JEAN JACQUES ROUSSEAU*

. . . From time to time certain general assemblies called congresses are convened among us, to which delegates from all states of Europe proceed solemnly, to return home again; where they assemble to say nothing; where all public affairs are discussed in detail; where they engage in common deliberation whether the conference table shall be round or square, how many doors the conference room shall have, whether one plenipotentiary shall sit with his face or his back to the window, whether another shall be allowed to enter the room as much as two inches on a formal visit; and a thousand questions of equal importance, vainly discussed for three centuries and certainly most worthy of occupying the attention of our statesmen.

It is possible that the members of one of these assemblies may be blessed with common sense some day. It is not even impossible that they will sincerely want to serve the public interest. And, for reasons to be discussed shortly, it is also conceivable that after ironing out many difficulties, they will be instructed by their respective sovereigns to sign the charter of the General Confederation containing the following five articles:

* Jean Jacques Rousseau, *Extrait du Projet de Paix Perpétuelle de M. L'Abbé de Saint-Pierre* (Geneva, 1761). Translated by Eva Tamm Lijphart and Arend Lijphart.

1. The contracting sovereigns shall establish a perpetual and irrevocable alliance, and shall appoint plenipotentiaries to hold in a specified place a permanent diet or congress, in which all disputes between the contracting parties shall be settled and terminated by means of arbitration or adjudication.

2. The second article shall specify: the number of sovereigns whose plenipotentiaries shall have a vote in the diet; those who shall be invited to join the organization; the order, time, and method by which the presidency shall pass from one to another at equal intervals; and finally each member's financial contribution and the method of collecting it, to pay for the common expenses.

3. The Confederation shall guarantee to each of its members the control and government of all its present possessions as well as the rules of succession, elective or hereditary, as established by the fundamental laws of each country. Moreover, in order to eliminate once and for all the source of those constantly recurring territorial disputes, the contracting powers shall agree to regard the status quo and their last treaties as the basis of their mutual rights, and to renounce forever any anterior claim. All future disputed successions and other claims shall be settled by the diet by means of arbitration. Resort to force or taking up arms against each other shall not be permitted under any pretext whatsoever.

4. The fourth article shall specify the cases in which any member state breaking the treaty shall be put to the ban of Europe and proscribed as a public enemy: namely, refusing to execute the judgments of the grand alliance, making preparations for war, negotiating treaties harmful to the Confederation, taking up arms to resist it or to attack any one of the member states.

The same article shall also stipulate that the member states shall take collective military measures, at the common expense, against any state put to the ban of Europe, until this state lays down its arms, executes the judgments and rules of the diet, makes reparations for its wrongs, pays the costs, and makes amends even for preparations for war contrary to the treaty.

5. Finally, the plenipotentiaries of the European states assembled in the diet shall always have the power, on the instruction of their courts, to establish rules which they consider essential for the greatest possible benefit for the Confederation as a whole and for each of its members. Provisional rules shall be adopted by a simple majority of votes; definitive rules (after five years) by a

three-fourths majority. But no change in these five fundamental articles shall ever be made without the unanimous consent of the member states. . . .

37. *THE LEAGUE OF NATIONS AND THE UNITED NATIONS* / U THANT*

Next year the United Nations will celebrate the twentieth anniversary of its birth in San Francisco. It will have then been in existence for almost exactly the same number of years as the effective life of the League of Nations, its forerunner. Some comparison of the experience and development of the two organizations is therefore timely.

The word "failure" is often applied to the League of Nations, and the history, especially of its early and successful years, is not much studied now, or even mentioned. And yet in the closing years of World War II the victorious allies hastened to organize and build a new international organization which was, in fact, an improved and strengthened version of the old League. It was not the League, or the ideas behind it, that failed. Rather its members, in the critical years of the 1930's, failed to use and support it, and to rally under its banner against aggression and other dangers. It was thus that they finally had to face these dangers separately and in disarray in the terrible first years of the Second World War.

President Woodrow Wilson laid the first draft of the Covenant of the League before the Paris Conference in 1919 with the words "A living thing is born". Despite disaster and unfulfilled promise, these words have proved to be prophetic, as we can see when we look at the world today as represented in the United Nations. For this first great attempt to move toward a "worldwide political and social order in which the common interests of humanity could be seen and served across the barriers of national tradition, racial differences and geographical separation" (as the League's historian, Mr. Frank Walters, has described it) was a historical event of the very highest importance. The League embodied a concept which has fundamentally altered, in our own century, the entire conduct

* U Thant, "The League of Nations and the United Nations," *UN Monthly Chronicle*, Vol. 1, No. 1 (May 1964), pp. 70–75.

of international relations and even the general convictions which form the basis of public opinion.

Let us look for a moment at the meaning of this change. Before the League of Nations came into being, it was almost universally held that every state was the sole and sovereign judge of its own acts and was immune from criticism or even questioning by other states. The idea—now generally accepted—that the community of nations had a moral or legal right to discuss and judge the international conduct of its members was not embodied in any treaty or institution until the Covenant. From that time also dates the idea, now almost universally accepted, that aggressive war is a crime against humanity and that it is the interest, the duty and the right of every state to join in preventing it. That these ideas now seem commonplace is a measure of the vision of the authors of the Covenant of the League.

The Covenant was based on other ideas no less important or fundamental—a new respect for the rights of small nations, the recognition of the need for cooperation in social and economic affairs, the habit of public debate on even the gravest diplomatic issues, the formation of an international civil service. It is the lasting achievement of the League that such ideas are an essential part of the political thinking of our world. Thus the League, as the embodiment of certain ideals and ideas, is very much alive and with us today.

In its time the Covenant of the League was a tremendous step forward, a radical change in the concept of international order. It was a response to the bitter, futile and appalling experience of the First World War, and in retrospect it may be thought the step was too far-reaching to provide a firm foothold when new and terrible dangers threatened. When its basic ideas were reborn in the closing years of the Second World War, however, they were supported by a far greater public understanding and by an even more compelling necessity for success.

The world has changed so rapidly in the last 20 years that it is hard to remember what it was like in the 1920's and 1930's. Thus we tend to forget how much, in the context of the inter-war world, the League actually did or attempted, or how important were the new models of international organization and action which it devised and developed. Despite its fluctuating fortunes, the central purpose of the League remained constant—to be the constitutional embodiment of man's aspirations for peace and a rationally organized world. We, in our time, owe an immense debt to those who, in far harder times, kept this idea alive and did as much as they could to build upon it.

I have already mentioned their achievement in the realm of political ideas. In the practical sphere also, their efforts made it possible for the United Nations, when it came into being in 1945, to build on firm and already existing foundations. Quite apart from the central political structure, many of the new organizations continued and developed from the old with unbroken continuity. The International Labour Organisation was maintained and the Permanent Court at The Hague re-established as the International Court of Justice. The Economic and Social Council was modelled on plans made by the Bruce Committee in the last days of peace in 1939. The WHO and FAO and UNESCO grew out of the corresponding parts of the League Secretariat, while the Mandates System of the League was taken over by the United Nations Trusteeship System. The League Treaty Series was maintained without interruption by the United Nations, and many other activities such as the control of narcotic drugs and work for refugees passed from the old organization to the new one.

The basis of both the League of Nations and the United Nations is the pledge by sovereign states to cooperate, a pledge which involves some measure of sacrifice of sovereignty in the common interest. Both organizations were designed as an intermediate base between the international relations of traditional diplomacy, which had become obsolescent with the disasters of the First World War, and were proved inadequate, and even dangerous, with the Second World War, and the theoretical, ultimate aim of a world legislature, if not a world government. Both organizations therefore show the weaknesses of a transitional state–great aims with small means, great responsibilities with little authority, great expectations clouded by deep suspicions, and hopes for the future constantly blurred by fears and prejudices from the past.

National sovereignty is, understandably, a jealously guarded possession. The harmonizing of national sovereignty with the wider interest, in a way that is acceptable to the governments and peoples concerned, is the main task, and necessity, of international organization. The League's experience made this necessity clear, and we can already see a considerable advance since 1919. Certain European organizations in particular, such as the Coal and Steel Community and the Common Market, have gone far in the direction of pooling resources, coordinating policy and limiting national sovereignty in certain economic fields.

The Charter shows some formal advances over the Covenant in the matter of sovereignty. For example, it forbids the use of force by a state in a manner inconsistent with the purposes of the Organization and obligates the members to supply armed forces and other assistance to the Security Council and to apply measures called for by the Council.

In the United Nations there have also been practical indications of a changing attitude towards the sanctity of national sovereignty. The acceptance of a United Nations peace-keeping force on the territory of a sovereign state is one such instance, and the provision of contingents of national armies to serve under United Nations command is another. These are small beginnings, but impotant ones. There is also, I hope, an increasing recognition of the impartiality and objectivity of the United Nations Secretariat. Despite these changes, the United Nations still has only to a very limited extent a separate existence, and possibilities of action, independent of the will of member governments and the policies of member states. In a given situation it can advance no further than the parties concerned permit. As my distinguished predecessor pointed out, its capacity to act is, in fact, still to a large extent restricted by fundamental national reactions.

There were major differences in the origins and environment of the League and the United Nations. The League was directly linked with the outcome of the First World War and was thus, from the first, dominated by the European situation. The Covenant of the League was an integral part of the Treaty of Versailles. The League was therefore an aspect of the postwar settlement, with all the advantages and disadvantages of such a position. The United Nations Charter on the other hand was drafted before the end of the Second World War and was expressly *not* a part of the postwar settlement. In a sense the League was thus tied from the first to the *status quo* with strong overtones from the past. The United Nations Charter, on the other hand, starting with a statement of purposes and principles for the guidance of the Organization and its members, looks firmly to the future. It is this difference perhaps more than any other that has given the United Nations its vitality.

The Covenant was a remarkable document for its time. Its articles on the reduction in armaments, on aggression, on the judicial settlement of disputes and resort to the Permanent Court of International Justice, on sanctions and on the use of armed force to protect the covenants of the League, were great political innovations in the world of 1919 and have been taken up and developed in the corresponding articles of the United Nations Charter. Unfortunately, in the critical 1930's the leadership, the confidence and the courage to apply them effectively were lacking, and with disastrous results. The soundness of the principles underlying them was reinforced rather than invalidated by this failure.

In other respects the League's Covenant lacked the dynamism of the Charter. Thus the Covenant lacked a clear statement of such an important objective as development towards self-government or independence, and emphasis on the necessity of economic and social development and human rights as an essential complement to political and juridical, and even military, arrangements to establish a firm basis for peace. The United Nations Charter has provided, in practice, a more flexible instrument than the League Covenant, over a wider field. The abandonment of the over-all rule of unanimity which prevailed in the League Council and Assembly is one symptom of this flexibility. The Security Council has a far wider discretion than the League Council had in determining what constitutes an act of aggression; while the system of specialized agencies makes possible much wider and more functional operation in the economic and social field.

The world of the League was in some ways a far less articulate world than we have today. A large proportion of the world's population was then still in colonial status and played little or no part in the world's affairs. This fact gave a basic lack of representative balance to the League's position as a world organization, which was aggravated by other factors relating to membership. Despite the primary role of President Wilson in its creation, the United States, by one of history's major ironies, was never a member of the League. The USSR only became a member in 1934, at which time both Germany and Japan had given notice of their withdrawal, to be followed two years later by Italy. Thus the major effort to maintain peace and security in a critical time through the League devolved upon France and Great Britain and had an essentially European basis, which deprived it of much of the moral authority of a truly global organization.

In this regard, the history of the United Nations presents a striking contrast in its steady progress toward universality. Existing in a time of rapid historic change, its membership has more than doubled since its inception, and the majority of its 113 members now come from Africa and Asia. It is thus more broadly based and less dominated by the greater powers, although the great powers, of course, play an immensely important role in its activities.

It derives added strength and balance from the activities and efforts of the smaller nations, which protect it to some extent from the buffetings of great power rivalries. Unlike the League, from which 14 countries withdrew during its active history, leaving it with a membership of 53 in 1939, no country has ever withdrawn from the United Nations, however adverse its position in the United Nations might appear to be at any given time.

In its predominantly European setting the successive breaches of the Covenant in the 1930's by Mussolini's Italy, and later, Hitler's Germany, paralyzed the League and rendered it ineffective, while the rise of economic nationalism after the depression of 1929 overwhelmed the promise of its earlier efforts in the economic field. Undoubtedly the mood of the 1930's turned against the system of the League Covenant. It was a bewildering mood, and they were confused and dismal times, when it seemed as if mankind had obsessively condemned itself to learn all over again the clear lessons of the First World War. The League Covenant became the victim of ultra-nationalist propaganda from all sides. This propaganda, actively pursued by many people in positions of power and responsibility, frustrated the League's efforts, grudged its successes and rejoiced in its failures. Confidence in its promise was undermined, and the system went down to a tragic and inglorious defeat. Only after five years of world war did the victorious nations rally themselves to repeat, with a conviction born of horror, the noble experiment.

In practice it could be said that the League tended to be legalistic in the face of crisis, while the United Nations has been pragmatic. Since the Covenant condemned "resort to war", the Japanese action in Manchuria in the early 1930's was justified as a "police action". The world has learned, in the cruelest way, the danger of such euphemisms. The Charter, of course, expressly forbids the threat as well as the use of force. The successful peace-keeping operations of the United Nations have been essentially improvised responses to particularly urgent problems. None of these operations was clearly foreshadowed in the Charter. The world has become a much smaller and more closely interrelated place in the last 30 years, and trouble can now spread and escalate much faster and with infinitely greater devastation. The relatively greater speed and informality in action of the United Nations in meeting danger, as compared to the League, reflects this fact as much as it does the heightened determination of nations to avoid a third and even more terrible war.

There were also inherent reasons for this change of attitude and pace in the changing environment in which the United Nations has worked for its first 19 years. Due partly to the lack of unanimity among the great powers and partly to the radical change in the nature of war resulting from the development of nuclear and thermonuclear weapons, there has been a gradual change in general attitudes on questions of international security in the United Nations.

There has tended to be a tacit transition from the concept of collective security, as set out in Chapter VII of the United Nations Charter, to a more realistic idea of peace-keeping in a changing world. There has also been a change in emphasis, for the time being at least, from the use of the military forces of the great powers, as contemplated in the Charter, to the use in practice of the military resources of the smaller powers, which has the advantage of not entangling United Nations action in the conflicts of the Cold War.

Already the concept of absolute sovereignty of a state is unreal, for no country can now exist in isolation. The Charter of the United Nations has taken away the sovereign right to go to war, or even to threaten the use of force in any international dispute. The International Court provides a tribunal for the judicial settlement of legal questions between nations. Many states have given the International Court a wide compulsory jurisdiction.

In the political field, even when there has been open conflict between states, and armed force has been used or threatened, there has been an increasing tendency for the principles of the Charter of the United Nations, rather than military power, to prevail, and on a number of occasions since 1945, the Charter has been a factor in actually preventing or in halting war. The principles of the Charter are clearly acceptable to most of mankind. The acceptance of their practical application, however, involving as it does concepts of national sovereignty long held sacred, is a longer and more difficult task—a task in which the League of Nations failed. If the United Nations has, so far, had more success and has made practical progress in applying the principles of the Charter, it is largely because public thinking on international issues has made great advances and because the dangers to be avoided are greater than ever.

We are now moving away quickly from the world of compartmentalized self-sufficiency into a world where human solidarity daily becomes more essential. Already in humanitarian questions this solidarity is real, as we can see from international responses to natural and other disasters. It is becoming more real in the economic field, and it is clearly a necessity, though not yet a practical reality, in the political field. Here the governments of the world, associated in the United Nations, must realize the ideals which were already accepted in 1919 in the Covenant of the League and were reaffirmed in 1945 in the Charter of the United Nations.

We can thus see how far the world has actually come since 1919 in making the ideas and ideals of the Covenant of the League of Nations into acceptable reality. If we are to make the next step toward world authority and then onward to a world government, it will be by the growth in authority and prestige of the institutions and agencies of the United Nations, and by the development of the provisions of the Charter and the Statute of the International Court. If we can make those documents accepted as binding law, as every government in the United Nations is pledged to accept, then we are on the right path to world authority.

38. *TWO DIFFERING CONCEPTS OF UNITED NATIONS ASSAYED*/ DAG HAMMARSKJÖLD*

I

Debates and events during the year since the publication of the last report to the General Assembly have brought to the fore different concepts of the United Nations, the character of the Organization, its authority and its structure.

On the one side, it has in various ways become clear that certain members conceive of the Organization as a static conference machinery for resolving conflicts of interest and ideologies with a view to peaceful coexistence, within the Charter, to be served by a Secretariat which is to be regarded not as fully internationalized but as representing within its ranks those very interests and ideologies.

Other members have made it clear that they conceive of the Organization primarily as a dynamic instrument of governments

* Dag Hammarskjöld, "Two Differing Concepts of United Nations Assayed," *United Nations Review*, Vol. 8, No. 9 (September 1961), pp. 12–17.

through which they, jointly and for the same purpose, should seek such reconciliation but through which they should also try to develop forms of executive action, undertaken on behalf of all members, and aiming at forestalling conflicts and resolving them, once they have arisen, by appropriate diplomatic or political means, in a spirit of objectivity and in implementation of the principles and purposes of the Charter.

Naturally, the latter concept takes as its starting point the conference concept, but it regards it only as a starting point, envisaging the possibility of continued growth to increasingly effective forms of active international cooperation, adapted to experience, and served by a Secretariat of which it is required that, whatever the background and the views of its individual members, their actions be guided solely by the principles of the Charter, the decisions of the main organs and the interests of the Organization itself.

The first concept can refer to history and to the traditions of national policies of the past. The second can point to the needs of the present and of the future in a world of ever-closer international interdependence where nations have at their disposal armaments of hitherto unknown destructive strength. The first one is firmly anchored in the time-honored philosophy of sovereign national states in armed competition of which the most that may be expected in the international field is that they achieve a peaceful coexistence. The second one envisages possibilities of intergovernmental action overriding such a philosophy, and opens the road toward more developed and increasingly effective forms of constructive international cooperation.

It is clearly for the governments, members of the Organization, and for these governments only, to make their choice and decide on the direction in which they wish the Organization to develop. However, it may be appropriate to study these two concepts in terms of the purposes of the Organization as laid down in the Charter and, in this context, also to consider the character and the significance of the decisions of the Organization as well as its structure.

II

The purposes and principles of the Charter are set out in its preamble and further developed in a series of articles, including some which may seem to be primarily of a procedural or administrative nature. Together, these parts of the Charter lay down some basic rules of international ethics by which all member states have committed themselves to be guided. To a large extent, the rules reflect standards accepted as binding for life within states. Thus, they appear, in the main, as a projection into the international arena and the international community of purposes and principles already accepted as being of national validity. In this sense, the Charter takes a first step in the direction of an organized international community, and this independently of the organs set up for international cooperation. Due to different traditions, the state of social development and the character of national institutions, wide variations naturally exist as to the application in national life of the principles reflected in the Charter, but it is not too difficult to recognize the common elements behind those differences. It is therefore not surprising that such principles of national application could be transposed into an agreed basis also for international behavior and cooperation.

In the preamble to the Charter, member nations have reaffirmed their faith "in the equal rights of men and women and of nations large and small," a principle which also has found many other expressions in the Charter.

Thus, it restates the basic democratic principle of equal political rights, independently of the position of the individual or of the member country in respect of its strength, as determined by territory, population or wealth. The words just quoted must, however, be considered as going further and imply an endorsement as well of a right to equal economic opportunities.

It is in the light of the first principle that the Charter has established a system of equal votes, expressing "the sovereign equality of all its members," and has committed the Organization to the furtherance of self-determination, self-government and independence. On the same basis, the Charter requires universal respect for and observance of human rights and fundamental freedoms for all "without distinction as to race, sex, language or religions."

It is in the light of the latter principle—or, perhaps, the latter aspect of the same basic principle—that the Charter, in Article 55, has committed the members to the promotion of higher standards of living, full employment and conditions of economic and social progress and development as well as to solutions of international economic and related problems. The pledge of all members to take joint and separate action, in cooperation with the Organization, for the achievement of these purposes has been the basis for the far-reaching economic and technical assistance channelled through or administered by the Organization, and may rightly be considered as the basic obligation reflected also in such economic and technical assistance as member governments have been giving, on a bilateral basis, outside the framework of the Organization.

It would seem that those who regard the Organization as a conference machinery, "neutral" in relation to the direction of policies on a national or international basis and serving solely as an instrument for the solution of conflicts by reconciliation, do not pay adequate attention to those essential principles of the Charter to which reference has just been made. The terms of the Charter are explicit as regards the equal political rights of nations as well as of individuals and, although this second principle may be considered only as implicit in the terms of the Charter, they are clear also as regards the demand for equal economic opportunities for all individuals and nations. So as to avoid any misunderstanding, the Charter directly states that the basic democratic principles are applicable to nations "large and small" and to individuals without distinction "as to race, sex, language and religion," qualifications that obviously could be extended to cover also other criteria such as, for example, those of an ideological character which have been used or may be used as a basis for political or economic discrimination.

In the practical work of the Organization these basic principles have been of special significance in relation to countries under colonial rule or in other ways under foreign domination. The General Assembly has translated the principles into action intended to establish through self-determination a free and independent life as sovereign states for peoples who have expressed in democratic forms their wish for such a status. Decisive action has in many cases been taken by member governments, and then the United Nations has had only to lend its support to their efforts. In other cases, the main responsibility has fallen on the Organization itself. The resolution on colonialism, adopted by the General Assembly at its fifteenth session, may be regarded as a comprehensive restatement in elaborated form of the principle laid down in the Charter. Results of developments so far have been reflected in the birth of a great number of new national states and a revolutionary widening of the membership of the Organization.

The demand for equal economic opportunities has, likewise, been—and remains—of special significance in relation to those very countries which have more recently entered the international arena as new states. This is natural in view of the fact that, mostly, they have been in an unfavorable economic position, which is reflected in a much lower per capita income, rate of capital supply and degree of technical development, while their political independence and sovereignty require a fair measure of economic stability and economic possibilities in order to gain substance and full viability.

In working for the translation into practical realities in international life of the democratic principles which are basic to the Charter, the Organization has thus assumed a most active role and it has done so with success, demonstrating both the need and the possibilities for such action.

Further, in the preamble to the Charter it is stated to be a principle and purpose of the Organization "to establish conditions under which justice and respect for the obligations arising from treaties and other sources of international law can be maintained." In these words—to which, naturally, counterparts may be found in other parts of the Charter—it gives expression to another basic democratic principle, that of the rule of law. In order to promote this principle, the Charter established the International Court of Justice, but the principle permeates the approach of the Charter to international problems far beyond the sphere of competence of the Court. As in national life, the principle of justice—which obviously implies also the principle of objectivity and equity in the consideration of all matters before the General Assembly or the Security Council—must be considered as applicable without distinction or discrimination, with one measure and one standard valid for the strong as well as for the weak. Thus, the demand of the Charter for a rule of law aims at the substitution of right for might and makes of the Organization the natural protector of rights which countries, without it, might find it more difficult to assert and to get respected.

The principle of justice can be regarded as flowing naturally from the principles of equal political rights and equal economic opportunities, but it has an independent life and carries, of itself, the world community as far in the direction of an organized international system as the two first-mentioned principles. It has deep roots in the history of the efforts of man to eliminate from international life the anarchy which he had already much earlier overcome on the national level, deeper indeed than the political and economic principles which, as is well known, were much later to get full acceptance also in national life. Long before the United Nations and long before even the League of Nations, governments were working toward a rule of justice in international life through which they hoped to establish an international community based on law, without parliamentary or executive organs, but with a judicial procedure through which law and justice could be made to apply.

The Charter states and develops the three principles mentioned here as a means to an end: "to save succeeding generations from the scourge of war." This adds emphasis to the concept, clearly implied in the Charter, of an international community for which the Organization is an instrument and an expression and in which anarchic tendencies in international life are to be curbed by the introduction of a system of equal political rights, equal economic opportunities and the rule of law. However, the Charter goes one step further, drawing a logical conclusion both from the ultimate aim of the Organization and from the three principles. Thus, it outlaws the use of armed force "save in the common interest." Obviously, the Charter cannot, on the one side, establish a rule of law and the principle of equal rights for "nations large and small" and, on the other hand, permit the use of armed force for national ends, contrary to those principles and, therefore, not "in the common interest." Were nations, under the Charter, to be allowed, by the use of their military strength, to achieve ends contrary to the principle of the equality of members and the principle of justice, it would obviously deprive those very principles of all substance and significance. One practical expression of this approach, which may be mentioned here, is that the organs of the United Nations have consistently maintained that the use of force, contrary to the Charter as interpreted by those organs, cannot be permitted to yield results which can be accepted as valid by the Organization and as establishing new rights.

In the Charter, the right to the use of force is somewhat more extensive than may seem to be the case from a superficial reading of the phrase "save in the common interest." Thus, apart from military action undertaken pursuant to a decision of the Security Council for repression of aggression—that is, for upholding the basic Charter principles—the Charter opens the door to the use of armed force by a nation in exercise of its inherent right to resist armed attack. This is a point on which, both in theory and in practice, the development of international law is still at a very early stage. As is well known, no agreement has been reached on a definition of aggression, beyond that found in Article 2, paragraph 4, of the Charter, and the Organization has several times had to face situations in which, therefore, the rights and wrongs in a specific case of conflict have not been clarified. It would be a vitally important step forward if wider agreement could be reached regarding the criteria to be applied in order to distinguish between legitimate and illegitimate use of force. History is only too rich in examples of armed aggression claimed as action in self-defence. How could it be otherwise, when most cases of armed conflict are so deeply rooted in a history of clashes of interests and rights, even if, up to the fatal moment of the first shot, those clashes have not involved recourse to the use of armed force?

In recognition of this situation and in the light of historical experience, the Charter makes yet another projection into international life of solutions to conflicts tested in national life, and establishes the final principle that the Organization shall "bring about by peaceful means and in conformity with the principles of justice and international law, adjustment or settlement of international disputes or situations which might lead to a breach of the peace." This principle, as quoted here from Article 1 of the Charter, is further developed specifically in Article 33, which requires parties to any dispute, the consequence of which is likely to endanger the maintenance of international peace and security, to "seek a solution by negotiation, inquiry, mediation, conciliation, arbitration, judicial settlement, resort to regional agencies or arrangements, or other peaceful means of their own choice." It is in this sphere that the Security Council has had, and is likely to continue to have, its main significance, both directly as a forum before which any dispute threatening peace and security can be brought up for debate and as an organ which directly, or through appropriate agents, may assist the parties in finding a way out and, by preventive diplomacy, may forestall the outbreak of an armed conflict. It seems appropriate here to draw attention especially to the right of the Security Council under Article 40 to "call upon the parties concerned to comply with such provisional measures as it deems necessary or desirable" for the prevention of any aggravation of a situation threatening peace and security, and to the obligation of members to comply with a decision on such measures.

It is in the light of the approach to international coexistence in our world today, which is thus to be found in the Charter, that judgment has to be passed on the validity of the different conceptions of the Organization which in recent times have become increasingly apparent. As already pointed out, the basic principles regarding the political equality of nations and their right to equal economic opportunities are difficult to reconcile with the view that the Organization is to be regarded only as a conference machinery for the solution, by debate and joint decisions, of conflicts of interest or ideology. It seems even more difficult to reconcile these principles with a view according to which equality among members should be reflected in the establishment of a balance between power blocs or other groupings of nations. The same difficulty is apparent as regards the principle of justice and the principle of prohibiting the use of armed force. It is easier to apply the conference concept to the principle of prevention of conflict through negotiation, but also on this point the difficulties become considerable if it is recognized that such solutions as may be sought by the Organization should be solutions based on the rules of equality and justice.

III

The General Assembly, the Security Council and other collective organs of the United Nations have features in common with a standing international diplomatic conference, but their procedures go beyond the forms of such a conference and show aspects of a parliamentary or quasi-parliamentary character.

While decisions of a conference, in order to commit its participants, must be based on their subsequent acceptance of the decisions, the organs of the United Nations act on the basis of voting, with the decisions being adopted if supported by a majority. However, the decisions of the Assembly have, as regards member states, only the character of recommendations (except for financial assessments and certain other types of organizational action) so that obligations like those arising out of an agreement, coming into force after a conference, do not normally flow from them. But although the decisions, legally, are only recommendations, they introduce an important element by expressing a majority consensus on the issue under consideration.

Naturally, such a formula leaves scope for a gradual development in practice of the weight of the decisions. To the extent that more respect, in fact, is shown to General Assembly recommendations by the member states, they may come more and more close to being recognized as decisions having a binding effect on those concerned, particularly when they involve the application of the binding principles of the Charter and of international law.

Both those who regard a gradual increase in the weight of decisions of the General Assembly as necessary, if progress is to be registered in the direction of organized peaceful coexistence within the Charter, and those who oppose such a development, have to recognize that, with certain variations in individual cases, the practice still is very close to the restrictive Charter formula. Experience shows that even countries which have voted for a certain decision may, later on, basing themselves on its character of merely being a recommendation, refuse to follow it or fail to support its implementation, financially or in other respects.

What has been said applies generally to the collective organs of the Organization, but, as is well known, the Charter has gone one step further beyond the conference concept, in the direction of the parliamentary concept, in the case of the Security Council. In Article 25 member states of the United Nations have agreed to "accept and carry out the decisions of the Security Council in accordance with the present Charter," thus, by agreement, making the decisions of the Council mandatory, except, of course, when such decisions take the form of "recommendations" within the terms of Chapter VI or certain other Articles of the Charter. They have further, in Article 49, undertaken to "join in affording mutual assistance in carrying out the measures decided upon by the Security Council."

This agreed mandatory nature of certain Security Council decisions might have led to a demand for unanimity in the Council, a unanimity which was the rule for the Council of the League of Nations. Even so, however, the arrangement would have gone beyond the conference principle with its requirement that no decision reached in an international organ should be binding on an individual member short of his agreement. With the present arrangements, requiring a majority of seven and the concurring votes of the permanent members, a bridge between the traditional conference approach and a parliamentary approach is provided by the commitment in Article 25 to agree to the carrying out of the decisions in the Council which should be considered as giving the Council its authority by general delegation as indeed stated in Article 24, paragraph 1.

What clearly remains within the Council of the traditional conference and agreement pattern is the condition that its decisions of a nonprocedural character must be supported by the unanimous vote of the five permanent members, thus avoiding for those members the risk of being bound by a decision of the Council which has not met with their agreement. It may be observed that this special position for the permanent members, apart from other reasons, has the justification that, without such a rule, the other members of the organization, in complying with a Security Council decision, might find themselves unwillingly drawn into a big power conflict.

In spite of the delegated authority which the Council may be considered as exercising, and the condition that decisions must be agreed to by the permanent members, the experience of the Organization, as regards the implementation of Council decisions, is uneven and does not indicate full acceptance in practice of Article 25. In this case also, examples can be given of a tendency to regard decisions, even when taken under Chapter VII, as recommendations binding only to the extent that the party concerned has freely committed itself to carry them out; there is here a clear dichotomy between the aims of the Charter and the general political practice at its present stage of development. Such cases refer not only to members outside the Council, or, perhaps, members inside the Council, who have not supported a specific decision, but also to members within the Council who have cast their votes in favor of a decision but who later on are found to reserve for themselves at least a right to interpret the decision in ways which seem to be at variance with the intentions of the Council. The ambiguity of this situation emerges with special force in cases where such attitudes have been taken by permanent members of the Council, who are considered to shoulder the responsibility for the maintenance of peace and security which is reflected in the special position they hold within the Council. Obviously, the problem whether the intended legal weight is given to decisions of the Security Council arises in practice not only in cases of noncompliance but also in cases of a refusal to shoulder the financial consequences of a decision of the Council.

These observations—which have been limited to a reminder of the Charter rules and a factual reminder also of the experiences in practice—point to a situation which in any evaluation of the United Nations must be given the most serious consideration by members. For the judgment on the various concepts of the United Nations which are put forward, it is one thing to note what the Charter stipulates; it is an entirely different but ultimately more important question as to what the situation is in practice and what, in fact, is the weight given to decisions of the Organization when they go beyond the conference pattern of agreement.

For those who maintain the conference concept of the Organization, it is natural to side-step the mandatory nature of decisions by the Security Council. For those who take a different view, it is equally natural and essential to work for a full and general acceptance of the Charter rules. Were those to be right who hold that the Charter, on the points discussed here and, maybe, also as regards the five basic principles discussed in the first part of this introduction, is ahead of our time and the political possibilities which it offers, such a view still would not seem to justify the conclusion that the clear approach of the Charter should be abandoned. Rather, it would indicate that member nations jointly should increase their efforts to make political realities gradually come closer to the pattern established by the Charter.

In the light of such considerations, the significance of the outcome of every single conflict on which the Organization has to take a stand and the weight given to its decisions in such a conflict stand out very clearly. A failure to gain respect for decisions or actions of the Organization within the terms of the Charter is often called a failure for the Organization. It would seem more correct to regard it as a failure of the world community, through its member nations and in particular those most directly concerned, to cooperate in order, step by step, to make the Charter a living reality in practical political action as it is already in law.

Were such cooperation, for which the responsibility naturally rests with each single member as well as with all members collectively, not to come about, and were the respect for the obligations flowing from Article 25 of the Charter to be allowed to diminish, this would spell the end of the possibilities of the Organization to grow into what the Charter indicates as the clear intention of the founders, as also of all hopes to see the Organization grow into an increasingly effective instrument, with increasing respect for recommendations of the General Assembly as well.

What this would mean for the value of the Organization as protector of the aims, principles and rights it was set up to further and safeguard is obvious. The effort through the Organization to find a way by which the world community might, step by step, grow into organized international cooperation within the Charter must either progress or recede. Those whose reactions to the work of the Organization hamper its development or reduce its possibilities of effective action may have to shoulder the responsibility for a return to a state of affairs which governments had already found too dangerous after the First World War.

IV

The growth of the United Nations out of the historic conference pattern—which, as observed earlier in this introduction, at all events naturally remains the starting point in all efforts of the Organization—is clearly reflected in what, in the light of experience, may seem to be a lack of balance in the Charter. While great attention is given to the principles and purposes, and considerable space is devoted to an elaboration of what may be called the parliamentary aspects of the Organization, little is said about executive arrangements. This does not mean that the Charter in any way closes the door to such arrangements or to executive action, but only that, at the stage of international thinking crystallized in the Charter, the conference approach still was predominant, and that the needs for executive action, if the new Organization was to live up to expectations and to its obligations under the Charter, had not yet attracted the attention they were to receive in response to later developments.

The key clause on the executive side may be considered to be Article 24, in which it is said that "in order to assure prompt and effective action by the United Nations, its members confer on the Security Council primary responsibility for the maintenance of international peace and security."

On that basis the Security Council is given the right, under Article 29, to establish such subsidiary organs as it deems necessary for the performance of its functions, the right under Article 40 to decide on so-called provisional measures, the right to use, for the purposes of the Charter, under certain conditions, armed forces made available to the Council, the right under Article 48 to request from governments action on the Council's behalf, as well as the right to request of the Secretary-General to "perform . . . such functions as are entrusted to him" by the Council.

The various clauses here briefly enumerated open a wide range of possibilities for executive action undertaken by, and under the aegis of, the Security Council. However, no specific machinery is set up for such action by the Council, apart from the Military Staff Committee, with planning responsibilities in the field of the possible use of armed force by the Security Council under Chapter VII of the Charter. In fact, therefore, the executive functions and their form have been left largely to practice, and it is in the field of the practices of the Organization that cases may be found in the light of which it is now possible to evaluate the ways in which the Organization may develop its possibilities for diplomatic, political or military intervention of an executive nature in the field.

The forms used for executive action by the Security Council—or when the Council has not been able to reach decisions, in some cases, by the General Assembly—are varied and are to be explained by an effort to adjust the measures to the needs of each single situation. However, some main types are recurrent. Subcommittees have been set up for fact-finding or negotiation on the spot. Missions have been placed in areas of conflict for the purpose of observation and local negotiation. Observer groups of a temporary nature have been sent out. And, finally, police forces under the aegis of the United Nations have been organized for the assistance of the governments concerned with a view to upholding the principles of the Charter. As these, or many of these, arrangements require centralized administrative measures, which cannot be performed by the Council or the General Assembly, members have to a large extent used the possibility to request the Secretary-General to perform special functions by instructing him to take the necessary executive steps for implementation of the action decided upon. This has been done under Article 98, as quoted above, and has represented a development in practice of the duties of the Secretary-General under Article 97.

The character of the mandates has, in many cases, been such that in carrying out his functions the Secretary-General has found himself forced also to interpret the decisions in the light of the Charter, United Nations precedents and the aims and intentions expressed by the members. When that has been the case, the Secretary-General has been under the obligation to seek guidance, to all possible extent, from the main organs; but when such guidance has not been forthcoming, developments have sometimes led to situations in which he has had to shoulder responsibility for certain limited political functions, which may be considered to be in line with the spirit of Article 99 but which legally have been based on decisions of the main organs themselves, under Article 98, and thus the exclusive responsibility of member states acting through these organs. Naturally, in carrying out such functions the Secretariat has remained fully subject to the decisions of the political bodies.

This whole development has lately become a matter of controversy, natural and, indeed, unavoidable in the light of differences of approach to the role of the Organization to which attention has been drawn earlier in this introduction. While the development is welcomed by member nations which feel a need of growth as regards the possibilities of the Organization to engage in executive action in protection of the Charter principles, it is rejected by those who maintain the conference concept of the Organization. The different opinions expressed on the development are only superficially related to this or that specific action and the way in which it is considered to have been carried through. They are also only superficially related to the choice of means used for translating decisions into action. The discussion regarding the development of executive functions is basically one confronting the same fundamentally different concepts of the Organization and its place in international politics, which could be seen also in the different attitudes toward the legal weight of decisions of the Organization.

It is in this context that the principle embodied in Article 100 of the Charter is of decisive significance. This principle, which has a long history, establishes the international and independent character of the Secretariat. Thus, it is said that the Secretary-General and the staff of the Secretariat "shall not seek or receive instructions from any Government or from any other authority external to the Organization," and that they "shall refrain from any action which might reflect on their position as international officials responsible only to the Organization." In the same Article, the members of the United Nations undertake to respect "the exclusively international character of the responsibilities of the Secretary-General and the staff and not to seek to influence them in the discharge of their responsibilities."

The significance of the principle stated in Article 100 is a dual one. It envisages a Secretariat so organized and developed as to be able to serve as a neutral instrument for the Organization, were its main organs to wish to use the Secretariat in the way which has been mentioned above and for which Article 98 has opened possibilities. But in doing so, the principle also indicates an intention to use the Secretariat for such functions as would require that it have an exclusively international character.

In the traditional conference pattern, participants in a meeting are mostly serviced by a secretariat drawn from the same countries as the participants themselves, and constituting a mixed group regarding which there is no need to demand or maintain an exclusively international character. It is therefore natural that those who favor the conference approach to the United Nations tend to give to Article 100 another interpretation than the one which the text calls for, especially in the light of its historical background and its background also in other clauses of the Charter.

There is no reason to go more deeply into this special problem here. Suffice it to say that, while the Organization, if regarded as a standing diplomatic conference, might well be serviced by a fully international Secretariat but does not need it, the other approach to the Organization and its role cannot be satisfied with anything less than a secretariat of an exclusively international character, and thus cannot be reconciled with a secretariat composed on party lines and on the assumption that the interests represented in the main organs in this manner should be represented and advocated also within the Secretariat. Thus, again, the choice between conflicting views on the United Nations Secretariat is basically a choice between conflicting views on the Organization, its functions and its future.

In order to avoid possible misunderstandings, it should be pointed out here that there is no contradiction at all between a demand for a truly international Secretariat and a demand, found in the Charter itself, for as wide a "geographical" distribution of posts within the Secretariat as possible. It is, indeed, necessary precisely in order to maintain the exclusively international character of the Secretariat that it be so composed as to achieve a balanced distribution of posts on all levels among all regions. This, however, is clearly something entirely different from a balanced representation of trends or ideologies. In fact, if a realistic representation of such trends is considered desirable, it can and should be achieved without any assumption of political representation within the ranks of the Secretariat, by a satisfactory distribution of posts based on geographical criteria.

The exclusively international character of the Secretariat is not tied to its composition but to the spirit in which it works and to its insulation from outside influences, as stated in Article 100. While it may be said that no man is neutral in the sense that he is without opinions or ideals, it is just as true that, in spite of this, a neutral Secretariat is possible. Anyone of integrity, not subjected to undue pressures, can, regardless of his own views, readily act in an "exclusively international" spirit and can be guided in his actions on behalf of the Organization solely by its interests and principles and by the instructions of its organs. . . .

39. *THE DISUNITED NATIONS** / *CHARLES DE GAULLE*

The United Nations Organization and its institutions were created in 1945 on the basis of a Charter, and with purposes which France at that time approved. I was, myself, at that time at the head of my country and in this capacity I was one of the founders of the United Nations at the request of President Roosevelt and then of President Truman, who were its promoters.

There was an executive council, the Security Council, which was a sort of Government composed of the five big powers, that is to say, the United States, the Soviet Union, Great Britain, China and France. And then there was a kind of non-legislative deliberative parliament, the General Assembly. The General Assembly, at that time, was supposed to debate only on subjects which were submitted to it by the Security Council. I will add that the General Assembly then included only about forty States, which had been in existence for a long time, which were endowed with cohesion and unity, and which were used to international relations and to the traditions, obligations and responsibilities which these relations entail.

In the Security Council each of the members—each of the big powers—had the veto power. And then finally in the General Assembly, in accordance with what France had wanted and had obtained in San Francisco, it was necessary—and it still is—to have a two thirds majority in order to pass a resolution.

It seems that all these procedures would enable the States to establish contact with each other, to examine world questions jointly and to promote peace while restricting demagogic activities.

As for the Charter, it was designed to prevent the Organization from interfering in the affairs of each State and it could intervene only on the explicit request of a government.

Finally, among the intentions which had inspired its creation there was the desire, perhaps the illusion of the Western nations—in any case of the Americans—to bring the Soviets to cooperate with the West. We know what has happened.

* Ambassade de France, Service de Presse et d'Information, *President De Gaulle Holds Fourth Press Conference* (New York, 1961), pp. 7–8. Reprinted by permission.

Today it must be said that the United Nations really do not in any way resemble what they were or ought to have been at the start. First of all, the Security Council no longer comprises—is far from comprising—only the big powers, but also several powers elected in turn, and then there is an undetermined number of delegations attending all debates of the Security Council, depending on the subjects under discussion. As for the General Assembly, at the present time it has assumed all powers. It can deliberate on everything, without and even against the advice of the Security Council, which is thus dispossessed of its essential prerogative. In addition, this General Assembly now includes the representatives of more than one hundred States—soon they will number one hundred twenty—most of which, at least many of which, are improvised States and believe it their duty to stress grievances or demands with regard to the older nations, rather than elements of reason and progress.

As for the Charter, it now inconveniences every one and there is no one who can enforce its application. As regards the hoped-for cooperation between East and West within the United Nations, we can see its results.

So that now the meetings of the United Nations are no more than riotous and scandalous sessions where there is no way to organize an objective debate and which are filled with invectives and insults proffered especially by the Communists and by those who are allied with them against the Western nations.

And then, as the United Nations becomes a scene of disturbance, confusion and division, it acquires the ambition to intervene in all kinds of matters. This is especially true of its officers. It is anxious to assert itself—even by force of arms—as it did in the Congo.

The result is that it carries to the local scene its global incoherence, the personal conceptions of its various agents and the individual partiality of each of the States which send their contingents with their own orders—send them, then withdraw them.

Under these conditions, France does not see how she can adopt any other attitude toward the United, or Disunited, Nations than that of the greatest reserve. In any case, she does not wish to contribute her men or her money to any present or eventual undertaking of this organization—or disorganization. Of course we hope that the day will come when common sense will again prevail and when the reasonable nations, noting the results of experience, will wish to resume this great world undertaking on a new basis.

In my opinion, this will be achieved if Europe succeeds in organizing itself and consequently in asserting its power, its reason and its experience in the world. Then Europe will be able to take the necessary steps.

FUNCTIONALISM AND REGIONALISM

XIII

THE SPIRITUAL FATHER OF THE FUNCTIONAL approach to international organization is David Mitrany, of Princeton University's Institute for Advanced Study. The first selection—an article which appeared in the British journal *International Affairs* in 1948—is a stimulating presentation of his views. Mitrany's best known book is *A Working Peace System.*

The second selection is by an outstanding practitioner of functionalism: Paul Hoffman. The author is Managing Director of the United Nations Special Fund, a program of economic and technical assistance to the developing countries.

The most exciting experiment in regional-functional organization is the European Economic Community. The third selection is a speech by Walter Hallstein, President of the E.E.C.'s Commission, to a joint meeting of Harvard University and the Massachusetts Institute of Technology on May 22, 1961.

40. *THE FUNCTIONAL APPROACH TO WORLD ORGANIZATION* / DAVID MITRANY*

It seems to be the fate of all periods of transition that reformers are more ready to fight over a theory than to pull together on a problem. At this stage I can only ask to be given credit for the claim that I do not represent a theory. I represent an anxiety. At home, when we want change or reform, we state our objectives in such terms that all may see how we may attain them. When it comes to the international world, where we are faced with old and stubborn habits of mind and feeling and political dogmas, where the change we have in mind must close one of the ponderous tomes of history and open up a new one, it seems that nothing will do but the perfect goal and winged results.

If we compare the general mood of 1919, when everybody was keen to get back to what had gone before, with the mood of 1948 one generation later, when the need for an active international society is almost universally taken for granted—we are justified in regarding the change as progress indeed; a change in outlook without which all schemes for international peace would, as in past centuries, remain but noble dreams. Yet, even with that change, present schemes may likewise remain noble dreams if they are beyond the reach of the ways and means of human government. "Government is a practical thing," Burke wrote to the Sheriffs of Bristol, and we should beware of elaborating political forms "for the gratification of visionaries." It is the task of experts, whether individuals or groups, to pass now beyond fine appeals and ideal formulae. Expert vagueness will merely result in popular vacuousness. If that popular receptiveness to the idea of international organization is to ripen into an informed public opinion, it must

* David Mitrany, "The Functional Approach to World Organization," reprinted by permission of the Society for a World Service Federation from *A Working Peace System,* published by Quadrangle Books, Inc.

now be fed with a diet of hard facts and practicable measures, so that it may know how to press and support Governments in the pursuit of an active international policy. How otherwise can it be explained why, with such broad goodwill and sense of urgency, so little has been fulfilled?

The general outlook, therefore, is promising. When we come to examine present trends more concretely, two stand out above all—the trend for national self-government, and the trend for radical social change. The two are at work in different strengths in different parts of the world, but they merge into each other. Even in Europe, where state-making seems near to completion, the transformation of society is taking place on a national basis; while in the Middle East, in South-East Asia and elsewhere, the new States express social revolution as much as political revolution. Speaking internationally, therefore, there is in this social nationalism or national socialism an actual danger of regression. The modern political trend has led increasingly to the splitting up of the world into independent States; the idea of national self-government was taken as the guide of the peace settlement of 1919 and is still strongly at work in the Middle East, in South-East Asia, and is stirring in Africa too. At the same time the modern division of labour had tended to weld peoples and countries together, and it is that unity which is in danger of being loosened by the new conception of the State. It is not my part to discuss whether the trend is desirable or inevitable, but merely to establish that these are the conditions from which our international house-building must start. We are favoured by the need and habit of material co-operation, we are hampered by the general clinging to political segregation. How to reconcile these two trends, both of them natural and both of them active, is the main problem of political architecture at present.

In the light of that problem ideas and schemes for international organization can be brought, speaking broadly, under one of three categories: (i) a general and fairly loose association, like the League of Nations and the United Nations, (ii) a federal system and (iii) functional arrangements.

The League of Nations and now the United Nations, as their names imply, rest upon national separateness. They are loose associations for occasional specific joint action, in regard to each of which each member remains on the whole free to participate or not. They are clubs which make joint action easier, if wanted, and in the

United Nations facilities for economic and social action are much improved; but they cannot prescribe such action, much less take it on their own authority.

Our short but tense experience since the creation of the United Nations has shown that such a loose arrangement is inadequate in scope and uncertain in working. Hence, no doubt, the widespread interest in the federal idea, in a variety of forms. Federalism is one of the great inventions of political theory and life. It came to us from the New World and has been adopted in a number of places especially in newer political groupings. It has served admirably where a number of adjacent and related provinces or countries, while retaining separate identity, wanted to join together for some general purpose. Federation has been the political equivalent of a company with limited liability. Habitually, federal experiments rest upon a number of similar elements: a degree of close kinship or relationship, a will to unity, but with it a clear intent to manage most affairs severally. How does all this apply to the international scene?

We are presented with a choice of proposals for international federation, advocating variously and vaguely European federation or Western federation or democratic federation or, more ambitiously, world federation. The fact that there are so many differing proposals show that they do not rest on any inherent element of kinship or close relationship. Any of them may be desirable, but we have no proof that any is desired. The will to unite is not self-evident. Indeed most of these ideas, like that for European federation, are pressed from outside upon countries which themselves have shown no sign of taking the initiative, as a corrective to their former individualistic ways—a novel idea of political marriage by sentence of the court. Or alternatively they are urged to federate so as to be able to stand up to other political groupings. The advice may be sound, but it is an argument for a new nationalism not for a new internationalism. Hitherto federation has indeed merely created a new separate political unit which in the process, as in Germany, did bring peace within the group. There is no evidence that it would necessarily contribute to peace between it and other groups. The prospect of two powerful federations, for instance, facing each other in Europe is not enchanting. It would not check one of the present general trends, that of political division: it would change the dimensions of nationalism, but not its nature.

Let us take the most hopeful view as to the will of the countries to unite, and leave aside for the moment this negative view of peace. The main question is—would some kind of international federation under present conditions strengthen the trend for material integration, so as to make of it a general and positive foundation for peace? A federation comes into being for certain specific ends, and for those *only*. A federation unites, but it also restricts. It rests on a rigid division of powers and functions between territorial authorities which have equal status; and that division is usually and necessarily laid down in a written constitution provided with an armoury of safeguards against its being lightly tampered with. In the volume of essays on Federal Planning[1] Professor Wheare granted that federal government is by its nature conservative and legalistic. Every attempt to give the central government some new function and power has to knock at the massive and rusty gates of the constitution. The efforts of the Canadian Government to change the fiscal arrangements of the federation have been blocked so far, in spite of long discussion and patent need. In Australia repeated efforts for economic and social action have been similarly defeated; and the recent decision to nationalize the banking system has shaken the political structure and temper of the country. Even in such a dynamic country as the United States, the sin of unconstitutionality has plagued efforts at social reform—such as the prohibition of child labour in factories—and killed or maimed most of the original New Deal measures. The now universally admired and imitated T.V.A. scheme had to sustain, on grounds of unconstitutionality, fifty-one suits before the Supreme Court before it was allowed to settle down to its great work.

It is curious how those who urge the use of the federal idea internationally have neglected this central characteristic of it. Jefferson, who politically was wise beyond a man's measure, foresaw this and would have liked the constitution to include a provision for its periodical revision every ten years. It so happens that such a provision and for such a term was part of the Austro-Hungarian federal arrangement, the so-called *Anschluss*, with the result that every term became a crisis with a threat of dissolution—which led the irrepressible Vienna wits to speak of it as "Monarchie auf Kündigung." Yet such a refractory attitude is not unreasonable. New functions and new powers allowed to the supposedly co-equal central authority, however beneficent the social purpose, have a cumulative effect politically, and a sufficient number of them would

[1] P. Ransome, Ed., *Studies in Federal Planning* (London, Macmillan, 1943).

before long permanently change the balance upon which the federation was established. It took almost twenty years of difficult negotiation, as Professor Brady points out,[1] to find a basis for the federation of Australia, and the reluctance to see it changed is therefore understandable. An international federation, to come into being at all, would have to start upon a very narrow basis and very rigid arrangements as to form and functions; and the reluctance to allow these to be disturbed would be correspondingly deeper.

In an international federation every adaptation, every amendment, would have to pass the gauntlet of jealous discussions between countries which have newly come together and differ in their political background. Even in agreed common matters the pace is that of the slowest member of the federation; issues which divide deeply have to be skirted. But in our time conditions and needs and problems are apt to change rapidly. The constitution would have to be continuously adapted, or the difficulty of doing this would hobble the life and government of the federation. Can such an instrument be made to fit the revolutionary mood which, whatever we may think of it, is surging in most parts of the world? Some may have been puzzled that the most revolutionary of all governments, which ideologically believes in world unity and in the proscription of the State, at the United Nations, and on every possible occasion, insists on a strict observance of national sovereignty. The explanation may be found in a recent article on sovereignty by Professor Levin,[2] a leading Soviet jurist, who uses this very argument—that any and every people must be free to transform its social organization with full power of its own to do so, and without external interference or complications. Professor Levin is obviously right in assuming that this would not be possible under some rigid and comprehensive form of political association. If a federal House cannot be half free and half slave, neither can it be half capitalist and half communist. Every attempt at deep change in one part would put in jeopardy the persistence of the whole; for the alternative would appear to the legalists as disruption, and to the reformers as stagnation.

A federal system has many bright virtues. But in form and working it is a combination of rigidities—rigid in its framework,

[1] Alexander Brady, "Dominion Nationalism and the Commonwealth" (*Canadian Journal of Economics and Political Science*, February, 1944, p. 9).

[2] J. D. Levin, "The Problem of Sovereignty in the U.N. Statute" (*Sovetskoe Gosudarstvo i Pravo*, No. 1, 1947, p. 16).

whether geographical or ideological; rigid in its consititution, which has to be formal and unchallenged; rigid in its general life, because of the limits and obstacles it places to fresh common action. If under present conditions of political nationalism an international federation is difficult to achieve, under present conditions of social revolution it would be difficult to maintain. It would have little prospect, except on the lowest common denominator as regards membership—such as the Benelux or the Scandinavian groups—or lowest common denominator as regards federal activity. But if a dynamic federal grouping is not possible, a laggard federal grouping would be meaningless now.

When the present federations came into being, their chief central functions were common defence and foreign policy. These are indeed the functions, with a common budget for their purpose, that Mr. Lionel Curtis considers sufficient to start the federal arrangement which he has advocated so eloquently and devotedly. But does this not again neglect the historical perspective? Not only do the number of functions which need to be carried out jointly change; their character is apt to change even more rapidly. A hundred or even fifty years ago defence and foreign policy were limited affairs in relation to the total life of the community. Now they embrace between them control of material resources and of the organization of industry, control of manpower and of training, and even control of communications as of education and opinion—with corresponding sweeping control of trade and of fiscal and financial policy.

Federation, to sum up, was invented and adopted when, in general, the functions of government were limited, and those of central government were deliberately intended to be restricted; now we live somewhat feverishly and precariously in an era of centralized planning. It was born in times of enthusiasm for constitutions; now we are in a pragmatic mood that scorns formal rules and restrictions. Federalism was meant to put into the hands of central authority the least possible functions of common life; now it could only mean leaving in the hands of the individual authority the least possible functions of local life. If federation were to do all the things for political security and for social security that present trends demand—inevitably through the instrument of central authority—it could only end in the paradox that the federal idea would be proclaimed only to be organized out of existence.

The foregoing examination of the difficulties of the federal idea is not made from any inclination to be critical. It is rather from a complete conviction that in this awkward field we cannot make progress by propounding schemes which have a pleasant symmetry without regard to the rough and shifty terrain on which they have to be grounded; and in looking at the federal idea against present conditions and needs I have really been trying to bring out the sociological framework within which any effort towards international government would have to work. That framework, shaped as it is essentially by the will for national distinctness and the need for social integration, shows that our end will be difficult to achieve simply by changing the dimensions of traditional political instruments. That being so, we are bound to look for a new political device, and the device which seems to fit that framework is the functional idea—not as a new invention, but as a new application.

It so happens that the functional approach has been used a great deal in established federations, very successfully by the New Deal, with the T.V.A. scheme as its outstanding example. It may be as well to deal here with two circumstantial points. If, it may be said, existing federations have been able to do all that, does not this break the argument that the federal idea cannot be helpful internationally? Existing federations can sometimes push aside or get round formal federal partitions because they *are* old-established federations. Generations of common life and experience have welded them into a community, with a common outlook and common problems expressed in the programmes of national parties; and common central government has come to be taken for granted, with state or provincial governments, with perhaps the exception of Quebec—a significant exception—more on the level of local administrative bodies. In most cases the problem, therefore, was not so much to create a common policy as to consolidate a group of similar or identical policies. And yet even in such old-established federations, in times of crisis, these collective doings were expanded not by changing federal arrangements but rather by circumventing them. In no case was there any deliberate change in the formal gradation of power; the federal governments took upon themselves many new tasks with tacit national consent, and thus acquired new power by functional accretion, not by constitutional revision. In the United States the one attempt at constitutional change, to increase the membership of the Supreme Court, was also the only issue on which President Roosevelt was utterly defeated, though its effect would have been mild compared with the tremendous impact of the New Deal.

The United States took this line boldly also in starting new connections with neighbouring States—not only in the close war-time arrangements with Canada, which were a matter of expediency, but in permanent measures. The Alcan Highway has created a strip of international administration running from the United States through Canada to Alaska; the arrangement with Mexico for the development of the Rio Grande has turned a dividing river into a joint enterprise; and pan-American developments are likely to follow the same line. These experiments have a particular lesson for the wider international problem. It is not only that they can be made, but that the United States has found it easier to complete the Alcan arrangement with Canada and the Rio Grande arrangement with Mexico than to get its own T.V.A. scheme going. The first two were made with sovereign countries which retained their sovereignty except in so far as it was pooled for a specific joint functional undertaking. The other experiment affected federal units which were reluctant to part with any of their share of power, and tried hard to maintain the balance laid down in the American constitution. In a more extreme way the point is illustrated by the insistence of the Australian Government, against American reluctance, that some form of international undertaking to work for "full employment" be included in the San Francisco Charter, with the purpose of getting in this way the right to take internal action which would otherwise be beyond its constitutional power—a striking and novel way of asking for international obligations to get over federal obstructions. The incident also illustrates how the content of "foreign policy" is changing. In the United States and in other federations, in other words, necessary joint action was possible in the face of constitutional obstacles because it could rely on an old and live sense of national unity. A new international federation would have no such unity, and the constitutional barriers would thus obstruct all the more starkly at every corner. And even those old federations have found it at times easier to make functional arrangements with foreign States than within themselves.

The truth is that by its very nature the constitutional approach emphasizes the individual index of power; the functional approach emphasizes the common index of need. There are many such needs which cut across national boundaries, and an effective beginning could be made by providing joint government for them. On such lines, the emergence of so many new national States, which politically adds to our difficulties, might even be put into the service of international unification. If they are to achieve a promising social foundation for their political independence they need many things in the way of material and technical help and service which are beyond their means and experience; and, as in the case of the Marshall Plan, such needs should be used deliberately and insistently to set up lines for joint international action.

The universal popular claim for social security could likewise be turned into a channel for international unity. For it is important to note that the new nationalism is everywhere a peculiarly social nationalism; like the nineteenth century nationalism, each wants to have its own national house but, unlike the earlier nationalism, it is especially intent upon a new social life within that house. There may be much to be said for one solid international block of flats, but as long as people choose to live in detached national houses we could go a long way by supplying joint social and other services. Only in some such way is there any prospect, for instance, of mending the breach in the political unity of India, and of leading gradually to a unity of natural common interests; whereas any suggestion for political reunion would only serve to make even such practical proposals suspect. Again, this seems the only possible hope of mending the division between Arabs and Jews in Palestine; and, indeed, of building some true unity among the Arab countries themselves, along the path so admirably mapped out by the Middle East Supply Centre during the war. In the Danubian region, in spite of much ideological fraternizing, Mr. Dimitrov's mere reference to a federal link-up at once brought a rebuke from Moscow, and little response from his neighbours; but those same countries are apparently working on a scheme for a Danube Valley Authority. Nor is there any other way of dealing with the vital problem of the Ruhr. If the region is to remain German, if French fears for security are to be assuaged, if the claims of neighbouring allied countries for a share of its products are to be met, and at the same time, German workers are to be given the prospect of a decent life, only a Ruhr Valley Authority under non-political international functional management would have any prospect of meeting these varied and mixed claims. Two points might be made on this which will bring out the contrast beetween the political and the functional approach: first, that an R.V.A. could be started at any time without waiting for a Western Union, while a Western Union would still have to work through an R.V.A.; and, secondly, that Soviet Russia could at any time be brought into the partnership of an autonomous R.V.A., but not in a Western Union. The enclosing of an R.V.A. within a full Western system would inevitably dig a moat against wider co-operation.

It would be instructive to examine the structure and working of the wartime functional arrangements, or the work of the international Labour Organization in giving a common direction to policies of social improvement without encroaching on State sovereignty. The French, Belgian and British Governments are now working out lines of co-operation for their African territories, ranging from sanitation, irrigation and soil conservation, to the common use of communications and other services, with a view to co-ordinating economic, educational and administrative policies.

It is not only to the field of government and economics that the functional approach brings relief. In the noteworthy sermon which the Archbishop of Canterbury preached before the University of Cambridge in November 1946,[1] he boldly admitted that all schemes of reunion between the English churches had failed because, as he insisted, they had tried a constitutional reunion, and he called for a different approach simply by the exchange of ministers and pulpits. "It is because I fear a stalemate," said Dr. Fisher, "that I venture to throw out this suggestion—Can we grow to full communion with each other before we write a constitution?" The evolution of the Flemish problem in Belgium is also instructive. The political separatist movement during the First World War created a bitter reaction in the country and almost led to civil strife. Since then, by gradual quiet changes, the Flemings have obtained complete autonomy in education—the University of Ghent is now completely Flemish and that of Liége completely French—and almost as wide autonomy in the administration of the Flemish area; in addition, there has been growing cultural association with Holland. The instructive point is that no constitutional provision has so far legalized this evolution, while talk of separation has died out among the Flemings.

Earlier in this paper I instanced the many varieties of the federal idea competing for public support as one proof of its weakness. There are as many, if not more schemes for functional experiment. Does that not show a similar fragility of conception? Perhaps nothing brings out more clearly how different is the core of the political from the functional approach. In the first the several

[1] Speech by Dr. Geoffrey Fisher, November 3, 1946 before the University of Cambridge. Reported in *The Times*, November 4, 1946.

schemes are mutually exclusive—a State cannot be in both a European or an Empire federation, or in both a European and a democratic federation. Functional schemes are at best complementary, each helping the others, and at worst independent of each other. Any one can be started at any time whether the others are accepted or not, and any one may live and prosper even if others fail or are abandoned. In such changing times they have the invaluable virtue of autonomous existence, and likewise of autonomous development. A scheme started by a few countries for transport, or for oil, and so on, could later be broadened to include belated members, or reduced to let reluctant ones drop out. Moreover they can vary in their membership, countries could take part in some schemes and perhaps not in others, whereas in any political arrangement such divided choice would obviously not be tolerable. Functional "neutrality" is possible, where political "neutrality" is not. In addition, functional arrangements have the virtue of technical self-determination, one of the main reasons which makes them more readily acceptable. The nature of each function tells of itself the scope and powers needed for its effective performance. All these elements are capable of concrete measurement, and unlike rigid political arrangements, they are therefore capable of concrete adjustment, in keeping with changes in the conditions of the function. The requirements of a federal authority for the conduct, for instance, of the common foreign policy must always be a matter of political bargaining. The requirements of a functional authority in charge of oil or aviation or of a Danube Valley Authority, at any given time for the clear-cut task entrusted to it, would be a matter of factual audit.

These characteristcis of the functional approach therefore help to mitigate the obstinate problem of equal sovereignty. In this approach it is not a matter of surrendering sovereignty, but merely of pooling so much of it as may be needed for the joint performance of the particular task. In such practical arrangements Governments have not, as in political systems, to safeguard their right to equal voting, but can allow a special position to the countries which have a special responsibility in the task concerned, so long as the service is performed for the benefit of all. All this is completely in keeping with the whole trend of modern government. Twentieth century government means less a division of powers than an integration of functions; administration and administrative law are its characteristic tools, and such functional arrangements would simply mean giving international range to administrative organs and administrative jurisdiction, in accordance with the nature of each task. They would also be in harmony with the social philosophy of our time. As Sir John Boyd Orr has said of his particular responsibility, "here in this world food plan we have the means whereby the nations could begin to co-operate on something which would do none of them harm and do all of them good."[1] If Governments have the welfare of their own peoples at heart they could let such organizations get to work; and if the organizations are successful and their number grows, world government will gradually evolve through their performance. From the point of view of normal daily life, to quote the late Professor Hobhouse, "the life of a community may be regarded as the sum of the functions performed by its members." And conversely, one might add, the performance of a number of common functions is the way to create a normal community. If one were to visualize a map of the world showing economic and social activities, it would appear as an intricate web of interests and relations crossing and recrossing political divisions—not a fighting map of States and frontiers, but a map pulsating with the realities of everyday life. They are the natural basis for international organizations: and the task is to bring that map, which is a functioning reality, under joint international government, at least in its essential lines. The political lines will then in time be overlaid and blurred by this web of joint relations and administrations.

Close association of States can be either comprehensive or selective. Clearly the first is the ideal—all countries working together for their common good. But if it cannot be comprehensive, if it has to be selective, it is better that it be selective on lines of special activities rather than of sectional groups. Any one country may join a particular activity, but a set group cannot help being exclusive; and, in the words of Dr. Johnson, "such is the disposition of man that whatever makes a distinction creates rivalry." Seen in this light the functional approach implies not merely a change of political device but a change of political outlook. It should help to shift the emphasis from political issues which divide, to those social issues in which the interest of the peoples is plainly akin and collective; to shift the emphasis from power to problem and purpose.

In all societies there are both harmonies and disharmonies. It is largely within our choice which we pick out and further. Since the end of the war we have had brutal illustration of this truth at peace

[1] Speech in the House of Commons, April 4, 1946, reported in *The Times*, April 5, 1946.

conferences, at meetings of the United Nations at which the new international life was supposed to be born. We must begin anew, therefore, with a clear sense that the nations can be bound together into a world community only if we link them up by what unites, not by what divides. In the second place, ways and means to that end must be fitted to that purpose. They have to be adequate, but they also must be relevant; and if they are to be relevant they must start from the conditions which are around us. They must avoid reaction, but also avoid Utopia. We can ask our fellow men to look beyond the national State; we cannot expect them to feel themselves at once members of a world State. During his first months as President, Jefferson wrote to a friend that he realized how short he would fall of achieving all that reason and experience justified, but "when we reflect how difficult it is to move or inflect the great machine of society, how impossible to advance the notions of a whole people suddenly to ideal right, we see the wisdom of Solon's remark, that no more good must be attempted than the nation can bear."

That is wise judgment. But in our case, and in our time, what the nations can bear shows a distinction. Taken by and large, they seem unable to bear much interference with their political independence, but they can bear quite a lot when it comes to economic and social action. That distinction gives a first guiding line for any international arrangement. The next question is, how such economic and social action might be organized to lead us to international community and international government. In our own countries we are getting accustomed to putting nearly all such action into the hands of central government. Are we ready to follow the same course in the international sphere? If so, a federation, with its restrictive political machinery, is in any case hardly the proper instrument. A federation leaving those social and economic activities in the hands of its national members would in this respect be little more than a replica of the United Nations, under a different guise and name. If, on the other hand, those activities are entrusted to a centralized international authority with corresponding powers and means, it will have to be hardly less than a full-fledged international government. These tasks must of necessity be performed jointly and controlled centrally; therefore, the true choice is not between the present competitive nationalisms and a lame international federation, but between a full-fledged and comprehensive world government and equally full-fledged but specific and separate functional agencies.

41. *A WAR ON WANT* / PAUL HOFFMAN*

Almost since its inception, the United Nations—dedicated to peace—has been engaged in a war, a good war that must be waged and won. It is a war against certain forces that breed war; against widespread impoverishment and ignorance, gnawing hunger and frustration.

True, these are ancient enemies. The vast majority of humanity had learned to coexist with them because they had no other choice. But, now that men know that such suffering need not be their fate, they will no longer endure it. They want and are determined to achieve a better life for themselves and their children.

Happily the less developed countries of the world are not poor because human or physical resources are lacking, but because they are under-utilized. In its potential, ours is a rich, rich planet. This has been amply demonstrated by the experience of the Expanded Program of Technical Assistance and of the United Nations Special Fund, both of which use the facilities of the United Nations family of agencies for assistance to the developing countries. Not only have they been able to identify many of the valuable resources in the developing countries; they have also demonstrated the possibilities of putting resources to fuller and better use. Work under these programs has shown the promise of development assistance in improving living standards in the low-income countries and in helping to expand the world economy.

But there is still a danger that this promise may not be achieved. Let me illustrate this danger with a brief analogy. Consider the case of a young man—basically able and ambitious—seeking a job that will make him self-supporting and give him a growing future. Without experience and education, he finds this kind of job impossible to get. But, without the income such a job would provide, he can't afford the education or obtain the experience. As a result, he's trapped. At best, he may earn a sub-marginal living. At worst, he may turn against society in anger and violence.

Just such a vicious circle presses in on whole nations which have not had the chance to develop their physical and human resources to the point where self-sufficiency is in sight. To help transform this vicious circle into an upward-mounting curve of development, the

* Paul Hoffman, "A War on Want," *UN Monthly Chronicle,* Vol. 1, No. 2 (June 1964), pp. 92–98.

United Nations and its family of agencies are engaged in an unrelenting war against world poverty. Their army is composed of scientists and researchers, doctors and nurses, meteorologists and hydrologists, educators and engineers, agronomists and animal health experts, and specialists in a host of other fields from manufacturing productivity to peaceful uses of the atom.

Some 13,000 of these specialists have been sent into developing countries by the Expanded Program of Technical Assistance during its 15-year history. In addition, almost 30,000 nationals of the developing countries have been trained under EPTA fellowships to further economic and social advance.

The United Nations Special Fund, a 5-year-old fledgling, has also sent many experts into the field; some 1,900 of them have gone out in teams with large quantities of equipment to help fight ignorance, economic stagnation and their ugly consequences. They are making their mark by the principles which guide them as well as by what they are accomplishing.

Principles and Achievements

The Special Fund is rooted in the conviction that all countries, rich and poor, have a common interest in speeding economic growth in the developing countries. The benefits will be shared and so must be the effort. Every country, therefore, regardless of the stage of its development, should be a full partner in this enterprise. This means that there must be a pooling of ideas and a harmonization of purposes, priorities and action.

One measure of this partnership in progress is the fact that 106 countries—from Afghanistan to Canada, India to the Netherlands, Senegal to Switzerland and the Soviet Union—are contributing cash to the central resources of the United Nations Special Fund. The more than $300 million thus far pledged is made up of annual contributions that have ranged from a few thousand dollars from the smallest countries, to some $36 million from the largest contributor, the United States. I would stress that it is not the amounts alone that count—though the more the better; it is the fact that each of these many countries contributes *voluntarily* to help, through this program, to defeat poverty in no less than 121 countries and territories.

Not only the money, but also the experts, equipment and

contracting services it pays for, come from poor and rich countries alike; indeed, we are proud that 12 per cent of the 1,300 experts now working in our projects come from the developing countries themselves.

A second premise fundamental to the work of the Special Fund is that the primary responsibility for development rests with the leaders and people of each developing country. Assistance achieves its maximum effectiveness when it is tied to maximum effort by the developing countries, and they have willingly acted upon this principle in the Special Fund. They are providing $502 million–60 per cent–towards the total cost of the 374 projects thus far approved by the Fund's Governing Council, leaving only $335 million to be provided by the Fund. Even more important than their contributions to project costs is their resolution and work to make these projects succeed.

All participating nations and organizations realize that development is an extremely difficult and relatively long-term task. It involves helping whole populations to raise their incomes and living standard to a level of decency and dignity.

Utility of Surveys

I mentioned earlier that most of the developing countries have physical resources sufficient to their needs. But resources cannot be put to work before they are explored, identified and appraised. Over $111 million of Special Fund assistance–about 33 per cent–is devoted to this task. Through surveys-in-depth of soils and subsoils, water and forests, rivers and oceans, the Special Fund helps to bring resources into productive use. Some of these surveys help mobilize capital to produce commodities not only for local consumption but also to earn precious foreign exchange. Others contribute to harnessing power for industry and for better living, and to developing transport networks that will not only give a farmer access to markets but bring to him inexpensive goods as incentives to further production.

The creation and expansion of industry is urgent in the developing countries. It should not, however, be forgotten that the vast majority of their people live on the land and must find their better-living standards from the soil. Nor should we forget that most people in the towns and cities must be able to get more and better food at reasonable prices.

This reminds me of an experiment which was described at the recent United Nations Conference on the Application of Science and Technology for the Benefit of the Less Developed Areas. Certain people in the town where the experiment took place were considered "lazy and irresponsible". Instead of working, they passed the day lounging under trees. Interestingly enough, when they were given one good meal a day they began to take new interest in life. They not only improved in health but showed ingenuity in seeking jobs and they worked well. The experiment demonstrated a simple fact that is too often overlooked: when man does not have enough to eat, nature requires him to conserve the little energy he has. Obviously, then, the soldiers of economic development, like all soldiers, move forward on their stomachs; other production often depends on food production and its availability to those who need better nutrition.

There is no doubt in my mind that the earth's resources can feed the earth's people, and that it can provide them with the raw materials they require and the creative work which is also their nourishment. Encouraging evidence of this is already emerging from the 148 physical resource surveys and industrial feasibility studies now being helped by the Special Fund and cooperating United Nations agencies.

In Syria, agriculture could not be substantially expanded without additional water. A survey assisted by the Special Fund and the Food and Agriculture Organization uncovered in the northern part of the country sufficient underground water to irrigate 250,000 acres. This land can now support three crops of cotton and wheat per year and provide a livelihood for 100,000 people.

In Mexico, Special Fund FAO assisted studies of forest resources are leading to a substantial expansion in the production of timber and wood products. Meanwhile, in Pakistan some 450 million tons of coal and 150 million tons of iron ore have been discovered, both of which can be used for the expansion of the country's industry. The United Nations is the executing agency for this project.

Attraction of Investment

These and other surveys open the way for indispensable investment. Eleven of them completed to date at a total cost of $10 million have already attracted almost $500 million of local and foreign investment for the development of resources in the low-income countries.

Another premise underlying the work of the Special Fund is that applied research and careful planning are essential to help make the available physical and human resources fully productive. Roughly $82 million, that is, 24 per cent of the Special Fund's financing, are being used for 83 projects in the fields of planning and applied research.

United Nations organs and experts have long urged the necessity of sound planning in the developing countries if resources, external as well as local, were to be used with minimum waste and maximum effectiveness. The Special Fund is extending to new dimensions the assistance given by our world community to train development planners and provide advisory services on problems of development programing and implementation. Three Special Fund assisted projects, administered by the United Nations, are for national planning organizations and three others are for regional economic and social planning institutes in Latin America, Africa and Asia.

Much information already exists which would be of direct value in raising production and productivity in the developing countries. The job is to get it tried, adapted to local conditions and applied on a broad scale to solve practical problems. Applied research can improve processes, increase output, introduce new products, find new uses for local material and thus raise levels of employment and income.

Research Institutes

The Special Fund is assisting 77 applied research institutes. In Argentina, for example, one such institute has brought management and labor together in boosting factory output. In the Sudan, another of these projects has improved the quality and productivity of the hides and leather industry. Still another of these institutes has helped industry in Thailand to eliminate waste of raw materials, to save production time and costs, and to produce better products.

No effort is spared to involve government departments, private industry and workers in these projects. This applies to farms as well as factories. Government extension services are strengthened and heavily relied upon to disseminate improvements such as the introduction of new agricultural methods, seeds and fertilizers. In other cases, business circles are involved in the research projects at a very early stage and continuously thereafter. Assisted laboratories and test stations are designed to be the strong and capable servants of industry and government in their efforts to raise production and productivity. So conceived, they can make notable and cumulative contributions to income and improved living standards.

The Special Fund gives particularly heavy emphasis to the human factor, and with good cause: it is people who will bring about development. Forty-three per cent of Special Fund money—$142 million—is devoted to increasing the knowledge and skills of people in the low-income countries. One hundred and forty-three advanced training and technical education projects are designed to prepare men and women for more productive lives and for development service.

Every Special Fund assisted project contains a training component, but many are designed exclusively to upgrade human skills. With the help of the United Nations, advanced training is being given in public administration, for example, in Ghana. The United Nations Educational, Scientific and Cultural Organization is cooperating to train engineers, architects, secondary school teachers, and a variety of technicians, from draftsmen to research workers. The International Civil Aviation Organization has joined forces with the Special Fund in training civil aviation flight and ground personnel; 1,000 pilots, navigators and other specialists have already been graduated. The International Labour Organisation is a major partner in projects to train managers, factory supervisors and vocational instructors. The World Meteorological Organization and the International Telecommunication Union are training key personnel in their respective fields.

The 45,000 middle and senior level persons already trained or now being trained in these projects will have a tremendous multiplier effect. Many are now teaching others to become teachers, and will undoubtedly continue to do so throughout their productive lives; others are teaching foremen, craftsmen and agricultual extension workers. In India alone, 1,500 industrial instructors have been graduated from five Special Fund ILO assisted institutes, and 1,000 more instructors are expected to complete their training this year. They will be of substantial help in producing the 750,000 additional skilled workers India needs by 1966.

Emphasis on Local Capability

In all projects—surveys, training and research—perhaps the most important contribution of the Special Fund and the cooperating agencies is to bolster the capacity of the developing countries to bring about their own economic and social advance. Our experts will depart. Their responsibility is to leave behind them cadres of highly trained people as competent institutions which will carry on and grow in strength.

In training projects, this means not only preparing people for immediate tasks, but also providing the personnel, programs and facilities to train others for future tasks. In applied research projects, technicians and institutes must be equipped and able to handle new problems as they arise. In survey projects, appropriate services and governmental departments are built or reinforced to help ensure appropriate follow-up and enable the country to undertake similar surveys on its own.

Thus, while Special Fund assistance has a beginning and an end, the results are expected to extend and expand steadily in the future. There is reason to believe that these aims are being achieved—both in projects under way and in those already completed.

Most of the credit for these successes goes to the governments concerned; but much credit is also due to the United Nations and nine of its related agencies which act as executing agencies for the projects. These agencies—ranging from the World Bank to the World Health Organization—together with our field officers assist governments in preparing requests for Special Fund help. They also assist in evaluating project applications, in drawing up the plans of operation for approved projects, and in actually implementing them.

Altogether, some two billion persons in more than 100 countries are involved in Special Fund assistance. Many of them participate through the contributions of their governments to the Fund's resources, and many also participate through the work of their governments as senior partners in carrying out projects within their own country. Not only those who are personally engaged in the projects, but all of these hundreds of millions of people can be proud of what their concerted efforts are accomplishing.

Integration of Programs

While valuable results have been produced by this cooperative program of the member countries of the United Nations and its related agencies, there is no room for complacency. The efficiency of our services should be further improved and our projects must be so oriented that they will do the absolute maximum to speed development. This means that no effort should be spared to integrate the diverse development activities of the United Nations family. In my opinion, approval of the proposals of the United Nations Secretary-General, U Thant, for the merging of the Expanded Program of Technical Assistance and the Special Fund—rather than their absorption into a new United Nations Development Program—would contribute greatly to the harmonization of these activities.

Streamlining United Nations assistance programs should also make governments willing—indeed eager—to channel more development assistance through our world Organization. There is without any doubt an urgent need for more of the kind of assistance the United Nations system is uniquely endowed to provide. The volume of requests for such assistance grows steadily and more resources are needed to meet legitimate requirements and promising opportunities.

The amounts involved are much less than many people believe. The immediate need of the United Nations family is for an increase of only $100 million a year in its pre-investment expenditures—50 per cent above the current level. That additional $100 million is but one-thousandth of what it costs every year to maintain the military establishments of the great powers. Yet this relatively small amount would be a potent long-range investment in peace and security. If it can help even indirectly to prevent economic tensions that might spread into political conflicts, it will be more than worth its price.

Are we willing to pay that price now, at mid-point in the United Nations Development Decade? The prize would be magnificent. We could thus move towards a world of expanding opportunity, a world substantially without want—a safer world for all. This is the good war we are fighting, the one we must win.

42. *ECONOMIC INTEGRATION AND POLITICAL UNITY IN EUROPE* / WALTER HALLSTEIN*

What I should like to discuss tonight is the political response that we in the West are making to the challenges that face us today.

* Walter Hallstein, *Economic Integration and Political Unity in Europe* (London: Information Service of the European Communities, 1961).

That which concerns me most directly is the creation of what is known as the European Economic Community—of whose Commission I have the honour to be President. In name, as you know, it is 'economic': but what I want to stress tonight is that it is also political. Note that I say 'it *is* political'—not just that it tends towards a political goal. That goal has been described by none less than Winston Churchill as 'a United States of Europe'. My aim tonight is to show that the future has already begun.

As you know, it was in 1950 that Germany, France, Italy, and the Benelux countries set up the European Coal and Steel Community. It was in 1957 that they set up Euratom—the Atomic Energy Community—and the so-called Common Market—the European Economic Community. These are economic organizations—but they are also highly political.

The Obligations of Membership

The question may arise: Why does the European Economic Community have only six members? Well, it is not because we are some kind of an exclusive club. Our number was not decided by those who joined, but rather by those who did not join. Our founding Treaty holds out two possibilities for European states—full membership, or association. Full membership means full acceptance of the Treaty and the institutions it establishes. It means acceptance of the political significance and dynamism of these institutions. A full member must agree to build common policy in a wide range of endeavour. Association, on the other hand, is only partial membership. An associate takes on only a part of the obligations of our Treaty and enjoys only a portion of the rights of full members.

The basic economic idea underlying the Common Market is that the resources of modern technology can only be used to the full if the economic area within which they are developed is large enough. In the economic sphere, the modern world is a world of continents, of markets and economies on the grand scale. Divided economies and divided markets mean small-scale efforts, which in turn mean waste and relative poverty. In the United States, with its huge common market of some 180 million people, some seventy million men and women—the working population—in 1960 produced the equivalent of more than 503 billion dollars. In the same year in the Community countries, with a combined population of nearly 170 million, a working population even larger than that of the United States produced the equivalent of only some 180 billion dollars–little more than one-third of what a smaller working population in America produced in the same time. You may say, quite rightly: 'But American industry is more capital-intensive.' But why is this so? Because it can afford to produce for the vast American home market, and can thus afford the massive investments that a large market both requires and makes possible. Only by establishing in Europe a home market of this scale can we hope to play our full part in producing and exploiting the world's wealth.

NOT JUST FREE TRADE

The idea of a single large home market, therefore, lies at the heart of the movement for economic integration. But this in itself involves political issues. It is not just a movement for free trade between separate economies. It is a movement to fuse markets–and economies–into one, and to establish within that 'common market' the conditions and characteristics of any single national market. This means sweeping away the classical barriers to trade, tariffs and quotas. It means removing less obvious barriers–various types of discrimination; legislative barriers; glaring tax differences, and so on. It means ensuring that private barriers do not divide the market–for example, market-sharing agreements and the activities of trusts. It means maintaining the external conditions of a single home market, by making uniform for the whole area the conditions in which imports may enter it. This entails merging the separate national customs tariffs *vis-à-vis* the rest of the world into one single, common tariff, and applying a single common policy for external trade. All these are matters of political importance.

A SINGLE ECONOMIC POLICY

And a common market goes even further than this. Within a home market, not only goods, but persons, services, and capital, can circulate freely. The same must apply to a common market composed of numerous states. A home market means a home market for agriculture: therefore it cannot be left out of a common market–or not, at least, without running into the risk of favouring one partner unfairly against another, and thus leaving the whole edifice not only incomplete but lop-sided. Nor, in the delicate matter of agriculture, where so many stubborn traditions and such deep political passions are involved, can things be left to look after themselves. A common market in agriculture inescapably involves a common agricultural policy to replace the often conflicting policies of the national states. Much the same is true of transport–another field where full and free competition is not yet a practicable goal. Finally, and most difficult of all, if we seek to establish a single home market and a single economy, we must progressively fuse into one our separate national policies and move towards one economic policy for the Community as a whole.

This, in a nutshell, is the philosophy behind the Common Market Treaty. But let me state it more concisely still. The statement is not mine. It comes from one of the last documents produced by the League of Nations, and issued by the United Nations in 1947. Here it is: 'For a customs union to exist it is necessary to allow free movement of goods within the union. For a customs union to be a reality, it is necessary to allow free movement of persons. For a customs union to be stable it is necessary to maintain free exchangeability of currency and stable exchange rates within the union. This implies, *inter alia*, free movement of capital within the union. When there is free movement of goods, persons, and capital in an area, diverse economic policies concerned with maintaining economic activity cannot be pursued'.[1]

Federal Institutions

Economically, therefore, those states that commit themselves to the Common Market commit themselves to a far-reaching process of integration into a single unit. Is this not a far-reaching political commitment? Let me continue the quotation that I cited just now. It goes on: 'To assure uniformity of policy some political mechanism is required'. Ladies and gentlemen, I do not need to remind you that our European Community has established an institutional mechanism whose salient features are federal. They are founded upon the principal of democratic control, embodied in the European Parliament, which is really the active beginnings of a Parliament: it has the one great power of overthrowing the executive organ of the Community, *i.e.* the Commission, and a number of much lesser powers, such as that of constantly putting questions, being legally

[1] 'Customs Union–a League of Nations contribution to the study of customs union problems', Lake Success, New York, 1947, p. 74.

entitled to an answer, and the right to be consulted on most occasions when the Community proposes to legislate. It is my belief that these powers must be augmented in the future, particularly when the Parliament—which at present is chosen by and from the national Parliaments—becomes the direct expression of democratic opinion by being directly elected by universal suffrage.

The Community institutions, then, are subject to democratic control. They are also subject to the rule of law. This finds its expression in the Community's Court of Justice—the nearest parallel, perhaps, to your own Supreme Court.

The representatives of the Member Governments sit in the Community's Council of Ministers. This, too, is a federal organ—since unlike those of international organizations, its decisions are taken, as a rule, by majority vote, thus making it often impossible for one Member State to impose its veto. This is a built-in guarantee of progress: it is vital to the success of the whole enterprise.

TASKS OF THE EXECUTIVES

I have left until last the so-called 'Executives' of the Community. These are fully independent of the Member States in that their Members—some of them ex-Ministers even—are no longer national representatives: they are expressly forbidden to take instructions, and are responsible exclusively to the European Parliament. Their discussions are not public, and once a decision has been reached, the Executive concerned has collective responsibility for it: decisions are reached, of course, by simple majority. I said just now 'so-called' Executives, because although the analogy with the executive branch of a classical constitution is a close one, it is not complete. The most important rôle of the Executives—apart from certain domains where they take and apply decisions directly affecting the Community as a whole—is threefold. The Commission is first a motor, to stimulate and initiate Community action. It has the sole right to propose action in a large number of fields, and its proposals can only be modified by a unanimous vote of the national representatives in the Council. Secondly, the Commission is a watchdog, one of the guardians of the Treaty, keeping Governments and others up to the mark. It must take offenders before the Court of Justice: in at least two cases, it has already done so. Thirdly, it plays the part of an honest broker, helping to bring about agreement among the Member States, and to ensure thereby that action is taken. Indeed, the basic secret of the Community's smooth working is the constant collaboration—and division of labour—between the national representatives in the Council and the independent Commission. I need not stress the crucial importance of all these rôles.

Nor, I think, do I need to point out that all this panoply of institutions is itself highly political. It is certainly, in the words of the League of Nations report I quoted earlier, 'some political mechanism'. Not only this, but the subject-matter of its actions is itself political. Let me make one final quotation from the League of Nations text: 'The greater the interference of the state in economic life, the greater must be the political integration'. For what we are doing, ladies and gentlemen, is not just integrating the action of employers, workers, merchants, or consumers. What is being integrated is the part played by the national states in creating the conditions within which economic activity takes place. I need not remind you how greatly the rôle of the state in this field has increased since, say, half a century ago, even in the freest and most liberal economies. Indeed, in some respects I think it may be true to say that the effect of economic integration is to make those economies more free, and certainly more liberal, than under a purely national economic régime. When one thinks of agriculture, for instance, it becomes clear that integration means a degree of liberation from innumerable national protective measures. It is also clear that this task is long, difficult, and delicate—precisely because its subject-matter is so highly political—and, indeed, politically explosive. Let me repeat: highly political. If we have learned anything in the years of experience which we have had since the European Coal and Steel Community first opened the common market for coal in 1953, it is this: that these apparently humdrum economic tasks are in reality very much more. And that 'very much more', which is political, is of the very greatest importance, not only to the Community, but also—and most particularly—to our friends in the rest of the world.

'We are not in business . . . we are in politics'

This is especially so, I think, in the case of the United States. It is important because it guarantees that we are serious—that we are in earnest. We are not in business to promote tariff preferences, to establish a discriminatory club, to form a larger market to make us richer, or a trading bloc to further our commercial interests. We are not in business at all: we are in politics. Our aim is to help ourselves, and so help others: to rid Europe of the crippling anomalies of the past, and enable her to pull her full weight in building tomorrow's world.

This task is urgent; and it is a task that does not concern us alone, or our economies alone. It is a political task, and a political task for us all.

THE CHALLENGE

Do I need to remind you, indeed, of how fast our world is changing? It is this single fact, I think, that distinguishes our age from the nineteenth century.

Only a few years ago, children's books were full of the wonders of the new twentieth century: automobiles, aircraft, telephones, radio. We all knew, we all said, that these inventions were going to transform our world, reducing distances, bringing peoples closer together. All this has happened. So rapidly have new wonders replaced the old that now, in the age of television, atomic energy, and space travel, we look back with affectionate nostalgia to the age of the early automobile, the biplane with fixed undercarriage, the Bell telephone, and the old crystal radio. Yet when we look at our political life, at our international relations, how far have we really accepted the political consequences of even those far-off inventions? And how much less have we applied to our whole way of thinking the consequences of more recent advance! We are running a race with destiny; we cannot afford to run it in period costume.

As I have suggested, there are signs of progress. After the first World War, a great President of the United States, Woodrow Wilson, outlined the famous 'Fourteen Points'. As a step forward at the time, this programme was remarkable. It sought to outlaw what were then seen as the causes of war: secret treaties, naval jealousies, the arms race, colonial rivalries. But seen from a distance of over forty years, the Fourteen Points look most remarkable as a symptom of their own age and a consecration of nationalism. In the words of a recent historian, their aim was to achieve justice 'by making states more perfect nation-states'.[2]

After World War II, attitudes had changed. The old League of Nations was replaced by the United Nations—and the change of name was significant. A new network of international organizations came into being, expressing the general recognition that even 'per-

[2] David Thomson: 'Europe Since Napoleon', London, 1957, p. 534.

fect' nation-states must acknowledge some degree of organized interdependence. But even this was only a belated attempt to face the political consequences of changes that had already occurred in the early years of this century. It was the first conscious effort to draw the logical conclusions from technical inventions now long past.

THE RESPONSE: INTEGRATION

It was not until 1950, in fact, that the process went one stage further, and the concept of the nation-state itself began to be modified in practice. Hitherto, the attempt to create a new order in the world had been limited to intensifying international co-operation between separate states. Now, for the first time, it began to take the form of integrating those states together, to reflect in their political life and political organization, the radical changes brought about in the first instance by technological advance. This, in fact, was the beginning of the European Community: it is yet another reason for stressing its political nature. For, if co-operation was the political response to the invention of automobiles, aircraft, telephones, and radio, then economic integration is the political response to those even more spectacular innovations of the jet age, of the atomic age, of which the latest instance is space travel by human beings.

Mention of this fact, I think, recalls that what we face, in this changing world, is more than a purely technological challenge. That challenge is political, too. Indeed, one may well ask whether the efforts which the countries of the European Community are making would have taken shape had there not been a direct political stimulus–I may even say a direct political threat. Certainly, the process of uniting Western Europe has been greatly accelerated by the fact that Europe as a whole is divided by the Iron Curtain. Paul-Henri Spaak, in his brilliant little book on NATO, takes as his starting point the thirteenth of March, 1948, when the Czech Foreign Minister, Jan Masaryk, committed suicide–or was murdered: but he rightly points out that this was only the culminating point in a whole series of events. Since the War, indeed, Europe has been menaced by political forces whose aim it is to destroy the Western way of life. Those forces are very close to us. They are very strong. They are constantly growing stronger. Driven by a pseudo-religious sense of mission, organized with great efficiency, and backed by ever-growing resources, they challenge us in all spheres—military, political, and economic. Locked in the military balance of power, we may yet find ourselves attacked in our political and economic life: all over the world, indeed, the struggle is on. Call it, if you will, 'competitive co-existence'; what is clear is that this kind of competition is no mere friendly rivalry, but a political and economic challenge that must be met by economic and political means. Faced on the one hand by Communist empire-building and on the other by Communist economic planning, we have to prove that our free system not only is better, but works better.

Never Purely Economic

In this context, can we regard the integration of Europe as a purely economic phenomenon? Is it, indeed, has it ever been, a purely economic affair?

As a matter of recent experience, the answer is 'no'. There was the plan—unhappily it came to nothing—for a European army, the European Defence Community. What more strikingly political proposal could be imagined? With it went the proposal for a European Political Community. Both failed—not so much because of a general lack of the will to achieve them, as because of particular political circumstances, among others a virulent and largely Communist inspired propaganda campaign against them.

But this failure was not the signal for retreat. Less than a year later came the Messina Conference and the proposals for the Common Market and Euratom. And their goal is not only, as I have said, the economic integration of Europe, with all the political overtones that this implies. It is also to carry one stage further an essentially political movement. It is no accident, for example, that the Euratom Treaty should contain the germ of a 'European University'. It is no paradox that the Community countries should now be feeling their way towards a unity of political action, partly under the stimulus of the suggestions made last year by President de Gaulle.

FROM CO-OPERATION TO INTEGRATION

All this, moreover, falls in line with the natural evolution of Europe itself. In that sense, in seeking political unity, we have history on our side. Even a generation ago, we used to speak of 'the concert of the Powers'. Traditionally, the structure of Europe consisted of a multiplicity of separate states with their own separate structures, which although they did not always act in total isolation from each other, came together only in temporary and *ad hoc* groupings. Basically, the system rested upon the balance of power between France and Germany, with—often—Great Britain in the rôle of moderator between them. It was a contrapuntal concert of Europe with conductors—sometimes—from outside the European continent.

That concert is silenced. It reached its finale in 1939—a bitter and tragic finale that continued for six years. Then, if not before, it became obvious that the nineteenth century system so masterfully employed by Bismarck could no longer endure in the twentieth century. It gave place to the system of Schuman, of Adenauer, of Sforza, of De Gasperi, of Spaak, and a whole new generation of statesmen. In place of the balance of power, they created the fusion of interests. In place of the *ad hoc* groupings of separate states, they proposed the pooling of problems and resources. In place of co-operation, they worked for integration. In place of the concert of the Powers, they set as their goal an ever closer union, shaped by common institutions, and built upon deeds, not words.

NEED FOR A POLITICAL CHOICE

These things did not happen automatically: in politics, nothing does. They demanded a clear choice, and a political choice. Need I add that this fundamental political decision has already borne unmistakably political fruit? In 1946, just a year after the War, Winston Churchill called for a reconciliation of France and Germany 'within a kind of United States of Europe'. Ladies and gentlemen, those words were prophetic. There has been a transformation of Germany's relations with France. Fifty years ago, my teacher in Mainz on the Rhine used to tell us that France was Germany's 'natural enemy', ordained by providence as such for all time. A few miles away, no doubt, little French boys were being taught the same pernicious nonsense—from the opposite point of view. Today, it would be laughable—if its past consequences had not been so tragic.

Those consequences themselves are a further political factor in the story. You in the United States are commemorating this year the hundredth anniversary of the Civil War. The War of 1939 to 1945, was, I sincerely hope, the last civil war in Western Europe. From your Civil War you emerged as a nation: from ours we emerged as a nascent Community. Nor is it by chance that the geographical area of the Six founder States of the European Community is almost identical with that which was brought to the brink of destruction, both materially, and psychologically, by the Nazi-Fascist monster and by the second World War. The former debased the concept of national sovereignty: the latter emptied it of substance. Frontiers seem less real when they can be flattened by tanks or ignored by intercontinental missiles.

IMMENSE POLITICAL CHANGES

But these brutal political facts–facts that we have had to face most clearly in Europe itself–are themselves only part of the immense political changes which have been transforming the whole world during this century. I said just now that in the economic sphere the world map is no longer made up of countries: it is made up of continents. This is true also in the political sphere. We are familiar with the idea of two great world powers–the United States and the Soviet Union. We are becoming familiar with the emergence of Communist China, with the rapid changes on the continent of Africa, with new prospects and new dangers in Latin America. Here, too, is a political challenge, but of a different kind. It is a challenge of scale, a challenge of size. In a world of giants, we cannot afford to be midgets. Here, then, is a further political motive for seeking real unity–political unity–in Europe.

Towards an Atlantic Community

This does not mean, of course, that we are seeking to create some kind of 'third force' in Europe, some kind of divisive factor within the Atlantic Alliance. Indeed, the same political challenge that is leading us to unite in Europe makes it all the more necessary for us to cement our European Community within the larger and perforce looser community that is the Atlantic Community. If we are seeking to create what has been called 'a second America in the West', it is because we wish to become a strong and valid partner for the 'first' America–to be one of the pillars upon which the Alliance itself is built. Not only do we believe in 'interdependence': we owe to it whatever progress we have achieved since the War. We shall never forget the foresight, the imagination, and the sheer generosity with which the United States helped to restore Europe after World War II. Today, that phase is over. Europe is on her feet again, and charity can be replaced by co-operation. And we need to co-operate —to defend ourselves, to help others, to fight poverty, to make a real attack on all those problems which not even the European Community as a whole, not even the United States as a whole, can tackle effectively alone. Can a so-called 'third force' maintain the NATO shield by itself? Can it meet by itself the needs of the developing countries? Can it alone solve the problems of booms and slumps, of currency reserves, of agricultural surpluses? Of course not. Ladies and gentlemen, we must rally the forces of the Atlantic Community to tackle these problems together, and to create a new economic order in the free world. What better way to begin than by uniting the European partners in this great venture? Already, indeed, the creation of the European Community is beginning to exert a cohesive effect. Without it, would Great Britain now be rethinking her whole relationship to continental Europe? Without it, should we have seen those other steps forward that have culminated in the formation of the O.E.C.D.? The stone once cast into the pool, the rings broaden out into ever widening circles.

I do not wish to claim too much for the European Community. But I do believe, and tonight I hope to have shown you *why* I believe—that the movement for European integration, far from being a mere movement for technocrats, for economists, is one that is essentially political, and therefore one that concerns all of us. It is a movement that is still in progress. Not all the problems are solved as yet—nor are all the dangers overcome, but we are determined, and we are hopeful.

Moreover, if there is one conclusion that emerges inescapably from what I have been saying here tonight it is that the political integration of Europe can only make its full contribution to the strength and safety of us all if it goes hand in hand with ever closer links across the Atlantic. It now takes less time to cross the Atlantic than it once took to cross the Mediterranean; and as the ocean that both divides and joins us, the Atlantic is indeed the Mediterranean of our own day.

A New and Creative Approach

I do not need to remind you of the many problems that we share, the many tasks that we must face together. Let me mention only three of them. There is the problem of our international monetary system, and the repercussions that even minor changes may have on the safety of all our currencies, the fruits of our thrift and industry, and even the stability of our political life. There is the problem of agricultural production in the age of modern technology—the problem of surpluses, and the problem of adaptation on the land. And finally, there is the pressing need to work together to help the world's developing countries—what Dean Rusk has rightly called 'a matter of life and death for freedom'. These are some of the problems that the new Organization for Economic Co-operation and Development will be tackling in the years to come—with the full participation of both the European Community and the United States, as well as of our other friends and partners in the free world. How important that partnership is I do not need to stress.

We for our part believe that the even closer partnership we are establishing in the European Community is one of the very few new political inventions that we in the West have made since World War II. We are determined to use it, in collaboration with the United States and with the West as a whole, to make a new and creative approach to the many other political and economic problems that face us all throughout the globe. With the help of our friends, with your help, we shall succeed.

INTERNATIONAL LAW

XIV

International law is one of the oldest attempts to bring a measure of order and peace to our troubled world. Hugo Grotius (1583–1645) is generally considered to be the "Father of International Law." The first selection is from the Prolegomena to his *On the Law of War and Peace.* In the Prolegomena, Grotius pays special attention to the nature and binding character of international law.

The second selection is by Philip C. Jessup, judge on the International Court of Justice in The Hague. Jessup made these remarks at the "Pacem in Terris Conference" held in New York in February 1965.

How effective can international law and international adjudication be? This question is examined in the third selection by the Belgian jurist Charles de Visscher. De Visscher also served on the World Court in The Hague.

43. *PROLEGOMENA TO THE LAW OF WAR AND PEACE** / *HUGO GROTIUS*

The municipal law of Rome and of other states has been treated by many, who have undertaken to elucidate it by means of commentaries or to reduce it to a convenient digest. That body of law, however, which is concerned with the mutual relations among states or rulers of states, whether derived from nature, or established by divine ordinances, or having its origin in custom and tacit agreement, few have touched upon. Up to the present time no one has treated it in a comprehensive and systematic manner; yet the welfare of mankind demands that this task be accomplished. . . .

Such a work is all the more necessary because in our day, as in former times, there is no lack of men who view this branch of law with contempt as having no reality outside of an empty name. On the lips of men quite generally is the saying of Euphemus, which Thucydides quotes, that in the case of a king or imperial city nothing is unjust which is expedient. Of like implication is the statement that for those whom fortune favors might makes right, and that the administration of a state cannot be carried on without injustice.

Furthermore, the controversies which arise between peoples or kings generally have Mars as their arbiter. That war is irreconcilable with all law is a view held not alone by the ignorant populace; expressions are often let slip by well-informed and thoughtful men which lend countenance to such a view. Nothing is more common than the assertion of antagonism between law and arms. . . .

Since our discussion concerning law will have been undertaken in vain if there is no law, in order to open the way for a favorable reception of our work and at the same time to fortify it against attacks, this very serious error must be briefly refuted. In order that we may not be obliged to deal with a crowd of opponents, let us assign to them a pleader. And whom should we choose in preference to Carneades? For he had attained to so perfect a mastery of the peculiar tenet of his Academy that he was able to devote the power

* Hugo Grotius, *De Jure Belli ac Pacis Libri Tres*, trans. Francis W. Kelsey (Oxford: The Clarendon Press, 1925), Vol. 2, pp. 9–18.

of his eloquence to the service of falsehood not less readily than to that of truth.

Carneades, then, having undertaken to hold a brief against justice, in particular against that phase of justice with which we are concerned, was able to muster no argument stronger than this, that, for reasons of expediency, men imposed upon themselves laws, which vary according to customs, and among the same peoples often undergo changes as times change; moreover, that there is no law of nature, because all creatures, men as well as animals, are impelled by nature toward ends advantageous to themselves; that, consequently, there is no justice, or, if such there be, it is supreme folly, since one does violence to his own interests if he consults the advantage of others.

What the philosopher here says, and the poet reaffirms in verse,

> And just from unjust Nature cannot know,

must not for one moment be admitted. Man is, to be sure, an animal, but an animal of a superior kind, much farther removed from all other animals than the different kinds of animals are from one another; evidence on this point may be found in the many traits peculiar to the human species. But among the traits characteristic of man is an impelling desire for society, that is, for the social life—not of any and every sort, but peaceful, and organized according to the measure of his intelligence, with those who are of his own kind; this social trend the Stoics called "sociableness." Stated as a universal truth, therefore, the assertion that every animal is impelled by nature to seek only its own good cannot be conceded.

Some of the other animals, in fact, do in a way restrain the appetency for that which is good for themselves alone, to the advantage now of their offspring, now of other animals of the same species. This aspect of their behavior has its origin, we believe, in some extrinsic intelligent principle, because with regard to other actions, which involve no more difficulty than those referred to, a like degree of intelligence is not manifest in them. The same thing must be said of children. In children, even before their training has begun, some disposition to do good to others appears, as Plutarch sagely observed; thus sympathy for others comes out spontaneously at that age. The mature man in fact has knowledge which prompts him to similar actions under similar conditions, together with an impelling desire for society, for the gratification of which he alone among animals possesses a special instrument, speech. He has also been endowed with the faculty of knowing and acting in accordance with general principles. Whatever accords with that faculty is not common to all animals, but peculiar to the nature of man.

This maintenance of the social order, which we have roughly sketched, and which is consonant with human intelligence, is the source of law properly so called. To this sphere of law belong the abstaining from that which is another's, the restoration to another of anything of his which we may have, together with any gain which we may have received from it; the obligation to fulfill promises, the making good of a loss incurred through our fault, and the inflicting of penalties upon men according to their deserts.

From this signification of the word "law" there has flowed another and more extended meaning. Since over other animals man has the advantage of possessing not only a strong bent toward social life, of which we have spoken, but also a power of discrimination which enables him to decide what things are agreeable or harmful (as to both things present and things to come), and what can lead to either alternative, in such things it is meet for the nature of man, within the limitations of human intelligence, to follow the direction of a well-tempered judgment, being neither led astray by fear or the allurement of immediate pleasure, nor carried away by rash impulse. Whatever is clearly at variance with such judgment is understood to be contrary also to the law of nature, that is, to the nature of man.

To this exercise of judgment belongs moreover the rational allotment to each man, or to each social group, of those things which are properly theirs, in such a way as to give the preference now to him who is more wise over the less wise, now to a kinsman rather than to a stranger, now to a poor man rather than to a man of means, as the conduct of each or the nature of the thing suggests. Long ago the view came to be held by many that this discriminating allotment is a part of law, properly and strictly so called; nevertheless law, properly defined, has a far different nature, because its essence lies in leaving to another that which belongs to him, or in fulfilling our obligations to him.

What we have been saying would have a degree of validity even if we should concede that which cannot be conceded without the utmost wickedness, that there is no God, or that the affairs of men are of no concern to him. The very opposite of this view has been implanted in us partly by reason, partly by unbroken tradition, and confirmed by many proofs as well as by miracles attested by all ages. Hence it follows that we must without exception render obedience to God as our Creator, to whom we owe all that we are and have, especially since in manifold ways he has shown himself supremely good and supremely powerful, so that to those who obey him he is able to give supremely great rewards, even rewards that are eternal, since he himself is eternal. We ought, moreover, to believe that he has willed to give rewards, and all the more should we cherish such a belief if he has so promised in plain words; that he has done this, we Christians believe, convinced by the indubitable assurance of testimonies.

Herein, then, is another source of law besides the source in nature, that is, the free will of God, to which beyond all cavil our reason tells us we must render obedience. But the law of nature of which we have spoken, comprising alike that which relates to the social life of man and that which is so called in a larger sense, proceeding as it does from the essential traits implanted in man, can nevertheless rightly be attributed to God because of his having willed that such traits exist in us. In this sense, too, Chrysippus and the Stoics used to say that the origin of law should be sought in no other source than Jupiter himself; and from the name Jupiter the Latin word for law (*ius*) was probably derived. . . .

Again, since it is a rule of the law of nature to abide by pacts (for it was necessary that among men there be some method of obligating themselves one to another, and no other natural method can be imagined), out of this source the bodies of municipal law have arisen. For those who had associated themselves with some group, or had subjected themselves to a man or to men, had either expressly promised, or from the nature of the transaction must be understood impliedly to have promised, that they would conform to that which should have been determined, in the one case by the majority, in the other by those upon whom authority had been conferred.

What is said, therefore, in accordance with the view not only of Carneades but also of others, that

> Expediency is, as it were, the mother
> Of what is just and fair,

is not true, if we wish to speak accurately. For the very nature of man, which even if we had no lack of anything would lead us into the mutual relations of society, is the mother of the law of nature. But the mother of municipal law is that obligation which arises from mutual consent; and since this obligation derives its force from the law of nature, nature may be considered, so to say, the great-grandmother of municipal law.

The law of nature nevertheless has the reinforcement of expediency; for the author of nature willed that as individuals we should be weak, and should lack many things needed in order to live properly, to the end that we might be the more constrained to cultivate the social life. But expediency afforded an opportunity also for municipal law, since that kind of association of which we have spoken, and subjection to authority, have their roots in expediency. From this it follows that those who prescribe laws for others in so doing are accustomed to have or ought to have some advantage in view.

But just as the laws of each state have in view the advantage of that state, so by mutual consent it has become possible that certain laws should originate as between all states, or a great many states; and it is apparent that the laws thus originating had in view the advantage, not of particular states, but of the great society of states. And this is what is called the law of nations, whenever we distinguish that term from the law of nature.

This division of law Carneades passed over altogether. For he divided all law into the law of nature and the law of particular countries. Nevertheless if undertaking to treat of the body of law which is maintained between states—for he added a statement in regard to war and things acquired by means of war—he would surely have been obliged to make mention of this law.

Wrongly, moreover, does Carneades ridicule justice as folly. For since, by his own admission, the national who in his own country obeys its laws is not foolish, even though, out of regard for that law he may be obliged to forego certain things advantageous for himself, so that nation is not foolish which does not press its own advantage to the point of disregarding the laws common to nations. The reason in either case is the same. For just as the national who violates the law of his country in order to obtain an immediate advantage breaks down that by which the advantage of himself and his posterity are for all future time assured, so the state which transgresses the laws of nature and of nations cuts away also the bulwarks which safeguard its own future peace. Even if no advantage were to be contemplated from the keeping of the law, it would be a mark of wisdom, not of folly, to allow ourselves to be drawn toward that to which we feel that our nature leads.

Wherefore, in general, it is by no means true that

You must confess that laws were framed
From fear of the unjust,

a thought which in Plato someone explains thus, that laws were invented from fear of receiving injury, and that men are constrained by a kind of force to cultivate justice. For that relates only to the institutions and laws which have been devised to facilitate the enforcement of right, as when many persons in themselves weak, in order that they might not be overwhelmed by the more powerful, leagued themselves together to establish tribunals and by combined force to maintain these, that as a united whole they might prevail against those with whom as individuals they could not cope.

And in this sense we may readily admit also the truth of the saying that right is that which is acceptable to the stronger, so that we may understand that law fails of its outward effect unless it has a sanction behind it. In this way Solon accomplished very great results, as he himself used to declare,

By joining force and law together,
Under a like bond.

Nevertheless law, even though without a sanction, is not entirely void of effect. For justice brings peace of conscience, while injustice causes torment and anguish, such as Plato describes, in the breasts of tyrants. Justice is approved, and injustice condemned, by the common agreement of good men. But, most important of all, in God injustice finds an enemy, justice a protector. He reserves his judgments for the life after this, yet in such a way that he often causes their effects to become manifest even in this life, as history teaches by numerous examples.

Many hold, in fact, that the standard of justice which they insist upon in the case of individuals within the state is inapplicable to a nation or the ruler of a nation. The reason for the error lies in this, first of all, that in respect to law they have in view nothing except the advantage which accrues from it, such advantage being apparent in the case of citizens who, taken singly, are powerless to protect themselves. But great states, since they seem to contain in themselves all things required for the adequate protection of life, seem not to have need of that virtue which looks toward the outside, and is called justice.

But, not to repeat what I have said, that law is not founded on expediency alone, there is no state so powerful that it may not at some time need the help of others outside itself, either for purposes of trade, or even to ward off the forces of many foreign nations united against it. In consequence we see that even the most powerful peoples and sovereigns seek alliances, which are quite devoid of significance according to the point of view of those who confine law within the boundaries of states. Most true is the saying that all things are uncertain the moment men depart from law.

If no association of men can be maintained without law, as Aristotle showed by his remarkable illustration drawn from brigands, surely also that association which binds together the human race, or binds many nations together, has need of law; this was perceived by him who said that shameful deeds ought not to be committed even for the sake of one's country. Aristotle takes sharply to task those who, while unwilling to allow anyone to exercise authority over themselves except in accordance with law, yet are quite indifferent as to whether foreigners are treated according to law or not. . . .

44. *ON THE WORLD COMMUNITY* / PHILIP C. JESSUP*

The encyclical [*Pacem in Terris*] that is the basis for all of our considerations at this Convocation does not cover the problem of law or the rule of law in detail. It would not be expected that it should. It does contain references to law and justice, and law cannot exist without justice. It also contains references to the need for international organization and specifically the United Nations, and law cannot exist apart from organization.

The rule of law has both simple and complex aspects. It is simple in the sense that every human society has regulated its interrelationships, whether of individuals or of groups, by some rule of law. That law which is established exists though it be violated. Unhappily, law and violation of law are facts confirmed to us all in our daily experience of life and in our daily reading of the headlines of the newspapers, whether they apply to situations inside states or to relations among the states of the world.

* Philip C. Jessup, Statement at the International Convocation on the Requirements of Peace held in New York City in February 1965, in *On the World Community* (Santa Barbara: Center for the Study of Democratic Institutions, 1965), pp. 11–12. Reprinted by permission.

But law is not only a group of prohibitions or provisions for penalties, as in what we call "criminal law." More importantly, perhaps, law is the method by which society has always created devices to enable people to work together for the accomplishment of their proper ends and for the common good. That is why, in our domestic system, basic institutions like those of marriage and the family are creations of law. The institution of property is a creation of law. Practically all of our economic and business life proceeds on the basis of a great legal creation—the corporation. The same thing has been true in the international field, although we grant that the development of international law has not been perfected to the extent to which law has been perfected inside national societies.

Take the Charter of the United Nations, which is itself a treaty, a contract, a legal document. It says that the members of the United Nations are "states." We take it for granted that we know what states are, just as we take it for granted that we know what "corporations" are in the business life of the community. But the "state" in the international sense is a legal creation; it is a notion that has evolved over the centuries.

The United Nations itself, as an international organization, is a legal device, in the same way as the corporation in national law is a legal device for accomplishing certain definite ends. Within the general family of organizations of the United Nations there is a nexus of international organizations by which the affairs of the world are carried on. Through these it is possible to post a letter in New York and have it delivered in Germany or in Hong Kong or in Buenos Aires; the world community is enabled to quarantine diseases or to check plague as it never could in the past; there is an exchange of weather information so vital now to air transport and to sea transport. All of these are developed by treaties, and treaties are law, and they so remain even when they are broken.

We are told, and it is true, that coexistence is not merely an aspiration but a fact. The Soviet Union and the United States coexist, but they do not coexist in a vacuum. States do not sit off, one here, and one there, and merely glare at each other. They have inter-relationships, and those inter-relationships must be—and are—determined by various legal rules. That is why, for instance, in the ordinary mechanics of international society, there is an exchange of ambassadors and consular officers who perform numerous functions that enable the relationships of states to proceed in an orderly way. That is why, for another example, there are agreements as to which planes of which countries may fly which routes, and agreements about the allocation of radio wave lengths so as to distribute these necessary services among the various states of the world without undue conflict.

There are those who talk of the need for gradual evolution of human institutions. There are others who are impatient and say, no, we must have a panacea, we must have world law tomorrow and that will assure the peace. But let us consider the Secretary-General of the United Nations as the super-apothecary of the world, to whom everyone comes with a prescription for peace. It seems to me that our super-apothecary must reply: the prescription for peace is compounded of elements drawn from all over the face of the globe. There is an herb that grows on some unclimbed summit of some great mountain; there is another that may be found in the swamps of impenetrable jungles in tropical areas; there is a third that blooms in the desert, perhaps when it rains once in ten years or even once in a millennium; and all of these, and others, must be gathered and brewed before we can succeed in finding the prescription for the panacea that the impatient ask for now.

If we think of the leader of the world organization as a physician who is asked to eliminate from the world the virus of hate, the virus of envy, the virus of jealousy, the viruses that poison international relations, he is bound to reply that there is no super-drug that will conquer these viruses. All that our medications can do is to counter the possible development of other ills which follow in the train of the virus and to which the system, weakened by the virus, may be subjected unless proper care is taken. And so it is with the rule of law. It is not a panacea, nor is it something already achieved.

One of the great difficulties standing in the way of the full development of law in the international community is the concept known as sovereignty. Sovereignty is a quicksand. If one tries to build upon it, the entire legal structure sinks and perishes. Sovereignty in the sense of the unregulated will of states to do as they please is absolutely incompatible with the international rule of law. People do not always realize that every time a state enters into a treaty—as, for example, a treaty limiting nuclear tests—it is not only *exercising* its sovereignty but *limiting* its sovereignty by prohibiting itself from doing certain things in the future.

I feel bound to say that the jurists and international lawyers of the Soviet Union do not share this point of view about sovereignty. To them the preservation of sovereignty is the keynote and the necessary foundation of the operation of the United Nations. Perhaps this is why, in the application of international law to the solution of international disputes, there are so few governments of the world prepared to submit their controversies to the existing international tribunal, the International Court of Justice.

It is necessary to add, however, that this unwillingness to submit disputes is not always related merely to an over-emphasis on state sovereignty but is sometimes inspired by the same considerations that lead attorneys in the domestic field to urge their clients to settle cases out of court by negotiation instead of submitting them to the hazard of litigation. Foreign offices of governments function with the aid of legal advisers. Since they are generally cautious lawyers, they say: Don't submit it to the Court, you might lose; whereas if you just sit back, perhaps nothing will happen. This is hardly the way to promote the international rule of law. On the other hand, it was Elihu Root who used to describe developments in international peace by way of the old English expression, "Leg over leg, the dog went to Dover." If Dover represents the ultimate goal of peace, we shall attain it only by that cautious, slow, and sometimes discouraging route.

In the meantime, there is law; there are institutions for the application of law; and it is possible today for governments, like individuals, to take the advice of Shakespeare and do as adversaries do in law, "Strive mightily but eat and drink as friends."

45. *REFLECTIONS ON THE PRESENT PROSPECTS OF INTERNATIONAL ADJUDICATION* / CHARLES DE VISSCHER*

Is the pessimism at present exhibited by certain scholars with regard to the current prospects of international law completely reasonable? More particularly, is it really justifiable to speak of a deterioration in the juridical methods of settling disputes between states? However disappointing the course of events may have been during the

* Charles De Visscher, "Reflections on the Present Prospects of International Adjudication," translated from the French by Eleanor H. Finch, *American Journal of International Law,* Vol. 50, No. 3 (July 1956), pp. 467–74. Reprinted by permission.

last ten years, it seems that certain evaluations, inspired by nostalgia for the past, to some extent lose sight of factual conditions which have always, in different degrees, limited the role of law in the solution of international conflicts. It is useful to recall such conditions at a time when excessive discouragement has succeeded unreasonable expectations.

Two questions concern us in this respect: (1) political resistance to submission to international jurisdiction; and (2) the contribution of international adjudications to the development of international law.

I

Every recourse of states to international adjudication proceeds from their free will. This voluntary agreement—whether it is expressed in the terms of a *compromis* or of a compromissory clause—is viewed by the jurist in its formal aspect: principle of recourse, object of the litigation, powers of the arbitrator or judge, obligatory force of the decision rendered, all combine for the jurist to deduce, by the ordinary method of interpretation, the will of the parties from its textual expression. This perspective leaves outside his field of vision the conditions of practical effectiveness of the voluntary agreement. Being inclined to see in the arbitral agreement an instrument of general use which is valid in all circumstances, this view, at the beginning of the century, advanced to a rapid and too often unreasoned extension of the methods of arbitral or judicial settlement. For the government official, for the observer of political realities, the efficaciousness of recourse to international justice is the fundamental problem. In our times, it offers a complexity which our predecessors could not foresee. This complexity is due to two essential causes. One is the abrupt entry into international relations of countries with civilizations obviously foreign to that which was at the basis of traditional international law and its procedures. The other is the intensity and duration of contemporary political tensions.

Recourse to an international court implies that, and is only completely effective when, the dispute is completely separated from politics; that is, both its submission to impersonal legal criteria and the renunciation by the parties of all individual action on the matter in controversy. This separation from politics requires habits and moral traditions which are not shared in equal degree by all peoples, and even less by those which only recently have acquired an independent position on the international scene. But, above all, recourse to the court is effective only on condition that the antagonism of the parties be henceforth reduced to *litis contestatio*, the juridical opposition of two contentions. A dispute is not actually non-political when it develops from the very text of the compromissory clause that the parties have not been able to agree on the terms of reference to the arbitrator or judge.[1] Neither is it non-political, notwithstanding appearances, when, in spite of the attempt made in the *compromis* to separate its object from the general political relations between the parties, the issue becomes embroiled at some time or another in a political tension which in fact dominates and absorbs it. The paralyzing action exercised on arbitration and judicial settlement by political tensions may be difficult to detect. This is because it rarely manifests itself openly, the majority of governments taking the greatest care to affirm their attachment to law and their respect for judicial methods. It has a no less injurious influence whether it prevents governments from stating their differences in terms of law which make them justiciable, or whether it removes from the dispute itself any specific definable subject and leads it into the obscure and shifting perspectives of politics.

Heretofore little thought has been given to the influence exercised by diplomacy in the development of arbitration. Our predecessors liked to emphasize what they considered the progressive emancipation from diplomacy of obligatory and universal arbitration.[2] There is much to be said on this subject. If it is correct that in the 19th century diplomacy frequently used arbitration as a useful instrument either as a means for governments to avoid taking irritating positions of no great political interest or as a means of relieving them of an embarrassing adjustment of a dispute, it is even more true that diplomacy has served arbitration by supporting its first steps. It has given a real purpose to its activities and assured the execution of its decisions. This was cruelly lacking at the beginning of the 20th century, when, under the urging of an impatient radicalism, clauses of obligatory arbitration were sometimes ac-

[1] Such a situation arose in the Asylum Case between Colombia and Peru before the International Court of Justice (1950–1951), [1950] I.C.J. Rep. 266, [1951] *ibid.* 71; 45 A.J.I.L. 179, 781 (1951).

[2] See for example the preface by de Lapradelle and Politis to the first volume of their Recueil des Arbitrages Internationaux.

cumulated without any regard for the order of importance of the interests involved. Ever-present politics blocked the efforts of doctrine to give what it called a rational definition to the political dispute or to classify political and juridical disputes in sharply distinct categories. The only result of these attempts was to put the governments on guard and make them determined to repeat the reservations to the arbitral agreement. Moreover, it had to be admitted that arbitral clauses, multiplied cheaply or drafted without reservation, fell useless if, at the time of putting them into operation, they were not supported by firmly pacific diplomatic action.

The arbitral agreement has all the more reality and effectiveness insofar as it is entered into *intuitu personae*. This is to say how little it lends itself to extension in some mechanical way such as was formerly contemplated. Its possibilities depend, on one hand, on a sufficient moral community between the contracting parties, and, on the other hand, on the condition of general political relations between them. This last observation must be kept in mind in order to place in their true perspective certain treaties of arbitration which contain particularly extensive enumerations of disputes declared to be justiciable. It is also advisable not to be deceived by the presence or number of reservations in the arbitration agreement. Experience has shown that agreements accompanied by maturely thoughtful reservations are often those which are the most carefully observed. Most of the above remarks apply to judicial settlement as well as to arbitral clauses. To be convinced of this it suffices to compare the imposing list of jurisdictional clauses of the International Court of Justice with the meager use made of them by the signatory states.

This recollection of experience explains the very reserved reception given by certain governments of the States Members of the United Nations and the Sixth Committee of the General Assembly to the Draft Convention on Arbitral Procedure adopted by the International Law Commission at its 4th session and revised by it during the following session (June 1–August 14, 1953). As is known, this draft in its definite form was submitted to the Tenth General Assembly (1955), which was to determine the action to be taken upon it.[3]

[3] On recommendation of the Sixth Committee, the Assemby sent the Draft Convention on Arbitral Procedure prepared by the International Law Commission back to the Commission so that it might consider the comments of governments and the discussions in the Sixth Committee. The resolution also

The draft is remarkable in its technical qualities and brings to light the difference between the point of view of the jurist who is inclined to draw from the arbitral agreement all of its logically deducible effects, and that of the statesman who is careful above all to maintain in arbitration the flexible qualities which at all times have kept arbitration in certain favor with governments. The draft, by endeavoring—as was formerly done at Geneva with regard to Article 15, paragraph 8, of the League of Nations Covenant—to plug up all the openings and to foresee every loophole, in a word, to enclose arbitration within a rigid framework, runs the risk of hindering its development. As the Netherlands Government observed, perfectionist aspirations threaten to end up by "petrifying" the evolution of arbitral practice.[4] The observation applies particularly to Article 2 of the draft which, before the establishment of the arbitral tribunal, confers upon the International Court of Justice, in cases of disagreement, the power to decide whether the existing dispute belongs in the category of those envisaged by the agreement to arbitrate. As has been pointed out, no distinction is made here between legal disputes and political disputes.[5] In that respect there is, apart from an important derogation from customary law, a certain misunderstanding of the present possibilities of international adjudication. Governments appear in no way disposed to reinforce the arbitral agreement by submitting to the obligatory decision of the Court the essential question of the arbitrability of their disputes. Their attitude, which is still so reticent with regard to the obligatory jurisdiction of the Court, is itself significant on this subject.

The attention of the International Law Commission was equally directed to the eventuality of one of the parties attempting to evade the obligation to arbitrate by failing to designate the arbitrator or

---

asked the Commission to report to the thirteenth session of the General Assembly, which would then consider convening an international conference of plenipotentiaries to conclude a convention on arbitral procedure. See Res. 989 (X), 554th Plenary Meeting, Dec. 14, 1955, U.N. General Assembly, Official Records, 10th Sess., Supp. No. 19 (Doc. A/3116), pp. 46–47.

[4] Report of the International Law Commission, 5th Session (June 1–Aug. 14, 1953), pp. 34–36. It is well to keep in mind the remark of Julius Stone: "The features of arbitration law which offer so many avenues of escape, and which serve in the Commission's eyes as excuses for 'shirking' international undertakings, may be the very features which attract States to enter into such undertakings." Legal Controls of International Conflict, p. 736.

[5] See particularly the observations of the Swedish Government, Report, *op. cit.*, pp. 36–37, and the remarks of the French delegate in the 6th Committee of the General Assembly of 1954.

arbitrators left to its choice. In this case, Article 3 of the draft provides that, within a determined period, this designation should be made by the President of the International Court of Justice. It may be thought that in this respect there is a certain excess of regulation. The suggestion has a practical interest in providing against the difficulties of joint designation of a third arbitrator. As to the refusal by the parties to designate arbitrators of their own nationality or of their personal choice, such refusal may be considered as very exceptional. If it should occur, the remedy offered will almost always be inadequate; such a refusal will imply a deliberate decision not to co-operate in the arbitration–hostility to its continuation. Moreover, one cannot disguise the embarrassing position of the President of the Court who may be called upon to make an appointment in such circumstances, nor especially the consequent dangers of non-execution of the arbitral decision.[6] This observation applies *a fortiori* to the case of withdrawal of an arbitrator, also envisaged in the Commission's draft (Article 7).

Needless to say, the proposals of the International Law Commission, considering them as purely permissive, may be retained wholly or partly by governments in concluding their particular arbitral agreements.[7] They are of too novel a character to be retained with a view to establishing them in a new common law of arbitral procedure intended to provide a remedy for refusal of one of the parties to perform its obligations. The arbitrability of the dispute, the establishment of the tribunal by the designation of its members at the choice of the parties, are questions too closely connected with the very principle of the obligation to arbitrate, to be left, through general provisions, to the decision of a third authority. An institution which derives its whole value from the voluntary agreement of states does not permit of confinement within such imperative formulas.

[6] It appears that the International Law Commission believed it saw an argument in support of its proposal in the refusal by the governments of Bulgaria, Hungary and Roumania to appoint their representatives to the Mixed Commissions established by the Treaties of Peace of 1947. (*Cf.* Advisory Opinion of the Court of July 18, 1950, [1950] I.C.J. Reports 221). One need only envisage the application to this case of the procedure suggested by the Commission to realize its largely illusory character. The bitter political tension in the general political relations of the states involved in the case was the basis for a complete refusal to co-operate. It would have made ineffective any clause delegating to a third authority the appointment of commission members.

[7] *Cf.* D. H. N. Johnson, "The Constitution of an Arbitral Tribunal," 30 British Year Book of International Law 152 *et seq.* (1953).

II

The excess of pessimism shown by certain authors on the subject of the rarity of recourse to international courts applies with even less justification to the appreciation of the value and legal force of decisions.

To a great extent there has been a recovery from the illusions which formerly prevailed as to the contribution of international tribunals to the protection of international security and peace. Even today, however, it is not unusual, in view of the political gravity of disputes between states, to disregard the value, however slight, of cases which are taken before an international court. We must be resigned to this. At a time when governments have a tendency to surround quite clearly legal disputes with opposing political tensions, disputes of an actual political significance are not easily set forth in terms of law. There is no doubt, however, that a part of the present disappointment with regard to international justice is due to the survival of a state of mind which has exaggerated the possibilities of recourse to courts for the maintenance of peace.

Yet if one puts aside these slightly messianic views in order to contemplate in its concrete realities the importance of the respective values of the arbitrations of the last century and those of recent arbitral or judicial decisions, it is evident that the comparison is not to the detriment of the latter. In fact the pacifist movement had certainly exaggerated the importance in international relations of the arbitral decisions of the second half of the 19th century. The reality is that today, as formerly, the international tribunal is generally only given jurisdiction of minor conflicts where the interests involved are limited. This does not prevent diplomatic action, impelled by the desire for even occasional agreement, to broaden at times the customary framework in order to submit to the Court serious disputes, even those which would put the national honor in issue. It is been properly noted that in such cases the agreement to arbitrate has greater value to peace than the decision itself. One need only recall the highly political significance of the *Corfu Channel Case* before the International Court of Justice.

Up to what point does the actual state of relations among states permit international adjudication to contribute to the development of international law? It should be observed first of all that the contribution of the judge is itself a function of the state of the law. In this regard one cannot deny the weakening influence upon international decisions, as well as upon recourse to international tribunals, exerted by the present poverty of the two essential sources of law juridically applicable, *i.e.*, treaty and custom.

The Second World War was terminated without a general peace settlement. Treaties of peace, whatever their defects may have been, have played a stabilizing rôle in the past. After ten years, the chaotic effects of their absence can be surveyed. Its consequences have been to remove a growing body of interests and relations from the rational criteria commonly accepted and to carry them far from jurisdictional paths into the political sphere of discretionary decisions. The sometimes excessive development of contractual regulation in areas of minor interests is not a cure for this state of affairs which, by being prolonged, daily tends more and more to put the impress of politics on international relations.

What is true in the realm of treaties is also true for partly the same reasons in the order of customary law. As flexible as it is, the growth of custom demands a minimum of stability. It cannot develop when state activities, because of their equivocal character and contradictory manifestations, cease to become crystallized in "a general practice accepted as law" (Article 38 of the Statute of the International Court of Justice). The margin allowed for abstention, tolerance, the slow consolidation by the action of time, recedes when the abrupt development of new needs impels governments to take unilateral positions which are often reckless and inspired by an individualistic conception of sovereign rights. It cannot be denied that the traditional development of custom is ill suited to the present pace of international relations.

We should be careful not to confuse this small productivity of custom with the tendency to particularize or individualize in the application of customary rules, which is already noticeable in certain recent judicial decisions. Certain authors have indicated uneasiness on this subject, and have expressed criticism of the jurisprudence of the International Court of Justice which appear hardly justified to us.

Some have reproved the Court for having followed too narrow a conception of custom so as to limit its field of application, and particularly for having avoided the exposition of firm and general criteria permitting the conclusion with certainty and, in some respects, *a priori*, of the existence of a customary rule.[8] Still less than any other custom, international custom does not lend itself to the establishment of such criteria. The selection of the factual elements which, viewed as a whole, lead in a given case to the admission of the existence of a customary rule is subject to extremely variable considerations; it hardly permits efforts toward systematization.

Other authors have devoted themselves with more justification to examining the logical process of the individualization of customary rules such as appears in certain decisions of the International Court of Justice, and more particularly in the *Fisheries Case* (United Kingdom–Norway, Judgment of December 18, 1951).[9] We do not believe that any contribution is made to the clarification of the question by reasoning in abstract terms on the general relations between rules and exceptions. There is too much risk of being confined to a "*petitio principii.*" What is really important in order to comprehend the exact significance of what the Court in the *Fisheries Case* envisaged, not as an exception but as an "application of general international law to a specific case,"[10] is to remember the function of custom and its necessarily evolutionary character. The customary rule is a source of living law only insofar as, by adhering to the flexibility of its own process, it is capable to providing courts "with an adequate basis for their decisions, which can be adapted to the diverse facts in question."[11] Far from denoting a disintegration of the law, these adaptations, as long as they are inspired by the realities of international practice and become operative under the control of the judge, are proofs of the progress of the law. By being individualized in its applications, the rule of law becomes more refined; it is enriched by new additions which permit it to be adapted to situations which are not yet envisaged and to meet the necessities resulting therefrom.

[8] Max Hagemann, "Die Gewohnheit als Völkerrechtsquelle in der Rechtssprechung des internationalen Gerichtshofes," in Annuaire Suisse de Droit International, 1953, p. 61 *et seq.*

[9] See particularly the interesting observations of Sir Gerald Fitzmaurice, "The Law and Procedure of the International Court of Justice, 1951–1954: General Principles and Sources of Law," 30 British Year Book of International Law 1–70 (1953).

[10] [1951] I.C.J. Rep. 131; 46 A.J.I.L. 359 (1952).

[11] Judgment of the International Court of Justice, *loc. cit.*, p. 133. The consent theory, which purports to base custom on tacit agreement between states, leads to a different and necessarily more static concept of the role of custom. Traces of it may be seen in the criticisms of the Judgment of Dec. 18, 1951.

It is also from the point of view of a certain individualization or particularization that the Court rendered its Advisory Opinion of May 28, 1951, concerning Reservations to the Genocide Convention.[12] It carefully pointed out the particular characteristics of such a convention. Its origins, its characteristics, and the requirements necessary to its collective purpose, all combined to make it appear profoundly distinct from conventions of a reciprocal character in which the fundamental question of the exact equilibrium of rights and obligations leads to the non-recognition of a reservation as valid unless it is accepted by all the contracting parties without exception. Moreover, without admitting that this concept of the absolute integrity of the convention had ever acquired general authority, the Court recognized the necessity for a greater flexibility in the appraisal of the legal effects of reservations insofar as these are compatible with the purposes of the collective convention.

In conclusion, and all things considered, the present slowing down of judicial activities must be attributed much less to a deterioration in their spirit or to the imperfections of their methods than to external factors of a strictly political nature which paralyze the role of all international law in international relations. Extreme political tensions today weigh heavily upon the attitude of governments, which are already naturally little inclined to divest themselves of the settlement of their disputes in favor of international tribunals. They fear both the effect of the process and the repercussions, however distant, of the judgment. It is better to recognize this reality clearly than to wander afield in the search for procedural reforms which remedy nothing. Order in peace remains the fundamental need of the Society of Nations. Without a minimum of order, justice is powerless. We conclude with these words of a jurist who was a tireless defender of international adjudication:

> It is thought that justice will bring peace because it is believed that justice can do away with war. It is rather the contrary which is true. The reign of justice presumes peace. In an atmosphere saturated with passions, rivalries and hostile attitudes, the judge is powerless, because his weapon, the law, loses all value before force.[13]

12 [1951] I.C.J. Rep. 15; 45 A.J.I.L. 579 (1951).
13 N. Politis, La Justice Internationale, pp. 253–254.

DISARMAMENT AND ARMS CONTROL

XV

This chapter deals with disarmament in the broadest sense, including the reduction and control of armaments. In his famous encyclical *Pacem in Terris*, Pope John XXIII made a stirring plea for disarmament. This part of the encyclical is reprinted as the first selection in this chapter.

Disarmament agreements have been very hard to achieve, and hopes for a halt to the arms race have remained largely unfulfilled in the postwar world. One exception is the Antarctic Treaty signed on December 1, 1959. This treaty, signed by twelve states including the United States and the Soviet Union, provides for complete demilitarization coupled with effective inspection, but it is, of course, limited to the

Antarctic only. The relevant articles are included in the second selection.

A more significant development was the Nuclear Test Ban Treaty signed in Moscow on August 5, 1963. The text of the treaty is the third selection.

Approximately two months before the Test Ban Treaty was signed, President John F. Kennedy discussed the rationale behind his efforts for peace including steps toward disarmament. He delivered his widely hailed speech "Toward a Strategy of Peace" at commencement exercises of The American University in Washington, D.C., on June 10, 1963.

A vital issue in disarmament negotiations is inspection. If we reduce our military strength, how can we be sure our treaty partners will live up to their part of the bargain? Seymour Melman discusses the question of inspection in the fifth selection. Melman, Professor of Industrial Management and Engineering at Columbia University, is the author of *Inspection for Disarmament.*

Finally, Jerome D. Frank discusses the disarmament question from a psychological point of view. Frank is Professor of Psychiatry at the Johns Hopkins University School of Medicine.

46. *DISARMAMENT* / POPE JOHN XXIII*

. . . it is with deep sorrow that we note the enormous stocks of armaments that have been and still are being made in more economically developed countries, with a vast outlay of intellectual and economic resources. And so it happens that, while the people of these countries are loaded with heavy burdens, other countries as a result are deprived of the collaboration they need in order to make economic and social progress.

The production of arms is allegedly justified on the grounds that in present-day conditions peace cannot be preserved without an equal balance of armaments. And so, if one country increases its

* Pope John XXIII, *Pacem in Terris,* text as published in *The New York Times* (June 11, 1963), p. 18. © 1963 by The New York Times Company. Reprinted by permission.

armaments, others feel the need to do the same; and if one country is equipped with nuclear weapons, other countries must produce their own, equally destructive.

Consequently, people live in constant fear lest the storm that every moment threatens should break upon them with dreadful violence. And with good reason, for the arms of war are ready at hand. Even though it is difficult to believe that anyone would deliberately take the responsibility for the appalling destruction and sorrow that war would bring in its train, it cannot be denied that the conflagration may be set off by some uncontrollable and unexpected chance. And one must bear in mind that, even though the monstrous power of modern weapons acts as a deterrent, it is to be feared that the mere continuance of nuclear tests, undertaken with war in mind, will have fatal consequences for life on the earth.

Justice, then, right reason and humanity urgently demand that the arms race should cease. That the stockpiles which exist in various countries should be reduced equally and simultaneously by the parties concerned. That nuclear weapons should be banned. And that a general agreement should eventually be reached about progressive disarmament and an effective method of control. In the words of Pius XII, our predecessor of happy memory: "The calamity of a world war, with the economic and social ruin and the moral excesses and dissolution that accompany it, must not be permitted to envelop the human race for a third time."

All must realize that there is no hope of putting an end to the building up of armaments, nor of reducing the present stocks, nor, still less, of abolishing them altogether, unless the process is complete and thorough and unless it proceeds from inner convictions: unless, that is, everyone sincerely cooperates to banish the fear and anxious expectation of war with which men are oppressed. If this is to come about, the fundamental principle on which our present peace depends must be replaced by another, which declares that the true and solid peace of nations consists not in equality of arms, but in mutual trust alone. We believe that this can be brought to pass, and we consider that it is something which reason requires, that it is eminently desirable in itself and that it will prove to be the source of many benefits.

In the first place, it is an objective demanded by reason. There can be, or at least there should be, no doubt that relations between states, as between individuals, should be regulated not by the force of arms, but by the light of reason, by the rule, that is, of truth, of justice and of active and sincere cooperation.

Secondly, we say that it is an objective earnestly to be desired in itself. Is there anyone who does not ardently yearn to see war banished, to see peace preserved and daily more firmly established?

And finally, it is an objective which will be a fruitful source of many benefits, for its advantages will be felt everywhere, by individuals, by families, by nations, by the whole human family. The warning of Pius XII still rings in our ears: "Nothing is lost by peace. Everything may be lost by war."

Since this is so, we, the vicar on earth of Jesus Christ, Saviour of the world and author of peace, and as interpreter of the very profound longing of the entire human family, following the impulse of our heart, seized by anxiety for the good of all we feel it our duty to beseech men, especially those who have the responsibility of public affairs, to spare no labor in order to insure that the world events follow a reasonable and human course.

In the highest and most authoritative assemblies, let men give serious thought to the problem of a peaceful adjustment of relations between political communities on a world level: an adjustment founded on mutual trust, on sincerity in negotiations, on faithful fulfillment of obligations assumed. Let them study the problem until they find that point of agreement from which it will be possible to commence to go forward towards accords that will be sincere, lasting and fruitful.

We, for our part, will not cease to pray God to bless these labors so that they may lead to fruitful results.

47. *ANTARCTIC TREATY* *

The Governments of Argentina, Australia, Belgium, Chile, the French Republic, Japan, New Zealand, Norway, the Union of South Africa, the Union of Soviet Socialist Republics, the United Kingdom of Great Britain and Northern Ireland, and the United States of America,

* *The Department of State Bulletin*, Vol. 41, No. 1069 (December 21, 1959), pp. 914–16.

Recognizing that it is in the interest of all mankind that Antarctica shall continue forever to be used exclusively for peaceful purposes and shall not become the scene or object of international discord;

Acknowledging the substantial contributions to scientific knowledge resulting from international cooperation in scientific investigation in Antarctica;

Convinced that the establishment of a firm foundation for the continuation and development of such cooperation on the basis of freedom of scientific investigation in Antarctica as applied during the International Geophysical Year accords with the interests of science and the progress of all mankind;

Convinced also that a treaty ensuring the use of Antarctica for peaceful purposes only and the continuance of international harmony in Antarctica will further the purposes and principles embodied in the Charter of the United Nations;

Have agreed as follows:

Article I

1. Antarctica shall be used for peaceful purposes only. There shall be prohibited, *inter alia*, any measures of a military nature, such as the establishment of military bases and fortifications, the carrying out of military maneuvers, as well as the testing of any type of weapons.

2. The present Treaty shall not prevent the use of military personnel or equipment for scientific research or for any other peaceful purpose.

Article V

1. Any nuclear explosions in Antarctica and the disposal there of radioactive waste material shall be prohibited.

2. In the event of the conclusion of international agreements concerning the use of nuclear energy, including nuclear explosions and the disposal of radioactive waste material, to which all of the Contracting Parties whose representatives are entitled to participate in the meetings provided for under Article IX are parties, the rules established under such agreements shall apply in Antarctica.

Article VI

The provisions of the present Treaty shall apply to the area south of 60° South Latitude, including all ice shelves, but nothing in the present Treaty shall prejudice or in any way affect the rights, or the exercise of the rights, of any State under international law with regard to the high seas within that area.

Article VII

1. In order to promote the objectives and ensure the observance of the provisions of the present Treaty, each Contracting Party whose representatives are entitled to participate in the meetings referred to in Article IX of the Treaty shall have the right to designate observers to carry out any inspection provided for by the present Article. Observers shall be nationals of the Contracting Parties which designate them. The names of observers shall be communicated to every other Contracting Party having the right to designate observers, and like notice shall be given of the termination of their appointment.

2. Each observer designated in accordance with the provisions of paragraph 1 of this Article shall have complete freedom of access at any time to any or all areas of Antarctica.

3. All areas of Antarctica, including all stations, installations and equipment within those areas, and all ships and aircraft at points of discharging or embarking cargoes or personnel in Antarctica, shall be open at all times to inspection by any observers designated in accordance with paragraph 1 of this Article.

4. Aerial observation may be carried out at any time over any or all areas of Antarctica by any of the Contracting Parties having the right to designate observers.

5. Each Contracting Party shall, at the time when the present Treaty enters into force for it, inform the other Contracting Parties, and thereafter shall give them notice in advance, of

(a) all expeditions to and within Antarctica, on the part of its ships or nationals, and all expeditions to Antarctica organized in or proceeding from its territory;

(b) all stations in Antarctica occupied by its nationals; and

(c) any military personnel or equipment intended to be introduced by it into Antarctica subject to the conditions prescribed in paragraph 2 of Article I of the present Treaty.

Article IX

1. Representatives of the Contracting Parties named in the preamble to the present Treaty shall meet at the City of Canberra within two months after the date of entry into force of the Treaty, and thereafter at suitable intervals and places, for the purpose of exchanging information, consulting together on matters of common interest pertaining to Antarctica, and formulating and considering, and recommending to their Governments, measures in furtherance of the principles and objectives of the Treaty, including measures regarding:

(a) use of Antarctica for peaceful purposes only;

(b) facilitation of scientific research in Antarctica;

(c) facilitation of international scientific cooperation in Antarctica;

(d) facilitation of the exercise of the rights of inspection provided for in Article VII of the Treaty;

(e) questions relating to the exercise of jurisdiction in Antarctica;

(f) preservation and conservation of living resources in Antarctica.

2. Each Contracting Party which has become a party to the present Treaty by accession under Article XIII shall be entitled to appoint representatives to participate in the meetings referred to in paragraph 1 of the present Article, during such time as that Contracting Party demonstrates its interest in Antarctica by conducting substantial scientific research activity there, such as the establishment of a scientific station or the despatch of a scientific expedition.

3. Reports from the observers referred to in Article VII of the present Treaty shall be transmitted to the representatives of the Contracting Parties participating in the meetings referred to in paragraph 1 of the present Article.

48. *NUCLEAR TEST BAN TREATY**

The Governments of the United States of America, the United Kingdom of Great Britain and Northern Ireland, and the Union of Soviet Socialist Republics, hereinafter referred to as the "Original Parties,"

Proclaiming as their principal aim the speediest possible achievement of an agreement on general and complete disarmament under strict international control in accordance with the objectives of the United Nations which would put an end to the armaments race and eliminate the incentive to the production and testing of all kinds of weapons, including nuclear weapons,

Seeking to achieve the discontinuance of all test explosions of nuclear weapons for all time, determined to continue negotiations to this end, and desiring to put an end to the contamination of man's environment by radioactive substances,

Have agreed as follows:

Article I

1. Each of the Parties to this Treaty undertakes to prohibit, to prevent, and not to carry out any nuclear weapon test explosion, or any other nuclear explosion, at any place under its jurisdiction or control:

(a) in the atmosphere; beyond its limits, including outer space; or underwater, including territorial waters or high seas; or

(b) in any other environment if such explosion causes radioactive debris to be present outside the territorial limits of the State under whose jurisdiction or control such explosion is conducted. It is understood in this connection that the provisions of this subparagraph are without prejudice to the conclusion of a treaty resulting in the permanent banning of all nuclear test explosions, including all such explosions underground, the conclusion of which, as the Parties have stated in the Preamble to this Treaty, they seek to achieve.

* *The Department of State Bulletin,* Vol. 49, No. 1259 (August 12, 1963), pp. 239–40.

2. Each of the Parties to this Treaty undertakes furthermore to refrain from causing, encouraging, or in any way participating in, the carrying out of any nuclear weapon test explosion, or any other nuclear explosion, anywhere which would take place in any of the environments described, or have the effect referred to, in paragraph 1 of this Article.

Article II

1. Any Party may propose amendments to this Treaty. The text of any proposed amendment shall be submitted to the Depositary Governments which shall circulate it to all Parties to this Treaty. Thereafter, if requested to do so by one-third or more of the Parties, the Depositary Governments shall convene a conference, to which they shall invite all the Parties, to consider such amendment.

2. Any amendment to this Treaty must be approved by a majority of the votes of all the Parties to this Treaty, including the votes of all of the Original Parties. The amendment shall enter into force for all Parties upon the deposit of instruments of ratification by a majority of all the Parties, including the instruments of ratification of all of the Original Parties.

Article III

1. This Treaty shall be open to all States for signature. Any State which does not sign this Treaty before its entry into force in accordance with paragraph 3 of this Article may accede to it at any time.

2. This Treaty shall be subject to ratification by signatory States. Instruments of ratification and instruments of accession shall be deposited with the Governments of the Original Parties—the United States of America, the United Kingdom of Great Britain and Northern Ireland, and the Union of Soviet Socialist Republics—which are hereby designated the Depositary Governments.

3. This Treaty shall enter into force after its ratification by all the Original Parties and the deposit of their instruments of ratification.

4. For States whose instruments of ratification or accession are deposited subsequent to the entry into force of this Treaty, it shall

enter into force on the date of the deposit of their instruments of ratification or accession.

5. The Depositary Governments shall promptly inform all signatory and acceding States of the date of each signature, the date of deposit of each instrument of ratification of and accession to this Treaty, the date of its entry into force, and the date of receipt of any requests for conferences or other notices.

6. This Treaty shall be registered by the Depositary Governments pursuant to Article 102 of the Charter of the United Nations.

Article IV

This Treaty shall be of unlimited duration.

Each Party shall in exercising its national sovereignty have the right to withdraw from the Treaty if it decides that extraordinary events, related to the subject matter of this Treaty, have jeopardized the supreme interests of its country. It shall give notice of such withdrawal to all other Parties to the Treaty three months in advance.

Article V

This treaty, of which the English and Russian texts are equally authentic, shall be deposited in the archives of the Depositary Governments. Duly certified copies of this Treaty shall be transmitted by the Depositary Governments to the Governments of the signatory and acceding States.

49. *TOWARD A STRATEGY OF PEACE*/ JOHN F. KENNEDY*

"There are few earthly things more beautiful than a University," wrote John Masefield, in his tribute to the English universities—and his words are equally true here. He did not refer to spires and

* John F. Kennedy, "Toward a Strategy of Peace," *The Department of State Bulletin,* Vol. 49, No. 1253 (July 1, 1963), pp. 2–6.

towers, to campus greens and ivied walls. He admired the splendid beauty of the university, he said, because it was "a place where those who hate ignorance may strive to know, where those who perceive truth may strive to make others see."

I have, therefore, chosen this time and this place to discuss a topic on which ignorance too often abounds and the truth is too rarely perceived—yet it is the most important topic on earth: world peace.

What kind of peace do I mean? What kind of peace do we seek? Not a *Pax Americana* enforced on the world by American weapons of war. Not the peace of the grave or the security of the slave. I am talking about genuine peace, the kind of peace that makes life on earth worth living, the kind that enables men and nations to grow and to hope and to build a better life for their children—not merely peace for Americans but peace for all men and women, not merely peace in our time but peace for all time.

I speak of peace because of the new face of war. Total war makes no sense in an age when great powers can maintain large and relatively invulnerable nuclear forces and refuse to surrender without resort to those forces. It makes no sense in an age when a single nuclear weapon contains almost 10 times the explosive force delivered by all of the Allied air forces in the Second World War. It makes no sense in an age when the deadly poisons produced by a nuclear exchange would be carried by the wind and water and soil and seed to the far corners of the globe and to generations yet unborn.

Today the expenditure of billions of dollars every year on weapons acquired for the purpose of making sure we never need to use them is essential to keeping the peace. But surely the acquisition of such idle stockpiles—which can only destroy and never create—is not the only, much less the most efficient, means of assuring peace.

I speak of peace, therefore, as the necessary rational end of rational men. I realize that the pursuit of peace is not as dramatic as the pursuit of war, and frequently the words of the pursuer fall on deaf ears. But we have no more urgent task.

Some say that it is useless to speak of world peace or world law or world disarmament—and that it will be useless until the leaders of the Soviet Union adopt a more enlightened attitude. I hope they do. I believe we can help them do it. But I also believe that we must reexamine our own attitude, as individuals and as a nation, for our attitude is as essential as theirs. And every graduate of this school, every thoughtful citizen who despairs of war and wishes to bring peace, should begin by looking inward—by examining his own attitude toward the possibilities of peace, toward the Soviet Union, toward the course of the cold war, and toward freedom and peace here at home.

The Possibilities of Peace

First: Let us examine our attitude toward peace itself. Too many of us think it is impossible. Too many think it unreal. But that is a dangerous, defeatist belief. It leads to the conclusion that war is inevitable, that mankind is doomed, that we are gripped by forces we cannot control.

We need not accept that view. Our problems are manmade; therefore they can be solved by man. And man can be as big as he wants. No problem of human destiny is beyond human beings. Man's reason and spirit have often solved the seemingly unsolvable, and we believe they can do it again.

I am not referring to the absolute, infinite concept of universal peace and good will of which some fantasies and fanatics dream. I do not deny the values of hopes and dreams, but we merely invite discouragement and incredulity by making that our only and immediate goal.

Let us focus instead on a more practical, more attainable peace, based not on a sudden revolution in human nature but on a gradual evolution in human institutions—on a series of concrete actions and effective agreements which are in the interest of all concerned. There is no single, simple key to this peace, no grand or magic formula to be adopted by one or two powers. Genuine peace must be the product of many nations, the sum of many acts. It must be dynamic, not static, changing to meet the challenge of each new generation. For peace is a process, a way of solving problems.

With such a peace there will still be quarrels and conflicting interests, as there are within families and nations. World peace, like community peace, does not require that each man love his neighbor; it requires only that they live together in mutual tolerance, submitting their disputes to a just and peaceful settlement. And history teaches us that enmities between nations, as between individuals, do not last forever. However fixed our likes and dislikes may seem, the tide of time and events will often bring surprising changes in the relations between nations and neighbors.

So let us persevere. Peace need not be impracticable, and war need not be inevitable. By defining our goal more clearly, by making it seem more manageable and less remote, we can help all peoples to see it, to draw hope from it, and to move irresistibly toward it.

Common Interests of U.S. and Soviet Union

Second: Let us reexamine our attitude toward the Soviet Union. It is discouraging to think that their leaders may actually believe what their propagandists write. It is discouraging to read a recent authoritative Soviet text on military strategy and find, on page after page, wholly baseless and incredible claims—such as the allegation that "American imperialist circles are preparing to unleash different types of wars . . . that there is a very real threat of a preventive war being unleashed by American imperialists against the Soviet Union . . . [and that] the political aims of the American imperialists are to enslave economically and politically the European and other capitalist countries . . . [and] to achieve world domination . . . by means of aggressive wars."

Truly, as it was written long ago: "The wicked flee when no man pursueth." Yet it is sad to read these Soviet statements—to realize the extent of the gulf between us. But it is also a warning—a warning to the American people not to fall into the same trap as the Soviets, not to see only a distorted and desperate view of the other side, not to see conflict as inevitable, accommodation as impossible, and communication as nothing more than an exchange of threats.

No government or social system is so evil that its people must be considered as lacking in virtue. As Americans we find communism profoundly repugnant as a negation of personal freedom and dignity. But we can still hail the Russian people for their many achievements—in science and space, in economic and industrial growth, in culture and in acts of courage.

Among the many traits the peoples of our two countries have in common, none is stronger than our mutual abhorrence of war. Almost unique among the major world powers, we have never been at war with each other. And no nation in the history of battle ever suffered more than the Soviet Union suffered in the course of the

Second World War. At least 20 million lost their lives. Countless millions of homes and farms were burned or sacked. A third of the nation's territory, including nearly two-thirds of its industrial base, was turned into a wasteland—a loss equivalent to the devastation of this country east of Chicago.

Today, should total war ever break out again—no matter how—our two countries would become the primary targets. It is an ironical but accurate fact that the two strongest powers are the two in the most danger of devastation. All we have built, all we have worked for, would be destroyed in the first 24 hours. And even in the cold war, which brings burdens and dangers to so many countries—including this nation's closest allies—our two countries bear the heaviest burdens. For we are both devoting massive sums of money to weapons that could be better devoted to combating ignorance, poverty, and disease. We are both caught up in a vicious and dangerous cycle in which suspicion on one side breeds suspicion on the other and new weapons beget counterweapons.

In short, both the United States and its allies, and the Soviet Union and its allies, have a mutually deep interest in a just and genuine peace and in halting the arms race. Agreements to this end are in the interests of the Soviet Union as well as ours, and even the most hostile nations can be relied upon to accept and keep those treaty obligations, and only those treaty obligations, which are in their own interest.

So let us not be blind to our differences, but let us also direct attention to our common interests and to the means by which those differences can be resolved. And if we cannot end now our differences, at least we can help make the world safe for diversity. For in the final analysis our most basic common link is that we all inhabit this planet. We all breathe the same air. We all cherish our children's future. And we are all mortal.

The Pursuit of Peace

Third: Let us reexamine our attitude toward the cold war, remembering that we are not engaged in a debate, seeking to pile up debating points. We are not here distributing blame or pointing the finger of judgment. We must deal with the world as it is and not as it might have been had the history of the last 18 years been different.

We must, therefore, persevere in the search for peace in the hope that constructive changes within the Communist bloc might bring within reach solutions which now seem beyond us. We must conduct our affairs in such a way that it becomes in the Communists' interest to agree on a genuine peace. Above all, while defending our own vital interests, nuclear powers must avert those confrontations which bring an adversary to a choice of either a humiliating retreat or a nuclear war. To adopt that kind of course in the nuclear age would be evidence only of the bankruptcy of our policy—or of a collective death wish for the world.

To secure these ends, America's weapons are nonprovocative, carefully controlled, designed to deter, and capable of selective use. Our military forces are committed to peace and disciplined in self-restraint. Our diplomats are instructed to avoid unnecessary irritants and purely rhetorical hostility.

For we can seek a relaxation of tensions without relaxing our guard. And, for our part, we do not need to use threats to prove that we are resolute. We do not need to jam foreign broadcasts out of fear our faith will be eroded. We are unwilling to impose our system on any unwilling people, but we are willing and able to engage in peaceful competition with any people on earth.

Meanwhile we seek to strengthen the United Nations, to help solve its financial problems, to make it a more effective instrument of peace, to develop it into a genuine world security system—a system capable of resolving disputes on the basis of law, of insuring the security of the large and the small, and of creating conditions under which arms can finally be abolished.

At the same time we seek to keep peace inside the non-Communist world, where many nations, all of them our friends, are divided over issues which weaken Western unity, which invite Communist intervention, or which threaten to erupt into war. Our efforts in West New Guinea, in the Congo, in the Middle East, and in the Indian subcontinent have been persistent and patient despite criticism from both sides. We have also tried to set an example for others—by seeking to adjust small but significant differences with our own closest neighbors in Mexico and in Canada.

Speaking of other nations, I wish to make one point clear. We are bound to many nations by alliances. Those alliances exist because our concern and theirs substantially overlap. Our commitment to defend Western Europe and West Berlin, for example, stands undiminished because of the identity of our vital interests. The

United States will make no deal with the Soviet Union at the expense of other nations and other peoples, not merely because they are our partners but also because their interests and ours converge.

Our interests converge, however, not only in defending the frontiers of freedom but in pursuing the paths of peace. It is our hope—and the purpose of Allied policies—to convince the Soviet Union that she, too, should let each nation choose its own future, so long as that choice does not interfere with the choices of others. The Communist drive to impose their political and economic system on others is the primary cause of world tension today. For there can be no doubt that, if all nations could refrain from interfering in the self-determination of others, the peace would be much more assured.

This will require a new effort to achieve world law, a new context for world discussions. It will require increased understanding between the Soviets and ourselves. And increased understanding will require increased contact and communication. One step in this direction is the proposed arrangement for a direct line between Moscow and Washington, to avoid on each side the dangerous delays, misunderstandings, and misreadings of the other's actions which might occur at a time of crisis.

We have also been talking in Geneva about other first-step measures of arms control, designed to limit the intensity of the arms race and to reduce the risks of accidental war. Our primary long-range interest in Geneva, however, is general and complete disarmament, designed to take place by stages, permitting parallel political developments to build the new institutions of peace which would take the place of arms. The pursuit of disarmament has been an effort of this Government since the 1920's. It has been urgently sought by the past three administrations. And however dim the prospects may be today, we intend to continue this effort—to continue it in order that all countries, including our own, can better grasp what the problems and possibilities of disarmament are.

The one major area of these negotiations where the end is in sight, yet where a fresh start is badly needed, is in a treaty to outlaw nuclear tests. The conclusion of such a treaty—so near and yet so far—would check the spiraling arms race in one of its most dangerous areas. It would place the nuclear powers in a position to deal more effectively with one of the greatest hazards which man faces in 1963, the further spread of nuclear arms. It would increase our security; it would decrease the prospects of war. Surely this goal is sufficiently important to require our steady pursuit, yielding neither to the temptation to give up the whole effort nor the temptation to give up our insistence on vital and responsible safeguards.

I am taking this opportunity, therefore, to announce two important decisions in this regard.

First: Chairman Khrushchev, Prime Minister Macmillan, and I have agreed that high-level discussions will shortly begin in Moscow looking toward early agreement on a comprehensive test ban treaty. Our hopes must be tempered with the caution of history, but with our hopes go the hopes of all mankind.

Second: To make clear our good faith and solemn convictions on the matter, I now declare that the United States does not propose to conduct nuclear tests in the atmosphere so long as other states do not do so. We will not be the first to resume. Such a declaration is no substitute for a formal binding treaty, but I hope it will help us achieve one. Nor would such a treaty be a substitute for disarmament, but I hope it will help us achieve it.

Peace and Human Rights

Finally, my fellow Americans, let us examine our attitude toward peace and freedom here at home. The quality and spirit of our own society must justify and support our efforts abroad. We must show it in the dedication of our own lives, as many of you who are graduating today will have a unique opportunity to do, by serving without pay in the Peace Corps abroad or in the proposed National Service Corps here at home.

But wherever we are, we must all, in our daily lives, live up to the age-old faith that peace and freedom walk together. In too many of our cities today the peace is not secure because freedom is incomplete.

It is the responsibility of the executive branch at all levels of government—local, State, and national—to provide and protect that freedom for all of our citizens by all means within their authority. It is the responsibility of the legislative branch at all levels, wherever that authority is not now adequate, to make it adequate. And it is the responsibility of all citizens in all sections of this country to respect the rights of all others and to respect the law of the land.

All this is not unrelated to world peace. "When a man's ways please the Lord," the Scriptures tell us, "he maketh even his enemies to be at peace with him." And is not peace, in the last analysis, basically a matter of human rights—the right to live out our lives without fear of devastation, the right to breathe air as nature provided it, the right of future generations to a healthy existence?

While we proceed to safeguard our national interests, let us also safeguard human interests. And the elimination of war and arms is clearly in the interest of both. No treaty, however much it may be to the advantage of all, however tightly it may be worded, can provide absolute security against the risks of deception and evasion. But it can, if it is sufficiently effective in its enforcement and if it is sufficiently in the interests of its signers, offer far more security and far fewer risks than an unabated, uncontrolled, unpredictable arms race.

The United States, as the world knows, will never start a war. We do not want a war. We do not now expect a war. This generation of Americans has already had enough—more than enough—of war and hate and oppression. We shall be prepared if others wish it. We shall be alert to try to stop it. But we shall also do our part to build a world of peace where the weak are safe and the strong are just. We are not helpless before that task or hopeless of its success. Confident and unafraid, we labor on—not toward a strategy of annihilation but toward a strategy of peace.

50. *THE POLITICAL IMPLICATIONS OF INSPECTION FOR DISARMAMENT* / SEYMOUR MELMAN*

Highly significant political opportunities have been opened up by the possibility of carrying out scientifically reliable inspection for disarmament. The possibility has been revealed by the scientific findings of recent investigations under the Institute of War and Peace studies at Columbia University. The results of the investigation indicate how international disarmament agreements can be implemented even in the presence of the international distrust which has been growing throughout the years of the hot and cold war. The results of the investigation have been set forth in the book

* Seymour Melman, "The Political Implications of Inspection for Disarmament," *Journal of International Affairs,* Vol. 13, No. 1 (1959), pp. 34–46. Reprinted by permission.

Inspection for Disarmament (New York: Columbia University Press, 1958). The purpose of this article is to review the scientific methods as well as the political opportunities for international disarmament inspection agreements.

I. Reliable Inspection Is Technically Feasible

The critical method of the investigation of inspection for disarmament was the effort to define crucial control points by which production of critical weapons could be reliably controlled. In this study, an effort was made to cope with the most difficult kind of disarmament problem, extensive types of agreement which would require reliable control over production of the most intricate matériél—long range intercontinental missiles.

Throughout the investigation an effort was made to utilize a multiple approach to each particular inspection problem. By this means the relative weaknesses of any particular approach could be compensated for by the possibilities of alternative methods. Thus, control over the production of certain instruments could be carried out by monitoring raw materials, production equipment, and the location of key technical personnel.

Owing to the extensive development of weapons technologies during recent decades there exist many opportunities for various kinds of disarmament agreements. Thus, our findings are pertinent to agreements on nuclear bomb-testing, control over high-altitude missiles testing, aerial inspection, production of fissionable materials, production of biological warfare elements, and production of long-range missiles and their various components.

When each of these elements was examined separately it was found that with reasonable outlays in manpower and equipment highly reliable systems of control could be set up to give mutual guarantees to the signatories to disarmament agreements. Our findings on the subject of nuclear bomb-testing, for example, were substantially confirmed by the recently concluded international meeting of technical representatives from the United States and the Soviet Union in Geneva.

The technically workable steps in disarmament agreements could be implemented at relatively modest cost in manpower material. The following table from *Inspection for Disarmament* gives a series of estimates of the direct field force that would be required in the continental United States for implementing the indicated types of disarmament inspection.

ESTIMATES OF THE NUMBER OF PEOPLE NEEDED FOR POSSIBLE ASPECTS OF INSPECTION FOR DISARMAMENT WITHIN THE UNITED STATES[1]

Type of Inspection	*Field Staff*
Aerial Inspection (Assuming 3 million square mile area. Including air crew, maintenance, and photo-interpreters).	550–750
Stations for Monitoring Nuclear Bomb Testing (15 stations: field and analytical staff)	225
Stations for Monitoring High-Altitude Missile Tests (15 stations–field and analytical staff)	180
Nuclear Reactors (300, including experimental and planned)	600–1,500
Fissionable Materials-Producing Plants (6 plants)	300–2,400
Uranium (and Vanadium) Mines and mills (637 in 1954)	1,200
Aircraft Assembly Plants (72 in 1954)	700–1,400
Aircraft Engines and Parts Plants (234 in 1954)	2,400–5,000
Aircraft Flight Instruments Plants (129 in 1954)	1,300–2,600
Radio and Radar Plants (225 in 1954)	2,250–4,500
Ordinance and Accessories Plants (493 in 1954)	5,000–10,000
Explosives Plants (74 in 1954)	750–1,500

Sampling inspection could be made in the following areas: i) biological laboratories; ii) metal-working plants; iii) U.S. government accounting; iv) scientific manpower.

Clearly, extensive disarmament inspection in the vast industrial complex of the United States could be carried out with the total requirement of about 40,000 men. The types of agreements which could be used for initiating the development of international disarmament could be carried out, as indicated, with a rather modest outlay in manpower.

[1] These estimates were constructed on the following bases: for aerial inspection and bomb and missile testing, the authors estimated the field staffs required for 24-hour functioning; checks on reactors could be maintained by as few as 2 to 5 men per reactor, depending on the need for 24-hour monitoring; in the fissionable materials plants, the range is due to readiness to rely on instrument monitoring vs. major reliance on human controllers; mines and mills could be covered by an average of about 2 men to each mill or mine; the various critical factories for missiles, aircraft, and explosives could be monitored by an average of 10 to 20 men per plant. Such estimates give an order of magnitude. They would be revised in accordance with detailed operating requirements of an international inspectorate.

II. Evasion of Inspection

Another major aspect of the study of the inspection for disarmament was the diagnosis of necessary conditions for successful clandestine evasion of disarmament agreements. Through studies of such efforts in Weimar Germany and in Palestine under the British Mandate, it was possible to infer a theory of successful evasion, which indicates the requirements for frustrating such evasion. Successful evasion, it was found, could be carried out if three conditions were satisfied:

A. A group of men exists which is prepared to carry out the clandestine production even at the cost of considerable personal sacrifice and risk. These men have strong allegiance to a guiding ideal.

B. The central working group is backed by a substantial part of a population, including a government or quasi-government, which backs up the operating groups and shields them from the inspecting authorities.

C. The operators of the clandestine production system learn how to simulate appearances that will seem to be ordinary and innocent in the eyes of the inspectors.

Where any one of these critical conditions is lacking or can be frustrated by an inspection system, the opportunity for successful evasion of inspection for disarmament is substantially curtailed.

The combined analysis of technique for evasion and for inspection yielded the judgment that the reliability of disarmament agreements is likely to improve with each particular success. The reason for this effect is indicated by the following reasoning from the general report on inspection for disarmament:

> Successful inspection, like successful evasion, requires more than technical feasibility. In the judgment of this writer, the final line of defense against evasion will be a condition of society in which such acts are widely regarded as unnatural and unthinkable. Even if some deadly weapons systems could be operated by as few as six men, those men could not make a military campaign; that would need the collaboration of at least a segment of a population. In this respect, the presence or absence of an "evasion mentality" could play an important part.
>
> Toward the end-in-view of diminishing or discouraging an evasion mentality, the early implementation of even partial steps

> for disarmament and international inspection is of the greatest importance. For every measure that relieves international tension and limits the fever of an arms race also limits the conditions that produce an evasion mentality. Stated differently: the introduction of particular disarmament measures in regard to highly destructive weapons, with reliable inspection, is bound to have a feed-back effect in reducing the pressures that lead to clandestine armament preparations. Thereby, conditions of mutual international assurance of compliance with disarmament agreements are improved.

The new knowledge at hand on the technical feasibility of inspection for disarmament clearly opens up political possibilities. This knowledge becomes important for political analysis, and for negotiation, in order to exploit to the fullest the political possibilities which inhere in international disarmament agreements. These opportunities involve a major alternative to the strategy of military deterrence which has dominated the international political scene.

III. The Failure of Military Deterrence

In the judgment of this writer, the strategy of military deterrence, a cornerstone of American foreign policy, now has major defects: the dangers of accidental triggering of nuclear wars are increasing; the addition of new countries to the nuclear weapons group vastly complicates the task of identifying an aggressor; possession of a clear lead in the arms race has become an improbable event; limited wars between the major powers have become less probable, leaving unlimited nuclear war the most likely event in a military contest.

A. WEAPONS OUT OF CONTROL

The very existence of weapons of mass destruction in large quantity opens up possibilities for these intricate military technologies going out of control. In the preface to *Inspection for Disarmament*, I indicated that:

> Undoubtedly, the designers of nuclear weapons have attempted to build into them certain mechanical safeguards against accidental firing—such as the requirement for a deliberate adjustment before such weapons become operative. There are no final safeguards, however, against the probability of human failure. As nuclear weapons are produced by the tens of thousands, and must be used by even more than that many men, the possibilities of world disaster through human failure cannot be ignored. One aberrant,

psychotic person, or person gone momentarily out of control, could explode nuclear weapons at a random place, or over any populated area. A space satellite could be mistaken for a ballistic missile.

Since military tactics and technologies have become geared to the idea of rapid retaliation, such accidents would require only one misjudgment in response to set the swift moves and countermoves of catastrophic nuclear war in motion. As nuclear weapons are increasingly available and dispersed in more hands, the probabilities of such an accident must necessarily increase. In the judgment of this writer, such possibilities weaken the assumptions of rationally calculated moves among military powers, which underlie the strategies of peace through mutual armed deterrence.

B. NEW COUNTRIES WITH NUCLEAR WEAPONS

One of the major assumptions of the mutual deterrence strategy will be drastically altered when many countries possess nuclear weapons. If a warhead should be set off in some city, it might be impossible to identify the aggressor, because of the number of countries possessing bombs, and the variety of possible ways for delivering nuclear explosives. Unless the aggressor were known, it would be clearly impossible even to threaten retaliation. Thereby, the strategy of a "balance of terror" fails as a way for deterring nuclear attacks.

Not many months ago, there was an accidental detonation in a Nike battery of anti-aircraft missiles in New Jersey. Since missiles of this sort may be equipped with nuclear warheads it is reasonable to speculate on the possibility of accidental detonations of such a battery of missiles.

The information reaching a military headquarters would be that a series of nuclear explosions have occurred in the New Jersey–New York area. There could be no indication as to the precise source of such explosions owing to the fact that nuclear warheads may be delivered to many points on the earth's surface by a great variety of means. These methods for delivery range from suitcase bombs to warheads encased in long-range missiles. At this writing, if the possibility of an accident were ruled out, military commanders might infer that the only possible source of such nuclear blasts was the government of the U.S.S.R. Accordingly, retaliation might be ordered.

In the foreseeable future, however, many nations will possess nuclear warheads. Then it becomes virtually impossible for any military group even to discover the source of control over such a nuclear blast. When the identity of a possible aggressor cannot be established, it clearly becomes impossible to carry out acts of retaliation, which are a necessary part of a strategy of military deterrence.

IV. A Decisive Lead in the Arms Race Has Become Improbable

The development of many alternative military technologies, in parallel, virtually excludes the possibility of any major power assuming a clear lead over the other in military technology. Where weapons systems must draw upon all the natural sciences and their range of engineering applications, it is reasonable to assume that there must be variation in the rate of development in these arts if only as a function of accidental factors of personality among the thousands of men engaged in such work in various countries. Moreover, both the United States and the U.S.S.R. are large countries, each able to devote thousands of able technical men to military tasks. It is unlikely that either country can develop a clear lead in technical intelligence. Nuclear warheads, for example, may be delivered by many alternative ways. It is virtually excluded for any one country to hold a clear lead with respect to all of these alternative possible ways. This is a critical affair because even one technique for delivering nuclear warheads could be sufficient to cause very great destruction. So long as one of the contenders in the arms race can utilize one of the available methods, the possibility of either side obtaining a clear military lead is virtually excluded. As a result, no military staff is now able to advise the government of a major power as to the sufficient steps for obtaining a military victory, either offensively or defensively.

At the very same time that military technologies have so developed as to yield a military impasse, with mounting dangers of accidental triggering of nuclear wars, these military developments have not served to deter the extension of the Soviet system. The government of the Soviet Union has proceeded to use political and economic methods for extending the scope of its rule throughout the world at the very same time that the arms race has developed into a military impasse. Accordingly, the military strategy of deterrence has failed in its avowed objective.

V. Limited Wars Among the Two Major Powers Are Unlikely

Finally, it is essential to underscore that limited wars are an unlikely event among the major powers. In the U.S.S.R. there is a tradition that militates strongly against military surrender. After World War II, Russian soldiers who had surrendered to the German army were severely punished for that act. In the United States, the recent discussion in the Senate on researches concerning possible strategies of surrender had the result of giving a fairly clear political directive to military commanders: surrender is not to be regarded as a reasonable, admissible act by senior military commanders of the United States.

Under these conditions, with surrender being excluded for senior Russian or American military commanders, any war in which these two military staffs are pitted against each other must soon change from a limited war by conventional weapons or tactical nuclear weapons, into an all-out nuclear war. As either side faces the danger of possible defeat, it must bring up the more powerful weapons needed to forestall such defeat, with its impermissible accompaniment of surrender. In that way, a conflict that began as an apparently limited military contest could develop into a world-wide holocaust.

Recent discussions of alternatives facing the United States have been formulated in terms of possibilities of surrender versus annihilation. In this writer's opinion, this formulation of alternatives is altogether realistic within the context of the general strategy of military deterrence. Indeed, there is only one way to escape such alternatives, and that is to adopt a different general political strategy which opens up new possibilities in international behavior.

VI. Political Opportunities in Inspection for Disarmament

International agreements that include systems of mutual inspection mean that distrust need no longer be an overwhelming obstacle to international agreements on particular disarmament elements. As a result there probably exists a new condition of political feasibility for disarmament agreements.

Agreements on particular disarmament matters necessarily do much more than cope with the particular matters involved. The implementation of each particular disarmament agreement produces a change in the situation within which the next step in disarmament must be taken. Just as each step of conflict and irritation during the cold war increased international distrust and tension, so would each success in international disarmament diminish distrust and tension.

It is, of course, possible to make the assumption that the Soviet Union or the United States, or both, represent substantially monolithic systems from the standpoint of international political agreements. When such an assumption is made, the effect is clearly to close off opportunities for almost any kind of agreement, for then one would give primary attention to the cold war history with its accompanying international deterioration. In the judgment of this writer, altogether different possibilities open up when one asks the question: What are the internal political effects within the Soviet Union and the United States from concluding particular disarmament agreements? What types of changes would be favored in each country by this situation and who would benefit from such changes? In the U.S.S.R., for example, the history of international tension has been a major device for justifying the maintenance and extension of dictatorial and brutal types of political control. The relaxation of international tension would favor those elements in Soviet society who themselves want a freer life.

This subject surely deserves the most extensive examination by political scholars, for the exploration of this area of results from inspection systems might very well open up hitherto unseen opportunities and effects from international agreements. Thus, it is entirely possible that scientists in the U.S.S.R., as a group, are disposed to favor international disarmament agreements, for such agreements would lay the basis for less political control over their occupations.

Disarmament and the promise of alternative use of vast human and industrial resources for peaceful purposes opens up the opportunity for a grand strategy that could very well have the most desirable effects throughout the world.

VII. Political Barriers to Disarmament Agreements

It is possible to pinpoint a number of factors which block international agreements on inspection for disarmament. These include:

an atmosphere of distrust and a tradition of evasive practices; occupational commitments to the arms race; the argument of relative military weakening as a result of disarmament; disarmament as a hazard to authoritarian practices; uninspectability of secret arms caches; and finally, the demand for foolproof inspection systems.

A. DISTRUST AND EVASIVENESS

Probably the most important single factor that militates against successful disarmament agreements is the development of fearful evasiveness as a common pattern of behavior in politics, and in other aspects of life as well. This factor is important in view of the considerable range of alternative technical possibilities in weapons systems that are open to military planners. In the presence of a widespread will to evade a disarmament agreement, coupled with the other necessary conditions for evasion which were cited above, the possibility is open for seizing upon one among many military technologies for designing and utilizing weapons of high destructiveness. Accordingly, the subject of evasiveness as a general feature of human behavior was given explicit attention in the study of inspection for disarmament.

Dr. Alberta B. Szalita wrote, in summing up her paper:

> The success of a disarmament agreement depends upon trust among peoples. Mistrust and evasiveness in individuals are the outcome of fear, loneliness, threats to security, lack of love, humiliation, helplessness, and the feeling of uselessness. When a society generates such effects as common conditions of life, then evasiveness and its concomitant ways become widespread and even acceptable features of behavior.
>
> Similarly, the need for, and hence receptivity to, "evasive" behavior and destructiveness can be mitigated. This occurs when conditions of living generate a widespread feeling of being needed and useful, and the allied senses of security, self-respect, and well-being.
>
> Under such changed conditions, evasiveness and destructiveness would become unnecessary.

A lessening of distrust and evasiveness would be a major derived effect from successful inspection for disarmament.

B. OCCUPATIONAL STAKES IN THE ARMS RACE

In every large country there is now a major labor force commitment to military design, production and application. This job stake in the arms race is another major source of pressure against the implementation of disarmament agreements. In the United States in 1956, it is estimated that about 15 per cent of the labor force was engaged in work on military orders. Such employment is concentrated in the capital goods industries.

The scientific and technical occupations are also especially effected by the emphasis on military related work. Various estimates indicate that the military budgets account for the financing of 30 to 50 per cent of all scientific and engineering research in the United States. These factors indicate the existence of a major human problem, for it means that many millions of men and women have developed occupational competence that is especially suited for weapons technologies. A major effort to shift away from the arms race necessarily entails a systematic effort to cope with the retraining of these people and the utilization of their capabilities for peaceful purposes. Moreover, it is only human to expect that these people will have developed a picture of their own worth in the community which is closely linked with the kind of work that they do. Accordingly, it is reasonable to expect that the people in these occupations, ranging from the worker on the plant floor to the highest paid executive, will seek to justify and continue the activities in which they have gained success in their livelihood. This suggests that the availability of practical plans for coping with a changeover to peacetime activities would itself play a part in curtailing the arms race.

C. RELATIVE MILITARY EFFECTS FROM DISARMAMENT AGREEMENTS

From a military standpoint it is often urged that no disarmament steps be taken which weaken one's own government in relation to international rivals. Such reasoning clearly assumes an ability to determine what military acts are in fact decisively advantageous—as among the major military powers.

I wish to argue that such calculations of relative military advantage are no longer possible. In detail: Nuclear warheads of major destructiveness can now be delivered by various ways, ranging from intricate missiles to the suit-case method, which bypasses many military defensive systems. As a result of such capabilities, no military staff is able to specify the sufficient actions to produce success either in offensive or defensive strategies. If this were not the case, if the necessary actions for military success could be specified, then it might be argued that a calculable military weakness would follow from the absence of some area of particular weapons capability. Such calculations cannot be made, however, owing to the alternative available methods by which nuclear warhead destruction can be applied. Accordingly, given the availability of nuclear arms systems, the argument of relative military disadvantage as a reason against particular disarmament steps becomes difficult to sustain. Similar reasoning is relevant to various non-nuclear weapons systems. Broadly, disarmament agreements which bear closely on one among many weapons technologies leaves a residue of military possibilities untouched.[2]

D. SECRET ARMS CACHES

International discussion of disarmament possibilities has frequently turned to the problem of secret arms caches. In a word, the fear is that the arms race has proceeded so far in many countries that secret stockpiles of arms could be (or already have been) put away before the inspection system for policing disarmament agreements goes into effect. Thereby, a weapons potential could be at hand despite the operation of even the most elaborate of inspection systems.

This possibility is altogether reasonable. It is realistic to assume that various military groups in each of the major powers would see to it that secret arms caches existed at the very time that disarmament agreements were being concluded and implemented. In the judgment of this writer, the critical question involved here is: Does the existence of secret arms caches, known to a relatively few persons in each of the major countries constitute a sufficient differential threat among the major powers to cause refusal to engage in disarmament agreements? Does a weapons stockpile necessarily equal military capability?

The early phases of disarmament agreements would clearly pertain to only certain sections of the available military technologies. Thus, agreements on nuclear warhead testing and high altitude missiles testing would leave in being the existing stockpiles and even production of missiles and weapons. As disarmament agreements encompassed more of the major military technologies and

[2] The interested reader will find illuminating confirmation of this thesis from an examination of a recent report of the National Planning Association entitled "1970 Without Arms Control" (National Planning Association, May, 1958).

were successfully extended from one sphere to another, one of the major accompanying effects would be the gradual growth of mutual trust and openness among the peoples of the earth. Under such conditions, the existence of secret caches of arms known to a few conspirators in each country could not constitute a major military threat to other countries of the world.

True, it is technically possible for a few men to deal a heavy physical blow through the use of highly destructive weapons. However, such an attempt becomes less probable as the political atmosphere in which such acts are regarded as natural and reasonable is altered, and the use of highly destructive weapons becomes increasingly an unthinkable, inhuman act. Furthermore, a heavy physical blow dealt by a few men does not constitute a military campaign. Such a campaign, aimed at taking over control of a major area of the earth requires the co-operation of millions of men. As the atmosphere of international fear and evasiveness is altered by the progressive extension of disarmament agreements, it necessarily becomes more difficult to secure such co-operation. Accordingly, a conspiratorial group, even heavily armed with nuclear weapons, thereby becomes effectively isolated as a military factor.

The weapons of secret arms stockpiles become a military factor only when there are large numbers of men who are willing and able to use them and have the backing of a major portion of society. The effect of progressive disarmament linked to appropriate inspection would be to diminish the conditions of social readiness which are necessary for rendering secret arms into operational weapons.

The gradual extension of international disarmament agreements will very likely involve, at some point, the establishment of an international military force. As such a force becomes important, relative to diminished national military establishments, the availability of secret arms caches in any one country necessarily becomes less of a military factor in terms of relative strength.

Finally, the meaning of a secret stockpile of arms needs to be examined in terms of a characteristic feature of modern weapons technology, namely the availability of many alternative ways for accomplishing highly destructive tasks. At the side of the destructive capability inherent in nuclear warheads, there are the possibilities of biological warfare utilizing micro-organisms or chemical agents. Biological warfare opens the possibility for highly destructive weapons being fashioned by relatively few men, with relatively primitive equipment.

In light of this analysis, I am compelled to the conclusion that the most important possible secret arms cache resides in the capability of human beings for making and using various types of destructive weapons. Owing to the many technologies which can be seized upon for destructive application, it is clearly the will of man to utilize his knowledge in this way, that is the critical weapons stockpile under modern conditions. In a word, the most dangerous military stockpile, the one most easily concealed, is the capability for making and using deadly weapons that can reside in the hands of determined men who are trained in modern technology and have the will to utilize this for destructive ends.

By this reasoning, the final line of defense against secret stockpiles must reside in the necessarily changed social atmosphere which would result from successful extension of disarmament agreements. Under present-day conditions, the greatest source of danger to mankind comes from the recognized willingness of people to fabricate and to apply weapons of mass destruction. Similarly, the safety of mankind will derive from the social atmosphere in which such acts are regarded as inhuman and unthinkable. Indeed, as such an atmosphere develops, the very existence of secret bombs caches becomes increasingly difficult to sustain. For the thousands of people who are needed to produce and then place large numbers of intricate weapons will very likely contain at least single persons who, in due course, could not bear the burden of being a party to the mass destruction of other human beings. Secret stockpiles of weapons, if they existed, would then be exposed.

E. THE HAZARD TO AUTHORITARIAN PRACTICES

Inspection for disarmament could lead to increased openness of society, as an inescapable requirement of the inspection process through more comprehensive agreements. This would result from the need for freedom of access to various types of premises, especially for controlling against illicit weapons production. As a result, internal security systems of all kinds would be pierced. These effects would remain even where inspection were carried out only by a formal agency. Such results would multiply if the methods of "Inspection by the People" were applied.[3]

Indeed, the internal political effects from the operation of inspection systems probably give the clue to understanding the

[3] See *Inspection for Disarmament, op. cit.*, pp. 38–44.

reluctance of various Soviet leaders to enter into such agreements. In my estimate, it is the inspection part of the nuclear test ban agreement that troubles them. An agreement on inspection by international teams would set a precedent whose internal effects would run counter to tight, unilateral systems of political control within the Soviet countries.

That does not mean, in my opinion, that the Soviets will necessarily continue to turn down inspection agreements. Pressure in that direction is bound to come within the Soviet sphere from the many people who could gain in their own freedom from a relaxation of international tensions and the reduction of internal police controls.

F. THE DEMAND FOR FOOLPROOF INSPECTION

The demand that inspection systems must be foolproof to be acceptable is tantamount to a rejection of the idea of inspection. For no such absolute condition of perfection is known in any sphere of man's knowledge or activity. There are always limits to accuracy. Variability and errors of estimation are characteristic of all observations of phenomena. Within such limits, we all do things that are useful and workable and predictable, though never perfect. We put insulation on wires and brakes on automobiles because they are workable, and we are vastly better off for having them despite occasional flaws. That is the understanding which is indicated for inspection systems. With such ends in view we can utilize and enhance the available inspection technique.

VIII. Alternative to the Arms Race

While calling a halt to the international arms race is an important end in itself, the steps necessary to achieve this goal give rise to a range of allied problems.

What use should be made of the human and material resources in the United States which are now devoted to arms development and production? Should present levels of taxation be maintained with the result that about 25 per cent of the national income is allocated through government decisions? By what means could one organize the allocation and expenditure of such funds while avoiding the development of highly centralized economic management with its concomitant concentration of political power?

What are the possibilities for international utilization of the resources formally devoted to the arms race? By what means could the application of such resources be organized? It has been estimated that at the present pace of arms expenditures, about fifteen hundred billion dollars would be expended for armaments between now and 1970.[4] Sums of this size are of the order of magnitude to accomplish a reconstruction of a major portion of the surface of the earth.

What are the consequences for internal affairs in the United States and in the U.S.S.R. in the event of a slowdown, and possible termination of the arms race? In the opinion of this writer, this is a question of major strategic importance, and the answers, however tentative, would serve as a major guide for policy-making. Thereby the achievement of disarmament with appropriate inspection systems could also be made to serve desirable political ends of freer society everywhere.

51. *EMOTIONAL AND MOTIVATIONAL ASPECTS OF THE DISARMAMENT PROBLEM* / JEROME D. FRANK*

Western nations today seem to be caught up in a maladaptive response to threat which seems analogous to that shown by certain mental patients in that the methods used to deal with a problem aggravate instead of solve it. The problem facing all nations today is how to assure human survival and achieve security in the face of massive, unprecedented threat posed by nuclear weapons. It is generally agreed that disarmament must be part of any solution. As the unanimous resolution of the United Nations Assembly of November 2, 1959 puts it: "the question of general and complete disarmament is the most important one facing the world today." So far, attempts to solve this question have consisted not of moves towards disarmament, but of the competitive development and accumulation of nuclear, chemical, and biological weapons of mass

[4] "1970 Without Arms Control," *op. cit.*

* Jerome D. Frank, "Emotional and Motivational Aspects of the Disarmament Problem," *The Journal of Social Issues*, Vol. 17, No. 3 (1961), pp. 20–27. Reprinted by permission.

destruction. Thus the means by which nations try to diminish the peril posed by modern weapons serve to increase it. Never have the nations of the world spent so much on armaments in an effort to achieve security, and never have they been so insecure.

One can find similar behavior in psychiatric patients, like the alcoholic who increases his anxiety and depression by trying to combat these feelings through drink, which aggravates them. It therefore may be worthwhile to explore possible parallels between the motivations and behavior of nations and individuals, recognizing, of course, that such analogies have only limited applicability (Frank, 1960).

The Nature of the Nuclear Threat

The unprecedented nature of the threat lies in the literally unlimited destructive power of nuclear weapons. This means that there can never be an adequate defense against them. There can be no passive defense because the attacker can always mount an attack sufficiently powerful to overcome it. By setting up certain arbitrary limitations, such as that the size of a nuclear attack shall be limited to 2500 megatons, it is possible to show that if certain drastic conditions are met—in itself highly unlikely—a country might survive a nuclear war. But the enemy is not bound by these limitations. America and Russia might choose to mount a 10,000 megaton attack against each other, in which case 75% to 80% of Americans and Russians would be killed outright and the rest would die within 2 years of radiation poisoning. "You might as well cross off both Russia and the United States from the map." (Glass, 1960, p. 11.)

Nor is it likely that there will ever be a successful active defense against these weapons, for the same thought processes which perfect a defense against a weapon at the same time devise ways of thwarting the defense. For example, we are now trying to develop a system for intercepting missiles through plotting their trajectories, and at the same time developing missiles which do not follow predictable trajectories. We boast of our means of confusing Russian radar, but they, of course, will be able to confuse ours equally well.

In the days of conventional weapons, a defense which worked reasonably well was good enough. Because of the massive destructive power of nuclear weapons, this is no longer true. Now a defense would have to be at least ninety percent effective—a level of effectiveness never achieved in history; and the likelihood of its being achieved when technology is advancing at such a fantastically rapid rate seems extremely remote.

Finally, the knowledge of how to make nuclear, bacteriological, and chemical weapons will never be lost. Therefore even if universal disarmament were achieved, it would always be possible for a nation secretly to build a few and blackmail its unarmed neighbors with them.

These considerations and others force one to a drastic conclusion, which has been succinctly stated in the following unanimous statement of 28 leading scientists from 8 nations: "In the end, only the absolute prevention of war will preserve human life and civilization in the face of chemical and bacteriological as well as nuclear weapons. No ban of a single weapon, no agreement that leaves the general threat of war in existence, can protect mankind sufficiently." (Proceedings of the Pugwash Conference, 1959, pp. 5–6.)

Some Maladaptive Responses to the Nuclear Threat

Before considering the possibilities that mankind might achieve the goal of the abolition of war, it may be well briefly to review some of the current responses to the threat posed by modern weaponry which are steadily propelling humanity towards disaster. These may be grouped into responses which have always beeen maladaptive, unreasonable, and known to make trouble, and those which always worked in the past but now for the first time in human history will not work any longer.

The grossly maladaptive responses have been described elsewhere (Frank, 1960; Osgood, 1959; Singer, 1958) so they will be merely mentioned here. Particularly important ones are:

1. *Ignoring* the danger. This is easy to do because it lies outside the experience of most of humanity. The human imagination has a remarkable capacity to make remote contingencies real, but it seems unable to grasp the immediacy and extent of the danger posed by weapons which do not impinge on any of the senses and whose full devastating power has never been actually experienced. The tendency to ignore the threat is reinforced by habituation and denial.

2. *Habituation.* Over and over again in the past 15 years we

have initially recoiled in horror from a weapons development, only to accept it calmly a few years later. We finally managed to become inured to the deaths of tens of thousands in a firebomb raid by the end of World War II. Now we consider with equanimity the deaths of millions. The point scarcely requires elaboration.

3. *Denial.* One common response to an overwhelming threat is "denial" in the clinical sense—that is, a refusal to admit the threat into awareness. Denial is not always pathological. The inability of most persons to contemplate their own deaths may be psychologically healthy. But denial in the form of failing to face the threat posed by modern weapons seriously impedes efforts to resolve the problem they present. Denial in this sense may take subtle forms. One is what David Riesman has termed "one man chess." (Personal communication, March 1960.) Each country plots its moves without considering what the moves of the enemy might be. For example, Senator Aiken, when told of the Russian threat to our bases abroad, is quoted as saying: "The first rocket to fall on the soil of our allies would be the signal for a rain of rockets on Russia." (Aiken, 1960, p. 1.) One looks in vain for the remainder of the thought "and a rain of Russian rockets on us."

A more subtle form of denial is a fallacious appeal to history: With the advent of each new weapon alarmists prophesied that it would destroy mankind and they were wrong; so those who say that nuclear, biological, and chemical weapons threaten the existence of humanity are probably also wrong. The fallacy lies in the proportionate increase in destructive energy made available by splitting the atom. At the dawn of history, when men killed each other with clubs and stones, a blow could scarcely kill more than one person. By 1944 mankind had so improved the destructiveness of weapons that an average firebomb raid on Japan killed four thousand. Thus the killing power of weapons increased by a factor of four thousand over half a million years or so. Today a moderate nuclear raid could kill fifty million people and nuclear weapons could be made in sufficient quantity to wipe out the entire human race. This represents an increase in destructive power over the most deadly non-atomic weapons by a factor of somewhere between 12,500 and infinity in a scant half-generation. Those who prophesy disaster, and their like-minded forebears, are in the position of the boy who cries "Wolf" too often, so that when the wolf really comes no one believes him.

4. *The effects of strong emotion.* To the extent that we do not

succeed in ignoring or denying the threat of modern weapons of mass destruction, we are made anxious by them. As is well known, anxiety and other forms of emotional tension tend to diminish flexibility of thinking and lead to a narrowing of alternatives. They also shorten the time perspective so that the anxious or emotionally aroused person clutches at measures which afford immediate relief despite the certainty that they will lead to increased suffering in the future. Like the alcoholic who uses alcohol to gain brief but immediate relief even though he knows it will eventually kill him, nations respond to each new threat by increasing the arms budget, which yields momentarily heightened feelings of security at the cost of increasing the likelihood and magnitude of ultimate disaster.

At the group level emotional tension is most seriously reflected in the formation of the stereotype of "the enemy." Whoever we are and whoever the enemy is, we gradually assume all the virtues and they become the incarnation of everything evil. Once we have cast another group in the role of the enemy, we know that they are to be distrusted. We then tend to twist all their communications to fit our belief.

The mutual distrust of enemies has two dangerous consequences. First, it tends to disrupt communication between them. Since the enemy is viewed as so diabolically clever, each side fears that the other will be able to use improved communications to its advantage. I am not suggesting that some enemies do not deserve to be mistrusted. But disruption of communication prevents gaining information which would help to rectify any incorrect perceptions of one's opponent. The second and greatest danger of the mutual stereotype of the enemy is that it tends to make itself come true by virtue of the mechanism of the "self-fulfilling prophecy" (Merton, 1957), which operates at both individual and group levels. Enemies may not be untrustworthy to begin with, but if the mutual posture lasts long enough, they eventually become so, as each acts in such a way as to justify the other's suspicion.

"*Adaptive*" *Responses to the Nuclear Threat*

The pathological, maladaptive nature of the responses described above is readily apparent. Therefore they are relatively easy to identify. More difficult to detect, and therefore perhaps ultimately more difficult to deal with, are responses to threat which have been highly adaptive in the past. Therefore they appear eminently reasonable and right today, though they are as maladaptive as the others in the face of weapons of limitless destructive capacity. Three of these warrant special comment because they are evoked by all conflict situations. They represent very deep-seated aspects of human nature, and any scheme for the abolition of war must include ways of taking them into account. They are the belief that superior destructive force is the final arbiter of conflict, the propensity to fight for one's ideals to the point of death, and the fact that any sign of weakness or fear encourages an opponent to attack.

1. *International relations since time immemorial have been based on the fact that in a showdown, conflicts are won by the side possessing superior destructive force.* Although behavior guided by this premise has regularly led to war, outcomes of armed conflicts have confirmed it, at least until the twentieth century. The intellectual conviction that no one can win a nuclear war in the sense of gaining the ends for which he fought can make little headway against agelong human experience to the contrary. So national leaders still speak of winning the nuclear arms race as if this statement made sense.

2. *In a conflict one must be prepared to give one's life for one's ideals and beliefs.* Whether in the long run the willingness of people to die for their ideals has been good or bad for mankind is debatable. The world would certainly be a poorer place today were it not for religious, national, and intellectual martyrs who sacrificed their lives for their convictions, but this propensity has also led to catastrophic conflicts over differences in ideologies which now seem utterly trivial, such as whether God is Unitarian or Trinitarian. None the less, when patriotic orators evoke the image of Patrick Henry, who preferred death to loss of liberty, most Americans feel a responsive thrill. Unfortunately a man can no longer die in battle for his ideals without dragging millions of people after him who have no choice in the matter. Nor can his death in a nuclear war possibly preserve the ideals for which he gave his life. However, any solution to the problems posed by weapons of mass destruction must permit people to sacrifice their lives, if necessary, for their beliefs, but in such a way that there is some hope of the sacrifice succeeding.

3. *One must not show fear in the face of the enemy.* There is no question as to the soundness of this principle, for fear undoubtedly encourages aggression. The time-hallowed way to maintain one's courage in the face of the enemy is to proclaim one's willing-

ness to die for his cause, and demonstrate by shows of strength and other means that he will not be intimidated. The series of Russian and American reactions precipated by the shooting down of the U-2 illustrate this response all too clearly. Each truculent gesture on one side evokes a corresponding one from the other, as a demonstration to itself and the other country that it cannot be intimidated. A world from which war has been abolished would have to include means for showing that one is not afraid, other than piling up arms.

Psychological Aspects of a World Without War

The crucial first step, psychologically, towards the ultimate abolition of war is the acceptance of the falsity of the first premise on which the policy of all nations today is based—that superior destructive force is the ultimate means of settling conflict. That is, one must begin one's thinking by ruling out resort to violence. The challenge is to devise non-violent means for resolving problems hitherto solved by war. This does not mean the abolition of conflict, but rather placing one's faith in the development of non-violent means of persuading, or even coercing, an opponent which have a chance of succeeding even if he has and is prepared to use superior destructive force.

The major ground for hope that this goal can be achieved lies in the actual demonstrations in recent years of the effectiveness of non-violent methods against an opponent who possessed and was prepared to use superior force. These include the non-violent campaigns in Norway and Denmark which demoralized the Nazi troops so badly that they had to be frequently rotated, the refusal of some Russian soldiers to fire on unarmed East Germans at the cost of their own lives, and, above all, the success of two large-scale, carefully planned non-violent campaigns—Gandhi's for Indian independence and Martin Luther King's for bus desegregation in Montgomery, Alabama. It seems probable that these leaders achieved a genuine break-through in human affairs, which we have barely begun to exploit. After the fact it is easy to explain away the success of these campaigns on the basis of certain special circumstances. The significant point is that in two different cultures both worked, when no one would have predicted their success in advance. This at least raises the hope that other successful non-violent ways of waging conflict can be developed for other situations, including even the arena of international conflict.

Because of the special conditions surrounding these campaigns, it is unwise to generalize from them, but in terms of this discussion they have at least demonstrated the possibility of meeting the needs mentioned above without threat of or resort to violence. Both these campaigns showed that non-violent methods of conducting conflict require as great a degree of dedication as violent ones, including the sacrifice of one's life. And the martyr would at least know his sacrifice might help to realize the aim for which he made it, as sacrifice of one's life in a nuclear war cannot.

Gandhi and King also succeeded in creating a set of group standards which made refusal to resort to violence a means of demonstrating one's fearlessness, thereby removing it from the context of cowardice.

Thus commitment to non-violent ways of resolving international disputes would immediately take disarmament out of the context of weakness and surrender. Disarming would become part of an over-all plan of promulgating our ideals, rather than a move away from them.

Finally, commitment to non-violence would take the teeth out of the threat of nuclear blackmail. That is, a world organized along non-violent lines would contain very powerful deterrents against any nation which was tempted to reinvoke the specter of superior destructive force. In such a world institutional means of resolving conflicts peaceably would have been developed, the standard of living would be rapidly rising as resources formerly squandered on armaments were expended for human welfare, and all peoples would be rejoicing in their release from fear of annihilation. Any government that contemplated taking advantage of the general disarmament to blackmail another country through threat of force would face extremely unpleasant consequences. First of all, such a move would have a profoundly demoralizing effect within the country that made it. Even an absolutely ruthless dictatorship cannot make major changes in policy overnight without consideration of the feelings of the population. An even more serious consequence would be that every country of the world would rearm as rapidly as possible and the aggressor would be the enemy of them all. Since the countries would still know how to make weapons of limitless destructive power and since some of these weapons—notably bacteriological ones—are very cheap and easy to produce, the government which threatened violence would have to be prepared to police the entire world. Finally, she would know that she would meet stubborn non-violent resistance in the countries she occupied.

There are powerful positive and negative incentives for applying ourselves to the development of means of non-violent solution of conflict. The negative incentive is that modern weapons of mass destruction have left no other alternative. As Dr. C. F. von Weizsacker, the eminent German physicist-philosopher, put it at a recent conference: "Renunciation of violence is no longer a pious hope but a necessity. The only question is whether it will come before or after a catastrophe." (Personal communication, July 1959.)

The positive incentive is the dazzling vista that opens up for mankind once our imaginations, freed from preoccupation with mutual annihilation, can turn to developing the constructive potentialities of the vast power now at our disposal.

References

1. AIKEN, GEORGE D. *Baltimore Evening Sun,* May 30, 1960, p. 1.
2. FRANK, JEROME D. Breaking the thought barrier: psychological challenges of the nuclear age. *Psychiatry,* 1960, **23,** pp. 245–266.
3. GLASS, H. BENTLEY. *Baltimore Morning Sun,* May 14, 1960, p. 11.
4. MERTON, ROBERT K. *Social Theory and Social Structure.* Glencoe, Illinois: Free Press, 1957.
5. OSGOOD, CHARLES E. Suggestions for winning the real war with communism. *Journal of Conflict Resolution,* 1959, **3,** pp. 295–325.
6. *Proceedings of Pugwash Conference of International Scientists on Biological and Chemical Warfare.* Pugwash, Nova Scotia, August 24–30, 1959.
7. SINGER, J. DAVID. Threat-perception and the armament-tension dilemma. *Journal of Conflict Resolution,* 1958, **2,** pp. 90–105.

PROSPECTS

part V

COLD WAR AND PEACEFUL COEXISTENCE

XVI

ENTERING THE LAST THIRD OF THE TWENTIETH century, where are we heading? In particular, what are the prospects for the relations among the major powers? Some of the basic issues on which any prognosis will have to be based are discussed in the debate between Nikita S. Khrushchev and George F. Kennan in the journal *Foreign Affairs*, which constitutes the substance of this final chapter.

Khrushchev was Chairman of the Council of Ministers of the Soviet Union and First Secretary of the Communist Party until his involuntary retirement in 1964. Although he is now out of office, most observers agree that his successors have not abandoned his foreign policy principles.

Kennan, Professor at Princeton's Institute of Advanced Study, is a former U.S. ambassador to the Soviet Union and former head of the State Department's Policy Planning Staff. He is the author of *Realities of American Foreign Policy*, *Russia, the Atom and the West*, and other works. He speaks here as a private—but highly influential—American citizen.

52. *ON PEACEFUL COEXISTENCE* / NIKITA S. KHRUSHCHEV*

I have been told that the question of peaceful coexistance of states with different social systems is uppermost today in the minds of many Americans—and not only Americans. The question of coexistence, particularly in our day, interests literally every man and woman on the globe.

We all of us well know that tremendous changes have taken place in the world. Gone, indeed, are the days when it took weeks to cross the ocean from one continent to the other or when a trip from Europe to America, or from Asia to Africa, seemed a very complicated undertaking. The progress of modern technology has reduced our planet to a rather small place; it has even become, in this sense, quite congested. And if in our daily life it is a matter of considerable importance to establish normal relations with our neighbors in a densely inhabited settlement, this is so much the more necessary in the relations between states, in particular states belonging to different social systems.

You may like your neighbor or dislike him. You are not obliged to be friends with him or visit him. But you live side by side, and what can you do if neither you nor he has any desire to quit the old home and move to another town? All the more so in relations between states. It would be unreasonable to assume that you can make it so hot for your undesirable neighbor that he will decide to move to Mars or Venus. And vice versa, of course.

What, then, remains to be done? There may be two ways out: either war—and war in the rocket and H-bomb age is fraught with

* Nikita S. Khrushchev, "On Peaceful Coexistence," *Foreign Affairs*, Vol. 38, No. 1 (October 1959), pp. 1–18. Copyright by the Council on Foreign Relations, Inc., New York. Reprinted by permission.

the most dire consequences for all nations—or peaceful coexistence. Whether you like your neighbor or not, nothing can be done about it, you have to find some way of getting on with him, for you both live on one and the same planet.

But the very concept of peaceful coexistence, it is said, by its alleged complexity frightens certain people who have become unaccustomed to trusting their neighbors and who see a double bottom in each suitcase. People of this kind, on hearing the word "coexistence," begin to play around with it in one way and another, sizing it up and applying various yardsticks to it. Isn't it a fraud? Isn't it a trap? Does not coexistence signify the division of the world into areas separated by high fences, which do not communicate with each other? And what is going to happen behind those fences?

The more such questions are piled up artificially by the cold-war mongers, the more difficult it is for the ordinary man to make head or tail of them. It would therefore be timely to rid the essence of this question of all superfluous elements and to attempt to look soberly at the most pressing problem of our day—the problem of peaceful competition.

II

One does not need to delve deeply into history to appreciate how important it is for mankind to ensure peaceful coexistence. And here it may be said parenthetically that the Europeans might have benefited a great deal in their day if, instead of organizing senseless crusades which invariably ended in failure, they had established peaceful relations with the differently-minded peoples of the Moslem East.

But let us turn to facts concerning the relatively recent past when the watershed between states no longer consisted of different religious creeds and customs, but of much deeper differences of principle relating to the choice of social systems. This new situation arose on the threshold of the 1920s when, to the booming of the guns of the Russian cruiser *Aurora* which had joined the rebellious workers and peasants, a new and unprecedented social system, a state of workers and peasants, came into the world.

Its appearance was met with the disgruntled outcries of those who naïvely believed the capitalist system to be eternal and immutable. Some people even made an attempt to strangle the unwanted infant in the cradle. Everybody knows how this ended: our people voted with their arms for Soviet power, and it came to stay. And even then, in 1920, V. I. Lenin, replying to the question of an American correspondent as to what basis there could be for peace between Soviet Russia and America, said: "Let the American imperialists not touch us. We won't touch them."

From its very inception the Soviet state proclaimed peaceful coexistence as the basic principle of its foreign policy. It was no accident that the very first state act of the Soviet power was the decree on peace, the decree on the cessation of the bloody war.

What, then, is the policy of peaceful coexistence?

In its simplest expression it signifies the repudiation of war as a means of solving controversial issues. However, this does not cover the entire concept of peaceful coexistence. Apart from the commitment to non-aggression, it also presupposes an obligation on the part of all states to desist from violating each other's territorial integrity and sovereignty in any form and under any pretext whatsoever. The principle of peaceful coexistence signifies a renunciation of interference in the internal affairs of other countries with the object of altering their system of government or mode of life or for any other motives. The doctrine of peaceful coexistence also presupposes that political and economic relations between countries are to be based upon complete equality of the parties concerned, and on mutual benefit.

It is often said in the West that peaceful coexistence is nothing else than a tactical method of the socialist states. There is not a grain of truth in such allegations. Our desire for peace and peaceful coexistence is not conditioned by any time-serving or tactical considerations. It springs from the very nature of socialist society in which there are no classes or social groups interested in profiting by war or seizing and enslaving other people's territories. The Soviet Union and the other socialist countries, thanks to their socialist system, have an unlimited home market and for this reason they have no need to pursue an expansionist policy of conquest and an effort to subordinate other countries to their influence.

It is the people who determine the destinies of the socialist states. The socialist states are ruled by the working people themselves, the workers and peasants, the people who themselves create all the material and spiritual values of society. And people of labor cannot want war. For to them war spells grief and tears, death, devastation and misery. Ordinary people have no need for war.

Contrary to what certain propagandists hostile to us say, the coexistence of states with different social systems does not mean that they will only fence themselves off from one another by a high wall and undertake the mutual obligation not to throw stones over the wall or pour dirt upon each other. No! Peaceful coexistence does not mean merely living side by side in the absence of war but with the constantly remaining threat of its breaking out in the future. *Peaceful coexistence can and should develop into peaceful competition for the purpose of satisfying man's needs in the best possible way.*

We say to the leaders of the capitalist states: Let us try out in practice whose system is better, let us compete without war. This is much better than competing in who will produce more arms and who will smash whom. We stand and always will stand for such competition as will help to raise the well-being of the people to a higher level.

The principle of peaceful competition does not at all demand that one or another state abandon the system and ideology adopted by it. It goes without saying that the acceptance of this principle cannot lead to the immediate end of disputes and contradictions which are inevitable between countries adhering to different social systems. But the main thing is ensured: the states which decided to adopt the path of peaceful coexistence repudiate the use of force in any form and agree on a peaceful settlement of possible disputes and conflicts, bearing in mind the mutual interests of the parties concerned. In our age of the H-bomb and atomic techniques this is the main thing of interest to every man.

Displaying skepticism about the idea of peaceful competition, Vice President Nixon, in his speech over the Soviet radio and television in August 1959, attempted to find a contradiction between the Soviet people's professions of their readiness to coexist peacefully with the capitalist states and the slogans posted in the shops of our factories calling for higher labor productivity in order to ensure the speediest victory of Communism.

This was not the first time we heard representatives of the bourgeois countries reason in this manner. They say: The Soviet leaders argue that they are for peaceful coexistence. At the same time they declare that they are fighting for Communism and they even say that Communism will be victorious in all countries. How can there be peaceful coexistence with the Soviet Union if it fights for Communism?

People who treat the question in this way confuse matters, wilfully or not, by confusing the problems of ideological struggle with the question of relations between states. Those indulging in this sort of confusion are most probably guided by a desire to cast aspersions upon the Communists of the Soviet Union and to represent them as the advocates of aggressive actions. This, however, is very unwise.

The Communist Party of the Soviet Union at its Twentieth Congress made it perfectly clear and obvious that the allegations that the Soviet Union intends to overthrow capitalism in other countries by means of "exporting" revolution are absolutely unfounded. I cannot refrain from reminding you of my words at the Twentieth Congress: "It goes without saying that among us Communists there are no adherents of capitalism. But this does not mean that we have interfered or plan to interfere in the internal affairs of countries where capitalism still exists. Romain Rolland was right when he said that 'freedom is not brought in from abroad in baggage trains like Bourbons.' It is ridiculous to think that revolutions are made to order."

We Communists believe that the idea of Communism will ultimately be victorious throughout the world, just as it has been victorious in our country, in China and in many other states. Many readers of *Foreign Affairs* will probably disagree with us. Perhaps they think that the idea of capitalism will ultimately triumph. It is their right to think so. We may argue, we may disagree with one another. *The main thing is to keep to the positions of ideological struggle, without resorting to arms in order to prove that one is right.* The point is that with military techniques what they are today, there are no inaccessible places in the world. Should a world war break out, no country will be able to shut itself off from a crushing blow.

We believe that ultimately that system will be victorious on the globe which will offer the nations greater opportunities for improving their material and spiritual life. It is precisely socialism that creates unprecedentedly great prospects for the inexhaustible creative enthusiasm of the masses, for a genuine flourishing of science and culture, for the realization of man's dream of a happy life, a life without destitute and unemployed people, of a happy childhood and tranquil old age, of the realization of the most audacious and ambitious human projects, of man's right to create in a truly free manner in the interests of the people.

But when we say that in the competition between the two systems, the capitalist and the socialist, our system will win, this does not mean, of course, that we shall achieve victory by interfering in the internal affairs of the capitalist countries. Our confidence in the victory of Communism is of a different kind. It is based on a knowledge of the laws governing the development of society. Just as in its time capitalism, as the more progressive system, took the place of feudalism, so will capitalism be inevitably superseded by Communism—the more progressive and more equitable social system. We are confident of the victory of the socialist system because it is a more progressive system than the capitalist system. Soviet power has been in existence for only a little more than 40 years, and during these years we have gone through two of the worst wars, repulsing the attacks of enemies who attempted to strangle us. Capitalism in the United States has been in existence for more than a century and a half, and the history of the United States has developed in such a way that never once have enemies landed on American territory.

Yet the dynamics of the development of the U.S.S.R. and the U.S.A. are such that the 42-year-old land of the Soviets is already able to challenge the 150-year-old capitalist state to economic competition; and the most farsighted American leaders are admitting that the Soviet Union is fast catching up with the United States and will ultimately outstrip it. Watching the progress of this competition, anyone can judge which is the better system, and we believe that in the long run all the peoples will embark on the path of struggle for the building of socialist societies.

You disagree with us? Prove by facts that your system is superior and more efficacious, that it is capable of ensuring a higher degree of prosperity for the people than the socialist system, that under capitalism man can be happier than under socialism. It is impossible to prove this. I have no other explanation for the fact that talk of violently "rolling back" Communism never ceases in the West. Not long ago the U.S. Senate and House of Representatives deemed it proper to pass a resolution calling for the "liberation" of the socialist countries allegedly enslaved by Communism and, moreover, of a number of union republics constituting part of the Soviet Union. The authors of the resolution call for the "liberation" of the Ukraine, Byelorussia, Lithuania, Latvia, Estonia, Armenia, Azerbaijan, Georgia, Kazakhstan, Turkmenistan and even a certain "Ural Area."

I would not be telling the full truth if I did not say that the adoption of this ill-starred resolution was regarded by the Soviet people as an act of provocation. Personally I agree with this appraisal.

It would be interesting to see, incidentally, how the authors of this resolution would have reacted if the parliament of Mexico, for instance, had passed a resolution demanding that Texas, Arizona and California be "liberated from American slavery." Apparently they have never pondered such a question, which is very regrettable. Sometimes comparisons help to understand the essence of a matter.

Travelling through the Soviet Union, leading American statesmen and public figures have had full opportunity to convince themselves that there is no hope of sowing strife between the Soviet people and the Communist Party and the Soviet Government, and of influencing them to rebel against Communism. How, then, are we to explain the unceasing attempts to revive the policy of "rolling back" Communism? What do they have in mind? Armed intervention in the internal affairs of the socialist countries? But in the West as well as in the East people are fully aware that under the conditions of modern military technique such actions are fraught with immediate and relentless retaliation.

So we come back to what we started with. In our day there are only two ways: peaceful coexistence or the most destructive war in history. There is no third choice.

III

The problem of peaceful coexistence between states with different social systems has become particularly pressing in view of the fact that since the Second World War the development of relations between states has entered a new stage, that now we have approached a period in the life of mankind when there is a real chance of excluding war once and for all from the life of society. The new alignment of international forces which has developed since the Second World War offers ground for the assertion that a new world war is no longer a fatal inevitability, that it can be averted.

First, today not only all the socialist states, but many countries in Asia and Africa which have embarked upon the road of independent national statehood, and many other states outside the aggressive military groupings, are actively fighting for peace.

Secondly, the peace policy enjoys the powerful support of the broad masses of the people all over the world.

Thirdly, the peaceful socialist states are in possession of very potent material means, which cannot but have a deterring effect upon the aggressors.

Prior to the Second World War the U.S.S.R. was the only socialist country, with not more than 17 percent of the territory, 3 percent of the population, and about 10 percent of the output of the world. At present, the socialist countries cover about one-fourth of the territory of the globe, have one-third of its population, and their industrial output accounts for about one-third of the total world output.

This is precisely the explanation of the indisputable fact that throughout the past years, hotbeds of war breaking out now in one and now in another part of the globe—in the Near East and in Europe, in the Far East and in Southeast Asia—have been extinguished at the very outset.

What does the future hold in store for us?

As a result of the fulfillment and overfulfillment of the present Seven Year Plan of economic development of the U.S.S.R., as well as of the plans of the other socialist countries of Europe and Asia, the countries of the socialist system will then account for a little more than half of the world output. Their economic power will grow immeasurably, and this will help to an even greater extent to consolidate world peace: the material might and moral influence of the peace-loving states will be so great that any bellicose militarist will have to think ten times before risking going to war. It is the good fortune of mankind that a community of socialist states which are not interested in new war has been set up, because to build socialism and Communism the socialist countries need peace. Today the community of socialist countries which has sprung up on the basis of complete equality holds such a position in the development of all branches of economy, science and culture as to be able to exert an influence towards preventing the outbreak of new world wars.

Hence we are already in a practical sense near to that stage in the life of humanity when nothing will prevent people from devoting themselves wholly to peaceful labor, when war will be wholly excluded from the life of society.

But if we say that there is no fatal inevitability of war at present, this by no means signifies that we can rest on our laurels, fold our arms and bask in the sun in the hope that an end has been put to wars once and for all. Those in the West who believe that war is to their benefit have not yet abandoned their schemes. They control considerable material forces, as well as military and political levers, and there is no guarantee that some tragic day they will not attempt to set them in motion. That is why it is so much the more necessary to continue an active struggle in order that the policy of peaceful coexistence may triumph throughout the world not in words but in deeds.

Of much importance, of course, is the fact that this policy has in our day merited not only the widest moral approval but also international legal recognition. The countries of the socialist camp in their relations with the capitalist states are guided precisely by this policy. The principles of peaceful coexistence are reflected in the decisions of the Bandung Conference of Asian and African countries. Furthermore, many countries of Europe, Asia and Africa have solemnly proclaimed this principle as the basis of their foreign policy. Finally, the idea of peaceful coexistence has found unanimous support in the decisions of the twelfth and thirteenth sessions of the United Nations General Assembly.

In our view, peaceful coexistence can become lasting only if the good declarations in favor of peace are supported by active measures on the part of the governments and peoples of all countries. As far as the Soviet Union is concerned, it has already done a good deal in this respect, and I am able to share some experiences with you.

As far back as March 12, 1951, the Supreme Soviet of the U.S.S.R. adopted a "Law on the Defense of Peace," stating:

> (1) Propaganda for war, in whatever form it may be conducted, undermines the cause of peace, creates the menace of a new war and therefore constitutes the gravest crime against humanity.
>
> (2) Persons guilty of war propaganda should be brought to court and tried as heinous criminals.

Further, the Soviet Union has in recent years unilaterally reduced its armed forces by more than 2,000,000 men. The funds released as a result have been used to develop the economy and further raise the material and cultural living standards of the Soviet people.

The Soviet Union has liquidated its bases on the territories of other states.

The Soviet Union unilaterally discontinued the tests of atomic weapons and refrained from conducting them further until it became finally clear that the Western powers refused to follow our example and were continuing the explosions.

The Soviet Union has repeatedly submitted detailed and perfectly realistic proposals for disarmament, meeting the positions of the Western powers halfway. But to solve the disarmament problem it is necessary for our Western partners to agree and desire to meet us halfway too. This is just what is lacking.

When it became clear that it was very difficult under these conditions to solve the complex disarmament problem immediately, we proposed another concrete idea to our partners: Let us concentrate our attention on those problems which lend themselves most easily to a solution. Let us undertake initial partial steps on matters concerning which the views of the different parties have been brought closer together.

It is perfectly clear that one of these questions today is the question of discontinuing atomic and hydrogen weapon tests. The progress achieved in this matter justifies the hope that an agreement on the discontinuation of nuclear weapon tests will shortly be reached. Implementation of this measure will, of course, be an important step on the way to the solution of the disarmament problem and the banning of nuclear weapons in general.

Attributing much importance to contacts and intercourse between statesmen of all countries, the Soviet Government a few years ago proposed that an East-West heads of government conference be convened in order to come to terms—taking into account present-day realities and guided by the spirit of mutual understanding—on concrete measures, the realization of which would help to relax international tension.

We also proposed that this conference consider those international questions for the settlement of which realistic prerequisites already existed. As a first step toward such a settlement, we proposed to the powers concerned that a peace treaty be concluded with Germany and that West Berlin be granted the status of a demilitarized free city. I want to emphasize particularly that we were guided primarily by the desire to put a final end to the aftermath of the Second World War. We regard the liquidation of the consequences of the Second World War and the conclusion of a peace treaty with the two German states—the German Democratic Republic and the German Federal Republic—as the question of questions.

Indeed, 14 years have already passed since the war ended, but the German people are still without a peace treaty. The delay has afforded wide scope for renewed activities of the West German militarists and revanchists. They have already proclaimed their aggressive plans, laying claim, for instance, to lands in Poland and Czechoslovakia. Of course, the German revanchists are thinking not only of a march to the East; they also know the way to the West. In the Second World War the Hitlerites occupied Western Europe before advancing against the Soviet Union.

Will the direction chosen by the modern German revanchists for their aggression be any consolation to the peoples of Europe if a global war breaks out on that continent? The lessons of history should not be ignored. To do so often ends in tragedy.

Some say: The Soviet people are unduly sensitive. Can one assume that Western Germany is now in a position to precipitate another world war? Those who put the question thus forget that Western Germany is at present acting in the world arena not alone but within the military North Atlantic bloc. She plays a paramount role in this bloc. And more than that, life has shown that the North Atlantic Alliance is being gradually converted into an instrument of the German militarists, which makes it easier for them to carry out aggressive plans. It is not at all impossible, therefore, that Western Germany, taking advantage of her position in the North Atlantic Alliance, might provoke hostilities in order to draw her allies into it and plunge the whole world into the chasm of a devastating war.

All this indicates how timely and realistic are the proposals of the Soviet Government for the conclusion of a peace treaty with Germany and for bringing the situation in West Berlin back to normal.

And yet, some of the Western opponents of the Soviet proposals say that if the Soviet Union really stands for peaceful coexistence it should even be asked to commit itself to the preservation of the existing status quo. Others argue that if the Western powers agree to the conclusion of a peace treaty with the two German states that would amount to a retreat on their part, and the Soviet Union should make some compensation for this "retreat."

There are no grounds whatever for these assertions, in our opinion. The task before us is to do away with the aftermath of the Second World War and to conclude a peace treaty. And any possibility of someone gaining and others losing, of someone acquiring and others making concessions, is out of the question here. All the parties concerned acquire a stronger foundation for the maintenance of peace in Europe and throughout the world in the shape of a peace treaty. Does this not accord with the interests of all the peoples?

At times, and of late especially, some spokesmen in the West have gone so far as to say that the abolition of the aftermath of the Second World War is a step which would allegedly intensify rather than ease international tension. It is hard to believe that there are no secret designs behind allegations of this kind, especially when attempts are made to present in a distorted light the policy of the U.S.S.R., which is intended to secure a lasting and stable peace, by alleging that it all but leads to war. It seems to us, on the contrary, that the Soviet position on the German question corresponds most of all to the present-day reality.

It now seems that no sober-minded leader in the West is inclined any longer to advance the unrealistic demand for the so-called reunion of Germany before the conclusion of a peace treaty, in as much as more and more political leaders are becoming aware of the fact that reunion in the conditions now obtaining is a process which depends upon the Germans themselves and not upon any outside interference. We should start from the obvious fact that two German states exist, and that the Germans themselves must decide how they want to live. In as much as these two states, the German Democratic Republic and the German Federal Republic, do exist, the peace treaty should be concluded with them, because any further delay and postponement of this exceptionally important act tends not only to sustain the abnormal situation in Europe but also to aggravate it still further.

As for Germany's unity, I am convinced that Germany will be united sooner or later. However, before this moment comes—and no one can foretell when it will come—no attempts should be made to interfere from outside in this internal process, to sustain the state of war which is fraught with many grave dangers and surprises for peace in Europe and throughout the world. The desire to preserve the peace and to prevent another war should outweigh all other considerations of statesmen, irrespective of their mode of thinking. The Gordian knot must be cut: the peace treaty must be achieved if we do not want to play with fire—with the destinies of millions upon millions of people.

In this connection it is impossible to ignore also the question of

West Berlin. It is commonly known that the German revanchists have made West Berlin the base for their constant undermining and subversive activity directed towards the provoking of war. We resolutely reject any attempts to ascribe to the Soviet Union the intention of seizing West Berlin and infringing upon the right of the population in this part of the city to preserve its present way of life. On the contrary, in demanding the normalization of the situation in West Berlin, we have proposed to convert it into a free city and to guarantee, jointly with the Western states, the preservation there of the way of life and of the social order which suits the West Berlin inhabitants best of all. This shows that the positions of the Government of the Soviet Union and the Governments of the Western states, judging by their statements, coincide on this question. We, and so do they, stand for the independence of West Berlin and for the preservation of the existing way of life there.

It is, therefore, only necessary to overcome the difficulties born of the cold war in order to find the way to an agreement on West Berlin and on the wider question of the conclusion of a peace treaty with the two German states. This is the way to ease international tensions and to promote peaceful coexistence. It would strengthen confidence between states and assist in the gradual abolition of unfriendliness and suspicion in international relations.

Implementation of the Soviet proposals would not injure the interests of the Western powers and would not give any one-sided advantages to anybody. At the same time, the settlement of the German question would prevent a dangerous development of events in Europe, remove one of the main causes of international tension and create favorable prospects for a settlement of other international issues.

The proposals of the Soviet Union were discussed at the Foreign Ministers' Conference in Geneva. The Ministers did not succeed in reaching an agreement, but the Geneva conference did accomplish a great deal of useful work. The positions of the two sides were positively brought closer together and the possibility of an agreement on some questions has become apparent.

At the same time, we still have substantial differences on a number of questions. I am deeply convinced that they are not fundamental differences on which agreement is impossible. And if we still have differences and have not reached agreement on certain important questions, it is, as we believe, with adequate grounds—a result of the concessions made by the Western powers to Chancellor Adenauer, who is pursuing a military policy, the policy of the German revanchists. This is a case of the United States, Britain and France dangerously abetting Chancellor Adenauer. It would have been far better if the NATO allies of Western Germany would persuade Chancellor Adenauer, in the interest of the maintenance of peace, that his policy imperils the cause of peace and that it may ultimately end in irreparable disaster for Western Germany. All this emphasizes again that the representatives of the states concerned must do some more work in order to find mutually acceptable decisions.

I believe that my trip to the United States and the subsequent visit of President Eisenhower to the Soviet Union will afford the possibility for a useful exchange of opinions, for finding a common tongue and a common understanding of the questions that should be settled.

V

We are prepared now as before to do everything we possibly can in order that the relations between the Soviet Union and other countries, and, in particular, the relations between the U.S.S.R. and the U.S.A., should be built upon the foundation of friendship and that they should fully correspond to the principles of peaceful coexistence.

I should like to repeat what I said at my recent press conference in Moscow: "Should Soviet-American relations become brighter, that will not fail to bring about an improvement in the relations with other states and will help to scatter the gloomy clouds in other parts of the globe also. Naturally, we want friendship not only with the U.S.A., but also with the friends of the U.S.A. At the same time we want to see the U.S.A. maintain good relations not only with us, but with our friends as well."

What, then, is preventing us from making the principles of peaceful coexistence an unshakable international standard and daily practice in the relations between the West and East?

Of course, different answers may be given to this question. But in order to be frank to the end, we should also say the following: *It is necessary that everybody should understand the irrevocable fact that the historic process is irreversible.* It is impossible to bring back yesterday. It is high time to understand that the world of the twentieth century is not the world of the nineteenth century, that two diametrically opposed social and economic systems exist in the world today side by side, and that the socialist system, in spite of all the attacks upon it, has grown so strong, has developed into such a force, as to make any return to the past impossible.

Real facts of life in the last ten years have shown convincingly that the policy of "rolling back" Communism can only poison the international atmosphere, heighten the tension between states and work in favor of the cold war. Neither its inspirers nor those who conduct it can turn back the course of history and restore capitalism in the socialist countries.

We have always considered the Americans realistic people. All the more are we astonished to find that leading representatives of the United States still number in their midst individuals who insist on their own way in the face of the obvious failure of the policy of "rolling back" Communism. But is it not high time to take a sober view of things and to draw conclusions from the lessons of the last 15 years? Is it not yet clear to everybody that consistent adherence to the policy of peaceful coexistence would make it possible to improve the international situation, to bring about a drastic cut in military expenditures and to release vast material resources for wiser purposes?

The well known British scientist, J. Bernal, recently cited figures to show that average annual expenditures for military purposes throughout the world between 1950 and the end of 1957 were expressed in the huge sum of about 90 billion dollars. How many factories, apartment houses, schools, hospitals and libraries could have been built everywhere with the funds now spent on the preparation of another war! And how fast could economic progress have been advanced in the underdeveloped countries if we had converted to these purposes at least some of the means which are now being spent on war purposes!

VI

It is readily seen that the policy of peaceful coexistence receives a firm foundation only with increase in extensive and absolutely unrestricted international trade. It can be said without fear of exaggeration that there is no good basis for improvement of relations between our countries other than development of international trade.

If the principle of peaceful coexistence of states is to be adhered to, not in words, but in deeds, it is perfectly obvious that no ideological differences should be an obstacle to the development and extension of mutually advantageous economic contacts, to the exchange of everything produced by human genius in the sphere of peaceful branches of material production.

In this connection it may be recalled that soon after the birth of the Soviet state, back in the early 1920s, the Western countries, proceeding from considerations of economic interest, agreed to establish trade relations with our country despite the acutest ideological differences. Since then, discounting comparatively short periods, trade between the Soviet Union and capitalist states has been developing steadily. No ideological differences prevented, for instance, a considerable extension of trade relations between the Soviet Union and Britain and other Western states in recent years. We make no secret of our desire to establish normal commercial and business contacts with the United States as well, without any restrictions, without any discriminations.

In June of last year the Soviet Government addressed itself to the Government of the United States with the proposal to develop economic and trade contacts between our two countries. We proposed an extensive and concrete program of developing Soviet-American trade on a mutually advantageous basis. The adoption of our proposals would undoubtedly accord with the interests of both states and peoples. However, these proposals have not been developed so far.

Striving for the restoration of normal trade relations with the United States, the Soviet Union does not pursue any special interests. In our economic development we rely wholly on the internal forces of our country, on our own resources and possibilities. All our plans for further economic development are drawn up taking into consideration the possibilities available here. As in the past, when we outline these plans we proceed only from the basis of our own possibilities and forces. Irrespective of whether or not we shall trade with Western countries, the United States included, the implementation of our economic plans of peaceful construction will not in the least be impeded.

However, if both sides want to improve relations, all barriers in international trade must be removed. Those who want peaceful coexistence cannot but favor the development of trade, economic and business contacts. Only on this basis can international life develop normally.

VII

Peaceful coexistence is the only way which is in keeping with the interests of all nations. To reject it would mean under existing conditions to doom the whole world to a terrible and destructive war at a time when it is fully possible to avoid it.

Is it possible that when mankind has advanced to a plane where it has proved capable of the greatest discoveries and of making its first steps into outer space, it should not be able to use the colossal achievements of its genius for the establishment of a stable peace, for the good of man, rather than for the preparation of another war and for the destruction of all that has been created by its labor over many millenniums? Reason refuses to believe this. It protests.

The Soviet people have stated and declare again that they do not want war. If the Soviet Union and the countries friendly to it are not attacked, we shall never use any weapons either against the United States or against any other countries. We do not want any horrors of war, destruction, suffering and death for ourselves or for any other peoples. We say this not because we fear anyone. Together with our friends, we are united and stronger than ever. But precisely because of that do we say that war can and should be prevented. Precisely because we want to rid mankind of war, we urge the Western powers to peaceful and lofty competition. We say to all: Let us prove to each other the advantages of one's own system not with fists, not by war, but by peaceful economic competition in conditions of peaceful coexistence.

As for the social system in some state or other, that is the domestic affair of the people of each country. We always have stood and we stand today for non-interference in the internal affairs of other countries. We have always abided, and we shall abide, by these positions. The question, for example, what system will exist in the United States or in other capitalist countries cannot be decided by other peoples or states. This question can and will be decided only by the American people themselves, only by the people of each country.

The existence of the Soviet Union and of the other socialist countries is a real fact. It is also a real fact that the United States of America and the other capitalist countries live in different social conditions, in the conditions of capitalism. Then let us recognize this real situation and proceed from it in order not to go against reality, against life itself. Let us not try to change this situation by interferences from without, by means of war on the part of some states against other states.

I repeat, there is only one way to peace, one way out of the existing tension: peaceful coexistence.

53. *PEACEFUL COEXISTENCE: A WESTERN VIEW* / GEORGE F. KENNAN*

In the public debate that has marked the progress of what is called the cold war, no term has been used more loosely, and at times unscrupulously, than the word "coexistence." In the article under his name, published in the last issue of *Foreign Affairs*, Mr. Khrushchev has given us an interesting definition of what he understands by this term. Peaceful coexistence, he says, signifies in essence the repudiation of war as a means of solving controversial issues. It presupposes an obligation to refrain from every form of violation of the territorial integrity and sovereignty of another state. It implies renunciation of interference in the internal affairs of other countries. It means that political and economic relations must be put on a basis of complete equality and mutual benefit. It involves, he says, the elimination of the very threat of war. It is something which "should develop into peaceful competition for the purpose of satisfying man's needs in the best possible way."

Not only has Mr. Khrushchev given us this definition but he has made it plain that he considers that the Soviet Union abides by these principles, has abided by them ever since the revolution of the autumn of 1917 and cannot help but abide by them in view of its social foundation; whereas there are still important elements in the Western countries who, in his view, do not abide by these principles, who "believe that war is to their benefit," who want to inflict "capitalism" by violent means on unwilling peoples and whose opposition must be overcome before peaceful coexistence can really be said to prevail.

* George F. Kennan, "Peaceful Coexistence: A Western View," *Foreign Affairs*, Vol. 38, No. 2 (January 1960), pp. 171–90. Copyright by the Council on Foreign Relations, Inc., New York. Reprinted by permission.

There could be few propositions more amazing than the assertion that the Soviet state "from its very inception . . . proclaimed peaceful coexistence as the basic principle of its foreign policy," and that the initial Communist leaders in Russia were strong partisans of the view that peaceful coexistence could and should prevail among states with different social systems.

One returns reluctantly to the record of those early years of Soviet power. One can well believe that authoritative circles in Moscow assess somewhat differently today the prospects for violent social revolution in the main industrial countries of the West, and perhaps even its necessity. One can imagine that they have a concept of the obligations of Russian Communists to the workers of those Western countries which is also somewhat different from that which prevailed in Moscow in 1917 and 1918. If this is so, then it would surely be better to let bygones be bygones, rather than permit the problem of coexistence in the present to be complicated by altercation over the attitudes of the past. The years 1917 and 1918 were, after all, a time of tremendous turmoil and tragedy in world affairs. Men acted, everywhere, in the spirit of violence and passion. Many things were done by both Communist and non-Communist sides which today, from the perspective of 40 years, appear clearly regrettable. Surely there could be very few people in the non-Communist world who would wish now to revive the controversies of that day or to associate themselves indiscriminately with the outlooks and prejudices of the period of World War I and its aftermath.

But if reference is to be taken prominently on the Communist side to the attitudes of Soviet leaders in 1917, as proof of the inviolable and inevitable attachment of Russian Communism to such principles as the repudiation of violence as a means of solving controversial political issues, the renunciation of interference in the internal affairs of other countries and the predominance of peaceful competition as between states of different social systems, then the Western scholar cannot refrain from registering his amazement and protest. It is surprising that there should be so little respect for the true history of the Russian revolutionary movement on the part of those who profess today to be its custodians and protagonists that they are willing to pervert it in this way for the sake of their own tactical convenience. One shudders to think what Lenin would have said to these preposterous distortions. Do the present leaders of the Russian Communist Party really profess to have forgotten that

Lenin regarded himself outstandingly as an *international* socialist leader? Who was it wrote, on October 3, 1918, "The Bolshevik working class of Russia was always internationalist not only in words, but in deeds, in contrast to those villains—the heroes and leaders of the Second International. . . ."? Who was it said, in that same document, "The Russian proletariat will understand that the greatest sacrifices will now soon be demanded of it for the cause of internationalism. . . . Let us prepare ourselves at once. Let us prove that the Russian worker is capable of working much more energetically, and of struggling and dying in a much more self-sacrificing way, when it is a matter not of the Russian revolution alone but of the international workers' revolution. . . ."?[1]

This is, as every good Communist in Russia knows, only a single quotation out of literally thousands that could be adduced to illustrate the devotion of the Bolsheviki in Lenin's time to socialism as an international cause—the devotion, that is, precisely to the duty of interfering in the internal affairs of other countries with the object of altering their system of government and mode of life.

The proposition that the political power dominant in the Soviet Union has always been on the side of coexistence, as defined by Mr. Khrushchev, also calls upon us to forget the long and sinister history of the relationship between Moscow and the foreign Communist Parties in the Stalin era. There is ample documentation to show for what purposes foreign Communist Parties were used during those years, by whom, and by what methods. There are many of us in the West who, again, would be happy to disregard these recollections when it comes to the political discussion of the present day. But it is another thing to suffer insult to one's intelligence; and if people in Moscow wish this unhappy history to be forgotten outside Russia, they must not blandly turn the facts of history upside down and ask that the resulting configuration be accepted as proof of the inevitable commitment of Russian Communism to the principles of coexistence.

Over a hundred years ago a distinguished Western visitor, the Marquis de Custine, wrote from Petrograd that: "Russian despotism does not only count ideas and feelings as nothing, but it remakes the facts, it enters the lists against the evident, and triumphs in the struggle."

People cannot hope to triumph in such a cause today. The very cultivation of these distortions, seeking as it does the obfuscation of

[1] V. I. Lenin, *Sochineniya* (Fourth Edition). Moscow: 1952, v. 28, p. 83.

public understanding of the historical development of the relations between the Soviet Union and the West, is itself a grievous disservice to any truly hopeful form of coexistence.

These statements of mine are not to be taken as implying a disposition to believe that the attachment of Mr. Khrushchev and certain of his colleagues to the principles of coexistence, as he has now defined them, is insincere and conceals sinister motives. This does not necessarily follow. The purpose is merely to point out that people in Moscow are not likely to strengthen belief outside Russia in the sincerity of their attachment to liberal and tolerant principles of international life by distorting the history of the Lenin or Stalin eras or by pleading that such an attachment flows inevitably from the nature of the social and political system prevailing in the Soviet Union. It is possible to conceive that the Soviet attitude in such questions may have changed; it is not possible to accept the proposition that it did not need to change in order to meet the requirements of peaceful coexistence, as Mr. Khrushchev has defined them.

III

In the statement of the Soviet view of coexistence, much stress has been laid on the attachment of people in the West to capitalism and on their alleged desire to see it triumph as a world system.

The Westerner of this day experiences a certain bewilderment when he hears the term "capitalism" used in this way. What is it that is meant by this expression? One notices that whatever the reality may be which it purports to symbolize, it is one which in Russian Communist eyes has not changed appreciably since the Russian Social Democratic Party came into being at the turn of the century. If there is any recognition in official Soviet thought of the fact that changes in the economic practices and institutions of non-Communist countries over this past half-century have been such as to affect in any way the elements of the classic Marxist view of Western capitalism, I am not aware of the place where this has found expression. Contemporary Soviet ideological material seems to suggest that there exists outside the Communist orbit a static and basic condition—a set of practices known as "capitalism" and expressed primarily in the private ownership of the means of production—which has undergone no essential alteration over the past 50 years, or indeed since the lifetime of Karl Marx; which continues to be the dominant reality of Western society; belief in which constitutes the essence of all non-Communist political philosophy; and to which the Western governments and "ruling circles," in particular, remain, as a matter of pride and tenacious self-interest, profoundly committed. It would presumably be to "capitalism" in this sense that Mr. Khrushchev was referring when he wrote that many readers of *Foreign Affairs* would perhaps think that capitalism will ultimately triumph.

It is hardly necessary to emphasize how far this seems, to many of us outside Russia, from the reality of this day. The principles of free economic enterprise and private ownership of the means of production have indeed had a prominent part to play in the economies of non-Communist countries everywhere over this past half-century. But in no two countries has this part been quite the same. Elements of public and social control have come in, everywhere, to challenge and modify the operation of these principles. The resulting balance between private control on the one hand and social or public control on the other now varies greatly from country to country. There is today not *one* social and economic system prevailing outside the Communist orbit: there are almost as many such systems as there are countries; and many of them are closer to what Marx conceived as socialism than they are to the laissez faire capitalism of his day. In each of them, furthermore, the balance between private and social influences is everywhere in a state of flux and evolution which makes it quite impossible to predict from the aspect it assumes today what aspect it is going to assume tomorrow.

This means that in the non-Communist world, where it is customary to attempt to relate the meaning of words to objective phenomena, the term "capitalism" no longer has any generic and useful meaning. It is only in Russia, where theoretical concept can still be spared the test of relevance to objective reality, that a meaning for this term still exists. Not only this, but there are numbers of issues of public life which today appear to most people in the non-Communist world as having a higher importance, from the standpoint of their general effect on the human condition, than the issues of the ownership of the means of production and the distribution of wealth with which the Marxist doctrine was preoccupied.

How absurd, in the light of these facts, to picture Western non-Communists as the passionate protagonists and devotees of something called "capitalism," and to suggest that there are influential people in the West who desire to bring upon the earth the miseries of another world war in the hope of being able to inflict the capitalist system on great masses of people who do not desire it. The question of who owns the machines is not the one that today dominates the thoughts and discussions of Western society and Western "ruling circles;" it is primarily the question of human freedom—of the right of people to choose and alter their own social and political systems as they like, to select those who shall govern them within the framework of those systems, and to enjoy, within that same framework, the civil liberties which relieve them of the fear of arbitrary injustice, permit them to practice freedom of the mind and enable them to walk with their heads up.

I am aware that Communists have long professed to see no value in either the parliamentary or judicial institutions of the liberal West. The classical Communist position has dismissed these institutions as frauds perpetrated on the helpless workers by the monopolists who exploit them. Is it too much to hope that people in the Communist world will now manifest their interest in coexistence by abandoning cynical and ridiculous extremism, in the face of which the whole development of British and American society over these last centuries becomes historically unintelligible?

That these liberal institutions are imperfect, most Englishmen or Americans would, I think, readily concede; but the overwhelming majority of us believe them to embody something that lies close to the essence of human dignity, as we have learned to see it, and something which is one of the most precious attainments of civilized man. It is to this, not to the system governing ownership and control of the industries of our country, that our deepest pride and loyalties relate. If, by the fair operation of these parliamentary institutions, and with preservation of all basic civil liberties, the arrangements governing ownership or control of the means of production should be drastically changed (and some already have been), most of us would view this as no final tragedy and would not see ourselves as defeated. But if it were the other way round, and if such changes had to be purchased at the price of the sacrifice of the rights and privileges which our parliamentary and judicial institutions now generally, if imperfectly, provide—then, and only then, would we consider ourselves to have suffered an irreparable defeat—only then would it seem to us that what was most essential had been lost.

We decline, therefore, to be depicted as the passionate protagonists of something called "capitalism" waging an ideological competition with the protagonists of something called "socialism." Least of all can we in America accept the charge of wishing to impose something called capitalism on other peoples. Several European countries have changed their social and economic institutions over the course of recent decades in ways that carry them very far from those prevailing in the United States. In this, they have not encountered the slightest opposition or hindrance from the American side. The basic ideological issue, as seen in the United States today, is not capitalism versus socialism but freedom versus its opposite. The disagreement between Moscow and the "leading circles" of the non-Communist world is not really a disagreement about which form of social system is most productive; it is rather a disagreement about what is most important, in the first place, in the lives of peoples.

IV

The fact that an ideological disagreement of this nature exists is in itself no reason why peaceful coexistence, as Mr. Khrushchev defines it, should not prevail. There is nothing new in the prolonged peaceful residence, side by side, of ideologically antagonistic systems. Many of the present peaceful relationships of international life, outside the Communist orbit, have evolved from ones which were originally relationships of profound ideological antagonism. There was, for that matter, no ideological affinity but rather a sharp ideological conflict between the Tsarist system in Russia and the world of American political thought. This did not prevent the two powers from existing in the same world, without hostilities, for more than a hundred years.

There are no doubt individuals scattered here and there throughout the Western countries who find intolerable this present antagonism of outlook as between the Soviet Government and the Western peoples and who cannot see how it can be either resolved or endured by means short of a world war. If one searches, one can even find, for quotation, public utterances of this view. But it would be generally agreed, I think, that these people are few and not very influential. The general attitude throughout the West would unquestionably be—and this goes for governments as well as for individuals—that while the social and political system now dominant in Russia is one that may not commend itself to us, its existence and prevalence there is not our responsibility; it is not our business to change it; it constitutes in itself no reason by a relationship of peaceful coexistence should not prevail.

The cold war, let it be said most emphatically, does not exist because people in the West object to the Russian people having socialism or any other system they wish. If, in fact, it were only a matter of ideologies, and only a matter of the relationship between the West and Russia proper, there would be no reason why the Soviet demand for "peaceful coexistence" should not be accepted without reservation.

But the Soviet Union is not only an ideological phenomenon. It is also a great power, physically and militarily. Even if the prevailing ideology in Russia were not antagonistic to the concepts prevailing elsewhere, the behavior of the government of that country in its international relations, and particularly any considerable expansion of its power at the expense of the freedom of other peoples, would still be a matter of most serious interest to the world at large.

And it is, let us recall, precisely such an expansion that we have witnessed in recent years. So far as Europe is concerned, this expansion had its origin in the advance of Soviet armies into Eastern and Central Europe in 1945. This advance was not only accepted at the time—it was generally welcomed in the West as a very important part of the final phase of the struggle against Hitler. But it has had a consequence which few people in the West foresaw in 1945 and which fewer still desired: the quasi-permanent advancement of the effective boundaries of Moscow's political and military authority to the very center of Europe.

The discussion of the question of coexistence on the Communist side is cast in terms which take no account of this situation and which ask us, by implication, either to ignore it or to pretend that it does not exist. The problem, we are told, is to "liquidate the consequences of the Second World War;" but this particular consequence, we are left to infer, is one which is neither to be liquidated nor to be spoken about.

Is this a realistic demand? One cannot agree that it is. The position of preëminence which the U.S.S.R. enjoys among the countries of the Communist bloc is not a secret. The Communist leaders of various countries do not ignore it when they themselves assemble to discuss international affairs. What people in the West should or should not do to change or affect this situation is another problem; but to demand that a situation which is perfectly well recognized *within* the Communist world as a significant factor in world affairs should be effectively ignored when it comes to the discussion of coexistence between East and West is surely neither reasonable nor helpful. The fact is that this extension of Russia's political and military power into the heart of Europe represents a major alteration in the world strategic and political balance, and one that was never discussed as such with Western statesmen, much less agreed to by them.

It is not just the *fact* of this situation which is of importance to the Western peoples; there is also the question as to *how* it came into existence and *how* it is being maintained. The truth is that it did not come into existence because the majority of the people in the region affected became convinced that Communism, as Mr. Khrushchev has put it, was "the more progressive and equitable system." This peaceful competition for the minds of men which the Communists today ask us to accept as the concomitant and condition of peaceful coexistence had precious little to do with the means by which socialist governments, on the pattern approved by Moscow, were established in the countries of Eastern Europe in 1944 and 1945 or with the means by which their rule was subsequently consolidated there. In the view of the West, formed on the strength of overwhelming historical evidence, these régimes were imposed by the skillful manipulations of highly disciplined Communist minorities, trained and inspired by Moscow, and supported by the presence or close proximity of units of the Soviet armed forces. They have been maintained in power by similar means.

It is not the intention here to attempt to judge these happenings from a moral standpoint. I do not mean to challenge the proposition that Russia has political interests in Eastern Europe and that these deserve the respect of Western governments as a matter of elementary political realism. Nor do I wish to deny that the present situation, whatever we may think of its origin, represents today a heavy commitment of the Soviet Government, which the latter cannot reasonably be asked to alter in any abrupt or drastic manner dangerous to its own political security.

There are, as Mr. Khrushchev knows, people in the West who have not despaired of finding ways to reconcile Soviet interests in this area both with the interests of the Western powers and of the respective peoples, and who have done what they could to pave the way for reasonable and moderate solutions of these difficulties. But the efforts of such people are bound to remain fruitless if the Soviet Government continues to give the impression that, having quietly pocketed this region, it is now saying to the West: "Coexistence begins at this point, and any curiosity on your part about the fate of these peoples will be a violation of it."

It was indicated above that the existence of the Soviet brand of socialism in *Russia itself* may well be regarded in the West as Russia's own business and need not be a barrier to peaceful coexistence. The Soviet régime is, after all, an indigenous régime throughout the greater part of the area of the Soviet Union. The processes in which it had its origin were not democratic ones in the Western sense, but they were deeply Russian ones, reflecting some very basic realities of the Russian political life of that day. It is indeed not the business of Americans to interfere with such a régime.

But when it comes to the governments of the Communist bloc in Eastern and Central Europe, then the problem is inevitably more complicated. These governments are not, in the main, truly indigenous. All this is of course relative; for seldom, if ever, is there *no* area of identity between the interests and sentiments of a people and the régime, however despotic, that governs it. But these régimes represent, in Western eyes, the fruits of a species of conquest and subjugation which was not less real for the fact that it did not generally involve hostile military invasion in the usual sense. And the thought inevitably presents itself: if such a thing could be done to *these* peoples, by means short of overt military aggression, and if we are now asked to accept it as something not to be discussed in connection with peaceful coexistence, to how many other peoples could this also be done, within the very framework of coexistence we are being asked to adopt?

The fact is (and it is one we have had impressed upon us in painful ways over these past four decades) that there are more ways than outright military aggression or formal political intervention by which the fate of smaller peoples may be brought under subjection to the will of larger ones, and more devices than those of the classic nineteenth century colonialism by which peoples can be kept in that state. There does exist, after all, such a thing as the science of insurrection—the science of the seizure of power by conspiratorial minorites, of the conquest of the vital centers of power, of the control of the streets, of the manipulation of civil conflict. Who would deny that this science had a part, and a very basic one, in the

Communist thinking and training of an earlier day? Revolutions may not be "made to order;" but that they normally flow only from the spontaneous impulses of the masses and are never influenced by the organizational and military activities of political "vanguards" is something that would scarcely be reconcilable with Communist doctrine of an earlier day, and something we certainly cannot be asked, in the light of historical evidence, to accept.

Mr. Khrushchev gives the impression that all this is not an important part of *his* thinking today. It would be wrong to assume automatically that there is no sincerity in this claim. (He has a point when he says that we should not look for the double bottom in *every* suitcase.) But even if this should be true in his particular case, it would scarcely be true of all of his present associates in the Secretariat and Presidium of the Communist Party of the Soviet Union; nor is there any reason to believe it to be true of the leaders of Russia's principal associate in the family of nations: Communist China.

Again, one must stress the fact that the historical record cannot be suddenly ignored. If the capitalist countries have, in Mr. Khrushchev's view, a past record to be explained away (he accuses us of having organized "senseless crusades" against Soviet Russia), so does Soviet Russia. In particular, it will be a long time before the foreign policies and methods of Joseph Stalin cease to be a determining factor in the consciousness of the West. In one sense, we are all, like Mr. Khrushchev himself, Stalin's pupils. It is from him that we learned a great deal of what we know about such things as ruthlessness and consistency and deception in international politics. Mr. Khrushchev must not now ask us to forget too quickly—certainly not more quickly than some of his own Russian and Chinese associates—the lessons we have learned from this eminent political teacher.

These reflections have an important bearing on the words "peace" and "peaceful" which are used so frequently on the Communist side in connection with the problem of coexistence. What is it that is meant by these terms?

The word "peace" has no meaning outside of the concrete conditions by which it is marked. Peace is not the mere absence of overt hostilities. We have peace today, in that sense. There is "peace," for that matter, in any well-disciplined prison. Peace is not an abstraction. Lenin understood this well. Thus he wrote in 1915: "The slogan of peace may be advanced either in connection with specific conditions of peace, or without any conditions at all—by way of struggle, that is, not for any specific peace but for peace in general (Frieden ohne weiters). It is clear that in the latter case we have to do not only with a slogan which is not a socialist one but is in general a senseless one, devoid of content."[2]

What content are we then to assign to the term "peace" in Communist usage? Is it unreasonable to ask Lenin's pupils to make this plain and to specify, when they use this term, precisely what sort of peace they are talking about: peace in whose interests? on what conditions? at what cost?

There is one kind of peace that is compatible with the true security of peoples; and this is one which is based on the principles of genuine national freedom. There is another kind of peace which represents the silence that reigns where the instruments of coercion are simply too formidable to be challenged by those against whom they are aimed.

The bandying about of the word peace as an abstraction evades, once more, the fact that there are ways in which peoples can be oppressed which do not necessarily involve at any given time the visible exertion of force across international frontiers—that sometimes the mere threat of force is enough. And it evades the fact that there have been instances, as in Hungary in 1956, where the Soviet attachment to "peace" did not inhibit the use of Soviet armed forces to determine the political situation in a neighboring country. Is it seriously supposed that people outside Russia can overlook these facts when the question of "peaceful" coexistence is duscussed?

V

Much is made, in Communist discussion of coexistence, of the military dispositions of the Western countries, particularly the United States. The United States Government is reproached for maintaining bases in various parts of the world; for being unwilling to agree to a total abolition and renunciation of atomic weapons and to a final ban on nuclear tests; for failure to match unilateral measures of reduction of conventional armaments which the Soviet Government claims (without very adequate proof) to have taken; for rearming the Germans within the framework of NATO, etc. All these facets of behavior on the part of the United States

[2] *Ibid.*, v. 21, p. 262.

Government are cited as inconsistent with a true disposition to abide by the principle of peaceful coexistence.

The writer of these lines has had his own differences with the military policies of the Western coalition in recent years. These policies have suffered, in his opinion, from several distortions. They have often reflected a certain mis-estimation of the true nature of the problem with which they were designed to deal. They seem sometimes to have been predicated on a view of Soviet intentions which, to anyone familiar with the history and psychology of Soviet power, can only appear crude and one-sided, drawn rather from the memories of past adversaries than from a dispassionate study of Russian-Communist principles and tactics. They have at times involved one-sided and unsound commitments to individual categories of weapons. They seem sometimes to have reflected an exaggerated confidence in the device of military alliance as a sort of panacea for all political ills, as though there were no dangers other than those of direct military aggression. They have on more than one occasion led to military dispositions which, however defensive in motivation, could well appear to a possible opponent as the reflection of an intention to initiate hostilities at some stage or other.

All this is true; yet none of it taken separately nor all of it taken together justifies the extreme interpretation Moscow has placed upon it. The Soviet leaders seem either unwilling or unable to take any proper account of the true measure of the shock wrought to the Western public by their exploitation, for purposes of political aggrandizement, of their military position in Eastern and Central Europe in the period 1945 to 1948; by their failure to match the demobilization of the Western armies; by the political attack launched by the Communists in Western Europe in the years 1947 and 1948; by the imposition of the Berlin blockade, and above all by the launching of the Korean War. To people in the West these actions seemed to reflect a hostility no less menacing in intent than would have been threats of overt military aggression by Soviet forces. Coming as they did on the heels of the Second World War, affecting as they did nerves already frayed and minds already prone to anxiety as a result of these fresh experiences, it is not surprising that they produced on a great many people in the West the impression that the security of Western Europe, having just withstood one fearful challenge, was now confronted by another one of scarcely smaller dimensions. Neither is it surprising that peoples' reaction to this impression should have been the intensive effort to re-create, within the framework of a Western alliance, something of the armed force which had been so hastily and trustingly demobilized in the immediate aftermath of the war. The history of Europe has been such that danger to the nation, within the period of historical memory, has generally been associated with the movement of armies over land frontiers. It is probably only natural that the peoples of the Continent should be obsessed with the *manie d'invasion* and should look to the creation of defensive military power as a means of protection even against pressures which are actually much more subtle and refined than those of regular military action.

In the questions raised from the Soviet side about the military rivalry there is room for discussion and room for compromise. But no useful purpose will be served by the willful misinterpretation and distortion of this subject in which people in Moscow stubbornly persist. The suggestion that there is a sizable or serious body of people in the West who, in the immediate aftermath of the horrors of 1939–1945, wish for new orgies of bloodshed and slaughter is too absurd to be entertained for a moment. The suggestion, in particular, that Chancellor Adenauer would be one of these people is so patently absurd, so wildly remote from the entire fabric of political realities in Germany today, and so mischievous in its obvious intent and implications, that its continued reiteration in Moscow is a grievous discouragement to those who hope for better understanding.

Mr. Khrushchev is right in viewing the weapons race of this day as inconsistent with any satisfactory form of coexistence. But the prospects for bettering this situation will not be promising so long as Moscow persists in viewing the military policies pursued in the Western coalition in recent years as solely the products of the lust of Western financiers and manufacturers thirsting for another war in the hopes of greater profits, and refuses to recognize that these policies, however misconceived or overdrawn, represent in large measure the natural and predictable reactions of great peoples to a situation which Moscow itself did much to create.

VI

A further component of the demand which is made from the Communist side in the name of peaceful coexistence relates to what Mr. Khrushchev has called an "increase in extensive and absolutely unrestricted international trade." Ideological differences, it is argued, should not be an obstacle to the development of trade. Without such trade, international life cannot be expected to develop normally.

This is, from the Western standpoint, an odd and somewhat puzzling requirement. If trade between the Soviet Union and non-Communist countries were of such a nature as to bring with it the normal incidental advantages of economic contact—extensive reciprocal travel and residence of businessmen in the other country, the establishment of close personal contacts and associations, the intermingling, in short, not only of the economic life but also of the people of two countries at least in a certain limited area of activity—then one would be able to see some relevance of the question of trade to the question of peaceful coexistence. But the Soviet Government, as is known, maintains a monopoly of foreign trade, conducts most of its transactions abroad, denies generally to foreign businessmen the privilege of residing and doing business on Soviet soil and takes most elaborate and unusual measures of precaution to see that Soviet citizens do not form permanent relationships of personal confidence or friendship with any foreigners whatsoever, whether through business contacts or otherwise.

In these circumstances, one might suppose, the virtues of increased international trade would of necessity be confined to the direct benefits such trade might bring to the economies of the respective partners. That there are such benefits to be obtained, at least in modest measure, cannot be disputed. But Mr. Khrushchev has himself denied that these benefits are of any vital significance to the Soviet Union. "In our economic development," he writes, "we rely wholly on the internal forces of our country, on our own resources and possibilities. . . . Irrespective of whether or not we shall trade with Western countries . . . the implementation of our economic plans . . . will not in the least be impeded."

In the case of the United States, it is hard to believe that trade with Russia could have a much greater significance than it has for the Russians. Except in time of war, trade between Russia and the United States has never assumed very large dimensions, either in the Tsarist or the Soviet period. The things which Russia normally has to sell are not such as to have any very sensational implications for the American economy; and the same would be true of the possibilities presented by the purchasing programs of the Soviet Foreign Trade Monopoly, to date.

In addition to this, the Western governments have to consider not just the possible advantages of trade with a foreign trade monopoly but also its possible dangers. Such trade is controlled and shaped at the Soviet end by a great government which has political as well as economic interests to pursue. This being so, one cannot look to a mere mutual economic advantageousness, as one does in the case of trade between countries with a free enterprise system, to provide the guarantee of stability. This is particularly the case when the government in question goes out of its way to emphasize how little dependent it is on this trade, how well it can get along without it. The non-Communist governments have always to reckon with the possibility that exchanges carefully built up over the course of the years and involving important commitments on the part of Western firms may be suddenly terminated by a switch in the purchasing policy of the other party, for reasons into which considerations of economic advantage do not enter at all. These things have happened in the past. Even if they had not happened in the past, there would be no guarantee that they could not happen in the future. This precariousness, arising from the absence on one side of the normal balance wheel of international trade—commercial self-interest—does not mean that trade with the Soviet Union is never safe or desirable; but it does place definite limitations on its possibilities.

One can well imagine that the emphasis laid on this factor by Mr. Khrushchev and other Soviet spokesmen rests on the fact that the expression of a desire for expanded trade relations has often (and particularly in Soviet diplomatic history) constituted the prelude to a political rapprochement or entente between two powers. But it would be difficult to persuade Americans to accept this view of the significance of commercial policy. In the American tradition, trade is a means of meeting real economic needs, not of expressing political feelings.

There have been in recent years, in the American position on questions of East-West trade, certain features which have been widely regarded by people in countries allied with the United States, and by some Americans, as distortions: as the expression of an undue timidity in the face of domestic criticism or of an exaggerated conception of the effect of such trade on Soviet military preparations. If a reëxamination of these attitudes would have, in Soviet eyes, a significance which would really be helpful in relaxing international tensions, then the suggestion is one that should not be lightly dismissed in Washington.

But even if this reëxamination were undertaken, we would still be faced with the fact that the existence in Moscow of a governmental monopoly of foreign trade creates a set of conditions for trade quite different from those to which people in the West are accustomed. This does not exclude the possibility of commercial exchanges; it does not even exclude the possibility of a considerable increase of Soviet-American trade over its present levels. It does place a ceiling on what can, from the Western standpoint, reasonably be expected. And this ceiling is such that it is difficult to see how foreign trade could enter very importantly into the problem of peaceful coexistence.

VII

One last reflection. Again, the values to which it relates are relative ones; but the difficulties which lie at the heart of the tensions between the Communist and non-Communist worlds will never be overcome if relative distinctions are to be ignored.

The reference here is to the concept of truth that prevails in Moscow (not to mention Peking) as opposed to that which prevails in most other parts of the globe.

We are all accustomed to hearing not only from the Communist propaganda machine but from the lips of senior Soviet statesmen propositions which are either so patently absurd or so flatly in contradiction to known facts that no child could believe them. If we were to take seriously what comes to us from the Soviet side we should have to believe, for example, that Russia has been governed for over 40 years by a group of men who differ so profoundly from all mortals who have existed before or elsewhere that they have—over this entire period—never made a mistake, never analyzed a problem incorrectly, never been guided by any sentiments other than those of most selfless dedication to the welfare of others. This we are asked to believe despite the fact that at one time or another over the course of these years numbers of these people, theretofore a part of this supposedly all-wise leadership, have been suddenly denounced by their associates as treacherous criminals and dealt with accordingly. Simultaneously we are asked to accept the thesis that with one or two possible exceptions the Western countries have been led—through an equally remarkable coincidence—exclusively by people who were unmitigated villains: either bloodthirsty, greedy capitalists or the spineless stooges of such capitalists. One could go on citing such examples at any length. One has only to think of the bland distortions of the historical record that enter constantly into the Soviet statements on foreign policy: the claims with respect to such matters as the outbreak of the Korean War, the origin of the difficulties in Southeast Asia, the nature of the Soviet action in Hungary, etc.

A characteristic but particularly serious extrapolation of this irresponsible attitude toward objective fact will be found in the anti-American campaign of recent years. While this campaign reached its apotheosis before Stalin's death, it did not, unfortunately, cease entirely with that event. The Western public generally is little aware of the fantastic distortion of the image of the United States which has been purveyed to the Soviet public, and particularly to the Soviet intelligentsia, over the course of the past ten years by those who control the informational media of the Communist Party of the Soviet Union. An image of America continues to be cultivated in which even those Americans who are critically inclined towards many manifestations of American life would not recognize the country they know—an image in which the real faults of American civilization find as little recognition as its real virtues.

Propaganda is propaganda; but surely, like everything else in life, it has its limits. What are we to conclude from the propagation of these fantastic misapprehensions about the United States?—that the Soviet leaders really believe them? or that, knowing them to be misapprehensions, they nevertheless find it in order that Soviet citizens should be encouraged to accept them as true? Either variant would have most questionable implications from the standpoint of the prospects for peaceful coexistence.

Nor is it much comfort to people in the West to be assured that if only tensions would be reduced and military preparations relaxed this stream of deliberate detraction would dry up as miraculously and suddenly as it once burst forth. People in the United States have much to correct in their civilization, but little to hide. They are as little interested in being artificially spared by others in the critical appraisal of American life as they are in being artificially disparaged. Let this appraisal be as critical and as skeptical as it will, provided only that it is honest.

Can one ignore, in the discussion of the problem of coexistence, the implications of this attitude toward objective reality—an attitude that characterizes not just the professional Soviet propagandist but the Communist Party of the Soviet Union as a whole, and the statesmanship which that Party inspires? It will always be difficult to know how much confidence can be placed in people who appear to be deliberately deceiving either themselves or others. Is it too much to ask the Soviet leaders to drop today this Byzantine dogmatism of political thought and utterance, for which a case might have been made in the early days of the revolutionary militancy of the Party, when it was still fighting for its ascendancy in Russia, but which is out of place on the part of a great government which asks for acceptance as a mature and responsible force in world affairs? Scarcely anyone, surely, is deceived today by these absurd extremisms. But there are many people in the non-Communist world to whom these recurring evidences of irresponsibility in the attitude toward truth are a constant source of misgiving about the prospects of any sound and enduring coexistence between Communist and non-Communist worlds. What can be the value of specific understandings, these people ask, if the underlying assumptions and beliefs are so grotesquely different? If the Soviet leaders really think us to be as evil as they depict us to their own people, how can they seriously believe in the possibility of coexisting peacefully with us? If, on the other hand, they are deliberately misleading their own people, how can we, on our side, have confidence in them?

The demand that must be made on Moscow is not in any sense a demand for the uncritical acceptance of other points of view. What we would like would be to see in the statements of Soviet leaders, and in the propaganda material produced under their direction, at least a reasonable effort to reconcile the picture they paint of world realities with the objective evidence they have before them. So long as the leaders of the Communist Party of the Soviet Union continue to hold that truth is what it is useful to the interests of the Party that people should believe, regardless of how preposterous or absurd this may be in the light of objective evidence—so long as they continue to deny the very existence of an objective reality and, accordingly, any obligation on their part to understand and respect it—even those people in other parts of the world who might most earnestly wish for coexistence as Mr. Khrushchev has defined it will have to put restraints on their hopes and expectations. The road to peaceful coexistence lies, admittedly, through many gates; but one of these is the abandonment by Russian Communists of the absurd contention that theirs is a party which has always had a perfect understanding of the human predicament and has never made a mistake.

VIII

If Moscow is sincere in the quest for peaceful coexistence, and if to this end it is prepared to envisage a *general* revision, on both sides, of the attitudes and practices that have produced, or have been produced by, this dangerous state of world affairs known as the cold war, there will then be no lack of people in the countries outside the Communist orbit prepared to lend their influence to this process, and if need be, at considerable personal cost; for it is not in Russia alone that the extent of the danger is apparent. But if it is conceived in Moscow that the adjustment has all to be made on the Western side, there will be little that anyone on this side of the line can usefully do to advance coexistence beyond its present uncertain status.

Could we not, all of us, now put aside the pretense of total righteousness and admit to a measure of responsibility for the tangled processes of history that have brought the world to its present dangerous state? And could we not, having once admitted this, drop the argument about whose responsibility is greatest and address ourselves at long last, earnestly and without recrimination, to the elimination of the central and most intolerable elements of the danger?